LEGISLATING BUREAUCRATIC CHANGE

SUNY Series in Public Administration
Peter W. Colby, Editor

Edited by PATRICIA W. INGRAHAM
and CAROLYN BAN

LEGISLATING BUREAUCRATIC CHANGE

The Civil Service Reform Act of 1978

State University of New York Press
ALBANY

Published by
State University of New York Press, Albany

© 1984 State University of New York

For information, address State University of New York
Press, State University Plaza, Albany, N.Y., 12246

Library of Congress Cataloging in Publication Data

Main entry under title:

Legislating bureaucratic change.
(SUNY series in public administration)
Chiefly papers presented at a symposium held
at the State University of New York at Binghamton
in the fall of 1981.
Includes bibliographical references.
1. Civil service—United States. I. Ingraham,
Patricia W. II. Ban, Carolyn. III. Series.
KF5337.L43 1984   342.73'085   83-26937
ISBN 0-87395-886-1   347.30285
ISBN 0-87395-885-3 (pbk.)

10   9   8   7   6   5   4   3   2

Contents

Acknowledgments

We wish to thank the State University of New York, which, through its "Conversations in the Disciplines" program, provided funding for the conference at which many of these papers were initially presented. We thank the participants at that conference who do not have papers in the book, but whose experiences with civil service reform provided invaluable discussion and comment: Ros Kleeman, of the U.S. General Accounting Office, George Nesterczuk, of the U.S. Office of Personnel Management, David Dresser of the U.S. Department of Housing and Urban Development, and Alan Campbell, the first Director of the U.S. Office of Personnel Management and a leading architect of the reform. We also thank the contributors to this volume for the uniformly high quality of their work, and for giving us the opportunity to work with such a fine group of people.

In addition, we are grateful to Susan Suarez of SUNY Press for providing excellent editorial advice and assistance, and to the anonymous reviewers for SUNY Press, whose comments were helpful in producing the final version of this book.

Last, but certainly not least, we thank Charlie and Bill for fine typing, great cooking, consistent moral support, and for listening to far more about civil service reform than they ever wished to hear.

Pat Ingraham
Kerry Ban

June, 1983

Civil Service Reform: Legislating Bureaucratic Change

CAROLYN BAN AND PATRICIA INGRAHAM

In the fall of 1981, academics, government managers, and other interested observers gathered at the State University of New York at Binghamton for a symposium on the early history of the Civil Service Reform Act of 1978 (CSRA).[1] Many of the papers included in this book were first presented at that symposium; additional papers were solicited for the book in order to provide a broader view of the Act's history and implementation.

The Civil Service Reform Act is important legislation. It has been called the most comprehensive reform of the federal civil service since the Pendleton Act. It is extraordinarily complex and touches on most aspects of the federal personnel system. The changes it proposed are far-reaching and include some reforms that are radical departures from the old system. It also contains highly technical changes in personnel procedures, along with some changes that represent little more than tinkering with existing procedures. The scope of the proposed changes reflects the scope of the issues the Act was intended to address.

What were those issues and why was civil service reform considered necessary? The problem definition process which preceded the legislation took place on essentially two levels.

First, there was a widespread public perception that public bureaucracies were bloated and inefficient. That perception stemmed partially from the rapid growth of the social programs of the 1960s and early 70s. In the twenty years prior to civil service reform, the federal government tackled problems that were, in many ways, intractable. In doing so, government moved into areas that were controversial, and even threatening, to some citizens. Excessively high expectations on the part of the public—generated in part by the political promises of the programs, the increasing size and vis-

ibility of the bureaucracy, and constantly increasing program costs—
contributed to the public's dissatisfaction. Political leadership consistently capitalized on this sentiment by campaigning against bureaucratic excess.

Second, career bureaucrats were aware of problems with the existing
personnel system. Their day-to-day experience with its many rigidities
led them to advocate change. Analysis of some specific problems
and suggestions for reform had been discussed for years. Proposals
for some type of senior managerial cadre had surfaced regularly at
least since the mid-1950s, for example. Various efforts to make the
career bureaucracy more efficient, more productive, and more representative had also surfaced regularly. Proposals for structural reform
with a personnel organization and a single appointed head who
would report directly to the President, plus a separate merit board,
date to the recommendations of the President's Committee on Administrative Management, in 1937 (the Brownlow Committee).

President Carter's election, in 1976, provided formal access to the
public policy agenda for these concerns and initiated the first step
in the process of drafting the Reform Act: The President's Personnel
Management Project (PMP). This project was a series of ten task
forces, composed of distinguished practitioners and academics assembled to provide a comprehensive overview of specific problems
and potential solutions.

Though the reforms were developed in an ostensibly decentralized
way, a common definition of the problems and a consensus on
appropriate solutions permeated the analysis. This consensus mirrored
long-held tenets of public administration, firmly anchored in the
scientific management movement of the early part of this century
and in the classical school of public administration.

Another factor which influenced the design of the reforms was
the public's long infatuation with private-sector management techniques. The drafters of the legislation borrowed heavily from private
management innovations, such as executive bonuses and performance
evaluation methods. The result of these influences was an approach
that emphasized the values of management flexibility and efficiency
and downplayed the traditional public personnel values of equity
and procedural uniformity.

The PMP report, consisting of problem analysis and program
recommendations from each of the task forces, was thorough and
comprehensive. Though its transition to a legislative package was
not exact, many of its elements were contained in the proposed
legislation. (See chap. 1 for a more detailed description of the history
and composition of the statute.) In retrospect, and perhaps even at
the time, it was inevitable that such a comprehensive reform—

emerging as it did from wide participation, discussion, and compromise—would contain some internal inconsistencies. The tensions created by the inconsistencies in the CSRA, however, have had significant implications for the implementation of the Act and for attempts to judge its success or failure.

DESIGN OF THE ACT

Three of the major inconsistencies contained in the Act provide good examples of the tensions and the problems they created.

The conflict between the desire for greater political responsiveness and the desire for greater managerial capability and independence. Traditionally, political leaders have been frustrated by their inability to control the bureaucracy. Major portions of the Senior Executive Service (SES) were designed to give political appointees greater control over career executives. The stated intent of SES, however, was to increase management competence and flexibility at the highest levels. This implies some measure of career independence and concentration on management problems, rather than increased attention to political directives.[2]

The conflict between the concept of a management cadre with a sense of identity and esprit de corps and the concept of competition to increase productivity. The SES, clearly modeled after the British Higher Administrative Class, a group with a distinct elite identity, was intended to create a team of generalist managers. The team would be loyal to public service and to improved management techniques, generally, rather than to programs or agencies. The members of this same group, however, would compete against one another for a relatively small pot of money for bonuses and rank awards. This process, which pitted managers against each other, was intended to increase and reward productivity, but would clearly erode esprit de corps.

The conflict between the goal of increasing managers' ability to fire problem employees and the goal of protecting whistleblowers. One of the rigidities in the system was the complex set of procedures for firing employees, particularly the lengthy appeals procedures. CSRA purported to make firing unproductive employees easier (although we would maintain that the changes were not as significant as heralded). In addition, the original system was perceived as permitting the abuse of employees who "blew the whistle" on inefficiency and mismanagement. CSRA created the Office of the Special Counsel within the Merit Systems Protection Board specifically to protect whistleblowers. Mismanagement, however, may be in the eye of the beholder, and a politician's whistleblower can be a career manager's pest.[3] Separating the real abuse from employee frustration is a difficult task; it clearly implies additional external intrusion into the merit system.

It should be noted that, despite the efforts at comprehensiveness that contributed to the above inconsistencies of the Act, the need for support and consensus caused some exclusions and some early modifications in the package President Carter proposed. The most prominent exclusion was the personnel classification system. There was clear consensus on its problematic nature, but there was no consensus on appropriate solutions. The labor-management provisions of the Act provide a good example of the role of a small, but powerful, group of special interests. The Act's labor-management relations section was not included in the original reform package. It was sent to the Hill later, as Title VII of the Act, in exchange for support of the Act as a whole by employee unions. Title VII created an independent Federal Labor Relations Authority, but did little to clarify the scope and meaning of other labor-related components of the legislation, such as the scope of bargaining.[4]

Veterans-preference provisions were also strongly influenced by interest group activity. The bill sent to Congress included provisions severely limiting veterans preference. The motive for these actions, as well as for the proposed elimination of the "rule of three," [5] was to enhance hiring possibilities for women and minorities. Organized veterans groups, however, strongly objected to these changes and mounted a major lobbying effort, which resulted in the exclusion of most of the provisions from the final legislation.

SELLING THE REFORM

One of the surprising things about CSRA is that it passed Congress almost intact. To understand this unusual outcome one must understand the process by which the legislation was sold. The selling took place on two fronts, which parallel the levels of concern discussed earlier. In selling the reform to Congress, the Carter Administration emphasized the need to improve management efficiency and to enhance political control. In selling the reform to the public, the Administration played to stereotypes of bureaucratic inefficiency, emphasizing the punitive aspects of the Act, especially the provisions for firing unproductive employees. This two-pronged selling effort was extraordinarily effective. Much of its success was due to the personal effort and political skills of Alan Campbell, then Chairman of the Civil Service Commission, and of his very able staff. The active involvement of President Carter was significant, as was the legislative leadership of Congressman Morris Udall, the floor leader for the bill in the House of Representatives. It should be noted that, while this strategy was successful in getting the Act passed, it was less successful in educating members of Congress about the true rationale for the reform and about potential ramifications of its passage. Campbell, later reflecting on this failure, noted that support for the Act was "a mile wide, but an inch deep." [6] This is important, because congressional failure to understand fully some components of the reform prior to passage resulted in continued congressional involvement during implementation. The SES bonus system, for example, was modified by Congress after the first agency had awarded bonuses.

Another effect of the two-pronged selling effort may have been the creation of unreasonable expectations for the Act. The simplistic emphasis on improving productivity overlooked the basic problems of *defining and measuring* public productivity. Public productivity is an amorphous concept. Public personnel systems, no matter how efficient or how reformed, may make only marginal improvements because other influences—frequently political—have greater impact. In addition, if other changes in the governmental system are occurring at the same time as reform efforts, factoring out reform impact may be impossible, but the inability to do so may lead people to see the reform as a failure.[7] For example, President Carter sold CSRA in terms of making it easier to fire public employees and strongly implied the existence of substantial "deadwood" in the public service. Yet, if the positive parts of the reform worked as expected, individual productivity would improve and there would be a diminished need for firing. In some quarters, the Act is now being ruled a "failure" because the number of firings has not increased.[8] Clearly, however, the correct measure of success should be increased productivity or efficiency, not increased firing. For many reasons, therefore, civil service reform has not lived up to expectations. Some of those reasons have nothing to do with the design or the legislative history of the Act, but rather with its experience in implementation.

IMPLEMENTATION OF THE REFORM

Just as the comprehensive nature of the Act was unusual, so too was the strategy for its implementation. The Carter Administration pursued a strategy that was high-risk in two regards. First, implementation was seen as a long-term process. Although the Act was passed in 1978, few of the major provisions took effect immediately. Rather, agencies were given several years to develop and implement new programs in such areas as performance appraisal and merit pay.

Though consistent with the private sector's experience in introducing such systems and also with bureaucratic stability, such a long-term strategy is at odds with the nature of the American political system, which is notoriously unstable and oriented toward short-term results. Second, the implementation strategy was highly decentralized. Agencies were free to design systems that met their own needs (within certain boundaries), to set their own timetables for implementation, and, if necessary, to make their own mistakes. The Administration knew that giving managers more flexibility would involve some abuse of that flexibility. This was a condition the Administration was willing to accept. The fact that other actors in the system, such as the General Accounting Office (GAO) and Congress, would be less tolerant of mistakes or of the slow pace of implementation may not have been considered.

The overall effect of this high-risk strategy was to leave implementation of the Act at the mercy of events. Its emphasis on decentralization resulted in many different experiences with implementation in the various agencies. In addition, the political changes engendered by the election of Ronald Reagan, with attendant changes in political leadership for the agencies, a changing view of government's role, and changing priorities throughout government profoundly affected implementation of the Act. While the Reagan Administration found some parts of the Act useful, its commitment to the underlying assumptions upon which the Act was built, or to the Act as a whole, is more doubtful. Further, the vast scope of the changes in many agencies caused by Reagan's cutbacks have overwhelmed the reforms. Even when implementation has gone forward, its effects have frequently been lost in the larger turmoil.

CIVIL SERVICE REFORM AND THE POLICY CYCLE

This brief analysis suggests that there are problems with civil service reform. There are, at this point in its history, few satisfied participants or observers. The lessons it has provided, however, are very important.

The lessons of the Civil Service Reform Act can be viewed from several equally valid perspectives. Obviously, CSRA has provided an unparalleled opportunity to study and evaluate alternative personnel management procedures. Similarly, the reform efforts have contributed to our understanding of large-scale organizational change and of organizational efforts to cope with an unstable and turbulent environment. The detailed organizational assessments which were conducted as part of the evaluation of CSRA[9] have made a major contribution to that body of literature related to implementation of public policy. Perhaps even more significant, however, the history of CSRA provides a rich case study of the public policy process in the U.S. To be sure, civil service reform has some unique characteristics. In this reform, for example, civil servants are both the problem and the means to its solution. Civil servants are the *targets* of reform policies; in other policy areas they are the "fixers" and those who deliver the services. Nonetheless, the lessons of the Reform Act are not limited to personnel management; they enhance our general understanding of problems faced by public policy makers and by public policy recipients. They illustrate well our inability to judge the success or failure of public policies that, as a result of compromise, concession, or simple lack of understanding, do not accomplish what we thought they would.

There are many explanations for this conundrum of policy reform: grandiose promises with limited effects. First, policy design may be flawed, or the solutions proposed may not fit the problem identified. In some instances, even problem diagnosis may be incorrect. In others, the solution may be incorrect or untested. In the case of civil service reform, many of the more sweeping changes had never undergone a pilot test or an evaluation in a governmental setting. Second, the implementation process may be so incomplete as to never allow a full test of the reforms. Or, even if full implementation has been achieved on paper, displacement or distortion of the goal may have occurred during the implementation process, with the result that the actual reform bears little resemblance to the initial intent. Some argue that this has been true with civil service reform.[10]

Finally, given the Act's comprehensive nature and its internal conflicts, we can anticipate dramatically different perceptions of success or failure and different reactions to overall effectiveness. Such perceptions can involve different actors in the system, different agencies, different components of the Act, and different criteria for evaluation. Academics, for example, have consciously pursued a stance of "critical observer," focusing on such issues as increased politicization of the career service. Academic analysis has also focused on a rather limited number of the Act's provisions, such as the Senior Executive Service and Performance Evaluation. The Office of Personnel Management's (OPM) early pronouncements tended to concentrate on the extent to which structural components of the Act were put into place quickly. The Civil Service Commission was dissolved and the OPM created, for example, with remarkable speed. OPM did attempt to create a long-term evaluation strategy to examine all major aspects of the Act, but this long-term strategy was overtaken by events, and much of it has been scrapped by the Reagan Admin-

istration. With few exceptions, individual agencies have not undertaken internal evaluations of civil service reform.[11]

Other evaluations of the Act, including those of Congress, have
been influenced by external interest groups, including several created
in response to the reform; the Senior Executive Association, for
example, was formed by members of the Senior Executive Service.

THE STRUCTURE OF THE BOOK

This book examines the Civil Service Reform Act of 1978 and the
early history of its implementation. In Part I, problems with the old
system and the design, intent, and legislative history of CSRA are
discussed and implementation strategy is examined. Patricia Ingraham
describes the Carter Administration's reform package and the changes
that congressional debate and action produced. Frederick Thayer
provides a differing interpretation of the intent of CSRA and of its
likely outcome. Carolyn Ban analyzes the general implementation
strategy for CSRA and examines the structural implications.

Part II deals with civil service reform as organizational change and
with the implementation of the major components of the Act. Charles
Bann and Jerald Johnson analyze employee receptivity to performance
evaluation and merit pay. Karen and Gregory Gaertner examine the
same provisions from the perspective of two agencies. Mark Abramson, Richard Schmidt, and Sandra Baxter share the experience of the
Department of Health and Human Services—one of the largest federal
agencies—with the implementation of the Senior Executive Service.
Carolyn Ban and Toni Marzotto describe a little-analyzed but important component of the reform, that of the delegation of examining.
Donald Parker, Susan Schurman, and Ruth Montgomery report on
the experiences of several agencies with the labor management provisions of CSRA. The final article in part 2, by David Rosenbloom
and Curtis Berry, examines the effects of civil service reform on
affirmative action practices in the federal government.

Part III focuses on civil service reform as public policy and examines
our ability to judge its success or failure. In a chapter that compares
the reform experiences in the United States with those of Great
Britain, David Dillman argues that reform is cyclical, with basic issues
emerging and re-emerging as new political coalitions are formed.
Gregory and Karen Gaertner examine one specific instance of political
influence on the reforms: that of the Reagan transition. Mark Abramson and Richard Schmidt assert that, in an unstable environment
such as that created by political transition or budgetary cutback,
positive outcomes of reform are unlikely. Frederick Thayer, returning
to the argument he presented in Part 1, argues that the design of

the reform guaranteed its failure. David Stanley, taking a historical perspective, asks, What if the reform Act had not been passed? What would be different? Finally, in the concluding chapter, Patricia Ingraham examines our ability to evaluate major public policies adequately and poses the questions, Do we know how to tell whether a policy has succeeded or failed? And what difference does it make?

The Civil Service Reform Act has been a major reform with an impact on virtually every federal employee. Its implementation has involved major costs, both human and economic. The lessons of civil service reform, and of reform as a political and institutional process, are important. We hope this book is of assistance in understanding those lessons and in applying increased understanding not only to future reform efforts—which will surely come—but to other policies and processes as well.

NOTES

1. The symposium ws funded by the Conversations in the Disciplines Program, State University of New York.
2. For discussions of the perceived problems with increased politicization, see Bruce Buchanan, "The Senior Executive Service: How we can tell if it works," *Public Administration Review* (May/June 1981): 349–358; Patricia W. Ingraham and Peter Colby, "Political Reform and Government Management: The Case of the Senior Executive Service," *Policy Studies Journal* (December, 1981): 304–317.
3. See Fred Thayer, chap. 13 of this book, for additional discussion of this point.
4. Toni Marzotto, Charles Gossett and Carolyn Ban, "Civil Service Reform and the Scope of Bargaining in Federal Labor Relations," unpublished paper, 1983.
5. The "rule of three", i.e., selecting an employee from only those three who had the greatest number of points on the relevant list, was considered too limiting and prejudicial in its impact. This was due, in large part, to the extra points veterans received in civil service competition. The Carter team proposed a list of seven for managerial consideration. This recommendation was eliminated in congressional debate.
6. Alan Campbell, remarks at the SUNY Binghamton Symposium on Civil Service Reform, Binghamton, New York, October, 1981.
7. For additional discussion, see Mark Abramson and Richard Schmidt, chap. 12 of this book.
8. Leonard Reed, "Bureaucrats 2, President 0," *Harper's*, November 1982. On the other hand, see Keith Sinzinger, "Discipline and Purpose," *Federal Times*, March 21, 1983, p. 2.
9. The U.S. Office of Personnel Management contracted to three universities for in-depth assessments of the organizational effects of CSRA:

Case Western Reserve University, the University of Michigan and the University of California at Irvine. Reports of the organizational assessments are available through the Office of Planning and Evaluation, U.S. Office of Personnel Management.

10. See, for example, Mark Abramson, Richard Schmidt, and Sandra Baxter, chap. 6, of this book.

11. A notable exception is the U.S. Department of Health and Human Services, which funded a major departmental evaluation. Chaps. 6 and 12 of this book are based on that research.

I

THE CIVIL SERVICE REFORM ACT: HISTORY, DESIGN, AND STRUCTURE

CHAPTER ONE

The Civil Service Reform Act of 1978: Its Design and Legislative History

PATRICIA W. INGRAHAM

What we should be doing is building the foundations of a personnel system that can endure for a generation, one that has the capacity to respond to at least the predictable changes in society.

—Jule Sugarman

Civil Service Reform is always necessary.

—David Stanley

INTRODUCTION

The U.S. federal personnel system is a large and complicated beast, not amenable to easy change. In the years after World War II, it grew, like Topsy, by leaps and bounds. In the 1960s, the new social programs of the Kennedy and Johnson Administration spurred its growth again. This period of our history saw federal bureaucrats assume responsibility for civil rights, expanded educational opportunities, expanded housing opportunities and health care for the elderly and the poor, employment programs for the poor, urban redevelopment efforts, nutrition programs, and many others. As former Chairman of the Civil Service Commission Alan Campbell noted, the emphasis at this time was on service delivery, while "talk of government efficiency was muted, because many perceived it to be a subtle, conservative attack on the new social programs." [1]

This growth in both the scope and size of the government bureaucracy occurred in a system popularly perceived to be objective, nonpolitical, and at least moderately competent. The growth also occurred in an environment that included an expanding economy and increasing social expectations. It was assumed that there was room for slack in our governmental system, and some bureaucratic inefficiency—in the name of humane delivery of services—was considered a necessary part of that slack.

Many factors contributed to a changed perception in the 1970s. Elsewhere in this book, David Stanley and David Dillman discuss some of them. Clearly, for example, Watergate and its aftermath caused many Americans to reconsider the role of government, as well as its size. The incredible growth and concomitant cost of many of the programs adopted in the 1960s, especially the health programs, dismayed elected officials and citizens alike. Declining economic conditions forced reconsideration of our ability to tolerate slack in the system and the inefficiencies it implied. As usually occurs when frustration is widespread but both problems and solutions are somewhat unclear, many looked for a scapegoat, and they found it in the bureaucracy. Just prior to passage of the Civil Service Reform Act of 1978 (CSRA), the *National Journal* began an article about bureaucratic reform this way: "Bureaucrats. If you're not one of them, you probably can't stand them. You figure that they're lazy and overpaid, that they arrive at work late and leave early and take long lunch hours. But you can't do anything about it, because it's impossible to fire a bureaucrat." [2]

This is not to suggest that all of the problems with the federal bureaucracy and its personnel system were figments of the public's imagination. Problems with the existing system were recognized by the public, by civil servants, by elected officials, and by academic observers. There was, in fact, remarkable agreement about the nature of the problems. Briefly, the list of problems generally included the following elements:

1. The dual function of the Civil Service Commission, that is, protecting the merit system in government while also overseeing, and advising on, presidential political directives, was compromising the commission's overall effectiveness.

2. Though designed for the protection of civil servants, some aspects of the merit system were, in fact, thwarting managerial capacity and the ability to utilize career talent appropriately. In addition, the protection was so complete that, in some cases, removing incompetent employees proved to be nearly impossible.

3. Despite the protections of the merit system, whistleblowers, or those who identified "waste, fraud and mismanagement" in the system, were not afforded adequate protection and were often shifted to less desirable jobs or to less desirable locations.

4. There was an additional concern that the merit system rendered federal personnel *too* immune from political directives of any kind. Presidents and appointed political executives perceived the career

bureaucracy to be independent, isolated, and resistant to carrying out new policy directives.

5. The lack of responsiveness to elected political leaders also indicated a general lack of bureaucratic responsiveness to the citizenry. Access to the public bureaucracy was considered to be limited and skewed toward large interest groups concerned with receiving benefits from public programs.

6. Inefficiency in the public bureaucracy was fostered by the stability and security of the system and by the automatic nature of many federal promotions and pay increases. Longevity, not performance, was perceived to be the key to bureaucratic success.

7. Finally, among some segments of the population, most notably women and minorities, there was a continuing—and accurate—perception that the career civil service and its management cadre were insufficiently representative of the larger society.

All these concerns surfaced on the national policy agenda with the election of Jimmy Carter in 1976. Though presidents before him had raged against the career bureaucracy, Carter made it central to his domestic legislative concerns.

During his election campaign he noted, "There is no inherent conflict between careful planning, tight management, and constant reassessment, on the one hand, and compassionate concern for the plight of the deprived and the afflicted, on the other. Waste and inefficiency never fed a hungry child, provided a job for a willing worker, or educated a deserving student." [3] In his 1978 State of the Union message, President Carter asserted that civil service reform was "absolutely vital."

THE PERSONNEL MANAGEMENT PROJECT

Carter based his proposals for civil service reform on a comprehensive review of the existing system that he initiated in the spring of 1977. The President's Personnel Management Project (PMP) was established under the chairmanship of Alan Campbell, Carter's appointed chairman of the Civil Service Commission. The PMP staff was headed by Dwight Ink, a distinguished professional with a long career in public service. The President made himself the chairman of the Executive Committee for the reorganization effort. Expectations for the PMP were high. In August 1977, Ink outlined some of the reasons for optimism:

> Certainly the Presidential interest . . . is a very, very
> important reason why we're optimistic about this effort. . . . I
> think the fact that the Congress and the President represent

the same party makes it somewhat easier for legislation to pass. . . . Drawing heavily from within government for the leadership of this undertaking, while drawing heavily on ideas and people outside of government means, one, we have an expertise brought to bear here that is generally not the case with these studies. Second, there are many people from within government who will be involved and, therefore, will have a better understanding of the reason for the recommendations. . . . And finally, it seems to me that there is a greater recognition now than ever before that we do need change. . . .[4]

To obtain the widest possible range of information, the PMP staff, members of the ten designated task forces, and members of the staff of the Civil Service Commission held seventeen hearings and meetings throughout the United States as well as in Washington. In an abrupt departure from earlier long-term studies, the PMP gathered information, prepared recommendations, and submitted them to the President in slightly less than six months. The general areas of concern identified by the PMP paralleled those outlined earlier: the contradictory functions of the Civil Service Commission, the difficulties in managing and motivating employees under the existing merit provisions, the problems with maintaining merit while still providing opportunities for the career service to become more representative of the larger society. The three-volume final report also contained full descriptions of current problems with testing procedures, with wage and salary setting procedures, and with labor management practices. This comprehensive laundry list of problems and potential solutions formed the basis for the civil service reform legislation that Carter submitted to Congress. Its very comprehensiveness, however, posed some of the first problems for the reform; clearly, there was a need to choose which of the proposed reforms were most necessary and most critical. In addition, the nature of some of the problems identified meant that solving one problem would exacerbate another. Though there was a desire to enhance presidential control of the career bureaucracy, for example, doing so would obviously endanger some merit principles.

The Carter Reform Package

This tension among some of the proposals contained in the reform became the focus of a great deal of debate. This was so primarily because the true intent of the reform could be interpreted in a number of ways. President Carter, for example, frequently spoke of the need to "remove the deadwood" from the bureaucracy. Alan Campbell, who became Carter's chief spokesman for the reform efforts, consistently spoke of the need to improve the productivity and efficiency of the federal civil service. As Lynn and Vaden[5] and others have noted, many career civil servants, including some who had participated in the PMP, perceived the proposed reforms to be a "return to the spoils system." Some external observers interpreted the various components of the reform package as the full emergence of punitive management techniques. (See F. Thayer, chap. 2 of this book, for a discussion of this interpretation.) It was amidst such controversy and skepticism that Jimmy Carter declared in his State of the Union Message, in January 1978, that his proposed reform would create "a government that is efficient, open, and truly worthy of our people's understanding and respect." [6] Shortly thereafter, in March, the White House sent the Civil Service Reform Act of 1978 to the Hill. The President also submitted, in May 1978, the proposed Reorganization Plan Number 2, which proposed to abolish the Civil Service Commission. If neither house of Congress disapproved the provisions of the Reorganization Plan within sixty days of its submission, it would become effective automatically at the end of that time. This occurred when neither house took adverse action on the plan. The Civil Service Reform Act, on the other hand, was the subject of full congressional hearings and emerged in a form somewhat altered from Carter's original package. The reform package submitted by the Carter Administration had contained the components described below.

The Office of Personnel Management and the Merit System Protection Board

In combination with Reorganization Plan Number 2, the Civil Service Reform Act proposed that the Civil Service Commission be replaced by two new agencies: the Office of Personnel Management (OPM), which would have responsibility for personnel management and agency advisory functions, and the Merit Systems Protection Board (MSPB), which would have responsibility for hearing appeals and protecting the merit system. The Office of the Special Counsel, within the MSPB, would investigate claims of prohibited personnel practices and protect whistleblowers. The proposed Act gave the Director of the OPM broad authority to delegate many functions, including the examining function, to the individual agencies. (For a discussion of the implementation of this provision, see Ban and Marzotto, chapter 7 in this book.) This decentralization was to emphasize OPM's role as monitor and evaluator, rather than as a day-to-day manager.

In creating the Merit Systems Protection Board and the Office of the Special Counsel, referred to as the cornerstone of civil service reform by Dwight Ink, the intent was to reaffirm the significance of merit principles and their protection. The bipartisan, three-member Board and the Special Counsel were to be given new powers to enhance their role, including subpoena authority, the power to initiate disciplinary action, and the power to impose fines.

The Federal Labor Relations Authority

The Reorganization Plan and the proposed Act also created a new Federal Labor Relations Authority and gave it a statutory mandate to govern federal labor-management activities and procedures. This action consolidated the activities of two previous programs (those of the Assistant Secretary of Labor for Labor Management Relations, and those of the part-time Federal Labor Relations Council) into one coordinated and strengthened effort.

Whistleblowers

The proposed Act strengthened the protections available to whistleblowers within the career civil service by giving the Office of the Special Counsel a specific mandate to protect them from "improper reprisals." It also created a formal mechanism whereby the allegations of whistleblowers could be reviewed and acted upon.

Performance Evaluation

The bill proposed a sophisticated performance appraisal system with criteria based on the job itself and greater reliance on the results of performance evaluation in personnel actions. At the same time, it proposed procedures that would simplify the removal of unsatisfactory career civil servants. The dismissal procedures would be clearly linked to performance appraisal. Employee appeals procedures were simplified and clarified. All of these actions were attempts to "accelerate the personnel action process, while protecting employees' rights to fair treatment." [7]

The Senior Executive Service

The Act proposed to create a new Senior Executive Service (SES). In an action advocated by many previous reform panels, as well as the President's Personnel Management Project, senior managers in the career service would become part of an elite cadre of more flexible, more mobile administrators. Open to careerists in Grades GS 16 through Executive Level IV, and entered through individual contracts between the manager and the agency, the SES would remove many of the protections and securities of the traditional system. In return, it would provide the opportunity to compete for special awards and bonuses, as well as other benefits, including increased training and development opportunities, and sabbatical leaves. Only 10 percent of the total number of SES government-wide slots could be reserved for political appointees.

In addition, the SES, departing from previous civil service practice, placed rank in person rather than in position. The potential for mobility that this implied, and SES's strong emphasis on increased financial motivation and reward at the top management levels of government, borrowed heavily from private sector experience and theory. This "debt" was clearly acknowledged in the Senate Report on the bill, which stated, "This provision [of S.2640] should foster the development and effective use of senior executives in the Federal service. It is the kind of system that has been highly effective in the private sector. . . ." [8]

Merit Pay

The proposed bill created a new merit pay system for mid-level managers in Grades GS 13 through GS 15. Like the performance evaluation provisions in the SES, this provision was intended to decrease automatic promotion and pay increases. Under the new system, individuals covered by merit pay would receive only half of the annual "comparability" pay increase automatically. They would have to compete for the rest of their raise, with higher raises going to top performers (as judged by the new performance appraisal systems) and no additional raise for marginal employees.

Veterans Preference

Carter's reforms proposed to curtail veterans preference. Under existing provisions, veterans received preference points in entrance examinations, preference in hiring, and preference in reductions in force. Under the proposed reform, preference in hiring for nondisabled veterans would be limited to a period that ended ten years after their separation from the service. Absolute protection in reductions in force would be limited to the first three years of civil service employment. Preference provisions for disabled veterans would remain the same in the Carter package.

Labor-Management Relations

The President's reform proposed to place the federal labor relations program on a statutory basis. Since the Kennedy Administration, federal employees' rights to collective bargaining had been provided by executive orders. The reform codified collective bargaining. It formulated procedures for reconciling impasses that might occur. (It should be noted that this title of the reform was not added until May, well after the original package had been sent up. These provisions, in combination with the creation of the Federal Labor Relations Authority, were an effort to assuage labor's fears about the reform bill and opposition to it.)

Affirmative Action

The proposed Civil Service Reform Act restated commitment to affirmative action principles and to the need for more women and minorities in the career federal service. Though it was anticipated that reduced veterans preference would increase opportunities for these groups, there were also additional provisions for increased recruiting.

Research and Development

The reform package proposed a larger emphasis on research and demonstration projects, the purpose of which would be to test new approaches to public personnel administration. As the designers of the reform had discovered, there were few systematic opportunities for the testing and evaluation of management techniques new to the public sector. As a result of this void, many of the components of the reform had never been rigorously tested in a governmental context. This title was an attempt to avoid that problem for future reformers.

The Carter Administration's general satisfaction with the reform package it had assembled was summarized by Alan Campbell:

> Some have argued that to solve the problems associated with federal personnel management would require the addition of even more rules and regulations. One could envision a system in which every action could have a check and balance, and every decision a mid-level review. This might eradicate abuse, but it would also thwart productivity. A balance must be struck between the freedom necessary to service the public's needs and the oversight required to protect the system's integrity.

The President's Reorganization Plan and the Civil Service Reform Act strike the appropriate and necessary balance. Their significance to the President demonstrates that personnel management has rightly taken its place among the top priorities of the federal government.[9]

THE POLITICS OF CIVIL SERVICE REFORM

As occurs with most legislation, the reform package submitted by the Carter Administration to the 95th Congress emerged in a slightly altered form. Given the comprehensive nature of the reform, however, and some of the dramatic changes it proposed in the federal personnel system, its legislative history is remarkable, not for the changes it produced, but for the extent to which the Carter package remained intact.

Clearly, submitting such a comprehensive bill had risks: this was acknowledged early on in the history of the reform. The strategy to minimize those risks had several parts. First, because it was anticipated that federal employees themselves would resist large-scale change, the inclusion of large numbers of careerists in the Personnel Management Project was intended not only to enhance the problem-definition phase of the reform process, but to convince career civil servants that their interests were being served by the proposed legislation. Second, because to a large extent civil service reform did play to the public's discontent with bureaucracy, there was an effort to publicize the need for reform and the proposed solutions in the popular media. Alan Campbell spearheaded this effort and was successful in getting editorials supporting reform in most of the major newspapers of the country. Though this phase of the selling job was successful in reawakening public interest in bureaucratic reform, some observers have noted that it had punitive overtones and was interpreted by members of the civil service as a negative effort that portrayed them en masse as bumbling incompetents.[10] Jimmy Carter himself contributed to what James Sundquist labels this "bash the bureaucrat" tone by his frequent references to inefficiency in the bureaucracy and by his penchant for discussing the difficulties in firing federal employees.

The final component of the selling strategy was directed toward Congress itself. This, too, was a long-term strategy. It included the formation of a legislative task group with the purpose of coordinating contacts with key congressional personnel and educating members about the reform proposals. Of this effort, Felix Nigro writes:

This voluntary effort was particularly needed because many members of Congress were not familiar with the details of federal personnel management. The legislative task group held meetings with members of the House and Senate Committees considering the legislation and with their professional staffs. Members of the legislative task group also arranged for the attended meetings between President Carter and these Congressional Committee members.[11]

The Administration anticipated that most of the opposition to its legislative package would come in the House of Representatives. The Senate's recently reorganized committee system permitted consideration of both the Reorganization Plan and the Civil Service Reform Act in the same committee—the Committee on Governmental Affairs. Further, because the Senate committee was new, there was not a long history of individual members opposing or supporting the various principles contained in the proposed Act. The House was expected to be more of a problem because the House Post Office and Civil Service Committee, and especially the Civil Service Subcommittee, had long-standing and strong ties to organized labor, one of the interest groups opposing some parts of the Carter legislation.

Nonetheless, Administration strategists hoped for quick consideration and action from both the House and Senate. In an interview just before congressional committees began work on the bill, Campbell stated: "Civil service reform is not a sexy issue and we know we wouldn't have gotten nearly this far without presidential involvement. We hope to get it this year, because it would be very hard to gear up public and congressional interest for civil service reform again." [12]

The Senate

As hoped, action on the bill by the congressional committees was fairly speedy. After receiving the bill in March, the Senate committee held twelve days of hearings in April and May. While most testimony supported the legislation, there were some predictable opponents. Veterans groups strongly opposed any changes in the provisions for veterans preference. Employee unions continued to argue for stronger collective bargaining language and other provisions favorable to labor. Other groups and individuals, including a former chairman of the Civil Service Commission, argued that some provisions of the reform package, most specifically those relating to the SES, offered undue opportunity for political manipulation. The Committee Report rejected the veterans preference limitations in the bill after narrowly defeating an amendment offered by Senators Jacob Javits and Thomas Eagleton that would have refocused veterans preference to emphasize assistance to disabled veterans and veterans of the Vietnam War. The committee also expanded the protections available to whistleblowers and decreased the delegation powers afforded the Director of OPM under the proposed legislation. Finally, it somewhat limited the potential for political intrusion in the SES when it included a provision mandating that the majority of SES performance review boards be career executives.

The bill as passed by the Senate did not differ dramatically from that reported out of committee. There was continuing concern expressed in the floor debate about the potential for politicization of the federal service and many references to the abuses of the merit system during the Nixon Administration. As a result, amendments were proposed and approved that further specified the kinds of positions in the SES that could be open to noncareerists, that severely limited the proposed delegation of examining, and that set more specific guidelines and oversight provisions for the new performance evaluation systems. In relation to veterans preference, the full Senate voted to eliminate job preference for retired military officers. The final Senate vote on the Civil Service Reform Act was 87 to 1 in favor of the legislation.

The House of Representatives

Consideration of the bill in the House was more troublesome. Though the Carter Administration scored a major coup when Congressman Morris Udall agreed to be the floor manager of the legislation, opposition to the bill was strong. Two members of the Civil Service Subcommittee had introduced legislation to provide statutory collective bargaining rights for federal employees. In addition, other members were interested in attaching amendments that would liberalize the provisions of the Hatch Act. Still others opposed the legislation because their constituencies were heavily weighted with federal employees who feared the possible politicization of the federal service if the Carter legislation was approved.

As reported out of committee, the reform package contained amendments that Nigro characterized as "distasteful to the Administration." [13] Among them were provisions liberalizing the Hatch Act and an amendment that broadened the scope of employee's bargaining rights. In an amendment strongly opposed by the Administration, the Senior Executive Service was proposed as a two-year experiment in three agencies. Because the SES was considered by many of the bill's architects to be the centerpiece of the reform, this amendment was viewed with considerable dismay.

Action on the House floor was equally difficult. All the issues that
had surfaced in committee debate remained on the agenda, and it
was necessary to bring the legislation to the full House twice before
the threat of killing it completely was dissipated. Again, as anticipated,
the issues of labor management and veterans preference remained
controversial, and veterans groups lobbied very strongly against provisions that would limit preference in any way. The Carter Administration also stepped up its campaign for the legislation. The fear
that it would not pass caused the intervention of President Carter
himself, primarily to resolve the impasse on labor-management relations, but also to assist in reaching a compromise acceptable to
those members of Congress still advocating liberalization of the Hatch
Act.

The leadership of Morris Udall proved decisive in reaching a
compromise on the labor relations title (Title VII) of the proposed
legislation. The range of proposed amendments to this title was far
reaching, and included one that proposed eliminating the title al-
together. Udall prepared and advocated a compromise amendment
in which the unions gained statutory authority for labor relations
programs, but which reserved considerable flexibility for management
in dealing with employee unions. This amendment was the one
included in the final House package.

The veterans preference debate on the floor included an attempt
to improve the position of Vietnam era veterans vis-à-vis veterans
from other time periods. The Administration continued its effort to
dilute the overall impact of veterans preference provisions on affirmative action and equal opportunity programs. However, arguing that,
because few women entered military service, it was only natural that
veterans preference should work to their disadvantage, veterans groups,
and many members of the House, claimed that changing the rules
of the game in relation to veterans was breaking the faith with a
group to whom the nation was collectively indebted. Rather than
approve the revisions proposed by the Carter legislation, the House
of Representatives approved an amendment that changed veterans
preference only slightly. Proposed by Congressman James Hanley,
that amendment retained all existing preference provisions except for
making ineligible those who retired at or above the rank of Major.[14]

Finally, House action added a major affirmative action program to
the Act. To formally encourage active recruiting of minorities and
women, Congressman Robert Garcia offered an amendment creating
the Federal Equal Opportunity Recruitment Program (FEORP).[15] (This
program and its effects are discussed in more detail by Rosenbloom
and Berry, in chapter 9.) Final passage in the House occurred in
September 1978. There were only ten dissenting votes.

The Conference Committee

Felix Nigro summarized the issues remaining to be resolved in this way:

> 1) The House standard for sustaining adverse actions was preponderance of evidence, the Senate's was reasonable evidence; 2) the Senate bill called for government-wide implementation of the SES, without any time limitation, but the House bill would launch the SES as a two year experiment in only three agencies; 3) the Senate bill would allocate to a merit-increase pool part of the annual comparability increases for GS 13–15 supervisors whereas the House measure would automatically grant the comparability increases; 4) the House bill would require agencies to pay employee attorney fees in cases of successful appeals to the MSPB, provided such payment was warranted. The Senate bill would require agencies to pay such fees if the MSPB rules that the agency had taken the adverse action in bad faith; and 5) the Senate wanted the OPM Director to be appointed for four year terms, coterminous with that of the President, and to be removable only for cause, while the House bill contained no such provision.[16]

The bill that emerged from the Conference Committee represented compromises on all of the above issues except the SES. The committee rejected the experimental plan included in the House bill, and declared that the SES would become effective nine months after passage. However, a five-year sunset provision was attached to the SES title.

The other provisions of the Conference Committee bill included "preponderance of evidence" for misconduct, but "substantial evidence" for performance cases; automatic payment of half the annual comparability adjustment for GS 13–15, with the other half to be set by new merit pay procedures; payment of attorneys' fees in cases where the employee prevails on merit, or where the agency's actions are without merit; and four-year terms for OPM Directors, which are not necessarily coterminous with those of the President, but power for the President to remove for reasons other than cause.[17]

The final bill was approved by Congress and signed by President Carter in October 1978, slightly less than eight months after its introduction. It was widely heralded as Jimmy Carter's "most impressive domestic political victory." (The full text of the Act is contained in the Appendix.)

THE POLITICS OF EARLY IMPLEMENTATION

In many ways, the Civil Service Reform Act of 1978 is a classic case study of attempts to impose rational change on an essentially political—and irrational—system. The conflict began early on in the life of the legislation, when some elements—such as methods of determining pay and setting pay scales—were excluded from the reform package because of their controversial nature. The early exclusion, and belated addition, of the labor-management title is another example. Further (as Parker, Schurman, and Montgomery indicate in chapter 8), the effect of the political debate and compromise on those provisions when they were included was to render them unintelligible to many charged with their implementation. The underlying rationality of the reform package was also eroded by some Carter Administration attempts to anticipate the impact of political compromise. Chairman Campbell has indicated, for example, that the issue of eligibility for SES merit and performance awards was one such case of miscalculation. Because the framers of the legislation assumed that the cash award system would be controversial and subject to compromise, the original legislation submitted to Congress contained the provision that 50 percent of an agency's SES members could be eligible for merit or performance awards. This number was considered unworkable for actual implementation, but the framers expected, according to Campbell, that this number would be reduced in the course of congressional debate and compromise. It was not.[18]

The anticipated reduction came later, during the early implementation of the SES. After the first round of awards had been given, Congress, reacting to what it believed to be an abuse of the system by Performance Review Boards and by members of the SES themselves, reduced the percentage of those eligible in an agency to 25 percent of the agency total. The Office of Personnel Management further reduced the number eligible to 20 percent. Both the timing and the dramatic nature of the cuts had a very destructive impact on the attitudes of members of the SES toward the reform.[19]

Thus, although the components of the CSRA closely resembled those in the original package submitted by Carter, the inevitable politics of passage had taken its toll. To the extent that there had been a coherence in the Administration's comprehensive plan—and there are those who argue that there was not—some part of its internal logic had been distorted by the time it emerged in final form. Other distortions and changes occurred in early implementation, as the reform managers at OPM encountered the many problems created by imposing large-scale changes on massive and somewhat resistant bureaucratic institutions. Additional change occurred because

Congress was reluctant to approve the additional resources necessary to carry out some of the legislative objectives. The staffing and full operation of the Merit Systems Protection Board was delayed for a substantial period, for example, by the lack of adequate resources. Finally, a major part of the Administration's plan for achieving effective reform had been an extended implementation period, which would allow for acceptance and institutionalization of the reforms with minimal disruption. The election of Ronald Reagan, in 1980, effectively destroyed that plan. Whatever Jimmy Carter's true intent in working for passage of civil service reform, he fully supported the legislation. Ronald Reagan and his appointees did not. In addition, the program and budgetary cutbacks imposed by the Reagan Administration added another layer of uncertainty to an already insecure and unstable bureaucracy. As Abramson and Schmidt argue (chapter 12), the experience of CSRA in the Reagan Administration suggests very strongly that reform may not be possible in a cutback environment. As the rest of this volume indicates, implementation of CSRA has been a complicated process and it is not clear that full implementation will ever occur. It is worth noting here, however, that the politics that marked the design of civil service reform and the debate surrounding its adoption did not go away with the passage of the legislation. Politics is a continuing part of the complexity of reform and of the reform cycle.

NOTES

1. Alan K. Campbell, "Civil Service Reform as a Remedy for Bureaucratic Ills," in *Making Bureaucracies Work*, ed. Carol H. Weiss and Allen H. Barton (Beverly Hills: Sage, 1980), p. 154.
2. *National Journal*, "Bureaucrats Under Fire," September 30, 1978, p. 1540.
3. Jimmy Carter, cited in Campbell, "Civil Service Reform as a Remedy," p. 166.
4. "Improving Management Through Reorganization," *Civil Service Journal* 18, no. 2 (October–December 1977): 3–4.
5. Naomi Lynn and Richard Vaden, "Bureaucratic Response to Civil Service Reform," *Public Administration Review* (July–August 1979): 333–43.
6. Jimmy Carter, State of the Union Message, 1978, cited in Alan K. Campbell, "Civil Service Reform: A New Commitment," *Public Administration Review* (March–April 1978): 99.
7. U.S., Congress, Senate, Committee on Governmental Affairs, Report No. 95–98b, Civil Service Reform Act of 1978, p. 10.
8. Ibid., p. 11.
9. Campbell, "Civil Service Reform: A New Commitment," p. 103.

10. For two perspectives on this public relations effort, see Felix Nigro, "The Politics of Civil Service Reform," *Southern Review of Public Administration* (September 1979), especially pp. 204–7; and James Sundquist, "Jimmy Carter as Public Administrator: An Appraisal at Midterm," *Public Administration Review* (January–February 1979): 3–11.
11. Nigro, "Politics of Civil Service Reform," pp. 209–10.
12. Harlan Lebo, "The Administration's All-out Effort on Civil Service Reform," *National Journal* (May 27, 1978): 838.
13. Nigro, "Politics of Civil Service Reform," p. 218.
14. For additional information on the House actions, see U.S., Congress, House, Committee on the Post Office and Civil Service, *The Civil Service Reform Act of 1978*, 95th Cong.; and *Congressional Record*, for the debates on August 11, 1978, and September 7 and 11, 1978.
15. Garcia first offered the amendment in a markup session of the House Post Office and Civil Service Committee, July 11, 1978, withdrew it until the Civil Service Commission agreement could be negotiated, then re-introduced it in the markup session on July 19. See House, 95th Cong., Markup of Civil Service Reform legislation, Public Law 95–454 USGPO, 1978, pp. 168–72, 253–4.
16. Nigro, "Politics of Civil Service Reform," pp. 227–8.
17. See U.S. Congress. Conference Committees, 1978. *Civil Service Reform Act of 1978: Conference Report to Accompany S. 2640* (Washington, D.C.: U.S. Government Printing Office, 1980) for a full discussion of these agreements.
18. Comments of Alan Campbell, State University of New York at Binghamton Symposium on the Civil Service Reform Act of 1978, Binghamton, N.Y., October 1981.
19. See, for example, Patricia W. Ingraham and Peter W. Colby, "Political Reform and Government Management: The Case of the Senior Executive Service," Symposium on Civil Service Reform, *Policy Studies Journal* (December 1982).

CHAPTER TWO

The President's Management "Reforms": Theory X Triumphant

FREDERICK C. THAYER

When the President proposes in a nationally televised speech "the most sweeping reform of the Civil Service System since it was created nearly 100 years ago," and when he labels this "the centerpiece of government reorganization during my term in office," we have an unparalleled opportunity to examine the dominant operational premises of public administration. For those of us who teach, undertaking such analysis is the equivalent of a civic duty, for seldom do political leaders spell out in detail the managerial concepts they bring to office. The Carter statement combines a bleak view of human nature, the needs of civil servants at work, and how managers can best perform their jobs, with an incredible contradiction concerning the treatment of "whistleblowers"—those who bring to public attention what the President terms "gross management errors and abuses." [1] This is not the only significant conceptual contradiction, but it is the most important one.

The President's proposals largely conform to the recommendations of the Civil Service Commission's Federal Personnel Management Project. This project began in June of 1977 and, in addition to a leadership contingent of four people and a working group of twenty-one others, included ten task forces comprising well over 100 other people. Supplementary comments were solicited from approximately 1,500 other individuals and groups in and out of government. Academics were among those consulted, and some of the project leaders have significant academic credentials. The 255-page *Final Staff Report*

Reprinted with permission from *Public Administration Review*, July/August, 1978. The author wishes to acknowledge the valuable suggestions of Charles N. Coleman, who reviewed an earlier draft of this paper.

of that project[2] must be seen as something of a consensus among academics and practitioners about the concepts that should guide us in teaching and practice. To put it mildly, "Theory X" not only remains dominant but is stronger than ever.

I begin by examining the proposal for a new elite group of senior managers, because some conceptual issues are best highlighted by such analysis. I proceed next to the dominant notion that management in the public sector can best be improved by copying allegedly more efficient approaches used in private business. I close with predictions as to where the President's reform of the civil service will take us, if it is enacted.

THE SENIOR EXECUTIVE SERVICE

Many have recommended the establishment of a group of senior managers who move from agency to agency in accordance with specific program needs of the moment. It thus seems attractive at first glance to read that a group of about 9,000 managers above grade GS–15 will be "held accountable for program success, goal-setting and achievement."[3] Indeed, there is little in the concept of increased "mobility" with which to find fault. The problem lies in the theory of how the Senior Executive Service (SES) *ought* to be managed.

The SES is to be managed primarily through a "rigorous SES evaluation system" featuring annual assessments of managerial performance and "incentive pay awards" for those deemed worthy. Those appraised "consistently mediocre" or "severely deficient" will be "easily" removed (i.e., returned to their career rank, in the case of the 90 percent of SES members who are to come from the career service). Since "removal from SES for less than fully successful performance as a manager would not be considered a disciplinary action," removal will indeed be easy; it will not be appealable.[4]

The incentive pay system includes five salary rates between $42,201 and $50,000, and the elimination of *all* longevity increases in favor of "annual performance awards." "Highly successful" SES managers will be able to increase their salaries as much as 20 percent, but not above a "cap" of $54,625 (on 1978 computations), and they also will receive improved retirement benefits. Up to 15 percent of them may be designated "Meritorious Executive" ($2,500 per year for five years), and 1 percent may be labeled "Distinguished Executive" ($5,000 per year for five years).[5]

The SES proposal reflects the President's assertion that the civil service now suffers from "inadequate motivation" ("too few rewards for excellence and too few penalties for unsatisfactory performance").[6]

Motivation, in other words, is to be tied to what management theorist Frederick Herzberg labels the "KITA" factors (Kick in the Ass). "Positive KITA" (carrot) includes such things as bonuses (bribes) and "negative KITA" (stick) includes swift dismissal for subpar performance.[7] The President's assumption is that the civil service is "ready and willing to respond to the risks and rewards of competitive life," [8] defined as an all-out struggle among colleagues for monetary favors from immediate superiors.

The President not only assumes that the best way to motivate administrators is to combine the threat of punishment with the enticement of bonuses, but he also seeks to "protect 'whistle-blowers'." [9] I will analyze in detail below what is likely to happen in the civil service, but I note here the contradictory situation that will face the SES. Many of them will be immediately subordinate to patronage appointees whose qualifications for assessing the competence of career subordinates are not immediately obvious. The most significant cases of "whistleblowing," moreover, are likely to occur at precisely that interface of political appointees and career administrators, but the latter will have to "jump for the jellybeans" (bonuses) doled out by the former.[10] The theory seems to be that those who already have demonstrated they are worthy of the highest public trust are best motivated by means which assume they cannot be trusted at all.

There is yet another important contradiction in the theory underlying the SES. These executives are, presumably, to be prized for their ability to move back and forth among federal agencies, acquiring in the process an appreciation of the broader multi-agency aspects of government problems and programs. Their greatest contribution, then, is to come from something other than intensive concentration upon the specific goals and programs of their own agencies. However, the yearly cash bonuses must necessarily be based upon productivity and efficiency in pursuing the specific goals of individual agencies. The SES seems intended to create one type of Senior Executive, but the KITA system is likely to create a different type.

The Dominance of Private Sector "Efficiency"

Wallace Sayre may have been correct when he asserted that public administration and business administration are similar in all unimportant respects. Paul Appleby may have been correct when he insisted that public administration *is* different. A panel of the National Academy of Public Administration, reflecting upon the Watergate affair, may have been correct in concluding that many of those involved had "displayed little appreciation or understanding of the special ethical responsibilities of public service." Even the authors of the Personnel Management Project's *Final Staff Report* may have had the right idea in labeling "public service ethics" as important subject matter, and in recommending training programs to make sure all administrators understand and grasp "professional ethical responsibilities which may be quite different than those in private industry." [11] Overall, however, the theory of the President and his advisers holds that public and business administration are different, but the difference lies in the superiority of business administration. The authors of the *Final Staff Report* indicate time and again that government personnel management can best be improved by searching out and copying, as the President put it, the methods "that are used widely and effectively in private industry." [12]

The effort to develop clearer performance standards will be necessary to provide *some* justification for the distribution of cash bonuses, whatever the difficulty of setting measurable standards. We are on notice as to the standards likely to be set. The President, in pointing out that only 226 federal employees, of a total of 2,000,000, were fired during 1977 for "inefficiency," clearly implied the figure was too low.[13] The *Final Staff Report* used the phrase "unrealistically low," [14] and Civil Service Commission Chairman Alan K. Campbell concludes that within-grade pay increases have become "automatic for most employees," citing as evidence that only 700 employees were denied them in FY 1977.[15] The proposed Office of Personnel Management will no doubt develop quantitative standards for the number of employees to be fired or denied pay raises each year if the government is to prove its diligence.

The belief that such methods are effectively used in industry seems only a belief, and one not buttressed by any evidence in the *Final Staff Report*. Meanwhile, other evidence indicates that industry and municipal government are not very successful at tying wage increases to productivity gains. The director of economic relations for General Motors, for example, announces that the company does not measure its productivity gains, because it cannot:

> We measure absenteeism, we measure profitability, we
> measure scrappage rates, we measure energy use, and every
> one of them can be called part of productivity. But it's
> difficult to measure productivity *period*.[16]

Another question raised by the new commitment to private business methods has to do with the renewed emphasis upon performance appraisals. Perhaps it is time to question the search for improved linkages between performance appraisals, productivity standards, cash bonuses, and more authority for superiors to fire subordinates. Having lived within a governmental performance appraisal system for many years, I can testify that many, indeed most, superiors do not and cannot *know* precisely what their subordinates *should* do and *do* do. Victor Thompson noted years ago that science and technology make "curiously distorted and unstable" the relationship of worker to boss, because the former is often a specialist in a field with which the latter is unfamiliar; despite increased reliance upon quantification or standardized adjectival performance ratings, "merit" becomes "an essentially subjective judgment of superiors," whatever we might wish it to be.[17] John Kenneth Galbraith's advice to Foreign Service officers becomes pertinent:

> I would urge your organization to look with concern on any administrative advice that encourages obeisance and bootlicking rather than independent expression and behavior. I have in mind especially the efficiency report. This device accords to the superior in an organization far too much power over both the manners and thoughts of his subordinates. . . . Co-workers and subordinates are often in a far better position to judge a man's competence and his capacity for leadership than his boss.[18]

So much of what modern administrators do occurs within those multiorganizational networks James Thompson labeled systems of "intensive interdependence" that the "absence or relative unimportance of authority" becomes obvious.[19] The President's approach seems obsolete at best.

Also worth asking is whether private business relies upon appraisal systems and firing to the extent the President and his advisers seem to believe it does. The *Final Staff Report* investigated the subject, but was content to say only that "the private sector has a wide variety of performance appraisal plans,"[20] thus indicating there is little agreement at all. Wide publicity is given to some corporate firings, but less attention is given to the generous financial settlements which frequently accompany such firings. There is evidence that corporations move around managers they deem incompetent, giving them meaningless titles and smaller offices as part of a general pattern of avoiding the ultimate act of punishment. Moreover, there is other evidence that successful corporations assume that the initial hiring of a manager is a partial guarantee of lifetime tenure, somewhat in the Japanese manner.[21] In sum, the President and his advisers may be relying upon an "ideal type" incorporating one normative premise (more people should be fired), while ignoring contrary operating premises (managers deserve humane treatment).

Still another question leads us to the mythology of classical microeconomics, the dominant subfield which deals with the behavior and decisions of individual producers and consumers. We in public administration tend to leave economics to the economists, even though *all* our conventional decision-making models are taken intact from microeconomic models of individual rational choice. Charles Lindblom, whose classic article is a highlight of this journal's history, reminds us that when we focus upon institutions such as legislatures, civil service, parties, and interest groups, we are "left with secondary questions." [22] Like those who now advocate the increasing use of market models in public administration, using as a label the phrase "public choice," the President and his advisers seem to rely upon a dubious mythology. It is reasonably clear by now that the ability of a private corporation to make a profit tells us nothing of its efficiency, but demonstrates only that it can set prices high enough to cover any and all *in*efficiencies.

One final question involves the needs of individuals in private business. The President and his advisers seemingly have a cynical view of what best motivates private sector employees to better performance. It is ironic that the emphasis upon threat and cash comes soon after a massive compilation of contrary evidence by the Department of Health, Education, and Welfare. Citing all sorts of survey data, some of it gathered by government itself, the department pointed out that "good pay" was not nearly so important as "interesting work," and that 70 percent of the nation's professionals and businessmen did not believe their jobs brought out their best.[23] Survey data cannot be conclusive, but the current reform movement might at least take it into account. To be sure, the *Final Staff Report* devoted one page to the topic "Improving the Quality of Working Life" but, even there, "bonus pay plans" was a prominent item.[24] The President ignored the large issue in his speech.

Coming full circle, I return to the issue of public versus business administration. Some analysts foresee the removal of distinctions between the two, and they suggest that the upcoming symbiosis may resemble what we take to be the norms of public administration.[25] Corporations are, more and more, compelled to deal with the consequences of their decisions for entire communities, even society at large, rather than restricting their analyses to consequences which affect only them. One example is corporate bribery, a problem exacerbated by the needs of corporation managers to survive in a highly competitive environment. Another example is phenomena encompassed by such words as "pollution" and "ecology," not to mention the search for the meaning of "social responsibility" on the part of corporations. In general, it is increasingly necessary to bring *inside* the decision-making process those factors economists label "externalities." The President's narrowly-based emphasis upon efficiency runs counter to this trend. Admittedly, coming to terms with such notions requires us to take up even broader issues, and I turn to them in the final section.

Can We Move Beyond Theory X?

In posing this question, I begin by outlining how the President's proposed reforms are likely to change organizational behavior. I earlier suggested that the twin emphases on protecting "whistle-blowers" and distributing cash bonuses were contradictory. Operationally, all of the following seem inevitable:

• Some senior executives will come to rely upon their annual 20 percent bonuses, and, hence, will not be disposed to "blow the whistle," "rock the boat," or otherwise "make waves." They will in some cases be extremely loyal to their patronage superiors; in other cases they may even "blackmail" superiors by threatening to "go public" if bonuses are not renewed; and, in all cases, they probably will attempt to remain close to their superiors, thereby negating the major objective of increased mobility.
• Other senior executives who believe they may be removed from the SES or denied a cash bonus, will trigger dubious cases of "whistleblowing." This is because the ability to make a case that they have been politically abused is one of the few ways to appeal the punishment meted out by superiors. This would seem to promise more and more public protests by administrators, and more extensive and expensive litigation.[26]
• Still other senior executives, those already removed or denied a cash bonus before being able to "blow the whistle," will become embittered careerists dedicated to damaging the images of their superiors and their agencies. This should lead to widespread "leaking" of documents, followed by wholesale rummaging through agencies to discover the culprits.

Other changes can be outlined by looking at the proposed system for dealing with middle level managers (GS–13 through GS–15), then at the newly revised definition of "due process" which is being proposed. Middle level managers are to be subject to an incentive pay system which permits as much as a 12 percent annual increase. This will be done without any increase in expenditures, and the explanation is ingenious and devious. Salaries are now raised each year by applying the "comparability principle," designed to keep federal salaries in line with private business. The increase usually amounts to 6 or 7 percent, an amount more correctly defined as "cost-of-living increase." This is to be cut in half, with only the first half being distributed to all administrators. The second half will form a "pool" from which merit increases will be distributed. How this will work is worth spelling out, as in the following chart, which assumes that administrators A and B hold the same rank and are paid $30,000 per year, a mid-range figure for middle managers.

Administrator A

Salary 1978	$30,000
2.5% comparability increase	750
12% merit increase	3,600
Salary 1979	34,350
2.5% comparability increase	860
12% merit increase	4,122
Salary 1980	39,322

Administrator B

Salary 1978	$30,000
2.5% comparability increase	750
0% merit increase	000
Salary 1979	30,750
2.5% comparability increase	770
0% merit increase	000
Salary 1980	31,520

This system, it can be seen, encourages exponential growth in salary differentials among managers holding the same rank and having comparable experience, with the ultimately huge differentials being justified solely on the basis of performance appraisals. It will be clear to many managers that denial of a merit increase is a fine levied by superiors to provide rewards for colleagues. If the two administrators used in the above example work together, the relationship will be one of extreme bitterness, in that the money with which the superior bribes A comes directly from B.

Such patterns are unlikely to change, once established, even though merit pay decisions are to be made year-to-year. For a superior to deny a subordinate a merit increase after having awarded such an increase the year before is to imply the superior made an incorrect decision the year before. Those agencies having long experience with performance appraisal systems as the basis for "up or out" personnel decisions (primarily the military and the Foreign Service), scan the records of officials administering ratings for consistency in awards.

We cannot expect superiors to demonstrate patterns of inconsistency, hence those awarded merit increases will continue to receive them, and those denied them will continue to be denied them. The predictable outcome among middle managers is "dog-eat-dog" competition, if not sheer hatred.[27]

The President promised his reforms would guarantee "due process" for employees subject to adverse action; as in the case of finding money for merit pay raises, however, this turns out to be dishonest advertising. Following the lead in the *Final Staff Report*,[28] the President completely reversed the meaning of "due process." While many punitive decisions will not be appealable to all, employees who can appeal will have to prove they were wronged. This version of "guilty until you prove yourself innocent" is enshrined in the legislation introduced following the speech.[29] Chairman Campbell summarizes the underlying philosophy as "A manager must have the right to be arbitrary in order to be effective."[30] While this approach will be threatening to everyone, minorities may see it as a major step backward.

Overall, it might be said that the President and his advisers rely upon the twin concepts of competition and authoritarianism. In doing so, they propose a system roughly parallel to those used in other career services (military, Foreign Service), but they seem not to understand some important nuances. At middle manager levels, for example, the other services use "up or out" methods, but in quite a different way. Those not selected for promotion are identified as probably not competent enough to serve at a higher rank, but terminating their service does not identify them as *presently* incompetent. The President's system depends upon redesignating as incompetent those earlier identified as competent at the same rank, then punishing them through decisions they cannot appeal. At lower levels of the military, the combination of an "all-volunteer" force and a "competitive pay" system has, as one military sociologist points out, led to a drive for unionism, the method commonly used by workers in private industry to make themselves less vulnerable to a competitive market situation.[31] It seems reasonable to predict that if the proposed system is installed, we will see a drive for unionism and collective bargaining among middle level public managers (GS 13–15). As to the reliance upon authoritarianism, the likely outcome is dangerous pathology:

> . . . autocratic management carries as its by-product a certain emotional immaturity. Fear leads to intellectual malfunctioning, which leads to ineffective response. . . . Not only does [the autocratic organization] lack that enthusiasm for accomplishing

>the mission or objective that we call motivation, it creates for
>itself the illusion of power and control. . . . Based on the
>obvious absence of overt resistance . . . it creates an inability
>to solve problems . . . partly because it systematically denies
>to itself access to information available in the lower echelon of
>the organization.[32]

With sycophancy identified as organization virtue, the future is not
promising.

Even broader questions are paradigmatic, and beyond the immediate reach of this analysis. No concept is dearer to the academic
heart of public administration than the presumed inability to distinguish "politics" or "policy" from "administration" or "implementation." Yet there remains a fairly clear legal and operational distinction between those who *make* policy (elected or appointed officials)
and those who *carry out* policy (careerists). Given the separation,
one recognized in the jargon of official Washington ("Smith is at the
policy level, Jones is at the administrative level"), it is difficult for
any president to advocate participation in the policy-making process
by supposedly neutral civil servants. Indeed, one cannot describe a
career service without accepting the premise that careerists are supposed to be apolitical, value-free instruments of policy. The logical
impossibility of the premise does not remove its existence. The
President's acknowledgment that "whistleblowing" can be useful,
even if his sincerity is questionable,[33] is a first step toward conceding
some need for participative management approaches. The same can
be said for the *Final Staff Report's* emphasis on ethical standards. If
we who study and write about public administration are to provide
a conceptual foundation which permits any president to go further,
we must look more closely at the nexus of political, economic, and
organization theories. The members of our community involved in
this proposal did not perform that task.

Finally, the immediate yardstick for successful reformation is apparently to be developed in an unusual way. The President did not
assert that many employees *are* "underworked, overpaid, and in-
sulated from the consequences of incompetence," only that the public
"suspects" this is so.[34] Chairman Campbell emphasizes that because
performance appraisals are not now used for demotion or separation,
"the image of the federal government as 'the incompetent's best
friend' is given credence, even if factually inaccurate." [35] Taken
together, these statements say that we may not have a problem at
all but, so long as the public *believes* there is a problem, leaders
must pretend the problem exists. Presumably, firings will be escalated
until opinion polls show the public no longer believes the government

is staffed by incompetents, even if many competent administrators must be removed in the process. Thus, Theory X is combined with Catch-22.

NOTES

1. Quotations are from U.S. Office of the White House Press Secretary. "Text to Address by the President to the National Press Club," March 2, 1978, 3 pp (mimeo). (hereafter, "President's Speech").
2. U.S. President's Reorganization Project, Personnel Management Project, Vol. 1, *Final Staff Report* (Washington, D.C.: Government Printing Office, December 1977). (hereafter, *Final Staff Report*.)
3. U.S. Civil Service Commission News Release [Fact Sheet], March 2, 1978, 21 pp. (mimeo). *Fact Sheet* 6.
4. Ibid.
5. Ibid.
6. "President's Speech."
7. Herzberg, of course, connects all KITA factors to "movement," not to "motivation," which can come only from improvement in the quality of working life. In Herzberg's theory, even "positive KITA" can only remove dissatisfaction and pain, not provide satisfaction. Frederick Herzberg, "One More Time: How Do You Motivate Employees? " in Fred A. Kramer, *Perspectives on Public Bureaucracy.* 2nd ed. (Cambridge: Winthrop Publishers, 1977), pp. 111–26.
8. "President's Speech."
9. Ibid.
10. Herzberg uses this phrase to criticize this use of "positive KITA" as a form of behavior modification.
11. The Sayre and Appleby observations are summarized in Howard E. McCurdy, *Public Administration: A Synthesis* (Menlo Park, Cal.: Cummings Publishing, 1977), p. 106. The Academy's report was published as Frederick C. Mosher and others, *Watergate: Implications for Responsible Government* (New York: Basic Books, 1974), p. 67; *Final Staff Report*, p. 135.
12. "President's Speech."
13. Ibid.
14. *Final Staff Report*, p. 40.
15. Alan K. Campbell, "Civil Service Reform: A New Commitment," *Public Administration Review* 38, no. 2 (March/April 1978): 101.
16. Brent Upson, quoted in Jerry Flint, "Productivity Just Won't Measure Up," *New York Times*, April 9, 1978. The article also notes that productivity has not proved useful as a guideline for wage increases in municipal government. While the issue cannot be explored in detail here, some of the more obvious problems are highlighted by the use of "body counts" in the Viet Nam War, and by testimony from New York City policemen that a requirement to meet quotas compelled them to issue parking summonses to legally parked cars and even to

nonexistent cars. *New York Times*, September 17, 1976. On the broader questions, see Kenneth H. Militzer, "The Fallacy of Linking Wages to Productivity," ibid., Business Section, August 19, 1973.

17. Victor A. Thompson, *Modern Organization*, (New York: Knopf, 1961), pp. 47, 98.

18. John Kenneth Galbraith, "Advice to the Foreign Service," *Foreign Service Journal* (December, 1969).

19. James D. Thompson, "Social Interdependence, the Polity, and Public Administration," *Administration and Society* 6, no. 1 (May, 1974): 15.

20. *Final Staff Report*, p. 142.

21. See, e.g., Allan J. Mayer and Michael Ruby, "One Firm's Family," *Newsweek*, November 21, 1977. This is an in-depth analysis of IBM's personnel management philosophy.

22. Charles E. Lindblom, *Politics and Markets* (New York, Basic Books, 1977), p. ix.

23. *Work in America*. Report of a Special Task Force to the Secretary of Health, Education and Welfare (Cambridge, Mass.: M.I.T. Press, n.d.), pp. 13, 41.

24. *Final Staff Report*, p. 209.

25. George C. Lodge, *The New American Ideology* (New York: Alfred A. Knopf, 1975), esp. chaps. 8–10; Harlan Cleveland, *The Future Executive* (New York: Harper and Row, 1972), esp. chaps. 1–4.

26. On the general treatment of whistleblowers (punishment by superiors), and the already enormous costs of resulting legal battles, see Helen Dudar, "The Price of Blowing the Whistle," *New York Times Sunday Magazine*, October 30, 1977.

27. While my direct experience is limited, my impression is that systems of this sort are in use at some universities and lead to the outcomes outlined here.

28. *Final Staff Report*, p. 41.

29. U.S., Congress, Senate, 95th Cong., 2d Sess., S. 2640, March 3, 1978, Title II, pp. 32–3.

30. J.F. terHorst, "Civil Service: It's Time for Reform," *Pittsburgh Press*, April 12, 1978.

31. Charles C. Moskos, Jr., "Compensation and the Military Institution," *Air Force Magazine* 61, no. 4 (April, 1978): 35.

32. David G. Bowers, *Systems of Organization: Management of the Human Resource* (Ann Arbor: University of Michigan Press, 1977), pp. 5–6.

33. After thorough investigation, three reporters concluded that concern over the leaking of information "has become as great as it was in the early months of the Nixon Administration." One internal investigation expert outlined the immediate objective as finding "an example—a case that would really slam an employee and possibly embarrass the news organization that dealt with him." While the Carter Administration was not using wiretapping and lie detector tests to locate whistleblowers, it was insisting upon sworn affidavits from those

considered possible sources of unauthorized leaks. *New York Times,* May 14, 1978.

34. "President's Speech."
35. Campbell, "Civil Service Reform," p. 101.

CHAPTER THREE

Implementing Civil Service Reform: Structure and Strategy

CAROLYN BAN

The implementation of new programs is a relatively recent interest for political scientists and students of public administration. While a principal focus of earlier work was how a bill became a law, it is only over the past twenty years that we have begun to realize that passage of the legislation is not the end of the process, but only the beginning of a second phase as fraught with problems and pitfalls as the legislative phase. We now understand that implementation of complex programs is far from automatic, and we have started to identify some of the likely sources of problems.[1] First, we have learned that the implementation process cannot be examined in isolation; it is a part of the policy process and its course is determined by the values, assumptions, planning (or lack of it), and compromises that drive the formulation of new policies. This is a point that Ingraham explores at greater length in chapter 15. We have also learned that implementation of complex programs frequently does not go smoothly. Indeed, in the bluntest formulation, implementation has been described as conforming to a "basic pattern: grand pretensions, faulty execution, puny results." [2]

To what extent has the implementation of the Civil Service Reform Act of 1978 (CSRA) succumbed to the many problems that lead to this pattern? Five years after the passage of the Act, it is not too

In writing this chapter, I have received help from people too numerous to mention. I would like to acknowledge all the staff members of OPM's CSRA Evaluation Management Division. In addition, I would like to thank the people throughout OPM who shared with me information and insights. And I acknowledge with gratitude the assistance of the excellent staff at OPM's library. Most of the material cited in this chapter, published and unpublished, can be found in their first-rate collection.

soon to analyze both the methods that were used to implement the Act and their effects.

As we have seen (chapter 1), CSRA was an enormously complex piece of legislation. The complexity that made implementation itself such a challenge makes it difficult to study the process of implementation. Given the many sections of the Act, its internal inconsistencies, and the many actors and organizations involved in its implementation, both practitioners and scholars have disagreed about what the Act was "really" about. This paper will focus on the creation of new agencies, and on these agencies' definitions of their new roles.

CREATING NEW AGENCIES: THE BIRTH OF OPM, MSPB,OSC, AND FLRA

Reorganization Plan Number 2 created two successor agencies to the old Civil Service Commission (CSC): the Office of Personnel Management (OPM), to be the management, or administration, voice on personnel matters, and the Merit Systems Protection Board (MSPB), to take over the appellate functions of the CSC. The Office of the Special Counsel (OSC) was created as a semi-independent organization within the MSPB, to protect whistleblowers and to investigate prohibited personnel practices. In addition, the reorganization plan created the Federal Labor Relations Authority (FLRA), a new agency that absorbed the functions of the Federal Labor Relations Council,[3] and that had new responsibilities as well. Finally, most of the CSC's responsibilities for equal employment opportunity in the federal government were handed off to the Equal Employment Opportunity Commission (EEOC), with the exception of the new Federal Equal Opportunity Recruitment Program (FEORP), which was housed in OPM. (Rosenbloom and Berry discuss some of the problems that EEOC has faced in handling this new responsibility, in chapter 9.)

Past experience in reorganizations at the federal level has shown that the process is rarely a completely smooth one. Past reorganizations have included combining several organizations into a new agency, such as the Department of Energy, the Environmental Protection Agency, or the Drug Enforcement Administration, or splitting out functions into separate agencies, such as the creation of the Department of Education and of Health and Human Services out of the Department of Health, Education and Welfare. In many cases, even several years after reorganization, new agencies are seen as less than fully successful in meeting their mission, and many have lingering morale problems.[4]

New agencies seem to share a common set of problems, which center around the clarity of their mission, the quality of their leadership, and the adequacy of resources available to them. But an examination of the structures set up by CSRA shows that they differed sharply in both the extent to which they faced such problems and the effectiveness with which they dealt with them.

FLRA and MSPB: Establishing Independence on a Tight Budget

Both FLRA and MSPB faced very similar start-up problems. While both inherited functions that had been performed by predecessor organizations, each was faced with the need to prove publicly both its independence and its competence. Both were faced with an increased work load in comparison to their predecessors as a result of broadened responsibilities. And both faced severe resource problems in their early years.

The Merit Systems Protection Board got off to a reasonably good start. The three members of the Board were selected quite early in 1979. Two of the three Board members had extensive experience in government.[5] The membership of the Board remained quite stable during the start-up period; there was no turnover until 1982. Further, their central mission, hearing appeals, was a concrete, clearly-defined task, and there has been no questioning of the legitimacy of the function or of their technical ability to perform it. The Board earned a reputation in its early days as a highly independent, professional body. There has been some dissatisfaction, however, with the highly legalistic, quasi-judicial model the Board has followed for its proceedings. Some observers feel that individuals appealing to the Board without counsel will fare less well than under the previous system.[6]

The pattern for the Federal Labor Relations Authority has been quite similar. The members of the Authority were in place early. The primary mission of the agency is clearly defined and, in many ways, flows from the work of a previously existing body, and leadership has changed only gradually. But while the FLRA was able to build upon the procedures of the earlier Federal Labor Relations Council (FLRC), it needed to prove that, unlike that body, it was a fully independent agency. Thus one critical early decision was that the FLRA was not bound by the precedents of the FLRC.[7]

The only major problems the new agencies have faced in defining their roles have been in areas where they have new responsibilities. For FLRA, this was its new role as investigator and arbiter of unfair labor practices, a function handled by the new position of General Counsel. The General Accounting Office (GAO) pointed out the problems created by the "delayed appointment and confirmation of the General Counsel (which) prevented the issuing of FLRA's regulations or the taking of dispositive action on unfair labor practice cases, resulting in a substantial case backlog.[8] Even after the appointment of a General Counsel, the management of this function had considerable shake-down problems. The number of unfair labor practices has more than doubled since passage of the Act, at least in part because the new procedures were cost free to the unions. FLRA has been taxed by this work load and is gradually beginning to explore ways to reduce the volume.[9]

MSPB faced similar although somewhat less severe problems in setting up the Merit Systems Review and Studies Office, charged with the new function of conducting studies of the merit system. Appointment of a Director was slow, and little was done during the first year. Further, as budgets have remained tight, this function has remained small and underfinanced.[10]

Both agencies shared major problems in the mundane but crucial area of resources, including budget, staff, and space. They started with severely inadequate budgets and ceilings on staff. Even where they had vacancies, finding qualified people was very time-consuming, and space was so inadequate that they sometimes avoided hiring needed staff because there wasn't any place to put them.[11] MSPB's first-year report conveys some of the flavor of these problems:

> . . . the first item of business facing the Chairwoman . . . was to create a workable, functioning agency. Given the circumstances surrounding the creation of the Board, this was no easy task.
> As a result of the unfavorable division of resources of the former CSC [Civil Service Commission] and the inadequate budgetary allocations provided to the Board, it commenced its existence unorganized, understaffed and underfinanced. [Space provided was] inadequate, seriously below acceptable standards and . . . ill-suited to the Board's functions. . . . During the past year, the Board has constantly been engaged in negotiations with the GSA for acceptable space. Although fruitless thus far these negotiations continue.[12]

GAO also detailed similar problems within the FLRA:

> The original 1979 level of the funding and the number of positions assigned to FLRA represented the resources required to continue a Federal labor-management relations program similar to that of EO 11491, before FLRA was established. As a result, the original funding did not provide for the new functions assigned by the CSRA. Many of these new functions

required hiring new professional staff. . . . The lack of
adequate space and resultant dispersal of staff have seriously
affected FLRA's efficiency and public image.[13]

At the end of two full years, GAO stated that these resource
problems "are slowly being resolved." [14]

The Office of the Special Counsel: A Problem Child

While OSC had start-up problems similar to those of the FLRA
and MSPB, its problems were greatly exacerbated by a lack of stability
of leadership and a failure to define its mission clearly. H. Patrick
Swygert, the first Special Counsel, lasted less than one year. Mary
Eastwood was then left in an acting capacity for a year and a half.
President Reagan appointed Alex Kozinski to the position, in 1981,
and he lasted only fourteen months before resigning under heavy
criticism. The newest Special Counsel, K. William O'Conner, was
appointed late in 1982.

The fact that OSC faced special problems was clear to the organization at the start. The OSC pointed it out in their first-year report:
"It is important to note that, unlike other government agencies which
result from reorganization, the OSC has been required to meet its
responsibilities without the benefit of a prior history of programmatic
activity." [15] This meant that OSC had to attempt to define clearly
some very soft concepts, such as whistleblowing, and to develop
procedures for how to investigate charges of prohibited personnel
practices, as well as strategies for how to proceed if, in the OSC's
judgment, a prohibited personnel practice had been committed. Setting up the function required a wide range of technical and administrative skills. There is some question as to whether such skills were
present. But, equally important, the OSC appeared to lack a strong
leadership that could provide both a clear definition of the agency's
role and the external visibility necessary to make the new office
really successful.[16]

These leadership problems were combined with the worst resource
problems of any of the new agencies. According to the OSC's First
Annual Report, the OSC received only nine professional and five
clerical staff members from the CSC. Their initial staff ceiling was
nineteen, plus six staff members loaned from the MSPB. By the end
of 1979, the staff had grown to forty-eight. (Their FY 1980 authorization was for 140 positions.) The report states:

> Until it received a supplemental appropriation in August,
> 1979, the Office was hampered by a lack of funds and staff,
> which prevented it from conducting needed investigations and

keeping current with the complaint caseload. Throughout the year, the central office staff was also handicapped by lack of private office space in which to work . . . thus making it difficult to afford the privacy necessary to effectively protect the rights of the Federal employees concerned.[17]

OSC's problems continued well into their second year. According to a GAO report:

In July 1980, the Congress rescinded 46 percent ($2 million) of OSC's fiscal year 1980 budget. The recission adversely affected all areas of operations, including near total curtailment of OSC's mandated responsibilities. In August 1980, OSC stopped all traveling and most other outlays and detailed about 60 percent of its staff to MSPB for about five weeks. Travel for investigations was not authorized until after January 1981. OSC continued to receive complaints during this time. As a result, we were told the case backlog increased, and OSC has not been able to fully recover.[18]

Such severe resource problems appear to be more than merely bad planning. It is difficult to apportion the blame for the initial staff ceiling, but it appears to be consistent with the theory that either the Administration or Congress, or both, saw the new Office of the Special Counsel as primarily a symbolic gesture, a sop to those critics concerned that the new reforms would undermine the merit system.[19] If either body had expected the protection of whistleblowers or the prevention of prohibited personnel practices would be serious problems, they would have seen the initial figures as ludicrous. The fact that the OSC has been kept on a near-starvation diet appears to reflect continued congressional skepticism about the Office's function, as well as dissatisfaction with the Office's leadership.

The OSC also faced a unique problem: its odd relationship to the MSPB. OSC is administratively housed within the MSPB, yet the Special Counsel is appointed by the president, and its budget requests are submitted directly to Congress.[20] The relationship between the two agencies has ranged from uncomfortable to disastrous. As GAO briefly described what was a long and rancorous conflict:

OSC operates independently of MSPB; however, OSC is organizationally part of MSPB for administrative purposes. This relationship is not clearly defined in the Civil Service Reform Act of 1978. In August 1980, the Chairwoman of MSPB issued directives concerning OSC's personnel authority, budget, and communications with the Congress and the news media. The Acting Special Counsel believed that adhering to

these directives would be contrary to the Civil Service Reform
Act. OSC requested a legal opinion from the Department of
Justice on OSC's relationship with MSPB. However, the issues
were not resolved. In November 1980, MSPB filed a lawsuit
against the Acting Special Counsel seeking to compel OSC to
comply with the August 1980 directives. The suit was
dismissed as moot, but the Special Counsel and MSPB must
work out a more satisfactory relationship.[21]

MSPB has gone so far as to submit a legislative proposal to separate
the Special Counsel from the Board and make it a completely independent agency.[22]

The net result of all these troubles is that, while the MSPB and
the FLRA have become established agencies, with high legitimacy,
the OSC is still struggling to find its identity and to gain acceptance
of its role. Reagan's first Special Counsel, Alex Kozinski, worsened
the organization's problems considerably. He was accused of bringing
the work of the OSC to a virtual halt and of politicizing the office.
Close to 50 percent of the central staff left during his tenure. The
controversy was so extreme that Representative Patricia Schroeder,
the head of the Civil Service Subcommittee, actually introduced a
bill to abolish the OSC, saying it "now protects management and
the administration from whistleblowers. It's the reverse [of congressional intent]." [23] While the bill has now been withdrawn, the new
Special Counsel has been put on notice that the position of the
organization is still tenuous.[24]

*The Office of Personnel Management: Redirection of an Established
Agency*

OPM had fewer resource problems than the other agencies, since
it was in fact, if not technically, the successor agency to the Civil
Service Commission[25] and inherited most of its budget and staff, as
well as its physical plant. But central to the concept of civil service
reform was a major change in the role of the central personnel
management agency, exemplified by Alan Campbell's statement, in
an address to the International Personnel Management Association,
that "personnel managers must be a part of management, rather than
either servants of management or policemen of the civil service
system." [26] The following section describes Campbell's attempts to
"turn the agency around," focusing particularly on OPM's strategy
for implementing the management-oriented reforms in CSRA. It then
turns to the role of OPM and its treatment of these reforms in the
Reagan Administration.

OPM Under Carter

Since Alan Campbell, the Chair of the CSC, and Jule Sugarman, a member of the Commission, were immediately made the first Director and Deputy Director of OPM, strong leadership with a clear sense of mission was in place, ready to move decisively on their agenda for the agency. Resources of the new agency were focused, to the extent possible, on implementing civil service reform. Thus, resources were pulled away from the more traditional CSC functions, particularly the job information and examining programs, and into programs designed to work directly with agencies in implementing civil service reform, as well as into research and evaluation.[27]

OPM's new leadership also strove for a change in values and attitudes on the part of OPM's staff, in line with the new direction they saw as appropriate for personnel management: away from the old style, which they clearly saw as hidebound, rigid, and negative (in line with the CSC's traditional role as the watchdog protecting the merit system against abuse), to a more active, positive, service orientation, with the personnelist seen as working with and assisting management. As one internal document put it:

> In its dealings with agencies OPM staff will adopt a "Yes, You Can" attitude and will help agency managers find practical solutions to difficult and persistent management problems. . . .[28]

This definition of OPM's new role was not greeted with unanimous enthusiasm by all CSC staff members. There was disagreement over the appropriateness of the new stance; some agency staff members greatly feared the politicization of a function that they felt should be strictly above politics. Others were uncomfortable with changing priorities and resource allocations.[29] But the feeling within OPM during Campbell's tenure of office was of an entire organization with clear-cut priorities; the major focus of the agency's energies was on the implementation of civil service reform, and particularly the management-oriented provisions.

For many people, the core of the Reform Act was the group of provisions aimed at improving the quality of management in the federal government, particularly the management aspects of the Senior Executive Service (SES), and the introduction of new systems of performance appraisal and merit pay. These provisions reflected a common concept of management, and OPM and the agencies generally saw them as a package and followed related strategies for implementing them.

The goal of the management reforms was to improve the quality of management in agencies via use of a management-by-objectives type of performance appraisal system that was linked to rewards and punishments. It was expected that such a system would lead to increased motivation on the part of both employees and mid- and upper-level managers and to increased communication between supervisors and subordinates about organizational goals and expected performance, and that it would give top managers the tools to control the work of their agencies.[30]

While one can argue whether this model of management is theoretically desirable,[31] the important thing from the point of view of implementation is that this is a management system, designed to be used by line managers. While the old CSC could always dictate personnel policy—via regulation—to agency personnel shops, to make this program work OPM had to reach a very different audience. Every supervisor and manager throughout the entire federal government had to be trained in the techniques of the new system. Moreover, managers at all levels had to understand and accept the purposes of the system. The implementation strategy OPM followed was posited on a number of assumptions. Among the central ones were:

- Top line management had to buy into the new systems, understand their underlying assumptions, and be willing both to commit resources to system development and then to use the system.
- The federal government was enormously complex. Agencies would have different needs, and would want to link new management systems to systems already in place. Further, agencies needed to design their own systems in order to have a sense of ownership, rather than having systems imposed upon them.
- Personnel functions as a whole should be decentralized to the extent feasible. This meant decentralization from OPM to agencies down as close as possible to the actual user of services. Line managers should become more directly involved in the personnel process.

In short, OPM's strategy was an attempt to rely less on the classic systems management model of implementation, which sees the process of implementation as a rational process organized hierarchically, and to depend more on a model of implementation as organizational development.[32] As Elmore characterizes this model:

The implementation process is necessarily one of consensus-building and accommodation between policy-makers and implementors. The central problem of implementation is not whether implementors conform to prescribed policy but whether the implementation process results in consensus in goals, individual autonomy, and commitment to policy on the part of those who must carry it out.[33]

The strategy OPM followed, based on these assumptions, was complex and ambitious. First, OPM's top leadership worked very hard to sell the Act to top managers in agencies. This process involved an enormous amount of direct personal contact by Campbell and Sugarman and by other top OPM executives. Individuals such as Assistant Secretaries for Management in the larger agencies were seen as crucial players, and their support was solicited both in passing the bill and in actively implementing the Act, once it had passed.

OPM also followed a process of consulting with line managers in developing its own strategy and procedures. Early in the implementation process, in October 1978, OPM held a major program development conference at Ocean City, Maryland, both to sell the reform and to give line managers a chance to provide input on implementation. The results of the conference[34] were fed into the OPM internal planning process.

OPM also attempted to open lines of communication directly to line managers both through such conferences as Ocean City and Cherry Hill the following year,[35] and through new publications, such as *Management*, targeted directly to line managers. While OPM could never directly reach all managers in the federal government, it could hope to win the support of "opinion leaders" who would sway others in their agencies.

In the area of designing the specifics of new performance appraisal and merit pay systems, OPM's early policy has been characterized as "let a hundred flowers bloom."[36] Actual system design and implementation was decentralized to agencies. OPM defined its role as providing training and technical assistance and approving agencies' plans, using quite broad guidelines as criteria for approval. The new Agency Relations Office played a central role in assisting agencies, identifying problems, providing technical assistance and handholding, and generally troubleshooting. Plan approval was somewhat of a bureaucratic stumbling block since, in theory, agencies' plans for performance appraisal systems for SES members, merit pay employees, and all other employees should be closely linked. Agencies were actually required to submit separate plans for each group, and the plans were approved by different offices within OPM. These offices did not coordinate their procedures and standards very effectively in the early stages of implementation; the plans of some agencies were accepted by one division and rejected by another. Furthermore, OPM changed standards in a number of cases in midstream, much to the distress of agencies that had already proceeded in implementing plans, which then had to be changed.

It is hard to convey the scope of the required implementation. The amount of work involved in training close to 130,000 line managers and SES members in the new systems, and in actually developing specific performance standards for a workforce of 2.3 million people is truly staggering. From the vantage point of several years of hindsight, a number of questions arise. First, were either OPM or the agencies up to the job? Developing performance appraisal systems and standards is a complex, technical task. OPM, a small agency, didn't have vast reservoirs of expertise in this highly technical field. There was a fair amount of throwing people into the breach, people who were often bright and committed, but who had little or no experience in the field, and frequently were given little training for their new assignments.

Agencies faced similar problems. Small agencies, in particular, complained that the implementation process taxed their limited resources and expertise. They frequently requested more structure and assistance from OPM. Even large agencies were stretched thin when it came to providing training and guidance to their line managers. People were often given cursory training and then expected to train others. As a result, there is some evidence that training in some agencies focused primarily on the specifics of the process, without conveying the necessary broader context of what these systems were designed to accomplish or how to use them.[37]

Some agencies recognized this problem and used consultants to design their systems, develop their training, and, in some cases, deliver the training. But many agencies found their experiences with consultants disillusioning. The perception that the expertise in performance appraisal in the private sector was far higher turned out to be not generally accurate.[38] Consultants sometimes brought in standardized packages, which they attempted to impose with little understanding of the setting. And relying on outsiders reduced the likelihood that agency staff would have a sense of ownership in the system.

In short, implementing such complex systems in every agency simultaneously may have overtaxed the resources available.

Further, while a decentralized and gradual strategy of implementation seems sensible in light of what we know about how agencies work, it was a high-risk strategy, given the shallow nature of political support for the reforms. OPM was fairly candid in recognizing that they didn't know enough to impose one specific design on all agencies. Rather, they proceeded in an atmosphere of experimentation; agencies would try different approaches, inevitably some would work better than others, and, as it became clear which approaches were most successful, OPM would share that information with other agencies and urge them to adapt their systems.

But a number of actors in the political environment were unwilling to sit back and let this gradual process take its course. The lack of depth of congressional support was evidenced very early, when Congress reduced the number of SES members who could receive bonuses. The General Accounting Office (GAO) has consistently failed to support OPM's decentralized strategy of implementation, pushing OPM toward tighter control.[39]

Most important, this gradual strategy assumed a stable political environment and relative continuity in government policies and programs. Thus, at the time of the 1980 election, agencies were still in the throes of setting up merit pay programs, as well as performance appraisal programs for all employees, with final implementation almost a year away. Further, at that point, in spite of OPM's active selling job, it is clear that agencies varied greatly in the degree to which they had accepted the underlying premises of the reforms. (See Gaertner and Gaertner, chapters 5 and 11, for comparisons of the approaches of two agencies, and chapter 6, Abramson, Schmidt, and Baxter, for the view from another agency.)

OPM Under Reagan

The 1980 election of Ronald Reagan had a far more pronounced effect on OPM than on the other agencies under study, since one of the effects of the reorganization was to transform OPM from the bipartisan commission model of the CSC to an agency headed by a single Director, appointed by the President. So this was the first "political" transition for the agency. For those in the midst of implementing civil service reform, there was a period of several months of uncertainty. How would the new Administration define OPM's role in general? And would they support civil service reform, or would they see it as tainted because it had been introduced by President Carter?

Reagan's appointment as Director of OPM, Donald Devine, is a conservative Republican who had been active in Maryland state politics as well as on the Reagan campaign. He has been an outspoken supporter of the President's general approach, in particular advocating sharp reductions in the size of the federal government and in the range of functions it performs.[40]

Devine also had definite ideas about the proper role for the federal government's personnel agency. He rejected the new orientation espoused by Campbell, who emphasized OPM's role as a service agency, and as a management agency. Devine stressed a "back to basics" approach. This included, first, a renewed emphasis on the policing function, that is, OPM's oversight responsibilities in ensuring compliance with civil service rules and regulations, including such "bedrock" personnel management concerns as proper application of position classification standards.[41] While budgets for many agency programs were cut, "funding for evaluation and compliance activities was increased by $0.7 million in 1981 in order to carry out an aggressive oversight function."[42]

OPM under Devine has also put less emphasis on decentralization of personnel management functions, at least in part because decentralization makes oversight and control more difficult. (See chapter 7 on delegations of examining.)

The new Administration also put highest priority on reducing costs of personnel programs, particularly on health insurance for federal workers and on pension plans and the costs associated with early retirement.

Inevitably, then, implementation of civil service reform did not dominate the attention of the agency as it had under Campbell. At the same time, Devine strongly stated his commitment to many parts of civil service reform, particularly to the management aspects of the reform. He saw performance appraisal as a major tool for managers, and stressed the importance of employee involvement in developing standards.[43] He also put a major OPM effort into ensuring that all agencies actually met the October 1981 deadline for implementation of new performance appraisal and merit pay systems. Further, he increased the size of the performance appraisal group, which many had seen as "seriously understaffed,"[44] and combined the performance appraisal and merit pay staffs into a single organization (an Office of Performance Management).

But Devine's approach to OPM's role in implementation differed markedly from the previous administration's. Consistent with his overall priorities for OPM, the emphasis shifted from technical assistance to oversight and compliance. Agencies were required to report formally to OPM on progress in meeting the October 1981 deadline, and to certify the number of people for whom standards were in place. At the same time, there was a de-emphasis on winning the support of top program managers and on networking, plus a renewed stress on working with "agency personnel directors, many of whom felt cast aside by the original OPM leadership."[45]

While OPM's leadership remained committed to much of civil service reform, it is important to note that final implementation took place in a period of turmoil and controversy over personnel management issues. Many agencies were going through major redefinitions of their role. Budgets were slashed, and, in several agencies, reductions in force (RIFs) were taking place or were threatened. Thus, in a number of agencies, the first use of the new performance appraisal systems occurred during a time of severe stress, with high levels of distrust between political and career staff, and with the fear that these performance appraisal results, from a new and untested system, would be used against individuals if a RIF occurred. (Chapter 5, on the transition, gives a vivid portrayal of this period.) As a result, although new systems for performance appraisal are in place and are being used, there is a real question whether they have been accepted by employees as fair and equitable.

PBIS, or Reforming CSRA

Within this context, OPM has been attempting to introduce, through the regulatory process, significant changes in the performance appraisal and merit pay systems, which are being sold as "bringing the spirit of the Civil Service Reform Act a big step forward." [46] The proposed changes, referred to as a Performance-Based Incentive System (PBIS), are quite technical, and they have gone through several permutations, but we can briefly summarize them.

First, the new regulations would impose more standardization on agencies' performance appraisal systems, including requiring all agencies to use a system with five levels of performance. While OPM sees this as "ensur[ing] that the new system is uniform in application and treats all employees fairly," [47] agencies that have invested considerable resources in developing their own systems, printing forms, and training staff may not take kindly to imposition of increased standardization.

Second, the new regulations propose linkages which are much more automatic between performance appraisal results and some personnel actions, such as within-grade increases. Further the proposed regulations make an individual's performance appraisal a major criterion for retention during a RIF, severely reducing the importance of seniority. They also significantly limit "bump" and "retreat" rights.

Proposed changes to merit pay are also quite significant. In addition to increasing standardization of the system, OPM proposes to guarantee that merit pay employees who receive a "fully successful" or higher rating would receive a pay raise at least equal to those given to nonmerit pay employees. This change responds to one of the most frequent gripes about the merit pay system, but while guaranteeing the full "comparability" raise reduces the risks of merit pay, it also significantly reduces the chances for sizeable rewards.[48]

As this book goes to press, the fate of these regulations is still in doubt. The protracted conflict over them has no doubt had an effect on the continued implementation of the original reforms by adding considerable uncertainty to the situation. Further, a study of OPM's attempt to introduce these changes, and of the reactions to OPM's initiative, sheds light on the policy process when there are high levels of conflict and little trust between all the major actors. One is tempted to describe the events of the past year as an example of politics as soap opera, with cliff-hangers, back-biting, and actions which are improbable, if not implausible.

In very brief summary, OPM issued draft regulations first in March of 1983, with a great deal of fanfare. The new regulations were described as "introducing pay-for-performance for *all* general schedule employees." [49] Initial reaction from all parties was strongly negative. The press focused largely on the RIF regulations, with headlines such as "Proposed Changes Bode Ill for RIFees." [50] Congressional reaction was also largely negative, and there was a feeling that the Administration was attempting, via regulations, to slip through major changes that should be considered by Congress.[51]

The regulations were redrafted to respond to comments and criticisms, and revised regulations were released in July and again in October. Even though these changes entailed significant revisions, and really did respond to many of the criticisms which had been raised, reaction from all parties was still largely negative.

When the third set of regulations was issued in October, OPM announced that, since attempts to reach a compromise with Congress had failed, OPM would implement the new regulations by November 25. At the last minute, Congress, in an attachment to a continuing resolution, banned OPM from using appropriated funds to implement the new regulations.[52] At this point, OPM came up with what can only be described as a creative interpretation of congressional intent, and decreed that the resolution only meant that OPM, MSPB, and FLRA could not spend money to implement. Therefore, all other agencies were to implement immediately, without OPM assistance!

Since Congress was not in session, the ball passed to the unions. NTEU brought suit to stop implementation of the regulations. In late December, they succeeded in getting a temporary restraining order against implementation, which OPM promptly pledged to appeal.[53] At this point, the policy process has deterioriated into a protracted, rancourous conflict with no end in sight.

One explanation for the sharpness of the reactions to the new regulations is that they were proposed at a time when conflict between career and noncareer employees was still high, in a number of agencies, and when many employees still did not trust the new performance appraisal system. But the strength of the reaction may also be a result of OPM's leadership style under the Reagan administration. Devine's detractors see him as overly ideological.[54] His relations with the Democratic leadership of House committees with oversight responsibility for OPM, including Reps. Patricia Schroeder and Mary Rose Oakar, have ranged from cool to stormy. And union leaders have branded him as both "anti-union," for his strong support for the firing of striking air traffic controllers, and "anti-federal employee," because of his commitment to shrinking the size of the federal workforce and reducing federal employees' benefits. Within this political context, it is easy to see why there was considerable distrust of OPM's motives in issuing the new regulations, and why many saw them as just one more was to "bash the bureaucrat."

These proposed changes are also a perfect example of why it is so difficult to study implementation. Simple models of a clear-cut new program, which is implemented over a certain period of years, after which its effects can be assessed, fall in the face of a complex reality in which the political environment changes rapidly and in which even the program we are examining continues to metamorphose.

CONCLUSIONS: THE STATE OF THE FEDERAL PERSONNEL SYSTEM

Five years after the passage of the Civil Service Reform Act, the federal personnel system is still mired in controversy. The MSPB and the FLRA face problems that center largely on resources. The Office of the Special Counsel has yet to show that its challenging mission is even possible, and its very existence is still tenuous. And OPM, under Devine, has been the center of repeated controversy. Some of this controversy has been a result of Devine's ideological and contentious style. But some people have had second thoughts about the wisdom of making the personnel function directly subject to political control. The issues of the politicization of the personnel system, and of its effects on the merit system, are still alive.[55]

The Splintering of the Personnel Function

We have focused thus far on the problems internal to each agency. Implementation of the Act also necessitated setting up new relationships between the separate agencies created to handle separate personnel functions. While relations have generally not been at the level of the discord between MSPB and OSC, they have frequently been prickly. Many of the problems can be traced to the Act itself, which attempted to create clearly separate functions, but which, in fact, left

a fair amount of overlap and ambiguity. For example, it handed off
equal employment opportunity programs to the EEOC, then turned
around and created a new EEO program, the Federal Equal Opportunity Recruitment Program (FEORP), and gave it to OPM, thereby
setting up problems of coordination and duplication of reporting that
were entirely predictable.[56] (See chapter 9 for more on this subject.)

In other areas, one agency was given the right to second-guess
another. OPM was given the responsibility to regulate in the personnel field, but MSPB was given an oversight responsibility, and
can rule OPM regulations invalid if MSPB believes them to require
the commitment of a prohibited personnel practice. While MSPB has
not often used this power,[57] the effects of such decisions can be
severe. The General Accounting Office has also gotten into the act,
through decisions, by the Comptroller General, ruling that OPM's
policies violate the law. Such rulings are binding. Similarly, in the
labor relations field, OPM is supposed to set policy for the federal
government, yet policy is, in reality, frequently set by FLRA and
court decisions in such areas, for example, as the provision of official
time and per diem to employees for union negotiations, or the role
of the unions in the new performance appraisal systems.

In short, many agency personnel specialists are confused as to
where to look for policy direction, or how to proceed in various
circumstances. This may have led to a more cautious, conservative
approach in such areas as firing or downgrading employees for poor
performance, precisely the opposite effect of that desired by the
authors of the Act. Indeed, one can question whether the newly
created organizational structures have succeeded in improving either
the protection of the rights of individuals or the clarity and efficiency
of the personnel function.

NOTES

1. Among the seminal works on implementation are Jeffrey L. Pressman
   and Aaron B. Wildavsky, *Implementation* (Berkeley: University of California Press, 1973); and Eugene Bardach, *The Implementation Game,*
   (Cambridge, Mass.: MIT Press, 1977). See also Robert T. Nakamura
   and Frank Smallwood, *The Politics of Policy Implementation* (New York:
   St. Martin's Press, 1980).
2. Richard F. Elmore, "Organizational Models of Social Program Implementation," *Public Policy* 26, no. 2 (Spring 1978): 186.
3. The Federal Labor Relations Council was created by President Nixon
   in 1969 (E.O. 11491). It was clearly a "management" body, comprised
   of the head of the CSC as Chair, the Secretary of Labor and the
   Director of OMB. See Toni Marzotto, Charles Gossett, and Carolyn

Ban, "Civil Service Reform and the Scope of Bargaining in Federal Labor Relations," unpublished.

4. For an interesting study of the reorganization that created the Drug Enforcement Administration, see Mark H. Moore, "Reorganization Plan #2 Reviewed: Problems in Implementing a Strategy to Reduce the Supply of Drugs to Illicit Markets in the United States," *Public Policy* 26, no. 2 (Spring 1978). On morale problems at the Department of Energy, see U.S. Office of Personnel Management, *Federal Employee Attitude Survey I: Department of Energy*, (Washington, D.C., U.S. Office of Personnel Management, 1980).

5. Ruth Prokop, who was named Chair, had extensive federal-sector experience. Ersa Poston had been a Commissioner of the CSC prior to the reorganization, and Ronald Wertheim had been in private practice.

6. Based on personal interviews with personnel officers in several agencies, 1980–81.

7. See Marzotto, Gossett, and Ban, "Civil Service Reform."

8. U.S. General Accounting Office, *The Federal Labor Relations Authority: Its First Year in Operation*, April 2, 1980 (hereafter cited as *Federal Labor Relations Authority*).

9. See, for example, U.S. General Accounting Office, *Steps Can be Taken to Improve Federal Labor-Management Relations and Reduce the Number and Costs of Unfair Labor Practice Charges*, November 5, 1982.

10. The Merit Systems Review and Studies Office recently received bad publicity, when a senior staff member quit with a public blast at the then head of the office, Kenneth Foran, for bringing the work of the office to a virtual halt. See Howard Kurtz, "Underused Bureaucrat Calls it Quits," *Washington Post*, April 20, 1983, p. A1. Shortly thereafter, Foran was reassigned to a nonsupervisory job. The office is currently headed by Dennis Little.

11. U.S. General Accounting Office, *Federal Labor Relations Authority*. The FLRA's space problems were so severe that GAO included photographs in the report to make the point graphically.

12. U.S. Merit Systems Protection Board, *First Annual Report*, 1980.

13. U.S. General Accounting Office, *Federal Labor Relations Authority*.

14. U.S. General Accounting Office. *Civil Service Reform after Two Years: Some Initial Problems Resolved but Serious Concerns Remain*, November 10, 1981.

15. Office of the Special Counsel, *First Annual Report to the Congress on the Activities of the Office of the Special Counsel*, 1980 (hereafter cited as *First Annual Report*).

16. U.S. General Accounting Office, *First Year Activities of the Merit Systems Protection Board and the Office of the Special Counsel*, June 1980, particularly faults the OSC for its lack of active leadership (hereafter cited as *MSPB and OSC*). U.S. General Accounting Office, *The Office of the Special Counsel Can Improve Its Management of Whistleblower Cases*, December 30, 1980, criticizes its administrative and case-handling procedures.

17. Office of the Special Counsel, *First Annual Report.*
18. U.S. General Accounting Office, *Observations on the Office of the Special Counsel's Operations,* December 2, 1981 (hereafter cited as *Office of the Special Counsel's Operations*).
19. See Bernard Rosen, "Merit and the President's Plan for Changing the Civil Service System," *Public Administration Review* 38, no. 4 (July/August 1978): 301–304, for an early expression of concern about the effects of the reform on merit.
20. Office of the Special Counsel, *For Merit and Honesty in Government: The Role of the Special Counsel,* 1980. It is interesting to note that this brochure, introducing the OSC to Federal workers, describes the OSC as an "independent Federal office," and never mentions the MSPB.
21. U.S. General Accounting Office, *Office of the Special Counsel's Operations.*
22. U.S. General Accounting Office, *MSPB and OSC.*
23. *Federal Times,* August 23, 1982. See also Keith Sinzinger, "Tactless in Technicolor," *Federal Times,* April 26, 1982.
24. Keith Sinzinger, "Staying Off Death Row," *Federal Times,* October 18, 1982. Schroeder has actually introduced a bill which would put not only OSC, but MSPB as a whole, along with OPM and FLRA, under a three-year "sunset," requiring formal reauthorization by Congress every three years. See Winston Wood, "Schroeder Takes Aim at Reform Act Units," *Federal Times,* October 24, 1983.
25. Technically speaking, the MSPB was the successor agency to the CSC, and OPM was a new entity, but in fact OPM kept the lion's share of CSC resources and space, and it was MSPB that started almost from scratch.
26. Alan K. Campbell, "Revitalizing the Federal Personnel System," *Public Personnel Management* 7, no. 6 (January-February, 1978): 59 (transcript of Keynote Address at the IPMA International Conference, in Chicago, Ill., October 3, 1977).
27. Approximately $5.6 million was reprogrammed in the first few months after passage of the Act. See "Implementation of Civil Service Reform: the First Steps," statement of Alan K. Campbell before the Committee on Post Office and Civil Service, U.S. House of Representatives, March 20, 1979.
28. U.S. Office of Personnel Management, "Organizational Change Goals for the U.S. Office of Personnel Management," Unpublished, 1979.
29. See U.S. Office of Personnel Management, "An Analysis of Workforce Input on the OPM Organizational Change Goals," Unpublished, 1979.
30. Such reforms were in the main line of contemporary organization theory. See, for example, W. Jack Duncan, *Organizational Behavior,* 2nd ed. (Boston: Houghton Mifflin, 1981), sections on motivation theories and on performance evaluation and organizational effectiveness.
31. See Frederick C. Thayer, "Civil Service Reform and Performance Appraisal: a Policy Disaster," *Public Personnel Management* 10, no. 1 (Spring 1981), as well as his contribution to this volume.

32. Elmore, "Organizational Models."
33. Ibid., p. 209.
34. See U.S. Office of Personnel Management, *Launching Civil Service Reform* (Summary Report of the Program Development Conference held at Ocean City, Maryland, October 22–25, 1978), (Washington, D.C.: U.S. Office of Personnel Management, November, 1978).
35. See U.S. Office of Personnel Management, *Toward a More Productive Government* (Summary Report of Second Annual Management Conference, in Cherry Hill, N.J., February 10–13, 1980), (Washington, D.C.: U.S. Office of Personnel Management, March 1980).
36. Merit Systems Protection Board, *Report on the Significant Actions of the Office of Personnel Management during 1980*, (Washington, D.C.: U.S. Merit Systems Protection Board, June 1981).
37. Frank Sherwood, "Wrong Assumptions, Wrong Strategies," *The Bureaucrat* (Winter 1982–3).
38. Ibid.
39. The most spectacular disagreement between OPM and GAO came over the implementation of merit pay, in which GAO unsuccessfully tried to get OPM to postpone the October 1, 1981, implementation date and did force OPM to change the amount of money included in the merit pay calculations. See U.S. General Accounting Office, *Federal Merit Pay: Important Concerns Need Attention*, March 3, 1981. See also U.S. Office of Personnel Management, *Merit Pay in 1980: Lessons Learned*, 1982, for a brief, cogent discussion of the effects of the GAO decision on the size of payouts.
40. See "OPM Director Devine Charts New Direction" (Transcript of Devine's remarks at the ASPA National Conference in Detroit), *Public Administration Times* 4, no. 9 (May 1, 1981): 4. See also U.S. Office of Personnel Management, *OPM, the Year in Review, 1981*, July, 1982.
41. Donald J. Devine, "A Fresh Look at the Status Quo," *Management* 2, no. 3 (Summer 1981): 2–5.
42. Efstathia Siegel, "Back to Basics and Looking Forward: a Personnel Management Perspective," *Management* 3, no. 2 (Spring 1982): 9–11.
43. Ibid.
44. Robert W. Brown, "Performance Appraisal: A Policy Implementation Analysis," *Review of Public Personnel Administration* 2, no. 2 (Spring 1982): 74.
45. Ibid., p. 78.
46. U.S. Office of Personnel Management, OPM Fact Sheet, "A Performance-Based Incentive System for the Federal Work Force," March 29, 1983.
47. Ibid.
48. The proposed regulations would remove two of the three sources of funds, i.e., one-half the comparability raises and the within-grade increase funds, from the merit pay pool. This would leave only the funds which the agency would have spent for quality step increases prior to the reform, a miniscule sum (in past years it ranged from 0.1 to 0.4 percent of payroll). The result would be, in essence, to eliminate

merit pay as a significant factor in setting pay for the group covered by it. For a useful diagram illustrating the contributions from various sources to the merit pay pool under the current system, see Patricia Power and Laurie Rothenberg, *Merit Pay in 1980: Lessons Learned* (Washington, D.C.: U.S. Office of Personnel Management, 1982).

49. U.S. Office of Personnel Management, OPM Fact Sheet.
50. Mike Causey, *Washington Post*, March 17, 1983, p. B2.
51. Mike Causey, "Administration Loses Round in Rules Change," *Washington Post*, May 12, 1983, p. B2.
52. See Winston Woods, "Hill Blocks OPM Rules Again," *Federal Times*, November 28, 1983, p. 1.
53. See *Federal Times* coverage on January 2, 1984, p. 3 and January 16, 1984, p. 1.
54. See, for example, Mike Causey, "Ideological Warfare: Devine v. House Unit," *Washington Post*, March 7, 1983, p. B2. Causey covered the PBIS controversy extensively, and also ran an informal poll to let Federal employees express their views on the new regulations, and was inundated by over 61,000 responses. About half the respondents supported "a system that ranks performance over seniority, if [they] thought that performance appraisals would be made fairly," but only about one-sixth of the respondents thought that such a system would work in their offices. See Mike Causey, "61,000 Answer Poll on Job Revision Proposals," *Washington Post*, May 22, 1983, p. C2.
55. See Bernard Rosen, "A Disaster for Merit," *The Bureaucrat* (Winter 1982–3): 8–17. See also Donald Devine's rejoinder (p. 18) and Rosen's reply (p. 19). Rosen strongly expressed his qualms about the reforms from the beginning. See Rosen, "Merit and the President's Plan."
56. See U.S. General Accounting Office, *Achieving Representation of Minorities and Women in the Federal Work Force*, December 3, 1980.
57. MSPB overturned OPM's regulations for taking adverse actions before new performance appraisal systems were completely in place in 1979 (*Wells v. Harris*). For a discussion of the impact of *Wells*, see Carolyn Ban, Edie Goldenberg, and Toni Marzotto, "Firing the Unproductive Employee: Will CSRA Make a Difference?" *Review of Public Personnel Administration* 2, no. 2 (Spring 1982): 92. MSPB also recently struck down an OPM rule barring employees from filing grievances against non-competitive promotion decisions. See Eric Yoder, "MSPB Strikes Down Rule on Promotion Grievances," *Federal Times*, February 13, 1984, p. 6.

II

CIVIL SERVICE REFORM:
THE RECORD TO DATE

CHAPTER FOUR

Federal Employee Attitudes Toward Reform: Performance Evaluation and Merit Pay

CHARLES BANN AND JERALD JOHNSON

How seldom, friend: a good great man inherits Honor or wealth, with all his worth and pains: It sounds like stories from the land of spirits if any man obtains that which he merits, Or any merit that which he obtains.
—The Good Great Man,
Samuel Taylor Coleridge

INTRODUCTION

Today, five years since the passage of the Civil Service Reform Act (CSRA), some of the reforms appear to be unraveling. Senior civil servants have been retiring in record numbers or have been looking for work in the private sector. Morale among federal employees is extremely low. And there is open concern that the fragile merit concept has been damaged. What has gone wrong? Much of the controversy centers around what many consider to be the pièce de résistance of the CSRA, the performance appraisal and merit pay package. In this chapter we propose to examine some of the problems encountered in implementing the new performance appraisal system.

The development of an effective performance evaluation process is neither simple nor automatic. In comparison with the old, the government has opted for a higher risk system. It has committed itself to fundamental changes in the way employees and supervisors interact with one another. And it has tried to put teeth into the system by linking evaluations of executives with their pay.

We are heavily indebted to Lisa Poster and, especially, Karen Blair for their tireless assistance in preparing this paper.

For this process to work successfully, the government is assuming that (a) its employees' level of confidence in the organization is high enough to support such changes; and (b) employees will accept the new system as an improvement over the old. We will examine these assumptions by first comparing the old performance appraisal system with the new. The advantages and disadvantages of the old performance evaluation process will be contrasted with the changes and conceptual underpinnings mandated by the CSRA. Second, we will use data from the 1979 and 1980 Federal Employee Attitude Surveys to examine employees' attitudes toward the performance evaluation process and their attitudes toward the federal workplace.[1] Third, we will explore the government's efforts to implement performance evaluation, and employees' reactions to these efforts.

THE OLD VERSUS THE NEW

What Is Performance Appraisal?

Lefton, Buzzotta, Sherberg, and Karraker define performance appraisal as:

> . . . (1) a formal discussion between a superior and a subordinate (2) for the purpose of discovering how and why the subordinate is performing on the job and (3) how the subordinate can perform more effectively in the future (4) so that the subordinate, the superior and the organization all benefit.[2]

The success of the 1978 Reform Act largely depends upon the successful implementation of such performance appraisal systems in each department and agency. Performance appraisals are supposed to be the basis for "training, rewarding, reassigning, promoting, demoting, retaining, and separating employees".[3] If properly implemented, supporters argue, the appraisal systems should provide such diverse benefits as protecting whistleblowers, enhancing participative decision making, and improving productivity and effectiveness in government programs.[4] Before evaluating the new performance appraisal system, it might be useful to look at the system that it replaced to see how it worked and to see why, in the eyes of many, it was inadequate.

The Old Performance Appraisal System

Under the system that predated CSRA, supervisors usually rated each of their employees on a number of traits, such as enthusiasm, dependability, integrity, loyalty, and the like, rather than on actual job performance. These traits—which tended to center on the employee's personality, motivation, and attitudes toward the organization—were described in nonquantifiable terms. That is, the evaluations often consisted of narrative accounts of the employee's traits or utilized some form of scoring system that was generally not replicable. This, of course, made it difficult to compare the ratings of different individuals in any systematic fashion, or to monitor changes in a single individual over time. The older evaluation instruments usually did not list job responsibilities or expected levels of performance, nor did they attempt to assess the employee's technical abilities and his or her performance on the job. (This system is not unlike rating a baseball team on the basis of how well the players "talk it up" rather than on the number of games they win.)

When the time came for supervisors to sit down with employees and discuss their ratings, the old performance evaluations proved more acceptable to the raters than to the ratees or to the organization. Since the rating system enabled the supervisor to be vague in evaluating the employee's actual work, it made the potentially uncomfortable task of reviewing the ratings with subordinates less painful.[5] Employees, on the other hand, received little in the way of information on what aspects of their jobs they were performing well or poorly, or on how they might improve their performance. The organization likewise suffered because it had an inadequate system for distinguishing between superior, average, and unsatisfactory employees.

In practice, employees were almost always given "satisfactory" summary ratings for their performance. Few were rated "above satisfactory," and virtually none were rated "below satisfactory." There was little or no incentive to give critical appraisals since supervisors found minimal support elsewhere in their agencies for disciplining poorly performing employees. When supervisors did make critical evaluations, the effect was often more negative than positive. Performance evaluations themselves meant very little in terms of pay raises or step-grade increases. However, critical reviews often hurt employees' feelings and lowered their morale.[6]

Despite its shortcomings, the old system did yield a number of unintended benefits to the organization and its employees. By providing the supervisors and their agencies with a justification for giving nearly every eligible employee a raise in pay (a satisfactory rating), the old performance evaluation system dovetailed nicely with the nearly automatic step-grade increase process. Granting merit increases to 99 percent of all eligible employees meant that most employees doing inadequate work were unjustly rewarded. Indeed, the system worked to the advantage of the marginal worker. Still, good workers were not disadvantaged, since virtually all employees doing satisfactory or superior work were also compensated. Such a system certainly met employees' security needs, even if it did little to identify superior or inferior work performance. Finally, the organization benefitted by maintaining a stable and predictable personnel system.

The New Performance Appraisal System: Potential

The new performance appraisal system is designed to alleviate many of the problems of the old. Under the terms of the CSRA, the following features must be included in all new federal government evaluation systems: (1) employees are to be rated on *performance*, not on *personality traits* or *motivational considerations*; (2) the specific performance areas to be evaluated, and their standards and objectives, are to be discussed and agreed upon by employee and supervisor; supervisors (or agencies) must list specific tasks as "critical," meaning that noncompliance in satisfactorily meeting any one of the critical tasks could lead to disciplinary action; (3) monetary rewards are to be linked to superior performance, not given simply on the basis of time-in-grade; and (4) for the highest levels (Senior Executive Service), rewards are part of a tradeoff that includes risks—political managers have the power to transfer employees, and may even move those who perform unsatisfactorily out of the SES.

There are some differences in the reward and evaluation criteria mandated for the various grade groupings. SES members have a bonus system that, as originally passed, could reward up to 50 percent of an agency's SES employees in any given year with bonuses unaffected by the current salary ceiling. All remaining employees, grades 1–18, are utilizing new, agency-developed performance evaluation systems. Under the new evaluation system, these employees will typically receive one of five possible ratings based on job performance: outstanding, above satisfactory, satisfactory, below satisfactory, and unsatisfactory.[7] For those employees classified as middle-level managers and supervisors (GS 13–15), the five ratings are tied directly to the size of their salary increases. The other non-SES employees also use the new evaluation *rating* system, but remain under the old step-grade *salary* system.

Neither the CSRA nor the Office of Personnel Management (OPM) specified the exact performance evaluation plans or methods to be followed. OPM preferred to let each agency create its own plan or plans according to its perceived needs, so long as they complied with the guidelines of the CSRA. It was expected that the evaluation forms would be developed in-house, with extensive consultation among agency employees. OPM's emphasis on extensive participation is important, as recent research underscores the necessity for employee involvement in the full evaluation process.[8] Because each agency developed its own evaluation system, there are major differences in the forms, ranging from highly complex plans based on numerical ratings (e.g., Navy; Health and Human Services) to relatively simple forms based primarily on narrative analysis (e.g., Bureau of Land Management).

As written into law, the federal system's performance appraisal guidelines incorporate many of the more innovative procedures utilized in the private sector. Scholars seem particularly impressed with the strong emphasis on performance-based evaluation and with the mandate for supervisors and employees to develop objectives mutually.[9] In fact, commentary indicates that these two provisions are at the cutting edge in the performance evaluation field.

The New Performance Evaluation System: Benefits

The new performance appraisal system is potentially beneficial to supervisors, employees, and the agency in other ways. For instance, the supervisor-manager can utilize a performance-based system to reinforce the annual work plan process. By segmenting and assigning responsibilities to subordinates at the beginning of each year, the supervisor can emphasize priorities, specify standards or quality, and stress important due dates. The new evaluation system would then require that supervisors devote a substantial share of their time in assisting subordinates—if for no other reason than that supervisors' own performance ratings depend upon their ability to motivate subordinates in achieving work plan goals. Cooperative behavior would also be encouraged by this process, providing benefits to both the agency and supervisors. Thus performance-based appraisals ultimately enhance the capacity of the organization to meet its goals.

The potential advantages to employees are just as great. For the first time, the federal government is actually signing de facto contracts specifying exactly what it feels is important for each individual to accomplish. It is also committing itself to specific quality standards. And it is required to recognize employees if such standards are exceeded.[10] In theory, this gives workers the leverage to make the government keep its personnel promises. And, one may hope, it will enhance the development of fast-track promotion ladders for high achievers.

Finally, the new appraisal system can go a long way toward improving communication inside the organization.[11] Bureaucractic organizations by their very nature tend to be extremely formal. This formality is accentuated by the vertical nature of public hierarchies, so that it is quite common for subordinates to complain of a lack of feedback from their superiors. The Federal Employee Attitude Survey (FEAS) indicates that this complaint is expressed at all levels of bureaucracy. Middle-level bureaucrats, claiming little communication with their superiors, were criticized in the same way by their subordinates. Virtually all employees at all levels indicated that they would like to receive more feedback on their performance. Since the CSRA mandates that supervisors and subordinates must work out performance appraisals together, communication between bureaucratic levels should become greater. As communication increases, and as performance is more effectively graded and rewarded, the organization ultimately benefits.

FEDERAL WORKERS' ATTITUDES TOWARDS PERFORMANCE APPRAISAL

We argued earlier that two things are necessary if OPM hopes to be successful in implementing the new performance appraisal system. First, members of the civil service must believe that the new evaluation system is, by and large, an improvement over the old one. Second, such extensive changes in the performance appraisal system can be successfully implemented only if employees have faith and confidence in the organization. In this section we examine to what extent these conditions are being met in the federal workforce, by looking at employees' attitudes toward performance appraisal and toward their work generally. Before examining the findings, however, we present a brief description of the data.

The Federal Employee Attitude Surveys

The implementation of CSRA calls for OPM to conduct periodic polls of the federal workforce to ascertain their opinions on a variety of subjects dealing with the civil service reforms. To date two such surveys, The Federal Employee Attitudes Surveys of 1979 and 1980 have been completed. Both surveys were designed and executed in-house by the staff at the Office of Personnel Management.[12] The first survey, also known as the Baseline Survey, included more than 250 questions dealing with a variety of subjects concerning federal employees' jobs and workplace. Among the subjects covered were: job satisfaction; attitudes towards the organization, supervisors, and co-workers; employees' attitudes toward affirmative action; attitudes toward the pre-CSRA performance evaluation and merit systems;

worker efficacy; organizational effectiveness; meaningfulness of work; and the like. The survey itself utilized a stratified random sample design of the federal civilian employee workforce. Mail questionnaires were sent to 20,000 employees, of which 13,862 were returned for a response rate of 69.1 percent.

The second survey, conducted in 1980, focused exclusively on senior-level employees (GS–13 and above). Approximately 75 percent of the 13,000 employees sampled in this survey filled out and returned their questionnaires.[13] Many of the same topics covered in the 1979 survey were also addressed in 1980. In fact, of the 250 questions included in the 1980 questionnaire, approximately 100 were first asked in 1979.

Satisfaction with Pre-CSRA Performance Appraisals

A significant number of the questions found in these two surveys dealt with federal workers' views concerning the pre-CSRA performance appraisal system, thus enabling us to construct an Index of Satisfaction with Performance Appraisals. This index measures the amount of confidence an employee had in his or her agency's performance appraisal process (the old pre-CSRA system). That is, we attempted to measure the extent to which each employee believed that the appraisal system was fair and accurate in assessing work accomplishments, and that it rewarded or punished accordingly.

To construct the Performance Appraisal Index we first selected a pool of items from the 1979 questionnaire that were judged by the members of our research staff to measure the concept, performance appraisal, as we have defined it. Items whose face content embodied the definition were included in the initial pool, while those items whose content seemed inappropriate to the definition were eliminated from consideration. Second, an index was constructed by summing the scores of all the items in the initial pool. The individual items in the pool were then correlated with the index itself. Those items that correlated 0.30 (Pearson's r), or above, were put into the final version of the Performance Appraisal Index. By this process we aimed to construct a measure that was both internally consistent and reasonably lengthy. The Satisfaction with Performance Appraisals Index contains thirty-two items. (The items comprising the Index are listed in the appendix to this chapter.)

Table 4.1 lists some of the items included in the Index of Satisfaction with Performance Appraisals, along with their frequencies. As the percentages indicate, there was little evidence that there was unanimous or even near unanimous acceptance of the old performance appraisal system. By the same token, there is little evidence of an overwhelming rejection of the old system by federal employees. In fact, the percentage of federal workers who agreed or who disagreed with any of the statements never exceeded 70 percent. What the items do show is that (1) some substantial proportion of the respondents believed that the old performance appraisal system was adequate, while a substantial proportion took the opposite view; and (2) from one-tenth to one-quarter of the respondents were simply undecided. The first two items in table 4.1 are typical. Thirty-nine percent of the federal workforce agreed that, "Promotions or unscheduled pay increases here ususally depend on how well a person performs on his/her job." Another 48 percent disagreed with this statement, while the remaining 13 percent were undecided. Similarly, 40 percent believed that supervisors took appropriate action when employees performed poorly, but 48 percent did not. The remaining items in the index give a similar picture.

Based on the distributions of opinions on a number of these items, some scholars have suggested that there was fairly widespread dissatisfaction with the old performance appraisal system in 1979.[14] This, in turn, seemed to indicate that civil service employees would be open to the changes proposed by the new system. Lloyd Nigro, for example, suggests that there was "considerable potential support" for the performance evaluation package. He concludes:

> Federal employees seem to be in general agreement with OPM Director Campbell's assertion that the CSRA addresses "real" problems and potentially effective solutions. At this stage of the game, existing attitudes appear to provide a reasonably firm foundation upon which to build a structure of policies and procedures that will energize the CSRA.[15]

While we do not dispute the empirical evidence, we do offer a cautionary note in interpreting federal employees' attitudes toward the pre-CSRA appraisal system. Since performance appraisal systems affect the career chances and salary increases of employees, one might reasonably expect that some individuals would find fault with almost any performance appraisal system, no matter how fair and just it may appear on its face. Consequently, it may be unreasonable to expect that any performance appraisal system would be acceptable to the vast majority of an organization's employees. Then too, what constitutes a *minimally* acceptable level of support for a performance appraisal system in a large organization is simply not known.

Since it really is not possible to tell if federal employees' overall satisfaction with the old performance appraisal system was "high" or "low," a better approach would be to ask federal employees to compare the old system with the new one. However, no questions contrasting the old system with a new one were included in either FEAS survey.[16]

Table 4.1 The Distribution of Opinions on Selected Appraisal Items
(Percent across)

ITEM	RESPONSES					
	Strongly Disagree	Disagree	Undecided	Agree	Strongly Agree	(N)
Promotions or unscheduled pay increases here usually depend on how well a person performs on his/her job.	18%	30%	13%	33%	6%	(13,753)
When an employee continues to do his/her job poorly, supervisors here will take the appropriate corrective action.	15	33	12	35	5	(13,742)
This organization considers performance appraisal to be an important part of a supervisor's duties.	4	15	24	47	10	(13,707)
Under the present system, financial rewards are seldom related to employee performance.	4	33	15	32	15	(13,712)
Performance appraisals do influence personnel actions taken in this organization.	5	17	19	49	10	(13,556)
There is a tendency for supervisors here to give the same performance ratings regardless of how well people perform their jobs.	4	28	13	36	19	(13,712)
My performance rating presents a fair and accurate picture of my actual job performance.	9	20	22	43	6	(13,720)
The standards used to evaluate my performance have been fair and objective.	6	14	26	45	9	(13,700)
My performance appraisal takes into account the most important parts of my job.	5	15	21	50	9	(13,683)
In the past I have been aware of what standards have been used to evaluate my performance.	4	19	17	54	6	(13,724)
I understand the performance appraisal system being used in this organization.	7	18	14	53	8	(13,705)

My job performance is carefully evaluated by my supervisor.	8	16	19	45	13	(13,712)

SOURCE: 1979 Federal Employee Attitude Survey. Except where noted, all tables utilize weighted frequencies. Weights were provided by OPM. See, U.S. Office of Personnel Management, *Federal Employee Attitudes. Phase 1: Baseline Survey, 1979. Government-wide Report* (Washington, D.C.: Government Printing Office, March, 1980 [Revised]), pp. 39–41.

Performance Appraisal and Attitudes Toward the Organization

Besides their views on performance appraisal, federal employees' attitudes toward the organization, their jobs, and their workplace are also important for the acceptance or rejection of the CSRA package. To examine their opinions concerning the organization, we constructed four indexes: Trust in the Organization, Trust in Supervisor, Work Efficacy, and Pride in Work. The definition of each index is listed below.

Trust in Organization. The belief that the organization is trustworthy, that it is concerned about its employees, that it functions effectively and efficiently, and that it treats employees fairly.

Trust in Supervisor. The belief that one's supervisor is interested in and genuinely concerned about the employees, that the supervisor is capable of overseeing work output and quality, and that the supervisor makes fair judgments with respect to employees.

Work Efficacy. The belief that one has control over his or her work decisions, that one can accomplish his or her tasks and achieve organizational goals, and the belief that change in the organization is possible and that one can play a role in producing that change.

Pride in Work. The amount of personal satisfaction, enjoyment, and sense of accomplishment an employee gets from his or her job.

These indexes were constructed following the same procedure used for the Index of Satisfaction with Performance Appraisals. The items included in each of the indexes are listed in the appendix to this chapter.

To examine the relationship between civil servants' satisfaction or dissatisfaction with the old system of performance appraisals and their work attitudes, we obtained the correlations between all five indexes (See table 4.2). The first four indexes, *Trust in Organization, Trust in Supervisor, Pride in Work, and Work Efficacy* are all substantially intercorrelated. There is a strong tendency for those who trust the system to also trust their supervisor, to take pride in their work, and to feel efficacious. By contrast, those who distrusted the organization also tended to distrust their supervisors, to take less pride in their work, and to feel relatively powerless in the workplace.

The most interesting finding in table 4.2, however, is the relationship between attitudes toward performance appraisal and the first four indexes. Those employees who were most content with the old performance evaluation system were also the ones most likely to trust the organization and their supervisors, to take pride in their work, and to exhibit high levels of work efficacy. Those most dissatisfied with the old performance appraisal system tended to have more negative attitudes toward the workplace.

These findings are underscored by the results in table 4.3, where we show in table form the relationship between the Performance Appraisal Index and a typical item from each of the other indexes. As the table shows, those least satisfied with the performance appraisal system were less likely to take satisfaction in their jobs, were distrustful of the organization's motives, did not trust their supervisor, and were less likely to indicate that they had a great deal of say over decisions concerning their jobs.

A number of conclusions may be drawn from tables 4.2 and 4.3. First, it appears that those who were most trusting of the organization and of the supervisors, who felt the most efficacious, who took the most pride in their work, and, hence, were most likely to be receptive to organizational changes, were the same individuals who were most satisfied with the old system. Second, those most dissatisfied with the old performance appraisal system also distrusted the organization. Consequently, the likelihood of their accepting the reform package was low. Finally, employees' attitudes toward various facets of career service appear to be quite strongly interrelated. The conceptual dis-

Table 4.2 Correlations Between the Five Indexes
(Pearson's *r*)

	Trust in Organization	Trust in Supervisor	Pride in Work	Word Efficacy
Trust in Supervisor	.62			
Pride in Work	.49	.49		
Work Efficacy	.67	.62	.66	
Satisfaction with Performance Appraisals	.68	.79	.54	.65

SOURCE: 1979 Federal Employee Attitude Survey. (N = 13,810)

Table 4.3 The Relationship between the Satisfaction with Performance Appraisal Index and Selected Work Attitudes

(Percent Down)

Work Attitudes	Very Low	Low	Middle	High	Very High
Trust in Organization Question 15					
Strongly disagree	4%	3%	6%	8%	16%
Disagree	9	22	31	42	52
Undecided	11	18	18	20	13
Agree	36	37	34	22	14
Strongly agree	40	20	12	8	6
N =	(2,682)	(2,780)	(2,783)	(2,743)	(2,748)
		tau-b = -.37			

Question 15: Employees here feel you can't trust this organization.

Work Attitudes	Very Low	Low	Middle	High	Very High
Trust in Supervisor Question 62					
Strongly disagree	26%	7%	3%	*	*
Disagree	36	27	16	9	3
Undecided	17	22	20	15	5
Agree	20	40	54	63	63
Strongly agree	2	5	7	13	29
N =	(2,695)	(2,767)	(2,763)	(2,740)	(2,743)
		tau-b = .47			

Question 62: My supervisor deals with subordinates well.

Work Attitudes	Very Low	Low	Middle	High	Very High
Work Efficacy Question 93					
Strongly disagree	27%	7%	3%	3%	1%
Disagree	46	40	34	22	12
Undecided	10	19	20	20	14
Agree	15	30	37	45	54
Strongly agree	3	4	6	10	19
N =	(2,696)	(2,771)	(2,778)	(2,738)	(2,751)
		tau-b = .37			

Question 93: I have a great deal of say over decisions concerning my job.

Work Attitudes	Very Low	Low	Middle	High	Very High
Pride in Work Question 81					
Strongly disagree	14%	3%	3%	1%	*
Disagree	24	15	10	5	1
Undecided	14	13	9	6	2
Agree	42	60	67	67	54
Strongly agree	6	10	12	21	43
N =	(2,693)	(2,767)	(2,777)	(2,739)	(2,753)
		tau-b = .39			

Question 81: In general, I am satisfied with my job.

SOURCE: 1979 Federal Employee Attitude Survey.
* Less than one percent.

tinctions between the work-related attitudes examined here and elsewhere in the CSRA literature may not be all that clear in the minds of civil servants. Rather, they tend to view the organization and its components as all of one piece. This suggests, contrary to Nigro, that low levels of trust in the organization need not be offset by more positive attitudes in other areas.

Performance Appraisal and the Characteristics of Federal Employees

We are also interested in examining the extent to which different classes of federal employees hold similar or contrasting views on the question of performance appraisal. Therefore, we looked at the relationship between the Index of Satisfaction with Performance Appraisals and a large number of background characteristics of the employees, such as race, sex, education, age, length of federal employment, agency, and grade. While it is not possible to present all the findings here, the results shown in table 4.4 are typical.

Drawing upon earlier research that suggests quite similar orientations among different categories of career employees, we hypothesized that few employee characteristics would show any important

Table 4.4. The Relationship Between Attitudes Toward Performance Appraisal and Selected Background Characteristics

| | (Percent across) | | | | | |
| | Performance Appraisal Index | | | | | |
Background Characteristics	Very Low	Low	Middle	High	Very High	(N)
Sex						
Female	18%	19%	22%	21%	21%	(4,941)
Male	21	21	20	19	20	(8,793)
Race						
White	19	21	21	20	19	(11,119)
Nonwhite	20	16	20	20	24	(2,557)
Number of Years as Federal Employee						
Under 1 year	7	17	24	26	26	(396)
1 to 3 years	15	21	22	20	22	(1,765)
4 to 9 years	22	22	20	19	18	(3,951)
10 to 29 years	20	20	21	20	20	(6,775)
30 years and over	20	18	16	24	23	(914)
Grade*						
GS 1–12	18	19	20	21	23	(9,651)
GS 13–15	15	18	21	21	25	(3,130)
SES (and Grades 16–18)	11	20	22	21	26	(970)

SOURCE: 1979 Federal Employee Attitude Survey.
* Based on unweighted sample.

distinctions. As table 4.4 indicates, career employee attitudes toward performance appraisals cannot be differentiated along the lines of sex or race. Most of the other employee characteristics we tested for also failed to show any differences in opinions concerning performance appraisals.

Yet, we also expected that the strong socializing influence of the organization might have some effect on the attitudes of federal workers. In particular, we believed that employees with lengthy careers in the civil service might take a more positive view of the old performance appraisal system than would newer employees. Similarly, we believed that employees at the higher grade levels would be more supportive of the old system than those in the lower grades. However, as the results in table 4.4 show, there is no support for either hypothesis.

Changing Attitudes among Federal Employees: 1979 to 1980

A number of researchers have found that federal employees' morale has taken a turn for the worse since 1979.[17] Fortunately, a considerable number of the items used in constructing our five indexes were repeated in the 1980 survey. With these items we constructed somewhat abbreviated versions of each index. (The items used in the short versions of the indexes are noted in the appendix to this chapter.) Even though they contain fewer items, the shortened versions of the five indexes are, for all practical purposes, equivalent to the original versions. (Correlations between the long and short versions of each index, using the 1979 data, ranged from 0.91 to 0.97.)

Table 4.5 presents the mean scores for our five indexes from the 1979 and 1980 surveys, for all employees grades 13 and above. As the table shows, there has been a decline in some of the employees' work-related attitudes since 1979. Specifically, federal employees registered declines in work efficacy, trust in their supervisors, pride in their work, and in satisfaction with the old performance appraisal system. In each case the declines are very small. However, there was no change at all between 1979 and 1980 in their levels of trust in the organization.

THE NEW PERFORMANCE APPRAISAL SYSTEM IN PRACTICE: IMPLICATIONS

Summary

Our analysis of the data contained in the two FEAS surveys provides some very important clues about the likelihood of developing

Table 4.5. Changes in Work Attitudes among Federal Employees GS–13 and Higher, 1979 and 1980

Work Attitude		Mean	Standard Deviation	Number of Cases
Work Efficacy Index*				
	1979	14.005	3.214	1,599
	1980	13.678	3.298	8,782
Performance Appraisal Index*				
	1979	49.802	11.649	1,599
	1980	48.675	11.652	8,782
Trust in Organization Index				
	1979	12.323	3.661	1,599
	1980	12.432	3.459	8,782
Trust in Supervisor Index*				
	1979	31.500	6.740	1,599
	1980	30.950	6.921	8,782
Pride in Work Index*				
	1979	36.153	4.929	1,599
	1980	35.849	5.188	8,782

SOURCE: 1979 and 1980 Federal Employee Attitude Surveys.
* Difference of the means significant at 0.05 level.

successful performance appraisal systems throughout the federal government. At the outset we stated that civil servants must believe that the new evaluation process is an improvement over the old. Although the two FEAS surveys do not allow comparison between the old and new systems, they do indicate that employee attitudes toward the pre-CSRA performance appraisal process were at best mixed. As we have shown, there was neither a wholesale rejection of the old system, nor unqualified support.

We also argued at the outset that changes are only successfully implemented when employees have a high degree of confidence in their organization. Our analysis indicates that the level of confidence found among federal employees may pose problems. We found that those most dissatisfied with the old system of performance appraisal (and presumably most open to a new system) were also unhappy with their jobs and with the organization in general. On the other hand, those who were relatively content with the old performance appraisal system also placed more trust in the organization and demonstrated greater satisfaction with their jobs.

Implications

The lack of employee commitment to performance evaluation relates to a simple balancing of advantages and disadvantages. The advantages—accurate appraisals, rewards for superior service, and better communication—have not come as fast or as completely as promised. The first bonuses given to SES employees demonstrate some of the current problems (see table 4.6). As this table indicates, many agencies selected their most senior employees for these first awards. Since in many cases these individuals were the panelists' immediate supervisors, it appears that the awards were bestowed more for the sake of prudence than for actual merit.[18]

The negatives—growing politicization of the civil service, lack of strong Office of Personnel Management leadership, few financial rewards, and inaccurate or indifferent appraisals—are of continued concern under the Reagan Administration. Particularly troubling is a growing feeling that the political appointees to OPM under President Reagan lack the will and perhaps the ability to provide strong leadership in this arena. Leaders have responded to major budget cuts in OPM by eliminating the professional staff in many critical areas.[19] The CSRA Evaluation Management Division, for example, has been drastically reduced, and many professionals from this section have left government employment.

As have many of its predecessors, the Reagan Administration appears to be giving civil service reform only secondary consideration.[20] Lacking strong OPM political leadership to push the CSRA to completion, we can safely argue that, over all, the decision makers most responsible on a continuing basis for the failures or successes of the Reform Act provisions are now high-level career public employees. Since the Act is designed to "motivate federal workers to carry out their responsibilities effectively and to take pride in their accomplishments" by a combination of reward and punishments,[21] success or failure of the Act will ultimately depend upon the bureaucrats' own appraisals of the personal advantages or risks of the changes in the new system. As we have indicated, the prognosis is not positive. There has been little to date suggesting that the CSRA

Table 4.6. First Round Bonuses for the Senior Executive Service

Grade	Number Eligible*	Number Received	Percentage
6	142	40	28.2
5	585	69	11.8
4	4,109	138	3.4
3	590	8	1.4
2	379	1	0.3
1	501	0	0.0
	(Theta = .44)		

SOURCE: Office of Personnel Management.
* Not all SES members at the lowest pay grade levels were eligible for awards, because of minimum time in grade requirements.

performance appraisal process has proven itself to be beneficial to either the employees or their agencies. As with so many reforms proposed within government, the promise remains more impressive than the actual results.[22]

APPENDIX

Work Efficacy Index

6. Overall, this organization is effective in accomplishing its objectives.*
9. It's really not possible to change things around here. (R) *
12. I have the authority I need to accomplish my work objectives.*
21. Employees do not have much opportunity to influence what goes on in this organization. (R)
79. I have a great deal of say over what has to be done on my job.
85. I have control over how I spend my time working.
93. I have a great deal of say over decisions concerning my job.*
117. I am satisfied with the chances I have to accomplish something worthwhile.

Performance Appraisal Index

5. When an employee continues to do his/her job poorly, supervisors here will take the appropriate corrective action.*
17. Promotions or unscheduled pay increases here usually depend on how well a person performs his/her job.*
19. There are adequate procedures to get my performance rating reconsidered, if necessary.
22. Under the present system, financial rewards are seldom related to employee performance. (R) *
23. There is a tendency for supervisors here to give the same performance ratings regardless of how well people perform their jobs. (R) *
26. I understand the performance appraisal system being used in this organization.
38. Performance appraisals do influence personnel actions taken in this organization.*
57. My supervisor considers the performance appraisal of subordinates to be an important part of his/her duties.*
58. My supervisor and I agree on what "good performance" on my job means.*
59. My job performance is carefully evaluated by my supervisor.
68. This organization considers performance appraisal to be an important part of a supervisor's duties.*
72. My supervisor discusses with me the specific reasons for the performance rating I receive.
74. My supervisor evaluates my performance on things not related to my job. (R)

80. My performance appraisal takes into account the most important parts of my job.
91. On my job, I know exactly what is expected of me.
92. The standards used to evaluate my performance have been fair and objective.
96. In the past I have been aware of what standards have been used to evaluate my performance.
106. Information that I receive about my performance usually comes too late for it to be of any use to me. (R)
107. My performance rating presents a fair and accurate picture of my actual job performance.*
120. I will be promoted or given a better job if I perform especially well.*
121. I can get the things I want from performing my job especially well.
122. My own hard work will lead to recognition as a good performer.*
123. I will get a cash award or unscheduled pay increase if I perform my job especially well.*
124. I will have better job security if I perform especially well.*
125. How often do you receive feedback from your supervisor for good performance? *
127. How often do you receive feedback from your supervisor that helps you to improve your performance?

In your opinion how much did your last performance appraisal help you to (Questions 129–33):
129. Assess your strengths and weaknesses in performing your job? *
130. Establish a plan for your training and development? *
131. Receive needed training?
132. Determine your contribution to the organization?
133. Improve your performance? *

Trust in System Index

2. The information that I get through formal communication channels helps me perform my job effectively.
4. When changes are made in this organization, the employees usually lose out in the end. (R)
7. In this organization, it is often unclear who has the formal authority to make a decision. (R) *
11. I am told promptly when there is a change in policy, rules, or regulations that affect me.
15. Employees here feel you can't trust this organization. (R) *
32. In this organization, authority is clearly delegated.*
35. I am not afraid to "blow the whistle" on things I find wrong with my organization.
37. It takes too long to get decisions made in this organization. (R) *
39. If I were subject to an involuntary personnel action, I believe my agency would adequately inform me of my grievance and appeal rights.

Trust in Supervisor Index

24. Management is flexible enough to make changes when necessary.
36. Supervisors in this organization take the time to help marginal and unsatisfactory workers improve their performance.*
54. My job duties are clearly defined by my supervisor.
55. My supervisor encourages me to help in developing work methods and job procedures.
56. My supervisor maintains high standards of performance for his/her employees.
60. My supervisor sets clear goals for me in my present job.*
61. My supervisor encourages subordinates to participate in important decisions.*
62. My supervisor deals with subordinates well.*
63. My supervisor gives me adequate information on how well I am performing.*
64. My supervisor insists that subordinates work hard.
65. My supervisor knows the technical parts of his/her job well.
67. My supervisor demands that subordinates do high quality work.*
69. My supervisor helps me solve work-related problems.
70. My supervisor handles the administrative parts of his/her job well.*
71. My supervisor asks my opinion when a problem related to my work arises.*
73. I am confident that my supervisor would not take action against me if I were to bring cases of inefficiencies or waste to his/her attention.*

Pride in Work Index

1. In general, I like working here.*
10. What happens to this organization is really important to me.*
25. I often think about quitting. (R) *
28. I care little about what happens to this organization as long as I get a paycheck. (R)
75. My job is challenging.
78. The work I do on my job is meaningful to me.
81. In general, I am satisfied with my job.*
84. My job makes good use of my abilities.
86. Doing my job well gives me a feeling that I've accomplished something worthwhile.*
88. My job gives me the opportunity to use my own judgment and initiative.
89. I work hard on my job.*
90. The things I do on my job are important to me.
94. All in all, I am satisfied with the work on my present job.
98. Doing my job well makes me feel good about myself as a person.*
100. I enjoy doing my work for the personal satisfaction it gives me.*
103. Working hard on my job leads to gaining respect from co-workers.

119. I am satisfied with the recognition I receive for public service.*
How important was each of the following factors in your decision to work
for the federal government?
136. Challenging work responsibilities?

NOTES

1. U.S. Office of Personnel Management, *Federal Employee Attitudes. Phase 1: Baseline Survey, 1979. Government-wide Report* (Washington, D.C.: Government Printing Office, March 1980 [Revised]).

2. Robert E. Lefton, V. R. Buzzotta, Manuel Sherberg, and Dean L. Karraker, *Effective Motivation Through Performance Appraisal* (New York: John Wiley, 1977), p. 2.

3. See Bernard Rosen, "A New Mandate for Accountability in the National Government," *Bureaucrat* 8, no. 1 (Spring 1979): 2–4.

4. See U.S. Office of Personnel Management, Personnel Management Project, *Vol. 1, Final Staff Report* (Washington, D.C.: Office of Personnel Management, December 1977).

5. The greater the interaction between supervisor and employee, the higher the overall final evaluation. By contrast, where the supervisors do not have to review the evaluation with the employee being rated, a nonspecific rating system allowed supervisors to give lower overall ratings. N. B. Winstanley, "How Accurate Are Performance Appraisals?" *Personnel Administrator* 25, no. 8 (August 1980): 55–58.

6. Pierson M. Ralph, "Performance Evaluation: One More Try," *Public Personnel Management* 9, no. 3 (1980): 149.

7. The number of categories and their definitions may vary from agency to agency.

8. See Robert L. Dipboye and Rene de Pontbriand, "Correlates of Employee Reactions to Performance Appraisals and Appraisal Systems," *Journal of Applied Psychology* 66, no. 2 (April 1981): 248–51. Early reports suggest that the federal government is falling far short of this objective. Most SES members have had minimal interaction in the development of their performance evaluation systems, and, in many cases, performance objectives are being developed exclusively by the supervisor or subordinate. See U.S. General Accounting Office, *Evaluations Called for To Monitor and Assess Executive Appraisal Systems* (Washington, D.C.: U.S. General Accounting Office, August 3, 1981), pp. 49, 60–66; see Gaertner and Gaertner, chap. 5, for recent experiences in two agencies.

9. Gary P. Latham and Kenneth N. Wexley, *Increased Productivity Through Performance Appraisal* (Reading, Mass.: Addison-Wesley, 1981), pp. 28–30.

(R) Scores on this item were reversed in constructing the index.
* This item is included in both the FEAS 1979 and the FEAS 1980 surveys.

10. By "recognition" we are stating that, with its strong emphasis on measurable objectives, the government is in a position where it is bound to honor these de facto contracts. If any employee has exceeded standards for the evaluation period, then the final overall rating must reflect those accomplishments.

11. Ed Yager, "A Critique of Performance Appraisal Systems," *Personnel Journal* 60, no. 2 (February 1981): 130; Don Bellante and Albert N. Link, "Are Public Sector Workers More Risk Adverse Than Private Sector Workers? " *Industrial and Labor Relations Review* 34, no. 3 (April 1981): 408–12.

12. The data in this study were made available by the Interuniversity Consortium for Political and Social Research. The questionnaires for the 1979 and 1980 Federal Employee Attitude Surveys were originally collected by the United States Office of Personnel Management. Neither the original collectors of the data nor the consortium bear any responsibility for the analyses or interpretations presented here.

13. *Federal Employee Attitudes. Phase 2: Follow up Survey, 1980, Preliminary Report.* Washington, D.C.: Office of Personnel Management, August 13, 1981.

14. Lloyd G. Nigro, "Attitudes of Federal Employees Toward Performance Appraisal and Merit Pay: Implications for CSRA Implementation," *Public Administration Review* 41 (January/February 1981): 84.

15. Ibid., p. 86.

16. In the first and second surveys, employees were not asked about the new system since it was not yet in place. As a result, there has been no opportunity to include in the FEAS surveys the very important question, "Is the new appraisal system, in your opinion, an improvement over the old? " It is hoped that questions contrasting the two systems will be asked when the next FEAS survey is conducted.

17. Bruce Buchanan warns of this danger in his article "The Senior Executive Service: How We Can Tell If It Works" *Public Administration Review* 41, no. 3 (May/June 1981): 349–58; see Leonard Reed, "The Joy of SES," *Washington Monthly* 12, no. 7 (September 1980): 43–48; also, William J. Lanouette, "SES—From Civil Service Showpiece to Incipient Failure in Two Years," *National Journal* 13, no. 29 (18 July 1981): 1296–9.

18. Some even suggest that most employees covered by the new pay systems have suffered financially since the change. See Eric Yoder, "OPM Merit Pay Looks at All Options," *Federal Times* 18, no. 38 (15 November 1982): 1, 12.

    There were numerous other complaints about the system, too. Some felt that it was used as a means of beating the pay cap for the most senior SES members. Others felt that the Boards reserved too many rewards for themselves, and still others saw rewards going to political favorites. See Lanouette, "SES," p. 1298.

19. Although Executive Order 12027, of December 5, 1977, gives the Civil Service Commission (now OPM) responsibility for "overall executive branch leadership," it is clear that major personnel-related decisions

are now being made elsewhere. See Sugarman's comments on the Carter Administration's goals for OPM in Jule Sugarman, "What the Administration Wanted," *Bureaucrat* 7, no. 2 (Summer 1978): 5–9.

20. Keith Sinzinger, "Devine Philosophy," *Federal Times* 17, no. 125 (8 June 1981): 2. The special issue of the *National Journal* listing new appointees devoted four pages and ten biographical sketches to the Office of Management and Budget (OMB); in contrast, OPM rated one-fifth of a page with no biographical sketches: *National Journal* 13, no. 17 (25 April 1981): 690–3, 49.

21. Personnel Management Project, *Appendixes to the Final Staff Report* (Washington, D.C.: Government Printing Office, December 1977), p. 5.

22. See Benton G. Moeller, "Whatever Happened to the Federal Personnel System?" *Public Personnel Management* 11, no. 1 (Spring 1982): 1–8.

CHAPTER FIVE

Performance Evaluation and Merit Pay: Results in the Environmental Protection Agency and the Mine Safety and Health Administration

KAREN N. GAERTNER AND GREGORY H. GAERTNER

INTRODUCTION

The Civil Service Reform Act of 1978 (CSRA) has been characterized at one extreme as a major overhaul in the way in which the federal government is managed, and at the other extreme as "much ado about nothing." In this paper we will analyze three key aspects of the reforms—performance standards, performance appraisal, and merit pay for managers—noting the ways in which these reforms, together and separately, have had an impact on agencies and their employees.

In our discussion we will make several points:

1. These three provisions should be seen as a performance management system in agencies rather than separate and distinct facets of the Reform Act. This is because each depends upon the others for success.

2. The performance appraisal activity should have two functions: first, to appraise past performance accurately and, second, to identify ways to improve performance in the coming year. When the latter occurs, the system is more likely to be used by

This research was supported by the U.S. Office of Personnel Management, OPM–23–80. These results are also reported in Karen N. Gaertner, and Gregory H. Gaertner, *Organizational Assessments of the Effects of Civil Service Reform*, FY 82 Annual Report. Washington, D.C.: U.S. Office of Personnel Management, 1982.

employees as a management system *and* a personnel system, rather than only the latter.

3. Employee participation in creating performance standards is important for increasing the acceptance, use, and quality of the standards.

4. So-called rating inflation, or high average performance ratings, has been identified as a problem with the system. Managers who try to control this inflation by lowering ratings after the fact compromise the integrity of the system and of their subordinate managers. A better way to manage the distribution of ratings is through the standards upon which performance is rated and through ongoing performance reviews.

5. Managers do learn from experience. Those who have had a good experience with their appraisal during the first year put more effort into their standards during the second year and use the standards for work management as well as appraisal.

THEORY

The Civil Service Reform Act of 1978 is well characterized as a redefinition of the conditions of work in the federal government. This is particularly true for the provisions with which we are interested in this chapter, performance appraisal based on written standards and merit pay. The Act both gives discretion to supervisors in the management of subordinates and their work and allows more clarity to subordinates regarding the criteria for excellence in their work (Gaertner and Gaertner 1979). The reforms were billed by many as an opportunity to "let managers manage" in the federal government and, for subordinates, as an opportunity to be rewarded with money for outstanding performance.

The central assumptions of these reforms are also well represented in the literature. Performance-contingent pay, hardly a new concept, has been identified as a significant means of rewarding employees at all levels if administered properly. (See Lawler [1981 and 1971] and Heneman and Schwab [1972] for cogent arguments regarding the appropriate use of money as a reward.) In particular, money may function as a reward for job-related behaviors insofar as

1. It is a valued reward in the eyes of the receiver
2. It is explicitly linked to the behavior in question in the eyes of the receiver
3. It is a fair or equitable reward, again, in the eyes of the receiver

Just as the concept and potential usefulness of merit pay are well represented in the literature, disagreement about its *actual* incentive value for managers is widespread. It has been argued that pay, an extrinsic reward, has the long-term effect of decreasing the value of such intrinsic rewards as a sense of accomplishment from the job (Deci 1975; Salancik 1975; Meyer 1975; Mikalachi 1976). It is implicit in the conditions stated above that if pay is to be effective it must be tied explicitly to a work-related behavior. At the managerial level this is very difficult, so the actual administration of pay in many organizations is more seniority-based than performance-based, lip service about merit pay notwithstanding (see, for example, Patten [1968], and more recently Loomis [1982]).

Merit pay has been no less controversial in the public sector than the private sector. Early studies of merit pay suggest that its effects on performance are inconclusive at best. O'Toole and Churchill (1982) find that the required objective basis for compensation decisions is elusive and that the available resources in the merit pay system are insufficient. They do find, however, that the various activities required by merit pay tend to enhance agency communication regarding goals and priorities. Pearce and Perry (1982) similarly find that employees do not perceive a strong link between their performance and compensation decisions, nor do they find that pay is a highly valued reward (it ranks between third and fifth on a list of nine rewards). Pearce, Stevenson, and Perry (1983) demonstrate that there is no relationship between merit pay and organizational performance in the agency they studied, interpreting their results as possible evidence that performance-contingent pay is not appropriate at managerial levels. Clearly, merit pay in the federal government has some rather formidable obstacles to overcome if it is to act as a significant reward for work performance.

Another critical aspect of the reforms is the creation of performance standards, or annual performance goals, as the basis for annual performance evaluation. The effect on performance of goal setting, apart from performance evaluation, is also well documented in the literature (see Latham and Yukl [1975] for a review). Essentially, employees having challenging but not unreasonable goals, with measurable accomplishments that have been set with their significant and substantial input, are more likely to perform at high levels than employees with no goals or goals determined in other ways or with other characteristics. Thus, goal setting itself, separate from annual appraisal and merit pay, if done as described above, should result in better work performance in the federal government.

Finally, performance appraisal, apart from its obvious links to performance standards and merit pay, can achieve performance improvement, if the appraisal focuses on future performance improvement in addition to past performance evaluation (Meyer, Kay, and

French 1965). Appraisals that focus only on past performance, even though accurate, tend not to help the subordinate understand what changes in work behavior might be appropriate for performance improvement. Further, appraisals that include some negative component are often met with defensiveness on the subordinate's part, resulting in little or no performance improvement in the coming year. However, appraisals that are forward-looking as well as accurate, given past performance, tend to produce changes in work behavior in the future. This is particularly true for people who have perceptions of themselves as competent, able employees. (See Shrauger [1975] for a discussion of self-image and performance appraisal.) Given these results, we would expect, in our population of managers in the federal government, that developmental, forward-looking appraisals would have a positive impact on their work behavior. As above, this effect is not necessarily dependent upon merit pay.

Our perspective in this chapter has several key characteristics that both take into account and go beyond the literature on performance standards, performance appraisal, and merit pay. We will argue that the three provisions taken together form a system that, if used only for performance appraisal and pay determination, will fail to enhance either and will not be accepted by employees as worthwhile additions to their conditions of work. Further, we will argue that this system, when treated as a management tool and integrated with the work of the agency, can contribute to improved performance and employee acceptance of the system.

As we discuss this new management system, we will do so in the context of agency mission and history, and in light of the reactions of top management to the first appraisal cycle. We will argue that top management's reaction to the first experience with the new system can be seen, via changes in agency policy, in new orientations toward performance standards and new merit policies. We will also argue that performance appraisal per se is more likely to be a function of subordinates' work relationships with their supervisors and the standards upon which performance is being appraised than of agency policy. This model (shown graphically in figure 5.1) will guide our discussion of the functioning of the system. In particular, we expect the following:

1. Employees who feel their standards are accurate, who put considerable effort into creating them, who feel they collaborated with their supervisor in creating them, and who use them for work management as well as appraisal will report a more satisfactory, developmental appraisal process than will others.

Fig. 5.1: Agency Policy, Supervisory Relations, and the Performance Management System

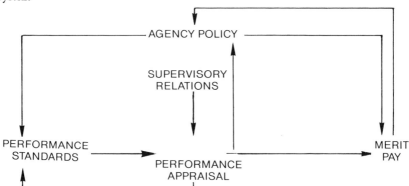

2. Employees who report good working relationships with their supervisor will report a more positive appraisal experience than will others.
3. Employees who feel that the new appraisal process is an improvement will be more likely also to accept merit pay based on that appraisal process than will others.
4. Acceptance of merit pay is a function of more than attitudes toward performance appraisal. Reactions to merit pay will also be a function of:
   a. Perceptions that those who deserved the raises got them
   b. Perceptions that the amount of money available for raises in merit pay is sufficient to motivate changes in work behavior
   c. Agency policy and managerial behavior regarding management of the distribution of performance ratings
   d. Perceptions regarding the good that merit pay can do for the agency
5. Performance standards that are written after experience with their use in an appraisal will reflect some of the qualities of that appraisal. People who have had a fair and developmental appraisal will be more likely to put in extra effort on their standards and to create useful standards than will others.
6. Agency policy regarding performance standards will be affected by the agency's past experience with appraisal and merit pay.

In summary, we will be looking for several key themes in the operation of the system: the effects of agency policy, stated or implied; the effects of collaboration in writing standards; the perceived quality of the standards and usefulness of standards as a work guide; the impact of supervisory relations compared with other factors in determining attitudes toward performance appraisal; and the impact of policy, managerial action, equity, and perceived agency gains on acceptance of merit pay.

METHODS

In this section we will highlight some of the important characteristics of the study from which the data used in this report are taken and provide some background information about the agencies.

We began our study of the effects of civil service reform in early 1980, collecting data in two installations of the Environmental Protection Agency (EPA) (headquarters and a large regional office) and three installations of the Mine Safety and Health Administration (MSHA) (headquarters and two field operations, located in the Northeast). Data collection has included systematic interviews with senior executives and middle managers; unstructured interviews with "key resource" people (a variety of people with information we felt we needed); mailed questionnaires to agency employees; collection and analysis of documents such as memoranda, policy guidance, training materials, sample performance standards and agency reports; and, to a limited extent, discussions with interested parties outside the agency (e.g., congressional staff). The interview and document collection activities have proceeded in a fairly continuous fashion, with increases in activity at about the time we distribute questionnaires. Questionnaires have been distributed at least twice in all sites: in late summer of 1980 (before full implementation) and early spring of 1982 (after implementation), in all sites except EPA headquarters, and in June 1980, May 1981, and April 1982, at EPA headquarters. The June 1980 questionnaire was a pretest for the study and in many ways is not comparable to the data collected later that summer in the other four sites. Thus, when we refer to pre-CSRA attitudes at EPA headquarters, we are using the May 1981 data collected at that site. These data were collected prior to the first performance evaluations and merit pay determinations in October 1981, but six to nine months after the data in the other sites. Return rates for all questionnaires in all sites vary from 58 percent at EPA headquarters to over 90 percent at the MSHA field installations.

Our analysis relies upon virtually all of these data sources. Quantitative data presented are all taken from questionnaires, while agency policy, culture, and background discussions derive from interviews and analysis of documents.

Results

In this section we return to the model depicted in figure 5.1 in order to assess the way in which the various components of the system act together and separately to influence attitudes toward its operation.

Performance Standards

We argued earlier that several aspects of performance standards were likely to affect attitudes toward performance appraisal. These included:

1. The extent to which standards had been developed collaboratively
2. The extent to which standards had been developed through a process of careful job analysis
3. The extent to which standards were an accurate representation of the job
4. The extent to which standards creation helped employees manage their work situation.

In this section we also include the effects that perceived suitability of performance standards, given the employees' job characteristics, might have on performance appraisal, recalling that one of the problems with performance-contingent pay systems for managers lies in measuring performance.

As seen in table 5.1, there were several significant differences between the agencies in attitudes toward performance standards during the first cycle of the system. In the first three columns we show the percentages of employees overall, and in the two agencies separately, that agreed with each of our measures for performance standards. In 1980, MSHA employees were more likely to agree than were EPA employees that they did a lot of thinking about their jobs when creating standards (78 percent versus 66 percent), that their standards were accurate (79 percent versus 63 percent), and that they liked using standards as a performance guide (59 percent versus 48 percent). Moreover, MSHA managers were less dissatisfied with their participation in creating standards (6 percent versus 26 percent), though employees in both agencies report about the same rate of collaboration with their supervisor (item 7). Finally, MSHA employees were more likely to feel that their jobs were certain and stable enough for standards to be useful than were EPA employees (item 4).

In sum, MSHA employees were more satisfied with the process by which their standards were created, more positive about the quality and usefulness of their standards, and more likely to feel that their

Table 5.1. Attitudes Toward Performance Standards in 1980 and Relationships Between Performance Standards Attitudes and Performance Appraisal Attitudes Among GS-13+ Employees[a]

	Percent "Agree" or "Strongly Agree"			Correlations with Performance Appraisal Attitudes[b]				
	All	EPA	MSHA	Clear Criteria	Accuracy	Perf. Improve.	Ident. for Awards	Overall Acceptance
Writing my current performance standards caused me to really think seriously about what I do in my job.	69	66 *	78	.23*	.20*	.21*	.27*	.22*
My current performance standards accurately represent the most important parts of my job.	67	63 *	79	.43*	.28*	.19*	.12*	.33*
My job duties do not translate very well into written performance standards.	48	51	41	-.11	-.11	-.23*	-.09	-.16*
My job is so uncertain and changing that performance standards aren't much good for me.	35	40 *	21	-.09	-.12	-.17*	-.05	-.20*
I like having written standards against which I can measure my own performance.	51	48 *	59	.11	.12	.17*	.18*	.16*
I wish I had more say in what my standards are.	22	26 *	6	-.21*	-.12	-.09	-.20*	-.05
% who worked with their supervisor at least 50–50 to create standards.	65	64	68	.27*	.12	.13*	.19*	.14*
N =	469	321	148					

[a] All questions, unless otherwise noted, were posed in a Likert-type format with response categories ranging from (1) strongly disagree to (5) strongly agree.

[b] Performance appraisal questions asked in spring 1982. Performance standards questions asked in summer 1980. See table 5.2 for exact question wordings of performance appraisal questions.

* Difference between EPA and MSHA or correlation statistically significant, $p \leq .05$.

jobs were appropriate for the use of standards. There are several possible explanations for these differences. One is that the process at MSHA was truly superior to the process at EPA. Though this is not consistent with the similar levels of collaboration reported by employees in both agencies, it is consistent with attitudes toward the training for performance standards. MSHA managers were more than twice as likely as were EPA managers to rate their training for performance standards as relevant (about 65 percent versus about 25 percent, data not shown).

A second possibility is a function of relative change rather than absolute change in the status quo. The CSRA afforded MSHA its first opportunity to do anything more than a checkoff performance appraisal, while EPA had a somewhat more sophisticated performance appraisal system in place prior to the CSRA changes. Thus, for MSHA employees, the change brought by the CSRA was greater than for EPA employees. The differences in responses could be the result of the magnitude of change over the pre-CSRA way of doing things rather than to the absolute levels of collaboration and job analysis that went into standards. Our interview data support both of these explanations.

The remaining data shown in table 5.1 provide moderate support for our hypotheses concerning the impact that performance standards would have on attitudes toward performance appraisal. In particular, we find that those who put a lot of effort into their standards and those who felt that their standards were a good reflection of their jobs are more positive than are others about the performance appraisal experience in all respects. This is particularly true for perceptions of clarity of criteria in the appraisal and overall acceptance of the new system. The bottom of the table also shows that those who collaborated more in writing their standards, and those who are satisfied with their role in writing standards, are more satisfied with the new performance appraisal system, though the relationships are not as strong as those discussed above. In other words, belief that one has high quality standards, as well as satisfaction with the process for creating the standards, contribute to reports of positive experiences with the subsequent appraisal, though quality of the standards seems to have greater impact on attitudes than satisfaction with the process for creating them. Indeed, we note with some interest that satisfaction with the process is not related to either overall evaluation of the new system (last column) or with perceptions of performance improvement as an outcome of the appraisal (sixth column). A collaborative process for creating standards seems most clearly to result in perceptions of clearer criteria for the appraisal and belief that the appraisal identifies those who deserve an award. The communication that takes place between supervisors and subordinates in the process of creating standards seems to result in greater understanding by subordinates of how and why appraisal decisions are made, but not in the belief that their own appraisals were accurate.

We also note that those who report that they are able to use their standards to help them with their work during the year are only slightly more likely than others to approve of the new system (r = .16) and to feel that they learned how to improve their performance during the coming year as a result of their appraisal (r = .17). In general, this aspect of performance standards did not have as strong an impact on the performance appraisal as we had expected. As we shall see in later sections, the usefulness of standards as a work guide becomes more important as a *result* of the first experience with the cycle.

Finally, we note that perceptions of problems with the work situation (items 3 and 4) are not related to perceived accuracy of the rating, perceived clarity of criteria for the rating, or perceptions that the new system identified those who deserved an award. They are, however, related to the probability of performance improvement coming from the appraisal and overall acceptance of the new system. This suggests that, when job uncertainty is high, the appraisal process may be flexible enough to be perceived as accurate to about the same extent that the process is seen as accurate in more certain job situations. However, concrete directions for future performance improvement are not as available from the appraisal in uncertain situations, and this may result in perceptions that the new system is not better than the old.

In sum, our expectations concerning the impact of performance standards on subsequent appraisal are supported in these two agencies. Those who put more effort into, and wrote more accurate, standards report more positive appraisal experiences in all ways, while those who collaborated in writing their standards report more understanding of the appraisal process, though not much more direction for future performance improvement than others. People who feel their jobs are not appropriate for standards are less likely than others to say that the new system is better than the old and less likely to feel they gained insights into how to improve their performance than their colleagues in more stable positions. Finally, using standards as a performance guide is related to performance improvement coming from the appraisal, belief that the new system identifies people deserving a bonus, and overall acceptance of the new system, but the relationships are not strong.

Performance Appraisal

Let us look more closely at the performance appraisal process per se. In table 5.2 we present attitudes toward the October 1981 performance appraisal and the relationships between these attitudes and overall acceptance of the new system.

In our earlier discussion we argued that the new performance appraisal system would be accepted insofar as it: (1) was perceived to be accurate; (2) was perceived to help employees improve their future performance; and (3) differentiated between people well enough to identify those deserving of larger merit raises. We also argued that the appraisal was likely to be positively related to the ongoing work relationship between supervisor and subordinate.

Table 5.2. Attitudes Toward Performance Appraisal and Relationships Among Performance Appraisal Attitudes Among GS–13+ Employees

| | Percent "Agree" or "Strongly Agree" | | | Correlations with | |
	All	EPA	MSHA	Overall Acceptance of New System (item 5)	Work Relations with Supervisor[a]
The performance appraisal system used in 1981:					
Was based on criteria that are clear to me.	64	62	66	.25*	.35*
Accurately rated my job performance.	44	45	41	.37*	.33*
Helped me improve my performance.	17	17	19	.45*	.26*
Identified people who deserved a cash award.	21	22	19	.33*	.18*
Was better than the old (pre-CSRA) system overall.	26	27	24	—	.14*
N =	479	338	141		

[a] This scale is the average of responses to the following items:
  1. My supervisor often lets me know how well he/she thinks I am performing my job.
  2. I can communicate well with my supervisor.
  3. My supervisor encourages me to give my best effort.
  4. My supervisor shows me how to improve my performance.
  5. My supervisor lets me know what is expected of me.
  6. I trust my supervisor to keep my interests in mind when he/she makes decisions.
  7. I respect my supervisor's judgment on most issues.
* Correlations statistically significant, $p \leq .05$.

As seen in table 5.2, most of our predictions were accurate regarding performance appraisal. There are no significant differences between the two agencies (despite the differences in performance standards noted in the last section); work relationship with one's supervisor is related to several aspects of performance appraisal; and specific aspects of the appraisal are all positively related to overall acceptance of the new system.

However, though our predictions were met, we see in table 5.2 rather negative attitudes toward the new system. Though nearly two-thirds felt the appraisal was based on clear criteria, and 44 percent felt it was accurate, very few (17 percent) report that it helped them improve their future peformance; only 21 percent believe it identified those deserving a cash award; and about a quarter felt the new system was better than the old system, overall. Though we do not show these data, we also found that the only respect in which the new system is seen as significantly better than the old is with respect to accuracy of the appraisal. Moreover, the new system is perceived to be significantly *worse* than the old in its ability to help people improve their future performance. We would suggest that these two changes are related (Meyer, Kay, and French 1965). That is, as the new system allows people to view the past more accurately, they may de-emphasize the importance of planning for the future. Stand-ards-based appraisal tends to focus attention on past performance, and the benefits of looking ahead during a performance appraisal may be sacrificed in the process.

We also note in table 5.2 that the strongest correlate of overall acceptance of the new system is precisely that aspect which has suffered; performance improvement ($r = .45$). Further, the aspect about which people are most positive, clarity of criteria, is the weakest correlate of overall acceptance ($r = .25$). This suggests that managers in agencies might want to refocus some of their attention toward future performance and not worry too much about improving the understanding of criteria to be used in the appraisal. Our results suggest that the very fact of having performance standards probably accomplishes the latter. What managers might want to think about in the appraisal is those things that standards do not almost auto-matically accomplish, such as identifying ways of improving perfor-mance for the coming year or two.

Finally, we see that work relationship with one's supervisor has a consistent and substantial impact on the reported quality of the performance appraisal (items 1, 2, and 3), but less influence on the more global or system-level attitudes about the system (items 4 and 5). Thus, while the work relationship with the supervisor has only a small impact on overall acceptance of the new system ($r = .14$), it has a substantial impact on perceived accuracy of the appraisal (*r* = .33).

These data suggest that performance standards and appraisal based on those standards yield improvements in the perceived accuracy of the appraisal, an important component of any pay-for-performance system. The cost, at least in the short run, appears to be that performance appraisal has become more accomplishment-oriented and less improvement-oriented. Although focusing on accomplishments is a key requirement of an appraisal system in which pay will be tied to those accomplishments, it is not the only purpose for performance appraisal. Indeed, our data suggest that it may not be the most important purpose, particularly because very few employees feel that the *system* is functioning to identify high performers accurately (item 4). Employees in these two agencies place more emphasis on the developmental character of the appraisal in their overall evaluation of the new system than on its accuracy (at a personal or a system level), suggesting that employees see value in the appraisal *not* as part of a compensation system, but as part of a performance management system. We will highlight the importance of this distinction in subsequent sections.

Merit Pay

Let us turn now to the last step in the cycle, merit pay. In table 5.3 we show employees' attitudes toward various aspects of the merit pay activities in 1981 as well as the impact that overall attitude toward the appraisal had on acceptance of merit pay. We argue here that merit pay events are linked to performance appraisal, but are also a function of several other factors, including:

1. Belief that merit pay will yield some efficiency and/or accountability benefits for the agency
2. The use of managerial discretion
3. Perceptions of equity
4. Perceptions of the incentive value of the raises available

We also include in table 5.3 a measure of the employees' belief that their position has been correctly classified as a merit pay position to assess the effect of their personal acceptance of the situation on their evaluation of merit pay.

As we look at the results in table 5.3, we see only two differences between the agencies, one that is easily explicable given what we know about agency policy differences, and another that is more mysterious. The latter relates to the incentive value of raises (item 7). MSHA employees are significantly more likely than EPA em-

Table 5.3. Attitudes Toward Merit Pay and Relationships Among Merit Pay Attitudes Among GS–13+ Employees

	Percent "Agree" or "Strongly Agree"			Correlation with Belief that Merit Pay is an Improvement (item 8)
	All	EPA	MSHA	
Merit pay has made this agency more effective by encouraging people to work harder.	10	9	10	.55*
One effect of merit pay has been to increase a supervisor's control over subordinates.	44	46	37	.34*
All in all, I think my job *should* be classified as merit pay.	48	51	42	.54*
The merit pay pool manager changed too many performance ratings.	46	50 *	39	-.23*
People who deserved a big raise got a big raise under merit pay.	5	6	4	.35*
I am satisfied with the way in which the merit pay funds were distributed.	13	14	9	.39*
There is enough difference between a satisfactory and an outstanding rating in the size of the raise to make the extra effort worth it.	20	15 *	31	.23*
I think merit pay for supervisors and managers is an improvement over the old way of determining raises.	29	31	24	—
The performance evaluation in 1981 was better than old (pre-CSRA) system overall.	26	27	24	.57*
N =	479	338	141	

* Differences between EPA and MSHA or correlations statistically significant, $p \leq .05$.

ployees to agree that the potential raise is worth the effort (31 percent versus 15 percent). This does not appear to be because MSHA managers *value* money as a reward more than EPA managers, nor is it because MSHA managers perceive a stronger link between pay and performance than EPA managers (data not shown). It is a particularly surprising result because EPA's merit pay system is structured to differentiate between satisfactory and excellent performers *more* than is MSHA's. Clearly, this structural difference is not reflected as a perceived difference among those affected by merit pay.

The other difference between the two agencies regarding managerial discretion in lowering performance ratings is a clear result of different choices made by managers in the two agencies when faced with a very high or "inflated" distribution of performance ratings. Both agencies had high ratings (average rating on a 5 point scale was about 4.2 in both agencies). But different steps were taken in response to these ratings in the two agencies. In fact this table conceals a major difference among EPA employees. At the regional site, a policy decision was made to change no ratings at a higher review level. Thus virtually no one at this site agreed with the statement presented in item 4. At headquarters, over 60 percent of the employees agreed with this statement. While there was no explicit policy regarding changing ratings at EPA headquarters or at MSHA, there was a tacit policy at EPA headquarters that ratings could and should be changed in order to lower the overall distribution. This had been done during this agency's pilot merit pay experience the previous year (Gaertner and Gaertner, 1981) with results much the same as those we see here. Moreover, EPA's system placed more emphasis on managerial discretion, thus producing a climate in which changing ratings was seen as legitimate by the executives responsible (though not their subordinates). MSHA had no policy regarding changing ratings nor had they a pilot experience upon which to draw, though some of the executives did indicate to their subordinates that some distributions would not be tolerated. From interview data, we conclude that ratings changes were far less frequent at MSHA than at EPA headquarters, which accounts for the difference in attitudes that we see in table 5.3.

These agency differences aside, the data in table 5.3 suggest fairly consistently that there is ample room for improvement in the merit pay aspects of the CSRA. Very few employees in either agency believe that merit pay will make the agency more effective (10 percent), and fewer than half feel that supervisors will be able to control their subordinates more as a result of merit pay (in both cases these attitudes have deteriorated by about 10 percent since the summer of 1980). Moreover, fewer than half of these employees overall feel that their jobs should be classified as merit pay, even though over 75 percent of them are in unambiguous merit pay positions. Thus, belief that merit pay will do the agency some good is not very strong, and personal acceptance of one's status in merit pay is similarly weak. Overall, fewer than 30 percent believe merit pay is an improvement (item 8).

Items 5, 6, and 7 have to do with the linkages between pay and performance. Again, the results for the system are not positive. Almost no one agreed that those who deserved big raises got them (item 5), suggesting that there is considerable belief that the pay-for-performance system is faltering. There was similar dissatisfaction with the overall distribution of funds in both agencies (item 6), lending further support to this argument.

In the right-hand column of table 5.3 we see the relationships between attitudes toward merit pay and evaluation of merit pay as a new system. Clearly, the attitudes with the largest impact on overall assessment of merit pay are: (1) whether the employee feels that merit pay will result in a more effective agency, (2) personal acceptance of merit pay, and (3) approval of the new performance appraisal system. Note that these are *not* the primary criteria suggested by performance-contingent pay theorists.

However there are substantial but smaller relationships between the incentive and equity characteristics of the pay decisions and overall assessment of merit pay. Those who are satisfied with the pay distribution, those who feel that deserving people were rewarded, and those who feel that the pay differential available to outstanding performers is adequate are all more likely than others to see merit pay as an improvement. These results suggest that some of the underlying assumptions of merit pay may be valid for these managers, despite the fact that they are not being met by the system in its present form, but that linkages to work management (item 1) might be more important.

Finally, we note a modest negative relationship between higher-level ratings changes and approval of merit pay ($r = -.23$). Those who approve of merit pay also tend to feel that ratings should not be lowered by higher-level reviewing officials. This is clearly an area in which agency policy can have some impact. We suspect that this relationship is weaker than it might be in other years because of the very high average ratings given in both agencies. Such high ratings make it nearly impossible to reward differential performers differentially because the systems assume an average rating closer to 3.5, rather than the 4.2 obtained. Thus, in the context of very high ratings, there may be more tolerance for lowering ratings than would normally occur. In any case, this action tends to have a negative impact on employees' evaluation of the system.

As noted earlier, merit pay and performance appraisal are cyclical processes. One important question for any evaluation of civil service reform is, What was learned? It is to this question we now turn our attention.

Performance Standards Revisited

We have argued that performance standards are the starting point for the operation of performance appraisal and merit pay. As such it seems likely that agency planners would choose performance standards as a place from which to influence the overall operation of the system. Thus, we would argue that attitudes toward performance standards may reflect some explicit as well as implicit policy redirections in each agency resulting from their first experience with the merit pay system.

In table 5.4 we present attitudes toward performance standards that resulted from the appraisal-payout process in October 1981. We have also reproduced attitudes toward standards for the previous year for ease of comparison.

Several rather startling changes are in evidence, particularly in MSHA. In this agency, attitudes deteriorated on virtually every dimension of performance standards about which we asked, and in most cases these differences are statistically significant. MSHA managers report less thought going into standards, less accurate standards, less appropriate jobs for standards (even though their jobs had changed very little), less willingness to use standards as a year-long performance guide, less participation in creating their standards, and less satisfaction with that process. These results are a clear outcome of a policy change made at the agency during the fall of 1981.

As noted earlier, MSHA's performance ratings were very high, on the average. In fact they were one of the highest in the entire Department of Labor. The culprit identified for these "inflated" ratings was performance standards. Standards had been made too lenient, so that very high ratings were inevitable. Moreover, agency planners discovered wide discrepancies between different field locations in standards, even though they were written for very similar jobs. Thus, several functional areas in the agency chose to centralize the creation of performance standards, drafting them at headquarters and sending them out to field installations for use. The result is very clear. Though we do not show the differences between headquarters and the field installations, the differences we would expect are in the data. Field employees show far less satisfaction with their standards and the uses to which they can be put than do headquarters employees.

Attitudes have deteriorated at EPA as well, though in no case are the changes statistically significant. This is because top management in this agency made no policy changes regarding performance standards as a result of the 1981 payout experience. If anything, the CSRA provisions were ignored by the new leadership in this agency until well into 1982. The slight decreases we see in the attitudes of EPA employees are probably a natural response to a new system that is not so new anymore, rather than a result of an explicit choice made by top management.

The change in participation (and attendant satisfaction) at MSHA is important because of the effects it has on all aspects of performance

Table 5.4. Attitudes Toward Performance Standards Before and After Experience Using Them Among GS-13+ Employees

| | Percent "Agree" or "Strongly Agree" | | | | | | Correlations with Overall Acceptance of New System | |
| | All | | EPA | | MSHA | | | |
	1980	1982	1980	1982	1980	1982	1980	1982
Writing my current performance standards caused me to really think seriously about what I do in my job.	69	60	66	63	78 *	54	.22*	.25*
My current performance standards accurately represent the most important parts of my job.	67	64	63	61	79	70	.33*	.23*
My job duties do not translate very well into written performance standards.	48	53	51	49	41 *	61	-.16*	-.25*
My job is so uncertain and changing that performance standards aren't much good for me.	35	44	40	45	21 *	42	-.20*	-.31*
I like having written standards against which I can measure my own performance.	51	50	48	50	59	50	.16*	.32*
Writing performance standards has helped me plan my work for the year.	—	32	—	30	—	34	—	.39*
My performance standards have helped me understand my supervisor's job.	—	30	—	28	—	33	—	.21*
I wish I had more say in what my standards are.	22	32	26	32	6 *	31	-.05	-.28*
Percentage who worked with their supervisor at least 50–50 to create standards.	65	57	64	60	68 *	49	.14*	.13*
N =	469	479	321	338	148	141		

* Differences between 1980 and 1982 or correlations statistically significant, $p \leq .05$.

standards. We found in this agency that those who collaborated with their supervisor in writing their standards were more likely than others to feel that their standards were useful to them as a work planning device and that their standards were accurate. They also report putting more thought into writing their standards. Further, those who were satisfied with their level of participation were more positive than were others about every aspect of performance standards, but most notably the usefulness of standards as a work planning guide and the accuracy and appropriateness of standards. In other words, people who felt that they had a sufficient amount of input in their standards appear much more motivated to use their standards constructively during the year and also appear to have a more accurate basis on which to be appraised in the coming year. As we know from table 5.1, this is likely to yield a more satisfactory appraisal process overall.

Aside from agency policy, the question still remains, How is performance appraisal related to the creation of future performance standards? In table 5.4 we see that correlations between overall approval of performance appraisal and attitudes toward new standards are quite similar to those between old performance standards and overall approval of the appraisal system. One clear exception is the increased importance of satisfaction with participation in creating performance standards (item 8). Here the correlation jumped from -.05 to -.28, suggesting that satisfaction with one's role in creating performance standards has become a much more important determinant of willingness to accept the new system. We also see that the strongest correlation between characteristics of the new standards and feelings about the new appraisal system is with the usefulness of standards in helping the employee plan work ($r = .39$) and use of standards as a performance guide ($r = .32$). The former question was not asked in 1980, so we do not know if this relationship has become stronger. However, use of standards as a performance guide was asked in 1980, and we see that this relationship has become substantially stronger with experience with the system (r's = .16 and .32). This suggests that one of the things learned from the first pass through the system is that using standards as a guide for work planning and work accomplishment is valuable and pays off in a better appraisal experience.

Finally, we might ask whether there were any specific aspects of the performance appraisal that had a disproportionately large impact on the character of performance standards for the following year. We have argued that agency policy regarding participation in creating standards had a substantial impact at MSHA. But were there things about the appraisal experience that were not a function of agency policy that might impact the quality of performance standards in the future? In order to answer this question, we looked at the relationships between specific attitudes toward the 1981 appraisal and specific attitudes toward the performance standards which were created following that appraisal. These relationships are shown in table 5.5.

The strongest relationship between almost all aspects of performance standards and the appraisal is the extent to which the appraisal showed the employee how to improve performance. The relationships are particularly strong for the usefulness of standards—the extent to which they helped the employee plan work for the year and the employee's understanding of his or her supervisor's job through

Table 5.5: Relationships Between Appraisal Experiences and Subsequent Performance Standards

The performance appraisal system used in 1981:	Writing my current performance standards caused me to really think seriously about what I do in my job.	My current performance standards accurately represent the most important parts of my job.	My job duties do not translate very well into written performance standards.	My job is so uncertain and changing that performance standards aren't much good for me.	I like having written standards against which I can measure my own performance.	Writing performance standards has helped me plan my work for the year.	My performance standards have helped me understand my supervisor's job.	I wish I had more say in what my standards are.	Percent who worked with their supervisor at least 50–50 to create standards.
Was based on criteria that are clear to me.	.19*	.29*	−.16*	−.13*	.15*	.17*	.18*	−.26*	.27*
Accurately rated my job performance.	.19*	.34*	−.09*	−.19*	.11*	.16*	.22*	−.34*	.13*
Helped me improve my performance.	.31*	.33*	−.23*	−.30*	.29*	.51*	.41*	−.24*	.22*
Identified people who deserved a cash award.	.26*	.22*	−.15*	−.18*	.22*	.35*	.31*	−.22*	.12*

* Correlations statistically significant, $p \leq .05$.

writing standards (r's $= .51$ and $.41$, respectively). This suggests that one clear effect of a developmental appraisal on future standards is to make those standards more useful for getting the work done in the agency and increasing the level of understanding between supervisor and subordinate regarding what is to be done. We interpret this as a sign of success for the system, as it indicates that the CSRA can have a positive impact on employees' ability to do their work well. Recall from table 5.2 that the relationship between a developmental review and various aspects of performance standards existing prior to the review were not particularly strong, suggesting that this is an area in which some real learning has taken place. In other words, these relationships were probably not a function of a self-fulfilling prophesy, but instead a function of a positive appraisal experience.

Insofar as this reinforcing cycle continues to exist, and insofar as developmental appraisals can be relatively independent of a particular set of performance standards (because the appraisal does not look back, but rather forward), this bodes very well for the new system and points us very clearly toward at least one conclusion for supervisors: during the performance appraisal, try to focus as much on how performance can be improved in the future as on how well goals were met in the past.

Certainly, this sort of advice can be converted into training and guidance regarding characteristics of a successful performance review. But as before, that review is a rather private matter and is ultimately not very susceptible to direction from top management. However, we would argue that very little of the training and orientation that accompanied the introduction of these systems emphasized the importance of a forward-looking review. Though our conclusions sound very commonsensical, it is our belief that many managers were so caught up in the details of accurately rating past performance based on standards that they overlooked the importance of a future orientation. Thus, as we see managers trying to incorporate both evaluative and developmental aspects into a single review, we would expect to see more and more use of standards as a work management tool, in addition to an appraisal tool, and greater acceptance of the new performance appraisal system as a result.

DISCUSSION AND CONCLUSION

In the beginning of this paper we argued that the three aspects of the CSRA with which we are dealing should be thought of as a system rather than separate parts because each interacts with the other. We are now in a position to expand that statement to recognize the independent contributions of each part. In particular, our results suggest that merit pay is not seen as a very useful activity by most managers in these two agencies. As a compensation system it is not perceived to be equitable, nor is there overwhelming agreement that the raises available are worth the effort required to obtain them. There is also considerable sentiment that there is not enough money in the merit pay system for it ever to function effectively. Thus, we are led to the same conclusion that other researchers have reached. Merit pay, as currently operating, is not having any positive impact on agency effectiveness, nor is it having any discernable impact on employee work behavior. Our analysis does not test the efficacy of pay-for-performance plans for managers in a very rigorous manner, yet it certainly lends no support to the argument that pay-for-performance is appropriate for managers, at least not for federal managers and with the current level of merit pay funding.

Our conclusions regarding performance appraisal and performance standards are rather different, however, and point to the CSRA as a work management system rather than a compensation management system. While there are certainly many people who do not feel that the new appraisal system is an improvement over the old, and while we have identified several problems with the way in which the new system operates, our results nevertheless suggest that, for those who do see the appraisal as valuable, there are changes in evidence in their performance standards that point to the standards becoming more useful for work management. That is, work performance is potentially improved through the use of performance standards, and this is most likely to be true among those who experience an appraisal that helps them identify ways in which to improve their performance. This suggests that the CSRA, as a work management system, has experienced small but significant success, while the CSRA as a compensation system for managers has not experienced such success.

Further, our results suggest several ways in which agencies may focus their efforts in order to make the system even more useful as a work management system. In summary, we found that:

1. Accurate performance standards are an important contributor to an accurate appraisal, and the CSRA seems to have fostered both. This aspect of standards and appraisal may need fine tuning, but no major investment of resources.
2. Participation in creating standards is an increasingly important aspect of the functioning of the system. In particular, the value that standards can have in helping employees plan their work is strongly related to participation in creating standards. Thus, if useful standards are to be written, participation is required.

Agencies that choose to centralize the creation of standards do so at a considerable cost to the utility of the standards.

3. Appraisals are best when they help employees improve performance in the future. Moroever, appraisals that do this are more likely to lead to useful performance standards for the coming fiscal year, which should enhance employee performance. Training and guidance on the value of developmental appraisals are areas in which agencies could devote resources to some benefit.

4. Employees do not see any positive value in merit pay. Given these attitudes and the current level of funding, merit pay should be viewed in practical terms as a bonus system rather than a major compensation and/or motivation system. De-emphasizing merit pay as a major management tool should help to focus attention on the parts of the system that have been more successful, namely, performance standards and appraisal.

5. Though we have not addressed this problem in great detail in this paper, there is considerable concern among top managers in federal agencies about so-called ratings inflation. (See Gaertner and Gaertner [1981].) We have seen in our results that post hoc attempts to lower the distribution of ratings does no good for merit pay or performance appraisal, and probably does some harm to the integrity of the system. We would make three points here. The first is that, until supervisors recognize some value in having a lower distribution of ratings (other than a guidance memorandum from a senior official), there is likely to be little movement toward a modal rating of 3 or 3.5 on the 5-point scale. Until managers wish to use the funds available in merit pay for making meaningful distinctions between managers, there is likely to be little reason in their minds to lower ratings. Second, as we have argued above, merit pay ought to be used as a bonus system, not a major compensation system. If this is the direction in which merit pay moves, there is very little reason to lower ratings. Finally, we would argue that under any circumstances, post hoc ratings changes are a poor managerial practice. Performance, like work, needs to be managed throughout the year. Ratings should come as no surprise to supervisor or subordinate, and higher-level reviewing officials should be aware, throughout the year, of the likely ratings among their employees. Failure to manage the process at the time that standards are written and during the year should not be "corrected" by changing ratings after the fact.

Clearly, the ultimate effects of these provisions of the Reform Act will not be known for several years. There are numerous effects that events apart from the Act had on the implementation and use of the Act, the presidential transition being but one, and we have not addressed these other events in any detail here. However, we feel that our results thus far, though of necessity tenuous, point to two major conclusions. The first is that merit pay is not working in our two agencies or in most of the other agencies in which evaluations are taking place. By not working, we mean that it is not widely accepted, it is not seen as an improvement, it is not rewarding deserving people fairly with significant raises, and it is not contributing to agency effectiveness. The second conclusion is that performance standards and performance appraisal may be working to improve the way in which employees are able to plan and accomplish their work goals. This general finding is endangered by a decrease in collaboration in writing standards, but is nevertheless an encouraging accomplishment for the CSRA and for the prospects for improving work effectiveness in the federal government.

References

Deci, E. L. 1975. *Intrinsic Motivation.* New York: Plenum.

Gaertner, Gregory H., and Karen N. Gaertner. 1979. "Proposal for the Organizational Assessments of the Effects of Civil Service Reform." Response to U.S. Office of Personnel Management OPM–RFP–24–79.

Gaertner, Gregory H., and Karen N. Gaertner. 1981. "Organizational Assessments of the Effects of Civil Service Reform: FY 81 Annual Report." Washington, D.C.: U.S. Office of Personnel Management.

Heneman, H. G., III, and D. P. Schwab. 1972. "An Evaluation of Research on Expectancy Theory Predictions of Employee Performance." *Psychological Bulletin* 78: 1–9.

Latham, Gary P., and Gary Yukl. 1975. "A Review of Research on the Application of Goal Setting in Organizations." *Academy of Management Journal* 18: 824–45.

Lawler, E. E., III. 1971. *Pay and Organizational Effectiveness.* New York: McGraw-Hill.

Lawler, E. E., III. 1981. *Pay and Organization Development.* Reading, Mass.: Addison-Wesley.

Loomis, C. J. 1982. "The Madness of Executive Compensation." *Fortune* (July 12): 42–52.

Meyer, Herbert. 1975. "The Pay for Performance Dilemma." *Organizational Dynamics* (Winter): 39–50.

Meyer, Herbert, E. Kay, and J. R. P. French. 1965. "Split Roles in Performance Appraisal." *Harvard Business Review* (January–February): 123–129.

Mikalachi, A. 1976. "There is No Merit in Merit Pay." *Business Quarterly* (Spring): 46–50.

O'Toole, Daniel E. and John R. Churchill. 1982. "Implementing Pay-for-Performance: Initial Experiences." *Review of Public Personnel Administration* 2, no. 3 (Summer):13–28.

Patten, Thomas. 1968. "Merit Increases and the Facts of Organizational Life." *Management of Personnel Quarterly,* (Summer): 30–38.

Pearce, Jone L., and James L. Perry. 1982. "Federal Merit Pay: A Longitudinal Analysis." Public Policy Research Organization Working Paper, Management Research Program, Graduate School of Management, University of California, Irvine.

Pearce, Jone L., William B. Stevenson, and James L. Perry. 1983. "Contingent Pay for Managers and Organizational Performance: A Time-Series Analysis." Public Policy Research Organization Working Paper, Management Research Program, Graduate School of Management, University of California, Irvine.

Salancik, Gary R. 1975. "Interaction Effects of Performance and Money on Self-Perception of Intrinsic Motivation." *Organizational Behavior and Human Performance* (June): 339–51.

Shrauger, J. Sidney. 1975. "Responses to Evaluation as a Function of Initial Self-Perceptions." *Psychological Bulletin* 82, no. 4: 581–96.

Chapter Six

Evaluating the Civil Service Reform Act of 1978: The Experience of the U.S. Department of Health and Human Services

Mark Abramson, Richard Schmidt, and Sandra Baxter

Introduction

The Department of Health and Human Services Evaluation Study.

This chapter presents findings from the first year of a three-year evaluation study of the impact of the Civil Service Reform Act of 1978 (CSRA) on motivating and improving the performance of individual executives in one large federal department. We offer tentative conclusions regarding the possibility that the Act will lead to demonstrably improved performance of governmental programs and services. We present the background of the Health and Human Services (HHS) study, how it came about, and why we decided on the study's approach. Later sections explore some of the findings that have emerged from the surveys and case studies we conducted. Finally, we discuss the goals of civil service reform and assess whether the Act is likely to produce the desired outcomes.

The Department of Health, Education and Welfare (HEW, which became the Department of Health and Human Services in May 1980) began evaluating the Civil Service Reform Act in the fall of 1979, shortly after the July 1979 inauguration of the Senior Executive Service (SES). In brief, the multiyear evaluation effort has several objectives:

The views presented in this paper represent those of the authors and should not be interpreted as representing the official view of the Department of Health and Human Services.

- To reach agreement on the objectives of civil service reform within HHS for which the Department was to be held accountable
- To ascertain, on an ongoing basis, to what extent those objectives are being achieved in HHS
- To recommend improvements in the HHS CSRA program to enable the objectives to be achieved
- When particular objectives are achieved in the HHS CSRA program, to understand the factors contributing to successful implementation
- When particular objectives are not achieved, to understand whether:
  a) the theory behind the intervention was flawed and not achievable;
  b) the implementation of the Act was incomplete;
  c) environmental factors prevented the intervention from succeeding.

The HHS evaluation of the CSRA is, in many respects, not traditional. Rather than independently assessing CSRA and returning in four years with a final judgment on its success or failure, this evaluation involves frequent interaction with the primary client, the HHS Assistant Secretary for Personnel Administration. The study is viewed as a diagnostic tool to understand and, where possible, to remedy problems in the implementation of CSRA in HHS. Whenever problems have been detected, possible remedies have been suggested. Future rounds of data collection will show whether remedial actions have resulted in improvement.

The HHS study of CSRA is focused on two aspects of the Act: (1) Title IV, which created the Senior Executive Service; and (2) the Department's "performance management" activities, consisting of Title II (performance appraisal), Title IV (Senior Executive Service), and Title V (Merit Pay). Throughout this paper, the term "civil service reform," or CSRA, will refer to the SES and performance appraisal aspects of the Act.

The findings reported here are based on the experience of HEW/ HHS in implementing CSRA from 1979 to 1982. We realize that these preliminary results may be not generalizable to other federal departments and may change over the next two years of the HHS study.[1] Instead, the paper presents a framework for assessing the success or failure of CSRA in HHS, which others may find useful in similar efforts across the government.

Just as the CSRA record differs from department to department, it differs across agencies within HHS as well. In many respects, HHS is a holding company, consisting of an Office of the Secretary and five operating divisions (OPDIVs). Comparisons across HHS, however, broaden our perspective on the problems of implementing a major innovation in a large department.

How to Evaluate the Civil Service Reform Act

At first, the thought of evaluating CSRA in HHS was intimidating. How could such a far-reaching management and personnel system be evaluated? Program evaluation only rarely confronts purely administrative processes. Because CSRA was intended to create far-reaching effects on management and on program performance, it seemed a worthwhile subject. Title IV of the Act is the only portion of the Act continuation of which is subject to review by Congress after five years, and it seemed especially important to evaluate it fully. Our first step was to specify and reach agreement on a model of the SES program that would structure the evaluation.[2] Chart 1 presents a design logic model of the HHS SES program, including the objectives for the SES program in HHS. The model was based on our analysis of the program's legislative intent and interviews with key policy makers. As can be seen from the table, the objectives are numerous and complex. While the key policy makers involved in creating and initially implementing the SES did not agree on the relative emphasis to be given to various components of the program, agreement did exist on its major objectives. At the end of Phase I, the Assistant Secretary for Personnel Administration agreed that the logic model accurately represented the SES program he would be administering. He further agreed that the program should be evaluated against the objectives presented in chart 1.

The logic model presents the components of the HHS SES program (events 1–12) and the agreed-upon objectives for the program (events 13–23). The objectives can be grouped into three categories, based on their proximity to the ultimate goals of CSRA:

- Immediate objectives
- Intermediate objectives
- Ultimate objectives

At the end of Phase I, the Assistant Secretary for Personnel Administration decided that the objective of increasing public confidence and satisfaction (event 23) was not plausible for the SES program in HHS, and that he could not assume responsibility for achieving it. The objective was dropped from the model and was not evaluated.

For the immediate and intermediate objectives, data from the first-year survey (personnel interviews and mail questionnaires) would

CHART I

HHS SES DESIGN LOGIC: POLICY MAKERS' AND PROGRAM MANAGERS' PERSPECTIVES

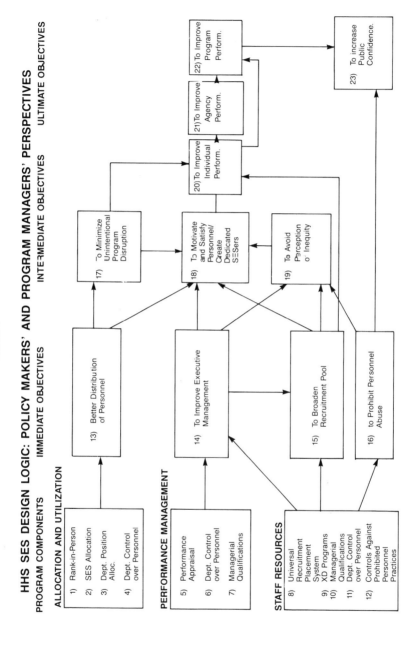

indicate whether the objectives were being achieved. If they were not, management interventions could be proposed to make them more achievable. The ultimate objectives are more difficult to assess and require several years' worth of data collection by less quantitative methods. Case studies could assess both the plausibility of achieving the objectives and evidence on their success or failure. We now turn to a discussion of general attitudes and the three sets of objectives for CSRA.

ARE CSRA OBJECTIVES BEING ACHIEVED?

General Attitudes

In many respects, CSRA can be viewed as an innovation. It is widely accepted that supportive attitudes are necessary if an innovation is to be accepted and adopted. The questionnaire survey of all SES members documented positive attitudes regarding dedication to their job and agency. Table 6.2 presents these findings. This is consistent with findings from other surveys of senior governmental managers.[3]

The SES members showed a high level of job satisfaction. We probed its sources during interviews. Nearly three-quarters attributed their satisfaction to their ability to influence public policy debate and to implement policy, once developed. Other sources included the opportunity to work with talented, dedicated colleagues and their ability to deliver important program services.[4] In discussing job satisfaction, respondents stated:

> I enjoy interacting with congressional committees about ways to modify programs and laws.

Table 6.2 Survey Findings: General Attitudes

HHS-SES members are dedicated.

  96 percent say that they are willing to exert much effort in helping their agency be successful
  91 percent say that they really care about the fate of their agency
  84 percent are proud to tell others that they are part of their agency
   8 percent stated that they feel little loyalty to their agency

66 percent of the HHS respondents expect to be working in the federal government two years from now. In a government-wide Merit Systems Protection Board study, only 57 percent responded yes to the same question.

SOURCE: *1982 Survey of SES Members in HHS: Chart Book,* Department of Health and Human Services, 1982.

My job satisfaction is derived from the decisions I make, the things I do, to make sure that the finest biomedical research in the world is supported.

The people I work with . . . are an extraordinarily competent, committed, skillful group with a true sense of integrity, and they are totally unrecognized.

This high job satisfaction is a solid base on which the innovation of CSRA might have been "sold" and implemented. However, much of the rhetoric surrounding CSRA and SES was negative, focusing on making bureaucrats more hard-working, dedicated, and responsive. In fact, most SES members already believe they possess those characteristics.

The above findings lead us to two conclusions:

- The high level of job satisfaction and agency commitment provide a basis for successfully implementing an innovation such as CSRA, so long as other components of the innovation are not viewed as detrimental. (This issue will be discussed further.)
- It was unrealistic to have expected SES to increase the level of dedication of senior federal managers. Based on survey data, there is very little room for improvement in this area.

Immediate Objectives

Table 6.3 presents survey findings regarding four immediate objectives (events 13–16) presented in the HHS SES logic model. Each objective is discussed below.

Better distribution and Utilization of Personnel. This objective was intended to operate on two levels, macro and micro. On the macro level, it was originally anticipated that both the Office of Personnel Management (OPM) and agencies would use SES allocations as a tool for responding to priority governmental problems or issues. In our interpretation, the original concept was based on an expanding (or at least a stable) government. A new program might be announced or given higher priority, and new or additional SES slots would then be made available to staff it. While this has happened, it has not happened as frequently as we anticipated. Instead, government is contracting in size, and SES slots are being reduced rather than increased. Many SES positions have gone unfilled. Although the agencies' allocation of SES positions may have been reduced, this has not created problems because of the large number of positions that have gone unfilled. Thus, on a macro level, this objective has

Table 6.3. Immediate Objectives

Objective	Is Objective Now Being Achieved?	Survey Evidence on Which Judgment Was Made
To Provide Better Distribution and Utilization of Personnel (event 13)		
Rank-in-Person System	No	27% of respondents expressed interest in a job change in FY 82; 58% of respondents do not know whether there are mechanisms in place to apply for a job change.
Improve Career/Noncareer Interface	No	5% of respondents reported that the interface had improved; 57% reported no change; 17% reported deterioration.
To Improve Executive Management (event 14)		
Departmental Performance Appraisal System	No	54% of respondents feel it is not worth the time it takes. Over 70% of respondents reported that performance appraisal had not influenced their work in the last 12 months.
Link Objectives of Organization, Program, and Individual	Yes	68% of respondents report that their program's objectives are included in their performance plan.
Increase Risk-Taking and Innovativeness	Partially	25% of respondents say that risk taking is included in their performance plan, while 40% say it is not.
Reward and Retain Good Executives	No	SES is viewed as having little impact in either reward or retaining good executives.
Executive Development Programs	Yes	Over 80% of respondents who have had an executive development experience express satisfaction with activity.
To Broaden Recruitment Pool (event 15)	No	Only 12% reported that civil service reform had made it easier to broaden the executive recruitment pool.
To Prohibit Personnel Abuse (event 16)	Yes	75% of respondents have not viewed any prohibited personnel activities taking place.

SOURCE: 1982 Survey of SES Members in HHS: Chart Book, Department of Health and Human Services, 1982.

not been totally achieved and is not as relevant as originally anticipated.

On a micro level, a major change introduced by the Senior Executive
Service was the "rank-in-person" concept.[5] Instead of individuals
being identified by their job grade level (the old supergrade system
assigned a grade, e.g., GS–16, to a position), SES members now
carry their own rank, as in the military. They can be shifted to
another position without losing rank. To many SES members, the
concept of rank-in-person is viewed as a double-edged sword.

- On one side, the rank-in-person provision allows *involuntary*
  transfers of individuals, starting 120 days after the appointment
  of a new Secretary. Many SES members feared, and continue to
  fear, that this power might be abused by punitively transferring
  individuals geographically across the United States. Several such
  actions were alleged to have taken place in other government
  agencies.
- On the other side, our study found many SES members eager
  for voluntary, *purposeful* reassignment. While many reassignments
  have occurred as a result of management initiatives, individuals
  continued to express disappointment at the infrequent use of
  reassignments for developmental purposes.

In personal interviews, we were told:

. . . there should be more mobility, which may mean creating
more SES slots.

There's an absence of opportunity for mobility assignments to
develop people.

I was hoping for lateral mobility but have not been able to do
it; I had hoped phone calls would be made across agencies,
based on the circulation of resume files and referrals, but
things are still wired. . . .

I thought someone would see it (SES) as a talent pool and
use it that way.

However, additional interviews with key departmental career officials revealed that the reactions of SES members to the concepts
of increased mobility and executive rotation were mixed. When
mobility was placed in an executive development context, respondents
split as to whether they viewed mobility as an individual responsibility or an organizational responsibility. Nearly half our respondents argued that mobility was an individual responsibility.

Executive development and mobility is an individual thing. SES members don't need training and development at this point in their careers.

Most executives did not view SES as a way to move every three years. They recognize that they have to work out their own executive movement.

An individual has two options: he can look at posted SES vacancies and apply for them, or he can discuss mobility with his supervisors or a senior level official. Much of this (mobility) is self-initiated. If you're a go-getter, go do it.

The remaining half felt that mobility was an organizational responsibility.

I think it is generally agreed that it is healthy for senior executives to have experience with more than one agency. But I think nothing will happen until someone in a leadership position dictates that it should. . . .

While some people find their own jobs, the tendency is for people to stay where they are. They [the department] tend to leave them there as long as they are doing a good job.

The PHS [Public Health Service] has taken the first step toward facilitating transfers in the case of SES members whose jobs have been abolished. Individuals are counseled by the ERB [Executive Resource Board] member from their organization. The ERB is ideal for this. Its members know where the jobs are, and the qualifications for those jobs. This might be a start to get at the mobility issue.

There was also mixed reaction to executive rotation mechanisms. Approximately half the respondents expressed a positive attitude.

A mindset has never developed which looks on rotational assignments as a positive. The perception is either that people are moved around like pawns, or that you are too highly valued to be moved.

The idea of executive rotation is a good one. I even find it attractive for myself. It would be an asset to rotate to see how other activities are carried out. It would be good to bring these skills back to my present position.

The remainder expressed a negative attitude toward executive rotation.

There is a productivity issue. I'm not sure how you backfill in behind people. This might create instability.

The problem with the idea is that senior executives generally are busy and hold important jobs. It's not easy to take them out of these positions to assign them somewhere else.

We reached two conclusions regarding the objective of better distribution and utilization of personnel:

1. The issue of mobility is complex. SES members seek *purposeful* mobility, while at the same time fear indiscriminate use of the reassignment authority. If the reassignment authority is consistently abused, Congress may eliminate the authority and make it difficult for anyone to be reassigned whether justified or not. The current lack of mobility demonstrates that the concept of rank-in-person still has not taken hold as envisioned by some SES members. Mobility is not yet viewed as either an executive development tool or a management tool that departmental leadership can use to either revitalize or improve a specific program. It may take time for the rank-in-person concept to gain acceptance in civilian agencies. Until then, mobility is likely to continue to be used in an ad hoc fashion.

2. The relationship between career and noncareer employees remains a fundamental problem for the government. We have no simple remedy for improving the relationship. It is crucial, however, that the two groups work together with mutual respect. We have suggested several activities that might be undertaken if a federal department desires such improvement.

   It should be noted that, since July 1979, when SES was inaugurated, the Department's SES members have worked under four Secretaries, each with his or her own staff and political appointees. While the working relationship between career and noncareer improved over time in each case, the frequent turnover makes it desirable that the two groups learn to work together as quickly as possible.

Improving executive management. As shown in table 6.4, this objective has many components. One of the most important is the use of performance appraisal as a tool for improving executive management. In many respects, performance appraisal is the foundation on which civil service reform rests. If components of CSRA are to succeed, performance appraisal must also succeed. It was hypothesized that the implementation of a performance-based appraisal system would serve:

- To reward (financially and nonfinancially) and to punish (pay reductions or dismissal) individuals for their performance
- To eliminate automatic pay raises, since pay would be linked to performance rather than longevity
- To clarify and link organizational and individual objectives
- As a tool by which departmental objectives could be communicated to agency and program staff
- To increase accountability for both individual and organizational performance

We received conflicting evidence regarding the relative success of performance appraisal. Accordingly, additional resources will be devoted in Year 2 to a better understanding of the dynamics of performance appraisal. After the first year of implementation, the SES managers interviewed were largely favorable to performance appraisal.

It provides a tool to review managers' performance and to spend additional time discussing issues that are arising.

The process allowed us to plan in a more comprehensive way; the need to specify goals and objectives was very helpful.

I have used performance appraisal plans to show supervisors how subordinates who thought they were good really weren't. For example, "X" makes good on one achievement but ignores the rest of the objectives on his or her plan.

However, performance appraisal was less successful in bringing SES members together with their own supervisors to discuss their SES performance plan:

My own plan went to a supervisor who didn't pay much attention to it.

I have not been able to talk with my supervisor about my plan because there has been a rapid succession of people heading the office.

The 1982 survey found much discontent with the performance appraisal system. The 1983 survey will probe whether distinctions are being made between the performance appraisal process for SES members and the process for merit pay members. The major problem with both systems is the perceived burden of the process. The eleven case studies also documented the perception of the appraisal process as a heavy burden.

The paperwork burden is the biggest problem.

[My agency] has created an unduly elaborate system of forms and reports. The structure is in the way.

Developing plans [and rating them] for people doing poorly has been very difficult because you have to painstakingly show why their work is bad.

After three years of experience with performance appraisal, the department's senior managers have mixed opinions about the likelihood of the system's improving or deteriorating into another "paper" process. A majority of our respondents felt that plans were improving, but that a sustained effort was needed to keep the process useful.

Yes, [plans have improved] very much. . . . We need to stick to it for a couple of years.

The plans have improved. People have learned to be more specific and have come up with things that can be quantified and rated.

Yes, the second round was better. The plans are becoming more general to avoid sounding trivial, yet more specific regarding management functions.

There were, however, many individuals who expressed disappointment with the performance appraisal process, and who stated that the plans were not improving or not serving the purposes for which they were intended:

I tell folks who report to me that I won't take the plans seriously. I'll give them all "excellents."

The system worked for two years but now the bloom is off.

The first-year plans were exacting, they had tough objectives. But the people who promised a lot, lost a lot. The second year's plans were more realistic. The third year's plans are more glamorous-sounding but lack substance and are more subjective.

There were several other positive findings regarding the goal of improving executive management. Many survey respondents reported that individual performance plans reflected the objectives of their programs, but additional research is required to verify this survey finding. Current research is seeking to understand whether the Department's performance appraisal systems have served to increase individual accountability and risk taking.

Executive development activities were also viewed positively. While only one-third of our respondents reported participating in executive development activities, those who did so were satisfied with their experience. SES members appear to enjoy meeting with one another in a seminar setting. Such activities can serve both to build *esprit de corps* among SES members and to develop executive skills. They are useful and relatively inexpensive.

To accomplish the goal of improving executive management capability within the government, the Civil Service Reform Act specified that OPM would be responsible for certifying the executive and managerial qualifications of all career appointees prior to their entrance into the SES. Thus far, few individuals across the government have failed to be certified. For the most part, career employees have lengthy experience in management prior to their entry into the SES. Thus, this provision has contributed little to improving executive management.

Another disappointment in the executive management area is that the CSRA is not yet viewed as having a positive effect in retaining senior federal managers. Table 6.4 presents data on this issue.

With the exception of salary, which was viewed as having a negative effective on retention, the predominant response was one of no change. Subsequent surveys may show improvement, but for the time being, SES does not appear to have significantly improved the executive management environment of the federal government.

Regarding executive management, we have come to the following conclusions:

Table 6.4 Factors Influencing Retention of SES Members

QUESTION 45: *In your opinion, have any of the following factors made it easier or more difficult to retain competent SES members?*

| | Percentage Responding* | | | |
	Easier	No Change	More Difficult	Don't Know
Bonuses	29	37	19	13
Rank Awards	20	47	12	18
Rank-in-Person	19	49	7	22
Salary	15	22	54	7
Sabbaticals	14	49	3	31
Executive Development Programs	7	63	5	22
Mobility Within HHS	5	58	10	24

SOURCE: *1982 Survey of SES Members in HHS: Chart Book,* Department of Health and Human Services, 1982.

* Figures do not add to 100 percent because some respondents did not answer this question.

- Performance appraisal should be viewed as the linchpin of the CSRA. Great effort will be needed to make the new system work. If it is to work, managers must view it as a management tool rather than as a bureaucratic nuisance. If it degenerates into simply another bureaucratic process, many other components of CSRA will also fail. To have its anticipated impact, it must be given more time. Further, more effort should be devoted to better understanding how to translate an individual's job into appropriate objectives and performance standards.
- Executive development should be viewed as a tool for both further developing management skills and increasing the sense of *esprit de corps* among SES members. While executive development is not viewed as a significant factor in retention, it is viewed as beneficial for those seeking further development and additional intellectual stimulation.
- The process of certifying career SES members for their managerial and professional qualifications appears to have had no effect.
- Civil service reform has not yet significantly altered the executive managment environment needed to retain SES members. While this goal is not yet achieved, it remains an important objective to be tracked over time.

To broaden recruitment pool. This objective has several aspects. It was hoped that SES would: (1) attract talented, dedicated people both from within and outside government; (2) attract minorities and women; and (3) remain attractive to a high quality group of SES candidates. Hiring freezes have both reduced the opportunity to bring outside talent into the federal government and restricted SES members already in the government from applying for new jobs. Correspondingly, there has been little turnover among SES members. The lack of turnover has reduced the number of opportunities to bring in new members, including minorities and women.

Table 6.5 presents survey data on whether the SES made it easier or more difficult to recruit individuals from inside the government. As with the question regarding retention, the predominant response is one of no change.

Because the achievement of this objective clearly rests on many factors beyond the control of the Department, we did not recommend any intervention that HHS itself might undertake. The recruitment issue is clearly a government-wide issue and not agency specific. The December 1982 lifting of the most recent pay cap may make future recruitment easier, provided that there are jobs open. In sum, we have concluded the following:

Table 6.5. Factors Influencing Recruitment of Executive Staff

QUESTION 46: *In your opinion, have any of the following factors made it easier or more difficult to recruit executive level management staff from inside government?*

| | Percentage Responding* | | | |
	Easier	No Change	More Difficult	Don't Know
Bonuses	28	36	11	22
Rank Awards	18	46	6	27
Salary	18	28	38	14
Rank-in-Person	14	45	7	25
Sabbaticals	14	45	2	35
Executive Development Programs	11	54	5	27
Mobility Within HHS	6	52	2	29

SOURCE: *1982 Survey of SES Members in HHS: Chart Book*, Department of Health and Human Services, 1982.

* Figures do not add to 100% because some respondents did not answer this question.

- There is little likelihood that the objective of recruiting new career staff from outside the government will be achieved in the near future, unless a variety of factors in the governmental environment are changed.

- Once the recruitment obstacles are removed, it remains to be seen whether SES will make it significantly easier to recruit from within the federal government. Survey data demonstrate that SES is not yet viewed as a significant factor in making recruitment easier.

- The candidate development program has been successful in HHS. Following intensive screening of more than 200 high-quality candidates, the Secretary selected 42 staff members from within HHS for the program, in July 1980. Of the first class, 10 have received SES appointments. More than 250 applications were received for the second candidate development class, indicating no shortage of Grade 14 and 15 employees interested in entering the SES.

To prohibit personnel abuse. To many SES members, personnel abuse continues to be an area of concern, although our HHS survey respondents observed few problems. This objective is crucial because the system must be viewed as fair, if it is to be taken seriously. Our case studies have also located no evidence to suggest that personnel abuse is occurring within HHS. This concern will continue to be monitored by our study. To date, we have concluded:

- There is no evidence that personnel abuse is taking place in HHS. While CSRA is viewed as being more open to such abuse, our survey respondents report very little evidence of it.

Intermediate Objectives

Table 6.6 presents survey findings regarding the three intermediate objectives (events 17, 18, and 19) cited in the HHS SES logic model. These objectives have been termed "intermediate" because they are hypothesized as dependent on the immediate objectives and a determinate of the ultimate objectives. SES might succeed in achieving the immediate objectives (events 13–16), but if the intermediate objectives are not met, improved program performance will not result. Each objective is discussed below.

To minimize unintentional program and organizational disruption. One aim of the SES was to provide stable program management from one administration to the next. As seen in table 6.6, our survey respondents stated that executive reassignments had not been disruptive in their agencies. Our case study findings also report little unintended disruption.

Table 6.6. Intermediate Objectives

Objective	Is Objective Now Being Achieved?	Survey Evidence on Which Judgment Was Made
To Minimize Unintentional Program and Organizational Disruption (event 17)	Yes	Only 11% of respondents view executive reassignment as disruptive to their agency's work.
To Motivate/Satisfy Personnel and to Create Dedicated SES Members (event 18)	Partially	HHS-SES members continue to express much satisfaction with their individual jobs; SES appears to have had little impact on increasing either job satisfaction or job dedication.
		68% of the respondents state that they would join the SES again.
To Avoid Perception of Inequitable SES System (event 19)	Yes	62% of respondents were satisfied with their last performance rating. 57% felt that the PRBs carried out their overall functions in a fair manner in FY 1981, while only 16% disagreed.

SOURCE: *1982 Survey of SES Members in HHS: Chart Book,* Department of Health and Human Services, 1982.

Program disruption has taken place, however, during the study period, but it was unrelated to the SES or civil service reform. Significant budget and personnel reductions in HHS have caused disruptions in some programs. In the minds of some, these disruptions have become confused with civil service reform, which occurred during the same time period. During the interviews, we were told:

> We have had too much turnover and turmoil over the past two years in this agency.

> The basic source of the morale problem is program instability, and not knowing which proposed reductions will be carried out. It creates a sense of unease for everybody.

> The morale problem in PHS is tied to the programs which expanded rapidly during the 1960s and held their own during the 1970s. SES members in PHS are program oriented. When their programs suffer, their morale suffers.

To motivate/satisfy personnel and create dedicated SES members. In evaluating this objective, it is proving difficult to sort out the problems associated with civil service reform from those problems associated with the general environment across government.

During our Phase I interviews, we were told frequently that morale was important. It was hoped that the creation of an elite cadre of senior managers would improve morale by creating a new sense of *esprit de corps* among government managers. This theme came up time and again in our interviews with SES members:

> [One objective] is hard to measure, it is an attitudinal thing . . . developing an *esprit de corps* among top executives.

> A federal executive is something beyond the GS grade structure . . . it is an elite service. [With the SES] now the term executive or manager may mean something.

We earlier reported that SES members express a high level of job dedication. Has SES changed that level of dedication? Many of our interviewees revealed that SES was not adding to their job dedication.

> I've probably been too negative in my responses, but the whole SES and Merit Pay systems affect me and most of my compatriots that way. The FDA [Food and Drug Administration] had always been, at least in the field, a *highly* motivated, hard-working team. The advent of competition for whatever money might be available has been destructive rather than constructive. The system has caused a falling away

of the carefully built structure of trust. It's too bad! I would hope it can be changed, someday.

. . . I believe most managers work hard and try to do what the boss wants; money [unless it is a large sum] will not cause a highly motivated manager to achieve [more]. I believe that my peers work as hard as they ever did, and so do I. The bonus system has become nothing more than another tool for public citizens to use against well-deserving employees. Perhaps we lost more politically than will ever be gained. . . .

The survey data also suggested that SES has added little to either the satisfaction or dedication level of SES members.

Table 6.7 presents survey findings concerning satisfaction with specific changes brought about by SES. Many of the mixed feelings and much of the dissatisfaction stem from alterations made in the SES program since its inception. Some components have been only partially implemented and others have never been implemented at all. The first major change occurred in July 1980, when Congress reduced the percentage eligible for bonuses from 50 percent to 25 percent. The Office of Personnel Management then lowered that figure to 20 percent. In September 1981, the 20 percent figure became law in the FY 1982 Continuing Resolution. Although the 50 percent figure was not universally applauded by SES members during our 1979 interviews, the reduction seriously affected their morale, especialy among those who were skeptical at the outset:

The breach of faith in reducing the bonus from 50 percent to 20 percent was really offensive.

The bonus process should be allowed to work as initially intended—50 percent rather than 20 percent.

During the first two and one-half years of SES, the salary of senior executives was capped at $50,112. The original pay system of six distinct levels enacted as part of CSRA was not implemented. That pay schedule ranged from $52,247 to $61,600. In October 1981, the pay cap was raised to $58,500, allowing for partial implementation of the pay system. Most SES members, however, remained at the cap. The pay ceiling was again raised in December 1982, but it was the period between July 1979 and October 1981 that created the most resentment. During that period, we were told:

The pay situation is a disaster. People should be getting decent salaries.

Eliminate the pay cap!

Table 6.7. Satisfaction with SES Changes

QUESTION 77: *How satisfied or dissatisfied are you with the changes SES has brought about in the following areas?*

	Satisfied	Percentage Responding* Mixed Feelings	Dissatisfied
Retention of annual leave	78	6	1
Opportunity for higher base salary	34	20	41
Opportunity for major bonuses or rank awards	28	25	45
Opportunity for sabbaticals	28	35	27
Opportunity for job mobility within your agency	21	48	21
Opportunity for mobility between agencies	17	48	25
Opportunity for presidential appointments	14	51	17

Source: *1982 Survey of SES Members in HHS: Chart Book,* Department of Health and Human Services, 1982.
* Figures do not add to 100% because some questions were not answered.

I will be leaving at the end of the year due to the pay cap.

The pay system was a major incentive for executives to join the SES. The original law envisioned SES members as being rewarded in two ways. First, an individual's pay rate could be adjusted along the six rates of pay. Based on such criteria as level of responsibility in an organization, stage of professional/managerial development, most recent performance appraisal results, and other indicators of performance, pay adjustments could be recommended to the Secretary. Second, bonus awards could be given to recognize outstanding performance in a given year. Since only the second reward system was available during the first three and one-half years of SES, it received much attention. Since salaries remained capped, bonuses became the only mechanism for increased financial reward, and the distinction between bonuses and the SES pay system became increasingly blurred. It is difficult to tell whether they will ever again be viewed separately. However, implementation of the SES pay rates now finally provides another mechanism to reward SES members, and the two systems can now work as originally intended.

Similarly, guidelines on sabbaticals were significantly delayed. The number of sabbatical-months alloted to each agency was not announced by OPM until the fall of 1981. The guidelines were more stringent than departments had hoped, and fewer members would be able to take sabbaticals than had been originally anticipated. Some departments have decided to allow no sabbaticals, given tight budgets. Thus, another component of the SES program now may be viewed as inconsequential.

Finally, as discussed earlier, hiring freezes and staff reductions have greatly slowed, if not halted, recruitment into the SES. While some new members have entered the SES, an infusion of larger numbers of new members who might further invigorate the system is needed. Based on preliminary evidence, newer SES members tend to be more satisfied with the system because it represents an improvement over their Grade 15 situation. Not having been part of the former supergrade system, they cannot compare SES to it. In addition, newer SES members are not as irritated over issues of "broken faith" as are the SES "charter" members, because newer members knew the extent of the SES program when they joined. Normal turnover among members and the infusion of new executives may have the effect, over time, of increasing support for the SES system.

Because of these problems, SES is now viewed by many members as having created new problems or exacerbated old ones, without many counterbalancing benefits. In addition to the above SES-specific problems, there continues to be a general malaise among federal employees. The following statements are illustrative:

> The reason for low morale is, since Eisenhower, everyone dumps on the federal employee. It's related to the politicians running for office against the bureaucrats.

> I find *intolerable* the lack of status, recognition, respect, the money [pay cap and bonus situation], and the constant abuse from Congress. I have a feeling that Congress enjoys hauling us up to the Hill for hearings so they can beat up on us.

> Government workers would be much better workers if Congress recognized their problems, their competence, and stopped using the bureaucrats as a whipping boy when a complex law isn't immediately implemented, or things don't turn out as Congress wants, or they don't see instant results.

Most of the departmental leaders we interviewed did not feel that HHS alone could remedy a government-wide morale problem, but many believed that the Department could do more to create a sense of community among HHS senior managers:

> The Department could be doing more to create a sense of identity among SES members. For example, they could put on seminars. If one is a physician, one attends the AMA convention every year; if one is in the SES, there is nothing comparable. A good set of structured presentations would be worthwhile. It would allow getting acquainted with counterparts in other agencies.

> I think the concept of an executive cadre here (in HHS) is viable. Anything we can do to help people think of themselves as part of the agency is a positive thing to do.

> If you want to build a community, you have to meet with people as a group. Even socially oriented meetings might help.

To avoid perception of an inequitable SES system. This objective has been viewed as crucial to the success of the CSRA. This objective directly affects the success of the previous objective of motivating/ satisfying personnel (event 18). If the SES is viewed as an inequitable system, it is likely that event 18 also will not be accomplished. A widespread perception of inequity would serve to deepen the existing sources of dissatisfaction already discussed. Failure here would also seriously damage the credibility of the entire SES system.

Although many factors could lead to a perception of inequity in the SES system, the bonus award process is viewed as the most crucial and potentially most troublesome aspect of SES. We probed this area in both our personal interviews and survey instrument.

Based on our evidence, we find the equity objective is being achieved in the Department of Health and Human Services. We cannot generalize beyond HHS, but it might be useful to view HHS as a good example of an SES system that is viewed as equitable. While more analysis is needed for a better understanding of all the factors influencing this event, several factors clearly stand out. First, HHS has put in place an elaborate and time-consuming Performance Review Board (PRB) process. Since 1980, more than 200 SES members have served on these boards. In the PRB context, the issue of "time-consuming" cannot be viewed as a criticism. To have avoided a perception of inequity, such effort was required. Service on a PRB was hard work, but the work appears to have paid off in ensuring fairness in the bonus process. The PRB review of SES performance plans at the beginning and end of the performance cycle contributed to the credibility of the bonus recommendations to the Secretary. We were told:

> The PRB was quite successful in getting changes made [in the SES plans]. Supervisors had to change the plan or be penalized. They learned after the first round.

> The biggest change was between years one and two, after decisions had been made based on the plans. Those who had not made suggested changes found themselves on the bottom of the list.

> It hurts people who don't put enough time and emphasis into the development of their plans. You won't find those individual's name on the bonus list.

Another factor contributing to the success of the PRB process in HHS is the large number of career employees who serve on the boards. Based on observations across the government, it is our impression that career employees devote more time than noncareer employees to civil service reform activities. The large number of career employees involved in the process appears to assist greatly in avoiding perceptions of inequity and abuse. It can also be speculated that by involving a large number of SES members in the Department, the process has served to educate numerous individuals into the operations of the PRB process. With this understanding of the process, fears of abuse might also have been lessened. However, the process must continue to be watched closely to ensure prompt action if perceptions of inequity arise.

Because of the crucial importance of equity in the award process, the Department has gone to great lengths to ensure as fair a process as possible. The effort appears to have been successful.

> The bonus system was very fair and took into account the difficulty of the job—the highest scorers did not necessarily receive bonuses.

> I was on the PRB and was recommended for a bonus—yet I never knew what was going on in my case because the PRB members kept it clean and confidential. I didn't want to know.

> It was an honest process through the PRB's. . . .

Our survey data also supports the above statements. While most respondents stated that the PRB was both effective and fair, approximately one-fourth of the respondents stated that they didn't know. Given that the SES had been in place for three years by the time the survey was fielded, the number of "don't knows" was quite high. We will follow the proportion in the Year 2 and Year 3 surveys. In many ways, they represent the swing votes who will decide whether the process if fair or not.

To summarize, we have concluded:

- In HHS, the SES performance appraisal system is currently viewed as fair and equitable. Although many members have reserved judgment, few have concluded that the process is unfair. It is crucial that the perception of equity continue if the SES is to remain credible.
- There are no shortcuts to making the bonus system work. It requires much time, hard work, and a commitment by the Department and PRB members to make the system work fairly. The current perception of the bonus system as a fair one is important to maintain in the future.

Overall, the survey data suggested that the three intermediate objectives in the SES logic model had been achieved to some extent. Programs, and the Department as a whole, have not suffered from unintentional disruption. The performance appraisal process, including the bonus component, is perceived as operating fairly and equitably. The senior executives are a highly dedicated group, although it is not clear whether their commitment has increased because of CSRA. We now turn to a consideration of the three ultimate objectives of the Act, which the immediate and intermediate objectives, in theory, make possible.

CAN CSRA AFFECT THE PERFORMANCE OF FEDERAL PROGRAMS?

Introduction

We now turn to a discussion of the final set of objectives of the Civil Service Reform Act. The first year of the case studies was designed to collect baseline information on the managerial and personnel practices in eleven programs prior to the creation of SES, in 1979. Thus, these studies have not yielded information as to whether the three objectives are achieved. This section, therefore, is largely conceptual, based on our observations of government both before and after the start of civil service reform. In Years 2 and 3 of the case studies, we will obtain information on the following questions:

- Have individual performance-tracking methods changed since the start of CSRA?
- Have program performance-tracking methods changed since the start of SES?

- Are changes in individual or program performance-tracking methods related to the Civil Service Reform Act?
- Are changes in the Department's new SES reward structure linked to changes in individual or program performance?

During Phase I of the project, we learned that CSRA, at least rhetorically, was conceived as an instrument to improve the services and programs operated by the government. Whether the Act was viewed seriously in that regard is not possible to determine, but we do know that those individuals involved with its initial design and implementation stated that clearly improved performance of programs constituted the "bottom line" for the Act. If demonstrable improvements did not occur, then they would hold the Act to be unsuccessful.

The questions we must now begin to address are:

- Is there agreement on what improvement means?
- If government services improved, would anyone know?
- Does the Act, with all other government systems in place, provide the necessary and sufficient set of conditions to yield, finally, satisfactory government performance?

While the case studies have not yet provided enough evidence to answer these questions, other information from our broader set of evaluation experiences can shed much light on the subject.

Is There Agreement on What Improvement Means?

Having examined the Act and the legislative history behind the CSRA, we are left with alternative propositions as to what was supposed to change as a result of the Act. The Act itself contains an implied criticism of the performance of government staff. A positive view might be that it was designed to provide positive incentives to improve the performance of individuals. During Phase I interviews, we were told:

- By the Office of Management and Budget, that improvement would be reflected in the number of bureaucrats fired (not through reduction in force, but fired);
- By OPM, that improvement would be reflected in the actual improvement in performance of government programs and services, although they had no means to judge such changes.

Some have argued that the expectation of improved program performance resulting from the Act was naive. The Act, they believe, was little more than a change (however substantial) in the way government manages its personnel function. Adopting this point of view lowers one's expectations for the program rather dramatically and limits interest in the Act to technical considerations of a personnel system.

With agreement from the HHS CSRA program manager—the Assistant Secretary for Personnel Administration—we adopted a program improvement model for CSRA. Over time, however, our expectations for improving program performance have grown increasingly modest as we have increased our understanding of the many other factors that affect the ability of the federal managers to improve their program's performance. Further, we have become increasingly aware of the rather limited ability of most observers to discern differences in program performance, even if they did occur.

It is now clear to us that the many views of the Act, and its intended or probable effects, are likely to produce a confused debate concerning the meaning of the knowledge generated by this or other study efforts. In this section, we try to clarify some of the issues involved in the attempt to improve program performance within the federal government.

If Government Services Improved, Would Anyone Know?

Assuming one can discover whether improvement is taking place implies the existence of a regular source of information about performance. From our experience, such sources are uncommon. Further, the CSRA provided for no additional resources. Based on information derived from the CSRA study and knowledge about the HHS program evaluation system, we know that no major change has taken place within HHS to facilitate the accumulation of more information about the performance of its programs.

There are a variety of factors that explain why more information is not generated. In brief, the conditions which demand that measurable program objectives be established are not yet in place. It is not that measurable program objectives are *never* established, only that they need not be established. Programs and entire federal agencies can be administered as sets of activities with limited, activity-oriented objectives (or with global and unachievable goals). In practice, we observe that Congress rarely sets measurable, achievable objectives for the programs it legislates into existence. Some believe that the key to legislative compromise and approval is ambiguity, settling on a program activity while avoiding any clear statement of what result is expected from its enactment and implementation.[6]

Thus, a major unanticipated problem that could prevent CSRA from actually improving performance is the difficulty we envision in attempting to determine whether any program improvement might be observed. A key to determining improvement is knowing what the current level of performance is. We believe that the general absence of formal agreements on program performance objectives and standards will inhibit, if not outright prevent, most observers from discovering whether or not government services have changed. This is not to say that no one will know whether any service has improved. Clearly, any government service in which the public experiences direct contact with government workers or services (Social Security, Internal Revenue, local welfare offices) will have its performance monitored fairly directly. Unfortunately, even in those cases, the performance measures (typically, client satisfaction) are crude and cover only a small part of the performance of the program in question. That they exist at all, however, is an advance over most programs.

Is CSRA the Missing Link in Government Performance Management?

A second major problem lies in the design of the CSRA. As with most federal programs, the Act represents a monumental leap of faith when examined in any depth. It is not that all programs are designed badly, but that there is such a disparity between the size of the problem and the program design and resources created to solve the problem. Many evaluation studies have failed badly, not because they were technically deficient, in a narrow sense, but because they essentially studied the wrong program, that is, they took too seriously the rhetoric used to carry the legislation through the debate process. Further compounding the difficulty, most legislation that defines programs appears to assume that the program under consideration is the only attack on the problem.

It is very useful to place the CSRA in the above context. If one defines its goal as improving the performance of federal programs, one must then define the current performance problems associated with governmental performance. Figure 1 sets forth a model of all the potential factors or problems that might cause government services to be inefficient and ineffective. If the table accurately describes the problems addressed by the Act—inefficient and ineffective performance—we must then ask exactly what the Act proposed to do about each one.

Government workers perform inadequately. One explanation, frequently favored by the public and Congress, is that federal employees simply perform at a level inadequate to the tasks that they are assigned. Workers might be badly trained, or simply not educated to do the work they are expected to carry out. Current incentives in government may provide inadequate motivation to produce good work, or federal workers may not be adequately managed by their career and non-

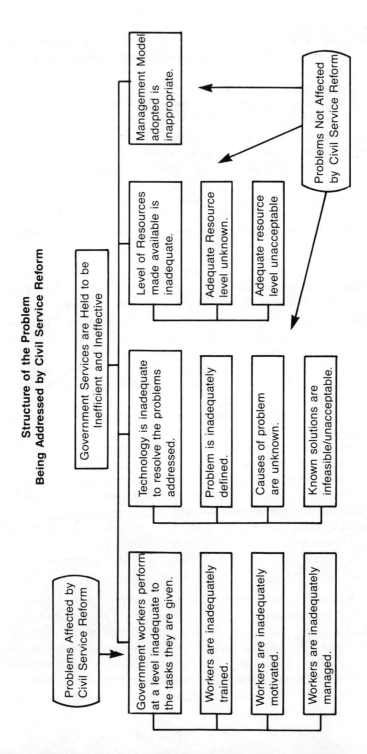

Figure 1

career supervisors. In this area, the Act sets forth a variety of components aimed at reshaping the federal workforce. At least for SES members, it includes provisions for further training (executive development), a new incentive system (bonuses), and a new approach to appraise the performance of individuals and the ways in which supervisors and employees interact (performance appraisal). The Act fails to provide much in the way of training and financial incentives (Merit Pay not withstanding) for workers below the SES, but at least one can clearly connect provisions of the Act with improved worker productivity and effectiveness.

Technology of federal programs is inadequate. Another explanation, not quite as popular, is that program performance is inadequate because the federal government is given so many jobs that no one knows how to do. This explanation has immediate face validity. One has only to consider the Office of Economic Opportunity (OEO), established to wage a war on poverty, or the Law Enforcement Assistance Administration, established to wage war on crime in the streets. While it was perfectly possible to "wage war" on all sorts of problems, it is quite another thing to demonstrate substantial impact on the problem being attacked. A frequently cited contrast to the above "wars" is President Kennedy's commitment to place a man on the moon within one decade. However technically challenging that task, one thing was quite clear—the President was serious and the technology for accomplishing the goal was within reach. In the areas of poverty and crime, the program technology was not so well advanced, and it is precisely in those areas that government has been so highly criticized for bad performance.

Resource levels. Another explanation for poor performance is inadequate resource levels. If an agency is told legislatively to resolve the medical human resources distribution problem and then given 10 percent of the estimated resources needed to accomplish that task (even assuming that we know enough), then achievement becomes difficult and "poor performance" becomes common.

Inappropriate management model. A final explanation for poor performance is that a specific program might be operating under an inappropriate management model. When Congress enacts legislation, its provisions often dictate how a program is to be administered— by revenue sharing, by block or formula grants, by direct (categorical) grants, or sometimes by direct provision of the service, as is the case for the FBI, the military, St. Elizabeth's hospital. Although these various management models are often viewed simply as different ways to parcel out the money, each method has certain constraining characteristics. The models fit some types of programs and objectives better than others. For example, if one decides to develop a technology to put a man on the moon within a decade, block grants would be an inappropriate model. If one wishes to redistribute tax revenues and constrain their use to certain areas, then block/formula grants are quite appropriate. Prescribing an inappropriate management model can adversely affect the ability of a federal manager to accomplish a particular objective, even if all other necessary conditions are present.

If we are correct that these other areas, technology, resource level, and management model are also necessary to improve federal program performance, then we must conclude that the CSRA, by itself, is an inadequate vehicle to bring about a more effective and efficient government. We have concluded that other conditions are also necessary to bring about improved program performance.

What Would an Improved Civil Service Reform Program Look Like?

After having examined the larger environment surrounding federal programs, it appears clear to us that CSRA introduced only limited changes, however profound, to the systems whereby federal staff are hired, plan and manage their work, and have their work appraised. It creates, ostensibly, an elite cadre of executives and managers, borrowing from both public and private sector models. But the big problems facing government managers, trying to deliver on the promises of civil service reform, really have very little to do with the Act itself. They are the problems that have always faced government, problems that were largely ignored in creating the Act. They have become important in the context of evaluating civil service reform, because of the need now to reconcile promise with performance and to come to some judgment on the plausibility of the "improved program performance" goal.

An improved civil service reform program would require additional elements from the set of conditions that appear to be necessary for success in government. The following elements represent a reasonable beginning:

- Top-level management emphasis on performance
- Alignment of incentive systems
- Effective design of federal programs

In the following discussion, the reader should keep in mind that, in some respects, each of these elements is already present within the framework of government and within HHS. We know from experience that they do occur, but only idiosyncratically. If government performance is to improve, they must be present and occur systematically.

Top-level management emphasis on performance. Former Secretary of the Treasury Michael Blumenthal, in a *Fortune* interview, remarked,

> . . . as in any organization, you have to decide where to put your energies. You learn very quickly that you do not go down in history as a good or bad Secretary in terms of how well you ran the place, whether you're a good administrator or not. You're perceived to be a good Secretary in terms of whether the policies for which you are responsible are adjudged successful or not: what happens to the economy, to the budget, to inflation, and to the dollar, how well you run debt financing, and international economic relations, and what the bankers and the financial community think of you. Those are the things that determine whether you are a successful Secretary.[7]

If one couples that belief with the fact that many noncareer top executives in government experience a brief tenure, generally less than two years, it is perhaps remarkable that top management in government pays any attention to the performance of existing programs. Most administrations take office with the goal of implementing a specific set of changes in national policy. With limited time and energy, devising and implementing the new policy generally represents the first priority. In private industry, the performance of ongoing operations is critical, even during periods of change, because it is the ongoing operations that generate money. In government, it is new policies that generate the political coin of the realm.

What is needed in government, then, is some systematic way for the Secretary and his or her top management staff to stress routinely the importance of performance. Note, we are not suggesting that this never happens, only that it does not happen systematically (in the same way, over a sustained period of time, covering an entire set of programs). Given the demands on the available time of top executives, it is not clear how to bring about such a change. One of the difficulties that would be encountered is that, unlike the private sector, government programs and services do not easily "add"; thus, it is not easy to conserve time by discussing aggregate concepts (such as profit/loss, market penetration, prices). Such concepts exist in government, of course, but their link to programs is rarely known empirically.

Alignment of incentive systems. A related problem is the confusion created by incompatible incentive systems. The CSRA created a straightforward incentive system for senior executives: the bonus. Although the relationship between performance and reward is clear, top career managers in government experience other signals, which also guide their actions. These include the budget, through which comes the money to operate their programs, staffing allocations when their staff slots are increased or decreased, space allocations in which their location, office space, and associated paraphernalia are allocated. Other, even less formal, methods exist for communicating what is important.

If managers receive signals from the Department, OMB, or Congress that their budgets will be increased or decreased regardless of performance, they may well become solely concerned about maximizing their budgets, even if that will not improve the performance of their programs. Managers observe carefully what kind of evidence is required to secure more staff, a larger budget, and bigger offices. Mainly, most government managers believe in their programs, want more money and more staff to operate them, and will pay more attention to actions that promise more of these things than to their potential bonuses.

A minimum requirement in aligning incentives with performance would be to insist that no performance bonus be awarded without demonstrable evidence of program improvement, or at least acceptable program performance (the equivalent of awarding bonuses in the private sector only when profits, or sales, warrant). At present, although bonuses are based on some performance dimension, that dimension is not necessarily program performance. It is by no means clear that other signals, budget, staffing, et al., can be aligned with performance. Legislators authorize programs and appropriate money for many purposes. What we need is some means for allowing and encouraging managers to operate programs according to conventional performance bases, without interfering with other political objectives.

Effective design of federal programs. It is perhaps pretentious to talk of designing federal social and economic programs as we might speak of designing an airplane, or a moon rocket. Yet, the absence of design inhibits performance management in subtle, but important, ways. The concept of "evaluability assessment" was devised to provide a means for overcoming the absence of design.[8]

One of the conclusions reached in devising evaluability assessment was that the members of Congress could not be expected to design programs beyond the broad conceptual level. They have neither the time nor the expertise to do so. Instead, it is the executive branch that must carry forward from where Congress leaves off to define the concept and convert it into a workable program. The design process might well lead to a conclusion that the concept contained in the legislation cannot be made to work, that is, produce the effect intended by Congress and the President. Most pieces of legislation contain concepts that are plausibly related to the problems they are designed to solve, although many miss the mark. As noted earlier, sometimes the problem is size, but sometimes we simply do not know enough. That is the purpose of research. But because success in Congress is often equated with passage of a bill, rather than elimination of a problem, we frequently encounter programs that do not, because they cannot, dent the problem they ostensibly address.

Design is essential at two levels within the Department. First, there is the level that combines several programs, the level at which one talks about such problems as health and human resources distribution. Within the Department, this level could constitute either a bureau or agency level program. Second, there is the level of the actual legislation authorizing the activity, which we commonly call a "program"—National Health Service Corps, Low Income Energy Assistance, Head Start. Each of these programs must be designed. Many people have argued that such an activity is unnecessary, because it is patently obvious what each program is supposed to do. We submit that it is not patently obvious, and that there are many different ideas concerning what would constitute success. There is at present no function within HHS clearly devoted to the actual design of new programs. Further, there is no process whereby program designs can be assessed and approved by higher authorities (by agency or operating division, for example). Without such design processes, it is impossible to determine unambiguously whether or not program performance is changing over time, or whether our managers have anything to do with any changes that are observed taking place. The basic concept of performance appraisal in relation to the performance of government services and programs will remain moot.

The idea laid out generally above is intended to link specifically to the design concept articulated quite early in our evaluability assessment of the Civil Service Reform Act within HHS. In that design, we posed three final events, really the basic end objectives of the Act:

1. That the performance of individual executives should improve
2. That the performance of organizations (bureaus, agencies) should improve
3. That the performance of services and programs should improve

This section of the paper has addressed the latter two events, with emphasis on the performance of programs and services. We imply, above, the need for some design work to provide a program for each organization, with the thought that bureaus, agencies, et al. should have defined areas of responsibility, much as we now assign responsibility to programs and program managers. We do not actually assign responsibility to program managers either, of course, but we expect a closer relationship between program success and individual manager performance at the program level than we expect at the bureau or agency level (because there are no programs at those levels). If we choose not to invent programs at these management levels, we still can insist on design and management accountability at the program manager level, but it should be borne in mind that many, perhaps most of the programs within the Department are actually managed by people below the level of SES. Without bureau/agency level designs and accountability, many SES members would be accountable only for the management work accomplished by lower-level staff. Conceptually, such a situation is problematic.

To summarize the arguments advanced in this section, we believe that:

- Civil service reform will not by itself lead to improved performance of government services and programs.
- The Department can take action to improve the probability of success by adding elements now either missing entirely or present in inadequate amounts.
- The Department's top leadership must develop and implement a systematic method to make it clear that performance of the Department's programs is critically important.
- The Department must attempt to ensure that incentive systems employed to motivate executives are aligned with the objective of program performance improvement.
- The Department should institute a new process to design and assess systematically the performance of its legislative programs.[9]
- The Department should institute a new requirement to design bureau and agency programs (areas of assigned responsibility that imply the responsibility to *resolve problems* important to the country) for which managers at these levels will be held accountable.

We recognize that many of these actions will be difficult to achieve, but we firmly believe that they are necessary if civil service reform is to deliver on its promise of more effective government.

CONCLUSION

What is the future of civil service reform? Based on our research to date and our government-wide observations, we are cautiously optimistic. We think that civil service reform can be made to work. Based on the first two years of implementation of civil service reform in HHS, to date, some components are indeed working in one federal department. Other components have yet to be fully implemented. We will continue to track many of the issues discussed here during the second and third years of the study.

We have been struck by the magnitude of the task necessary to make civil service reform work effectively. We have found no short-cuts to making CSRA an effective management tool in government, but we now have a better understanding of what it takes to make civil service reform work.

An agency head must be committed to taking civil service reform seriously and providing resources to support that commitment. Civil service reform is not a self-implementing piece of legislation. Each component of civil service reform needs to be tailored to a specific department or agency and then put in place. HHS provides an excellent case study of the hard work and effort necessary to make civil service reform work. In the case of the Senior Executive Service, there is, within the Office of the Assistant Secretary for Personnel Administration, an entire office devoted to SES and other executive personnel matters. In addition to that office, each Operating Division within HHS has a personnel office that devotes significant resources to staffing both the Executive Resource and Performance Review Boards. Again, we found no shortcuts to hard work.

We have been impressed by the continued need for the government to operate on a "good faith" principle. Civil service reform is based on the premise that managers will not abuse CSRA provisions. Negative effects often result when governmental systems are designed to prevent an abuse from taking place, rather than to accomplish a specific, desired objective. There is a danger that civil service reform may become laden with such bureaucratic checks. An overabundance of these checks will lead senior executives to believe that they are inherently distrusted and that adherence to process is more important than production of positive results. This phenomenon is what causes governmental systems to continue, seemingly by design, to produce limited results at high cost. If CSRA is to succeed, trust is required on the part of individual SES members and Departmental leadership. Without such trust, the system is likely to falter.

We have again been struck by the confounding variables that continue to influence the environment. The most recent example is the FY 1984 budget, which proposed a pay freeze for all federal employees. If adopted, this proposal will have a major impact on the Merit Pay system. Merit Pay plans will continue to be required, with the prospect of no payout for employees. Regardless of the soundness of the Merit Pay concept, the lack of payout may greatly hinder the seriousness with which plan development and plan review occur. Again, the difficulty of implementing a major innovation in a governmental setting is apparent.

Finally, we have gained a greater understanding of all the factors that influence governmental management. We now feel that CSRA tools need to be complemented by other management changes, or reforms. Although CSRA *alone* cannot improve the management of government, it is capable of providing a foundation on which further changes can be made. The demand for improved government performance will continue. Whether the demand will be satisfied is an open question.

NOTES

1. For a discussion of the differences between federal agencies in implementing CSRA, see Mark Abramson, "Civil Service Reform and Cutback Management" (Paper presented to American Association of Budget and Program Analysts, Washington, D.C., November 1982).
2. For a full discussion of the Phase I evaluability assessment, see Mark Abramson, et al., "Developing an Evaluation Design for the Senior Executive Service," *Review of Public Personnel Administration* 2, no. 3 (Summer 1982).
3. Specifically, the Merit Systems Protection Board's September 1981 "Report on the Senior Executive Service," and the Office of Personnel Management's first and second Federal Employee Attitudes Surveys, found high levels of job satisfaction.
4. We realize, however, that senior managers' dedication to their program and the delivery of public services can be viewed as a problem. This section of the paper is based on the premise that individuals, in both the private and public sectors, should be dedicated and committed to their jobs. It has been our experience that civil servants are willing to change program direction, whenever departmental leadership provides clear guidelines on new directions.
5. For a discussion of the rank-in-person concept, see Mark Abramson, "The Senior Executive Service as a 'Career Service'." (Paper presented to the National Capital Area Political Science Association Spring Conference, Washington, D.C., February 1982).
6. Charles L. Shultze, *The Politics and Economics of Public Spending* (Washington, D.C.: The Brookings Institution, 1968).
7. "Candid Reflections of a Businessman in Washington," *Fortune*, January 29, 1979.
8. For a detailed discussion of evaluability assessment, see Richard Schmidt, John Scanlon, and James Bell, *Evaluability Assessment: Making Public Programs Work Better*, Project Share Monograph Series No. 14, DHEW Publication No. OS–76–130, November 1979.

9. The idea espoused here is embodied in "Program Management in Government," a concept paper written by Richard Schmidt, in which he outlines the four responsibilities of a program manager: (1) ensuring that his program operates in compliance with the law; (2) ensuring that his program satisfies the intent of the law; (3) exercising such effective guidance and control that his program is implemented properly; and (4) exercising such effective guidance and control that his program demonstrates improved performance over time.

CHAPTER SEVEN

Delegations of Examining: Objectives and Implementation

CAROLYN BAN AND TONI MARZOTTO

Civil service reform was a broad-sweeping change of the personnel management system in the federal government. While most scholarly attention has focused on a few provisions of the Civil Service Reform Act (CSRA), most notably the Senior Executive Service (SES), Merit Pay, and Performance Appraisal, several other parts of the Act may have far-reaching effects on how the federal government manages its personnel resources. This paper explores one such provision: the delegation of examining. We look at the method the federal government used to examine and hire before CSRA, the debate about centralization versus decentralization in examining, the provisions of the Act that resulted from this debate, and their implementation. We end with a discussion of changes in policy in this area under the Reagan Administration.

BACKGROUND: HIRING BEFORE CSRA

Hiring is, of course, the first step in managing personnel. And, as any line manager can tell you, the ability to hire staff of good quality in a timely fashion is critical to getting the job done. Given the merit standards that underlie the modern civil service, which require open competition for jobs, the first step in hiring is examining. Examining generally consists of two steps: (1) determining which applicants

Reprinted, with permission from *Review of Public Personnel Administration*. The authors wish to thank Don Holum, Ed Komorous, Joe Howe and Alan Campbell, who graciously agreed to be interviewed for this paper. An especially warm thanks to Mary Ellen Finn, who gave most graciously of her time and expertise, both for sharing her ideas on delegations, and for reviewing the paper.

meet the basic qualifications for the job (which are published ahead of time), and (2) ranking the qualified candidates. The ranking process can be done ahead of time, as is the case when there is a standing register, or it can be deferred until a specific job is being filled, as is the case for mid-level positions. It is at this stage that points for veterans preference are added to the applicant's score. Also at this stage, "compensable preference eligible veterans," that is, those who have a 10 percent or greater service-connected disability, are automatically placed at the head of the list of eligibles, so long as they meet the minimum qualifications.

Through its history, the role of the Civil Service Commission (CSC), and of individual agencies, in this process, has gone through relatively rapid change, with the locus for examining moving from the agencies to the CSC and back again. At first, examining was done by agency personnel, sitting on Commission-supervised boards. When Theodore Roosevelt was Commissioner, the function was centralized in the CSC, in large part as a response to extensive political abuse of the system. Roosevelt is credited with greatly strengthening the merit system.[1] During the late 1930s and during World War II, the rapid growth of government would have overwhelmed the CSC, had it not delegated much of the examining function back to the agencies.[2] By the late 1950s, confusion reigned:

> . . . a crazy-quilt pattern emerged: a hodge-podge of boards with overlapping jurisdictions or gerrymandered boundaries defying explanation to the job-seeking public, Congress, and the employing agencies. Few people were happy about the arrangement.[3]

Decentralization during this period was so complete that, in one example, an individual applying for a secretarial job who was interested in being considered by all the federal agencies in an installation had to submit twelve separate applications, even though all the agencies to which she was applying were located in the same building.[4]

The reforms in the 1960s recentralized examining within the CSC. Examining took place at CSC's headquarters, and at its regional and area offices. This was the situation prior to civil service reform.

THE DEBATE OVER CENTRALIZATION VERSUS DECENTRALIZATION

Why these cycles of constant change? It would appear that each approach, centralized or decentralized, had advantages and disadvantages. The choice of approach was sometimes made to fit the needs of the federal government at the time, as during World War

II. But it may be that people are more sensitized to the faults of the system with which they are working at a given time, and this may make the obverse look more attractive.

The President's Personnel Management Project (PMP) task force on staffing[5] was familiar with the CSC experience under both centralized and decentralized examining. The greatest disadvantage with the centralized system that they cited was the untimely delivery of service, because of red tape and the rigidity of the system.[6]

In developing the recommendations that led to the Civil Service Reform Act, the PMP task force on staffing examined the hiring process in depth and used flow charts of actual personnel actions. The action they chose to show the problems was one in which almost everything went wrong. In that case, the action took 374 days from the time the recruitment effort began until a selection was made.[7] We should point out that, although this example was used to buttress the case for delegations, much of the delay took place in the agency, not in CSC.

In addition, the task force felt that the examination and rating of candidates was often being done by staff who were far removed from the hiring official. This meant that the rating officials, particularly in highly technical areas, were not trained in the field and did not have detailed knowledge of the jobs for which they were examining. Nor were they always familiar with the specialized needs of the hiring official. The result often was applicants who were not ideal for the job.[8] One measure of this was the fact that fully 44 percent of certificates were returned to CSC without a candidate having been selected.[9] Given the resources necessary to produce each certificate, this was a powerful indictment of the system.

But, needless to say, centralized examining does have some advantages, or the CSC would not periodically have returned to it. One of the strongest arguments in favor of centralization is cost. Particularly for jobs common to several agencies, it is simply more cost-efficient to have a single agency examine than to have each agency develop and administer exams and maintain registers, since economies of scale result. The other strong argument in favor of centralization is that it provides better safeguards of the merit system, since it is further isolated than agency personnel offices from political pressure.[10]

Further, centralized examining ensures that standardized criteria can be applied to selection for similar positions throughout the government. This principle of standardized treatment philosophically underlies much of the current federal personnel management system. Centralized examining also makes life easier for the job applicant, who can file one application rather than having to contact several different agencies individually.

A decentralized approach to examining also has fairly predictable advantages and disadvantages. Its primary advantage is expected to be speed; it should make it possible to hire people more quickly. Further, particularly for jobs requiring special skills, more direct involvement of agency personnel who really understand the work of the hiring unit should improve the fit between applicant skills and the needs of the position. Finally, if agencies can advertise when they have an opening, and make clear to the applicant where the job is located, rather than having to hire off an existing register for which people may have applied months before, they are more likely to come up with applicants who are interested in that specific job and who are still available.

The disadvantages of decentralization are the obverse of the advantages of centralization. It can be more costly, if agencies are examining separately for common jobs; it has greater potential for political abuse and for differential treatment of similar occupations; and it can make life harder for the job applicant.

The Personnel Management Project staffing task force, while they were aware of the strengths and weaknesses of each approach, clearly felt that the pendulum had swung too far toward centralization, and that the result was an overly rigid and slow system. The approach of the PMP in this area was entirely consistent with their overall approach, which stressed the need to give managers the tools they need to manage. In fact, in addition to delegated examining, they proposed other far-reaching reforms that would have given managers even more discretion in hiring.[11]

The bill as it was submitted by the Administration to Congress included a sweeping provision for delegated examining, which would permit the Office of Personal Management (OPM) to delegate examining for any occupation, with no limits. This broad approach was opposed in Congress. One crucial actor was Bernard Rosen, who, as Executive Director of the CSC had been responsible for the previous move to centralization, in the 1960s. In 1977, while he was serving as an adviser to the Senate Committee on Government Affairs, he warned about the dangers of overly sweeping delegations. As a result, the Congress placed a limitation on OPM's right to delegate examining authority to agencies:

> The Director may not delegate authority for competitive
> examinations with respect to positions that have requirements
> which are common to agencies in the Federal Government,
> other than in exceptional cases in which the interests of

economy and efficiency require such delegation and in which such delegation will not weaken the application of the merit system principles.[12]

The Act also called for OPM to establish standards that would apply both to its own activities and to those of other agencies to which it delegates authorities, and for OPM to establish and maintain an oversight program to ensure that activities under delegated authorities are in accordance with the merit system and with the goals of securing accuracy, uniformity, and justice in the staffing functions.

IMPLEMENTATION: 1978 TO 1980

OPM's implementation strategy was summarized in a task force report, "A Model Competitive Staffing System." [13] The model staffing system the task force described set forth three components:

Component A: agency-based staffing. This approach was considered appropriate for most jobs that were unique to one agency. For entry-level occupations or those for which the agency had a frequent need, such as air traffic controllers, Internal Revenue Service special agents, or Federal Deposit Insurance Corporation bank examiners, the agency could maintain a register. For higher-level jobs, the agency could examine on a case basis. OPM's criterion for jobs appropriate for delegation to agencies was whether the agency was the sole or predominant user in the relevant geographical area.[14]

Component B: OPM-based staffing. This component consisted of OPM "retention of staffing responsibility for certain designated occupational areas." This component was seen as appropriate for entry-level occupations and other occupations that are quite common and have well-defined, established, and readily applied rating and ranking procedures. This was considered to be the "work load best processed on a central basis, with obvious return-to-scale efficiencies and economies," and the workload that allowed for effective use of automation in examining and maintaining registers. These occupations would include typing, key punch operating, and other clerical work.

Component C: OPM-agency shared staffing. The task force also envisioned special situations that might require a hybrid system, with parts of the function divided between OPM and the agency. These would include systems in which OPM processes applications and issues notices of rating, and then the eligible candidates apply directly to the agency, which can either maintain a register or hire directly. The task force felt that no single category lent itself to these approaches, except summer jobs and PACE (Professional and Administrative Career Examination) positions. One example of such a combined approach, which is currently in use, is Department of Defense auditors, for whom examining is conducted by OPM, with registers maintained by each service. This system of separate registers was designed to reduce the declination rate.

It is very clear that, in the two years after passage of CSRA, OPM worked aggressively to delegate to agencies as much examining as possible. A great deal depended upon how one defined "common jobs." OPM defined the congressional restriction on delegating for common jobs as tightly as possible. Essentially, OPM maintained that each job at the GS–9 to GS–15 levels was considered different from other jobs in the same series and level. This meant that every agency was the sole or predominant user of that occupation. This strategy was most apparent in delegations of mid-level occupations.

It is also clear that, for Jule Sugarman, then the Deputy Director of OPM, delegated examining was closely tied to the goal of increasing the hiring of women and minorities. In addition to delegating examining, OPM revised the regulations concerning the public announcement of job openings. Formerly, the requirements for announcing a vacancy were quite specific, with minimum open periods and publicity areas defined for each occupation and grade level.[15] Initially, OPM changed these regulations for vacancies covered by delegated examining, permitting agencies more discretion in establishing recruitment requirements. Essentially, the only requirement for an agency hiring under delegated examining was to notify OPM and the Department of Labor (DOL), which would list the vacancy in the Job Information Centers. What was done to recruit beyond that was up to the agency. Agencies were encouraged to target recruiting specifically to those groups it was trying to attract, which might include women and minorities. OPM also permitted agencies to have a relatively brief open period during which applications were accepted, thus limiting a huge flood of applications for only a few openings. However, by mid-1981, after learning that some agencies had rather lax recruitment procedures, OPM revised all the outstanding delegation agreements, setting mandatory minimum recruitment requirements that were the same as those used by OPM.[16]

OPM's leadership worked aggressively to encourage agencies to accept delegations. While delegations were always on a voluntary basis, and agencies could always decline to accept a delegation, OPM made a concerted effort to convince agencies of the benefits to them of accepting delegations, through memos to agency Assistant Secretaries of Administration, phone calls and personal visists from top OPM officials, presentations to the Interagency Advisory Group, articles in OPM publications, and the like. While some agencies eagerly accepted delegations, others held back. Some agencies were concerned about the resource implications of accepting delegations. When examining had previously been centralized, agencies had given up resources to CSC. Now that OPM wanted to return this responsibility to them, it was unwilling to provide resources to go with the function. Alan Campbell, in discussing this problem with us, said that OPM's leaders were determined to resist this pressure for returning resources to the agencies; in the dynamics of the budgeting process, he explained, it was easier for other agencies to get more resources than for OPM to regain them, since it would be quite a small percentage of an agency's total budget, but a large percentage of OPM's.[17] While OPM was not willing to give agencies resources, it did provide technical assistance and training to help agencies assume this function.[18]

In addition to their concerns about resources, some personnel directors were anxious about the pressures they would encounter to violate the merit system. Their feeling was that, under a centralized system, if a political appointee came to them with a request to bend the rules, they could pass the blame to CSC, saying there was no way they could buck the system. But when they had more direct control over examining, that political pressure would fall directly on them and might be hard to resist. Nonetheless, OPM was effective in convincing many agencies to accept delegations. By the end of fiscal year 1981, 26 percent of new hires into the competitive service had come through agency examining.[19] Some research has shown that the agencies studied are generally satisfied with delegated examining and feel that it has improved quality and timeliness and that the resources required have not been onerous.[20]

In addition, OPM's Staffing Services Group was given the responsibility for the new oversight role that CSRA imposed on OPM in this area, and it regularly audits agencies' use of delegated examining. While no wide-scale abuses or scandals have surfaced, there has been a small amount of misuse. This has involved abuses of the merit system, including preselection, overly limited open periods for receipt of applications (in some cases as short as one day), and selection of individuals who did not meet the OPM-established minimum qualifications for the job. In a small number of cases, OPM has withdrawn the authority for delegated examining because of the seriousness of the abuse.[21]

DELEGATED EXAMINING IN THE REAGAN ADMINISTRATION

As we have shown, the policy of OPM under Campbell and Sugarman was to delegate examining as broadly as possible. They saw this as consonant with their general thrust of giving managers the tools to manage, and also tied to the goal of increased hiring of women and minorities. It is clear that they were willing to accept a certain amount of abuse, since, as Campbell told us, he believed that OPM should be a support agency rather than a police agency.[22]

The concerns of the Reagan Administration have been somewhat different. First, the new Director of OPM, Donald Devine, is particularly interested in ensuring that OPM's policies are in line with actual congressional intent. As one OPM senior official described the process by which he (Devine) reviewed OPM programs, "Devine starts with the law and reads it very carefully."[23] In reviewing OPM's policy of delegating examining very broadly, Devine raised questions of whether it was really appropriate for OPM to delegate mid- and senior-level jobs that were common to all agencies, such as policy analyst or budget examiner. Further, he felt that there was reason to believe that, in light of the legislative history, the PACE occupations were precisely those that Congress did not want delegated.

Devine has also been particularly concerned about possible abuses of the merit system under delegated examining. He is clearly less willing to view a modicum of abuse as an acceptable cost for giving agencies more direct control over hiring. There is certainly some legitimate basis for concern, since OPM is aware of instances of political pressure on personnel officers which has put them in a difficult situation. One response on OPM's part has been an increased emphasis on OPM's oversight function.

Finally, given the drastic cuts in the federal budget, cutting costs has been an overriding concern throughout this Administration. The issue of costs is clearly important to Devine. In the area of delegations, as in other staffing programs,[24] the new Administration has taken a hard look at the cost implications.

As a result of these concerns, in March 1982, OPM issued a significant revision of its guidance to agencies concerning delegated examining.[25] It cited a number of negative aspects that had resulted from OPM's "liberal policy of examining delegation," including delegation of examining for occupations that appear to be common to other agencies, duplication of examining efforts by agencies for similar occupations, increased burden on applicants who have to file multiple applications, and "some instances of apparent inadequate public notice of competitive examinations."

As a result, OPM announced that, in the future, it would no longer delegate examining authority for entry-level positions previously or currently covered by PACE, or for positions under the mid-level and senior-level examinations that are common to agencies. Further, in order to justify a delegation, an agency would have to be the predominant employer of the occupation in the relevant labor market area. This was defined as employing approximatey 80 percent or more of the employees in the occupation in the relevant labor market.[26]

OPM recognized that pulling back existing delegations should be gradual, to avoid disruption and to permit OPM to plan to absorb the increased work load. The FPM Letter (Federal Personnel Manual) announcing this change in policy was followed by a letter to Directors of Personnel, announcing that by July 1, 1982, OPM regions and the Washington area office would review all delegations under their jurisdiction for conformance with the revised guidelines. This review would lead to the development of a timetable for phasing out inappropriate delegations.[27]

There was some debate over both how drastic the effects of OPM's new policy would be and whether the change was warranted. First into the fray was the General Accounting Office (GAO), which issued a report less than four months after OPM's new policy was issued, calling into question whether the change was needed.[28] GAO's position can be stated succinctly: "If it ain't broke, don't fix it." The report stated that most agencies were quite satisfied with the results of delegated examining, and that they perceived positive effects from delegation both on timeliness and on the quality of candidates hired. GAO saw no significant evidence of abuses of delegations that would warrant a pullback. And GAO's General Counsel failed to support OPM's contention that the previous administration's more liberal interpretation of the law was incorrect. GAO also expressed skepticism about OPM's ability to handle the increased workload that would result from withdrawing a significant number of delegations; they were concerned that both timeliness and the quality of candidates might suffer. GAO concluded by recommending that OPM not go ahead with the planned withdrawal of delegations "without first determining that an abuse exists or that OPM could provide timely examining in a more cost-effective manner." [29]

In spite of GAO's advice, OPM has proceeded with the planned withdrawal of some delegations. At the time that OPM's revised guidance was released, 836 delegated examining authorities had been approved, and about 26 percent of hires in FY 1981 had been through delegated examining.[30] By June 1, 1983, OPM had completed negotiating pullbacks with all but one of the agencies involved. The pullbacks of delegations considered inappropriate will be phased over a three-year period, with one-third to be pulled back each fiscal year. Those pulled back in the first year are delegations that cover relativey small numbers of "new hires," so that OPM can adjust gradually to resource demands of withdrawing delegations.

OPM's original estimates were that up to 50 percent of delegated examining authorities might be withdrawn. In fact, as negotiated, the impact is somewhat less severe. The delegations being withdrawn cover primarily the mid-career and senior level. Many agencies have delegations covering not only these levels, but also several other occupations unique to their agencies. So most agencies have been able to keep some delegated examining authority, although the number of occupations covered has been narrowed. In fact, as of April 1983, the net drop in the number of delegations was only forty one.

How have agencies responded to OPM's abrupt change in policy, so soon after the delegations had been given? On the one hand, most agencies, after some initial reluctance, had accepted delegations willingly and were very satisfied with the results. In fact, at the time that OPM was conducting its review of the policy, several requests for new delegations were pending. On the other hand, the Carter and Reagan hiring freezes, and the present restrictions on hiring because of budget cuts, have made it difficult to get an accurate picture of how delegated examining works. Many agencies have made only limited use of the authority and expect to do little or no hiring this fiscal year. Further, as Don Holum pointed out to us, although most agencies had resolved the resource question in accepting delegations and now saw this as a less important issue than formerly, the FY 1982 budget cuts not only meant fewer hires, but may also have reactivated agency concerns about the resources associated with accepting delegations.[31]

Another point of view is presented in a recent article on the withdrawal of delegated examining by the Director and Deputy Director of the Civilian Personnel Command of the Department of the Navy.[32] They made a strong defense of delegated examining:

> The view that only the central personnel agency can examine for federal jobs is a narrow one; it doesn't recognize the complexities and diversities of the federal work force.
> Centralizing examining authority, even with a decentralized mode of operations, does not permit the flexibilities agencies need to adapt to varying needs in different employment and labor market settings.[33]

They further maintain that, although direct costs for centralized examining may be lower, a more sophisticated cost-benefit analysis would have to include the costs of keeping jobs vacant as a result of the delays of a centalized system.

In spite of these objections, agencies have accepted the withdrawal of some delegated examinations without major conflict. Certainly, this is largely because so few agencies are currently doing more than minimal hiring. The critical issue for the future will be the way OPM copes with this new responsibility. In order to handle the increased work load, OPM will need to rely heavily on increased automation of examinations involving written tests, but the GAO report claims that OPM's computerized system will not be in place nationwide for another two and one-half years.

In sum, the test of recentralizing examining will come when OPM has to cope with the full work load, in three years, and particularly, if the federal government once again enters a period of growth. If agencies again experience long delays, we can expect increased pressure for yet another cycle of decentralization.

Notes

1. Paul P. Van Riper, *History of the United States Civil Service* (Evanston, Ill.: Row, Peterson, 1958), pp. 176–207.
2. Ibid., p. 386.
3. Donald R. Harvey, *The Civil Service Commission* (New York: Praeger, 1970), p. 60.
4. Interview with Don Holum, Chief, Examination Planning Branch, Staffing Services Group, Office of Personnel Management, October 16, 1981.
5. U.S. President's Reorganization Project, *Personnel Management Project,* Option Paper No. 2 (September 6, 1977), p. 4 (hereafter cited as *Personnel Management Project*). Task Force 3, which was charged with examining the staffing process, was chaired by Charles E. Weithoner of the Federal Aviation Administration..
6. Ibid.
7. *Personnel Management Project,* vol. 3 (Washington, D.C.: Government Printing Office, 1977), Appendix XII, Chart 2.
8. *Personnel Management Project,* Option Paper No. 2. We should note that the procedures in existence prior to CSRA provided the option of agency participation in the rating panel. Actual agency involvement varied greatly under this system.
9. The above cited problems contributed to this return rate. Another important factor discussed by the PMP was veterans preference, which required compensable preference eligible veterans to be placed at the head of the list on the certification. One reason for returning a "cert" without making a selection is that a veteran is blocking all the desirable candidates. The Civil Service Reform bill sent to Congress proposed severely limiting veterans preference, but Congress would not accept this provision. See *Personnel Management Project,* vol. 1, p. 28.
10. Of course, even the CSC has not been immune to scandals arising from responsiveness to inappropriate political pressure. During the Watergate era, CSC was involved in a scandal in which the agency was charged with cooperating with requests for preferential treatment

in response to requests from political appointees. Interview with Joe Howe, Chief, Policy Coordination Division, Office of Personnel Management, October 5, 1981.

11. In addition to attempting to limit veterans preference (see note 9, above) OPM attempted to modify the "rule of three," thus enabling selecting officials to go further down the best eligible list to make an appointment.

12. See *Public Law 95–454*, October 13, 1978, Title II Par. 1104.

13. U.S. Office of Personnel Management, Staffing Services Group, *A Model Competitive Staffing System*. Task Force Report June 28, 1978. The Task Force was headed by John Fossum, then the Deputy Director of the Staffing Services Group, at OPM. Hence, the report is frequently referred to as the "Fossum plan."

14. The important thing here is that the appropriate geographical area differs, depending on the GS level of the position, all the way from the local commuting area for lowest-level jobs to the entire nation for the highest level. These guidelines were originally issued in FPM Letter 331–6, issued December 29, 1978. They were subsequently incorporated into FPM chap. 331, subchap. 4.

15. The PACE examination is no longer in use. See ch. 9 for a discussion of the Luevano consent decree and the demise of PACE.

16. *Personnel Manaement Project*, vol. 2, Task Force 3 Report, p. 3.

17. Interview with Don Holum.

18. Interview with Alan K. Campbell, former Director of the Office of Personnel Management, September 6, 1981.

19. The internal reorganization, as the CSC became OPM, was a tangible expression of Campbell's and Sugarman's priorities. They created the Agency Relations group, the function of which was to assist agencies, providing them with information and technical assistance, and simultaneously to serve as a conduit of information from the agencies to OPM. They also created the Workforce Effectiveness and Development group, the primary focus of which was on productivity and performance appraisal. They clearly downplayed OPM's compliance function, while increasing funds for broad research on personnel management.

20. Statistics provided by Examination Planning Branch, Staffing Services Group, Office of Personnel Management.

21. Institute for Social Research, University of Michigan, *Organizational Assessments of the Effects of Civil Service Reform*, 2nd Year Progress Report (1981), OPM Contract 22–80. The reader should note that this is an in-depth study of the effects of six major provisions of CSRA, which covers only five sites.

22. Interview with Don Holum.

23. Interview with Alan K. Campbell.

24. Interview with Don Holum.

25. Changes have already been made in OPM's policies concerning granting agencies the right to offer employees early retirement, based upon an analysis of the costs of the program.

26. *FPM Letter* 331–7, Office of Personnel Management, March 10, 1982.
27. The relevant labor market area differs by grade. See Guidelines for the Delegation of Competitive Examining Authority to Agencies, Attachment to *FPM Letter* 331–7, p. 2.
28. Interview with Don Holum.
29. U.S. General Accounting Office, "Better Guidance Is Needed for Determining When Examining Authority Should Be Delegated to Federal Agencies (GAO/FPCD–82–41), July 1, 1982.
30. Ibid.
31. Projected estimates for FY 1982 were 33 percent.
32. Interview with Don Holum.
33. Jan K. Bohren and Leland A. Goeke, Jr. "Undoing the Potential," *The Bureaucrat* (Winter, 1982–83): pp. 20–21.
34. Ibid., p. 21.

CHAPTER EIGHT

Labor-Management Relations Under CSRA: Provisions and Effects

DONALD F. PARKER, SUSAN J. SCHURMAN
AND B. RUTH MONTGOMERY

The Civil Service Reform Act (CSRA) has received a great deal of attention because it was intended to bring about major change in the human resource apparatus of the federal government. Among the Act's most notable features is its proactive tenor. Based upon the assumption that many federal workers are not competent and dependable (Lowman and Parker 1982) most of the Act's initiatives are designed to give management strong measures for coping with the supposed problems and to insure that the measures are used.

One section of the Act is different. Both the motivation for the inclusion of Title VII, Federal Service Labor-Management Relations, and its provisions are philosophically and operationally different from the remainder of the Act. Instead of mandating change in labor-management relations, the Act simply gives statutory recognition to collective bargaining in the federal government and specifies the minimum rights and obligations of both parties. Perhaps most important is the fact that Title VII provides a framework for change, but places the onus of deciding whether and how extensively to take advantage of the opportunities on the employees and their unions. Thus, the provisions of Title VII are generally viewed by students of federal labor relations as an opportunity to expand the scope of federal labor union influence that may or may not be exploited.

The potential for expanded union activity raises questions about Title VII's possible effects on the functioning of the federal agencies, on the unions, on the union members, and on the overall conduct of labor-management relations in the federal government.

The purpose of this chapter is to examine the law and the labor-management relations experience of five federal installations, using evidence accumulated in a longitudinal study of the effects of CSRA.

The first section addresses the law itself, including an overview of the development of federal labor relations, the legislative history and intent of Title VII, and a discussion of the law's specific provisions. The second section presents findings from the empirical investigation of the effects of Title VII on actual federal organizations. In the final section we consider likely future changes, in light of the organizational experience with the law to date.

BACKGROUND AND CONTENT

Development of Federal Labor-Management Relations

Title VII is based upon the rationale that collective bargaining safeguards the public interest, contributes to the effective conduct of public business, and facilitates amicable settlement of labor-management disputes. Its purpose as described in the Act is as follows:

> To prescribe certain rights and obligations of the employees of the federal government and to establish procedures which are designed to meet the special requirements and needs of the government. The provisions of this chapter should be interpreted in a manner consistent with the requirement of an effective and efficient government (Appendix, p. 279).

This statutory support for collective bargaining represents a rather dramatic shift from earlier attitudes toward organized labor in the federal government and reflects the growing strength of public employee unions. For many years, the 10th Amendment to the Constitution was interpreted as the source of sovereign governmental power, precluding public employee organization and bargaining (Rehmus 1974; Gershenfeld 1977). However, beginning in 1961, with Kennedy's Executive Order (EO) 10988, and followed by Nixon's EO 11491, federal labor-management relations have become increasingly more formal and centralized (Rehmus 1974), and federal unions have grown dramatically.

Title VII, in addition to providing a statutory basis for the existence and recognition of federal unions, contains provisions which potentially broaden their scope of bargaining. It also contains a number of provisions that clearly attempt to prevent the broadening of scope from going too far.

Legislative History and Intent

Title VII, like other sections of the Act, had its origin in the Personnel Management Project (PMP) set up early in President Carter's term of office.[1] The Labor Relations Task Force was one of ten established under the project. Proposals developed by the task force were used by the Administration's staff to draft what eventually became Title VII.

Title VII was submitted after the original bill as an amendment and was passed in near-original form by the Senate. In the House, however, two substitute bills were submitted that considerably broadened the scope of bargaining, including the right to strike, to negotiate wages, and to negotiate an agency shop.[2] Their substitute language was incorporated into the Administration's bill in committee, but as the bill moved to the floor, compromises were reached that brought it closer to the Administration's version. The right to strike and to negotiate over wages, and the agency shop, were all excluded from the final bill, and a number of management rights were restored. According to Marzotto, Gossett, and Ban (1981), this combination of bills resulted in crucial ambiguities that were of considerable concern to the Administration, centering around the provisions covering the scope of bargaining. It was feared that these ambiguities would widen areas of negotiability beyond what was intended. Marzotto, Gossett, and Ban cite remarks by Jule M. Sugarman, Deputy Director, OPM, as indicative of the extent of the ambiguities: "Title VII was referred to by the Senate staff as the 'Dark Continent' because nobody understood what was in it."

The legislative intent behind Title VII has remained ambiguous. It depends very much on whom you ask. Clearly Title VII was intended to provide a statutory basis for collective bargaining in the federal sector and to establish an impartially administered labor relations system. What is less clear is the extent to which Title VII was intended to strengthen the position of federal labor unions. That there are substantial differences of opinion among the various parties is evidenced by the statement of Alan Campbell, former director of both the Civil Service Commission (CSC) and the Office of Personnel Management (OPM):

> OPM, and agency management in general, have expressed concern at what we see as the use of peripheral legislative history and ambiguous statements to support interpretations of Title VII, which misread the essential legislative intent to codify Executive Order 11491, as amended.[3]

Provisions of Title VII

Title VII gives federal employees the right to form, join, or assist any labor organization, or to refrain from such activity. Among those it excludes from the definition of employee are supervisors, management officials, members of the uniformed services, Foreign Service employees, and, importantly, any person who participates in a strike against the government. Title VII applies to all executive agencies except the General Accounting Office, the Federal Bureau of Investigation, the Central Intelligence Agency, the National Security Agency, the Tennessee Valley Authority, the Federal Labor Relations Authority, and the Federal Service Impasses Panel.

Title VII's provisions can be grouped into three categories: those establishing new administrative structures and the powers and duties of these bodies; those that delineate the rights and duties of agencies and labor organizations; and those concerning negotiated grievance procedures.

Structural changes. Three provisions of Title VII affect structural aspects of federal labor-management relations; they involve the Federal Labor Relations Authority (FLRA), the General Counsel, and the Federal Service Impasses Panel (FSIP).

1. *The FLRA.* The major structural change mandated by the Act is the creation of the Federal Labor Relations Authority as an independent agency modeled after the National Labor Relations Board (NLRB), which administers the private sector's industrial relations system (Frazier 1979). The FLRA replaced the Federal Labor Relations Council (FLRC), a body that served only part-time and was composed of senior federal managers. The three members of the bipartisan FLRA are appointed by the President for five-year terms and can be removed only for cause; they serve full time and must have no other connection with the government.

The FLRA appoints regional directors and administrative law judges to carry out certain of its functions. Its other duties and powers include the following:

a. Determining appropriate bargaining units
b. Supervising representation elections
c. Determining unfair labor practice complaints, with the power to require an agency or union to discontinue violations of the Act and to take appropriate remedial action
d. Resolving negotiability disputes arising from interpretation of provisions in the Act regarding the scope of bargaining
e. Determining appeals regarding exceptions to arbitral awards
f. Providing leadership in establishing policies and guidance under the Act relating to labor-management relations

2. *The General Counsel.* The act provides for a General Counsel of the FLRA, appointed by the President for a five-year term, but who may be removed at any time. The role is analogous to that of

the General Counsel of the NLRB (Frazier 1979). The General Counsel's duties include the investigation of unfair labor practice complaints, making final decisions as to which cases to prosecute before the FLRA, and the actual prosecution.

3. *The FSIP.* The Federal Service Impasses Panel existed before CSRA, but was changed by Title VII into an independent entity within the FLRA (Frazier 1979). It continues to have the function of resolving negotiation impasses between agencies and unions.

Rights and duties of agencies and labor organizations. Title VII delineates the rights of both unions and agencies.

1. *Labor organization rights.* Exclusive recognition is granted to a labor organization if it is selected by a majority of employees voting in a secret ballot election. The FLRA conducts such elections upon petition of 30 percent of the employees in an appropriate bargaining unit where there is no exclusive representative.

The FLRA also has the authority to designate appropriate bargaining units, using an agency, plant, installation, functional, or other basis. It is thus possible for a site or agency to have several bargaining units and several unions. Where there is no exclusive representative at the agency level, those unions that are the exclusive representative of a substantial number of employees of the agency (as determined by criteria prescribed by the FLRA), are to be granted national consultation rights by the agency.

An exclusive representative must represent the interests of all employees in the unit, regardless of union membership. Such a union has the right to be represented at certain specified discussions between the agency's representative and any employee in the unit. An exclusive representative also has the right to dues-withholding upon request. Furthermore, employees representing the exclusive representative in the negotiation of a collective bargaining agreement are to be authorized official time and pay for conducting such activities. Official time may be used for other labor-management activities in amounts agreed to be reasonable by the agency and the union.

Unfair labor practices are defined in Title VII for both agencies and labor organizations, but only slight changes were made to those existing under the previous executive order (Klingner 1980). Both agencies and labor organizations are given the duty to meet and negotiate in good faith. Standards of conduct are outlined for labor organizations that include freedom from corrupt influences and maintenance of democratic procedures, and the FLRA may revoke recognition of a labor organization that participates in, or fails to take action to stop, a strike.

2. *Agency rights.* The management rights clause of Title VII is very broad and contains two basic categories of management rights. The first consists of those on which bargaining is permitted but not required. These include the numbers, types, and grades of positions assigned to an organization, project, or tour of duty; and the technology, methods and means of performing work. This category of permissible bargaining areas has been narrowed somewhat from the previous executive order; the second category has been expanded.

This second category designates management rights on which bargaining is prohibited. These include the right to determine the mission, budget, organization, number of employees, or internal security practices of the agency. Also included are the right to hire, assign, promote, direct, lay off, and retain employees, as well as the right to suspend, demote, discharge or take other disciplinary action in accordance with applicable laws.

These broad management rights, combined with the exclusion of matters affecting working conditions otherwise provided for by law (such as pay), create a scope of bargaining that is very narrow in comparison to private sector standards. However, agencies are required to negotiate with regard to the impact of, and the procedures used in, carrying out management rights. The ambiguities referred to earlier arise, in part, from this provision because some say that the requirement to bargain over impact and procedures constitutes de facto recognition of the right of unions to negotiate on the rights themselves.

Negotiated Grievance Procedures

The final major provision of Title VII concerns grievance procedures. The act mandates that all collective bargaining agreements must contain procedures for the settlement of grievances, including questions of arbitrability. These procedures must include binding arbitration for grievances that aren't satisfactorily settled at lower levels.[4]

A grievance is defined broadly to include any matter relating to employment with an agency and any claimed violation of any law, rule, or regulation affecting conditions of employment. Likewise, the scope of a negotiated grievance procedure is defined broadly, and matters that the parties do not wish to include must be specifically excluded in the collective bargaining agreement.

The negotiated grievance procedure is the exclusive means of redress for bargaining unit members on matters that are covered by the procedure, with the exception that, where a statutory appeals procedure exists, the employee may choose either, but not both. Arbitration awards may be appealed to the FLRA on limited grounds, but judicial review of arbitration decisions is available only for cases involving adverse actions and Equal Employment Opportunity (EEO) complaints.

These provisions strengthened considerably the negotiated grievance procedures in the federal sector. Previously, binding arbitration was allowed but not required; matters for which statutory appeals processes existed were excluded from the negotiated procedure; and grievability and arbitrability questions were decided by the Assistant Secretary of Labor for Labor-Management Relations.

Summary

Although Title VII did not automatically bring about major changes in federal labor-management relations on either the local or agency levels, many expected that having a statutory basis would provide new encouragement to labor organizations in the federal sector. Some believed that strengthened grievance procedures would provide new bases on which to appeal to federal employees. Additionally it was felt that a strengthened and impartially administered labor-relations system would eventually affect the conduct of labor-management relations at both local and agency levels. In the next section we examine the extent to which some of these expectations have been realized.

EFFECTS OF TITLE VII ON LABOR-MANAGEMENT RELATIONS IN FIVE INSTALLATIONS

The Study

The results and conclusions reported here are based on data collected as part of a three-year longitudinal study of the effects of CSRA on a sample of five federal installations. The study, one of three funded by the Office of Personnel Management, was conducted by a research team including the authors at the Institute for Social Research of The University of Michigan.[5] Five federal organizations were selected for study, representing a diversity of missions and work technologies. These include: a medical center of the Veteran's Administration; a regional and an area office of the Department of Housing and Urban Development; an Internal Revenue Service Center; several sections of the Internal Revenue Service's national headquarters; and an engineering/technical production facility of the Air Force.

Objectives. The study's objectives were to (1) document the implementation of the provisions of CSRA within each of the focal units and their parent agencies; (2) document the effects of the Act upon individual employees in different job categories and organization levels; (3) document the effects of the Act upon unit functioning and performance; and (4) evaluate and draw conclusions about the provisions of CSRA, the agencies' implementation strategies and processes, and the short- and long-term outcomes of implementation.

It is important to point out that the research design was intended to provide an organizational assessment of the effects of the legislation. Each study site was considered an intact, unique, functioning entity with its own distinctive mission, history, traditions and practices, and behavioral norms. The research aimed to understand how CSRA affected these different organizations and to understand the conditions that served to aid or impede the realization of the law's intent.

Method. The principal methods of study included: (1) interviews with key executives; (2) examination of documents to track the steps and stages of implementation; (3) two organization-wide surveys at the five study sites, administered in July 1980 and February 1982; (4) interviews with a representative sample of individuals at each site to obtain detailed insights into their encounters with, and responses to, the CSRA provisions; and (5) tracking of selected indicators of record at each site to detect changes in personnel and pay practices, labor-management relations, work performance, and budgetary performance.

The Sample. Table 8.1 displays selected demographic characteristics of the federal employees who completed the 1980 and 1982 surveys. The overall characteristics of the two samples on these measures are similar. In both cases they contain a majority of white female employees, although there were substantially more males and nonwhites among the 1982 respondents. The percentage of respondents eligible to join unions remained essentially constant from 1980 (71 percent) to 1982 (70 percent).

Early experience. Extensive interviews were conducted during the early months of the study with employees at each of the five sites and with appropriate representatives in the headquarters of the agencies having responsibility for the five installations. The principal purposes were to learn of actions being taken and progress being made to comply with the provisions of Title VII and to assess the familiarity of the employees with the labor-management provisions of the Act.

These interviews indicated that most federal employees had scarcely heard of the CSRA. It also became apparent that little change had occurred in labor-management relations in the study sites in recent

Table 8.1. Selected Demographic Characteristics of the Sample

	1980	1982
Total number of respondents	2,822	2,770
Number of respondents by site		
I	375	414
II	793	677
III	577	565
IV	598	625
V	479	489
Sex		
% Female	55.2	52.9
% Male	44.8	47.1
Race		
% White	76.4	64.7
% Black	21.1	22.4
% Other	2.4	12.9
Number eligible to join union	2,083	1,931
Percentage eligible to join union	71	70

years as a result of either CSRA or other occurrences. The usual question asked of the interviewers by federal employees at all levels was why they had been selected for questioning when they knew nothing about the CSRA.

As the interviews continued, it became more and more apparent that the labor-management provisions of the Act were known and understood by only a small group of personnel specialists (OPM 1980). Other employees at the sites had little information and few opinions about any aspect of CSRA, although most had been provided briefings or informational materials about the provisions of the new law.

Interviews with the small cadre of labor-relations experts, however, indicated that they viewed the provisions of Title VII as constituting a significant change. To them, Title VII represented an opportunity for unions, rather than a mandate for action by the federal government. Many, nonetheless, expected the Act to bring about significant changes in the relations between covered federal employees and the agencies who employ them.

Implementation

Data collected from the early interviews indicated that both the agencies responsible for carrying out various enabling actions and the agencies included in the study had been quick to take the necessary steps to comply with the new labor-management provisions. Shortly after the CSRA became law, the Civil Service Commission provided guidance to agencies on key actions to be taken to assure compliance.

The actions required of the units under study to comply with the new provisions were minor and were completed without difficulty or delay. The actions required were principally concerned with the assignment of certain responsibilities to personnel specialists, changes in record-keeping procedures, and measures needed to amend existing contracts and to negotiate new ones in accordance with the provisions of Title VII. All of the sites had taken the necessary steps shortly after their responsibilities were made known.

Subsequent Findings

Based upon the provisions of Title VII and information from the earlier interviews, several aspects of labor-management relations were selected for exploration by means of the questionnaires. A primary topic of interest was level of commitment to the local union and any subsequent change that might occur after the parties had experience with the new provisions of the Act. Measures of two kinds were developed to examine this topic. The first was an indication of support for the union as shown by membership among eligible employees. The second source of information on this topic came from items designed to tap attitudes and beliefs about the union in each site. Yet another topic of interest that was included had to do with each worker's philosophical position with respect to unions in general. Finally, the questionnaire contained a number of items designed to assess the employees' overall perceptions about labor-management relations in their workplaces.

Union support. The most obvious indicator of constituency support for a union is the proportion of eligible employees who pay union dues. Table 8.2 displays the number and proportion of union-eligible employees in the sample who reported that they pay union dues. Slightly fewer than 30 percent of the eligible workers reported being dues-paying members, with percentages ranging from 11 percent to 44 percent. The responses from the second survey indicated that the rates of overall membership decreased slightly from 1980 to 1982. Very small decreases were reported in the percentage of dues payers during the period in all sites, except Site III, where there was a slight increase.

When examined in terms of pay grade level, however, a somewhat different picture emerged. The percentage of eligible employees who paid dues appeared to be increasing slightly at the lowest General Schedule (GS) levels and throughout the Wage Grade (WG) levels. Site III, which had the greatest proportion of WG employees, con-

Table 8.2. Number and Percentage of Union Eligible Employees* Who Report Paying
Union Dues

	Total	
	1980	1982
Number	559	532
Percentage	29.1	28.0
Number of eligible employees	1,924	1,903

	By Site											
	I		II		III		IV		V		VI	
	1980	1982	1980	1982	1980	1982	1980	1982	1980	1982	1980	1982
Number	17	15	212	186	142	157	113	104	19	18	57	52
Percentage	11.3	9.4	44.4	43.5	33.9	36.2	23.3	21.4	14.8	12.3	21.5	20.7

	By Pay Grade									
	GS 1–4 WG 1–4 WS 1–4		WG 5–8		WG 9–15		GS 5–8		GS 9–15	
	1980	1982	1980	1982	1980	1982	1980	1982	1980	1982
Number	120	125	18	32	101	87	196	178	85	80
Percentage	27.2	30.9	31.6	45.1	55.5	57.6	30.5	27.6	16.8	15.0

* The category of union eligible employees excludes temporary employees and all
supervisors, except WS 1–4.

stituted the one site where an increase in the percentage of union
eligibles paying dues was observed. The observed increase of dues
payers among WG and low-level GS employees holds, however,
even when Site III is removed from the sample. A slight decrease
in membership occurred among people in the GS–5 through GS–15
levels. Despite the change in participation within pay grades, however, table 8.2 suggests that relatively little change occurred in overall
union membership between 1980 and 1982. Interviews tended to
confirm this finding and to indicate that what changes did occur
were brought about largely by local conditions.

Another indicator of the importance of the union to employees is
the extent to which employees report making use of the union
contract. As shown in table 8.3, the number of employees, both
supervisors and nonsupervisors, who reported having read the union
contract within the past six months had increased only slightly from
1980 to 1982. The majority of nonsupervisors in both surveys reported
never having read it.

Yet another indication of support for unions is provided by employees' general attitudes toward the union at their sites. Nonsu-

Table 8.3. Percent of Employees Who Report Having Read the Union Contract

| | | | Percentage | | |
			None	Once	More than once
How many times have you read the	Nonsupervisory	1980	62.5	20.0	17.5
union contract in the last six months?		1982	59.0	20.4	20.8
	Supervisors	1980	28.1	15.9	56.0
		1982	23.3	19.7	57.0

pervisory employees' attitudes toward the union did not change from 1980 to 1982. In both years the average response represented a neutral position—neither satisfied nor dissatisfied. Attitudes toward participation in union activities in 1982 were slightly negative, again with no change from 1980. This measure is taken from a scale composed of items measuring the likelihood of participation in union activities, including serving on a union committee, attending a union meeting, referring to the union contract in case of a problem, or filing a grievance if required. Another component of the union participation scale is a question that taps a more abstract notion, namely, that employees need a union to protect their rights. Here, as might be expected, nonsupervisors expressed more agreement than supervisors, but this too was unchanged from the 1980 value, indicating only slight agreement.

Perceptions of labor-management relations. Thus far, Title VII does not seem to have affected perceptions about labor-management relations. In 1980 most employees and managers regarded the relationship in neutral terms, and they continued this attitude in 1982. Table 8.4 displays several measures of these perceptions. As in 1980, differences in attitudes among sites in 1982 were more pronounced for supervisors than for nonsupervisors, but even these were not large. Responding to two items asked only in 1982, supervisors neither agreed nor disagreed that the union has a say in more things than it did a year ago, and nonsupervisors expressed similar neutral feelings about whether the union keeps management informed about changes and conditions that might cause problems.

Site-specific changes. In only two sites were there overall changes in any of the labor-management measures. In both sites, however, these changes are best attributed to internal management changes that are essentially unrelated to CSRA. In Site V, nonsupervisor data show a small increase in union involvement. It should be noted that, even with this increase, the response is still in the neutral range, and for the most part the change reflects an increase in two of the five scale

Table 8.4 Perceptions of Union-Management Relations

		I		II		III		IV		V†		VI	
		1980	1982	1980	1982	1980	1982	1980	1982	1980	1982	1980	1982
Cooperativeness of labor-management relationships (nonsupervisors)	Mean	4.0	3.9	4.0	3.9	3.9	3.9	4.0	4.0	3.8	3.7	3.7	3.8
	SD	.81	.78	.98	1.00	1.00	.91	.95	.96	.82	.84	.88	.97
	N	140	170	620	526	424	426	449	494	123	145	254	248
Cooperativeness of labor-management relationships (supervisors)	Mean	3.6	3.6	4.7	4.7	4.4	4.5	4.7	4.6	4.0	3.7	3.3	3.7
	SD	1.10	1.09	1.07	1.06	1.01	1.06	1.22	1.26	1.27	.91	.95	1.13
	N	218	231	146	140	139	121	97	90	31	39	35	36
Management acceptance of the union (supervisors)	Mean	4.7	4.8	4.9	4.7	4.2	4.0	4.8	4.7	5.0	4.8	4.0	4.3
	SD	1.35	1.41	1.17	1.18	1.29	1.35	1.33	1.29	1.02	1.30	1.52	1.68
	N	216	228	144	137	132	120	96	89	28	39	35	36
Management involvement of the union (supervisors)	Mean	3.4	3.5	4.7	4.7	4.3	4.4	4.1	4.4	3.8	3.6	3.1	3.7
	SD	1.33	1.33	1.13	1.11	1.15	1.22	1.47	1.22	1.16	1.38	1.23	1.19
	N	217	228	150	140	139	119	97	89	31	39	35	37
Union has a say about more things now than they did a year ago.* (supervisors)	Mean		4.2		4.2		4.2		4.3		4.1		4.0
	SD		1.30		1.21		1.25		1.22		1.63		1.20
	N		231		140		121		89		40		37
Union keeps management informed about changes and conditions that might cause problems* (nonsupervisors)	Mean		4.5		4.5		4.3		4.3		4.2		4.3
	SD		.96		1.12		1.21		1.18		1.05		1.18
	N		169		530		428		501		147		250

NOTE: Scale values range from (1) strongly disagree to (4) neither agree nor disagree to (7) strongly agree.
* Not asked in 1980.
† For this table, Site V was divided into its two distinctive units, one shown as Site VI.

components: the likelihood of referring to the union contract, or, going to the union in case of a problem. This rise coincides with marked increases among GS 1–4 level employees at Site V, both in reported acceptance of the union and in an item measuring overall satisfaction with the union. These observed changes in attitudes of employees may be related to the union's role in resolving an issue involving the transfer of a job function from the site. This link is only a tentative one, however, and it is too early to tell if the observed increase is more than temporary or if it has real significance.

The other site-specific change occurred at Site VI, where supervisor responses indicated an increase in self-reports by supervisors that they communicate effectively with the union. These supervisors also expressed significantly less overall dissatisfaction with the union. Such results may be the effect of higher union visibility or may merely reflect the supervisors' increased awareness of their role vis-à-vis the union. Again, these conclusions are somewhat premature and are, therefore, tentative.

At Site IV, there was no general change in any of the labor-management measures, but the data indicate that GS 1–4 and WG 1–8 level employees were more satisfied with the activities of the union in 1982 than in 1980. While these levels were still in the neutral range, the increase in satisfaction of lower-level employees does coincide with interview data concerning the union's efforts to increase its visibility and, taken together, suggest that the effort was somewhat successful. During the same period, GS 9–12 supervisors reported a decrease in their acceptance of the union, which may also be related to the union's attempts to increase its visibility.

In general, site-level changes appear to be unique to the individual sites rather than reflecting a pattern of change related to any effects of CSRA, but this is not to say that no effects will be observed in the long run. Much depends on the actions the unions themselves take. It seems important to note that those sites where changes did occur were sites where the unions had taken actions, either on a local or national level, that increased their visibility to the employees at the sites. The unions, however, face two important problems in their efforts to increase visibility: first, for many employees the union does not appear to be able to affect significant job-related problems; and second, the benefits of union representation can be obtained without paying dues.

Record Data

Record data pertaining to unfair labor practice charges are displayed in table 8.5. These data and records applying to grievances corroborate the general picture from measures already discussed of little change in labor-management relations. Contract grievances, while varying considerably from year to year at some sites, show no discernible pattern or trend.

Contract grievance procedures were found to be most heavily used for issues concerning the administration of leave, including absence without leave and charges of sick leave abuse, and issues arising from annual appraisals. Closely related to grievances arising out of annual appraisals are those concerned with promotions; these are also among the most frequently grieved issues. Promotion-related grievances most often concern the evaluation of the employee that is done in rating the applicant's suitability for a particular position.

Pay and overtime grievances are also very common, as are those relating to adverse or disciplinary actions. The grievance procedure is most commonly used for disciplinary actions, such as oral admonishments, written reprimands, and suspensions for fourteen days or less. The union-management contracts at three of the sites exclude adverse actions from appeal through the contract grievance procedure. The other sites include adverse actions within the purview of the contract grievance procedure. Even at these sites, however, adverse actions are generally appealed to the Merit Systems Protection Board (MSPB), if they are contested at all.

Most grievances at all the sites are resolved at early stages of the grievance process. The numbers are very small, and insufficient time has elapsed to draw any firm conclusions, but there may be an increasing tendency to use the arbitration process at some of the sites.

The low level of activity is the most notable aspect of the grievance procedures at the sites. Unfair labor practice charges likewise show no obvious changes. Although some had suggested it as a possibility (Marzotto, Gossett, and Ban 1981), there is no evidence indicating that unfair labor practice charges are being used as a relatively low-cost alternative to arbitration or bargaining. While it initially appeared that this might be a tactic of choice following the installation of a

Table 8.5. Number of Unfair Labor Practice Charges Filed

Site	1979	1980	1981	1982 1st Quarter
I	1	2	0	0
II	1	1	0	0
III	12	4	2	4
IV	0	0	0	0
V	0	1	0	0
VI	0	1	0	0

new union president at one site, the situation does not appear to be developing in that fashion.

Conclusions

The survey and interview data indicate that no abrupt changes have occurred in labor-management relations as a result of the Civil Service Reform Act. What appears to be occurring, instead, is a slow maturing of the labor-management relationships as both sides learn and test out various options they might pursue. At present it appears that most of the changes that are occurring can best be explained in terms of the personalities of key participants at each site, or particular events at that location.

Labor-management relations appear to be generally good at the study locations, and all of the changes observed have been in the direction of better, more businesslike interaction. None of the sites could be correctly described as having even slightly troubled labor-management relations.

Union membership is generally unchanged, although one of the unions seems to be achieving some success in increasing membership, primarily by heightening its visibility and involving more members in various union activities. And although most employees interviewed were aware of the events surrounding the Professional Air Traffic Controller's strike, in August 1981, most reported that their beliefs and attitudes toward union membership were unaffected by that action. The possibility of such a strike in any of the research sites seems highly unlikely under present conditions.

In an earlier report (OPM 1981), it was suggested that the character of local labor-management relations is determined more by local factors than by more general federal labor-management issues. The governing local factors include the personalities of local union leaders and management; the labor relations philosophy and strategy of local managements and unions, and their preferred style of interacting; and particular events and issues emerging from the local context. This view seems still to be valid. For the most part, such changes as have transpired in local labor-management relations over the course of the study stem primarily from specific changes in the local situation and not from the effects of Title VII. At no site does it appear that labor-management relations have a major impact on other organizational factors.

Future Local Issues

Although no major labor-management controversies exist at the moment, a few issues have come up often enough at the study sites to indicate that they could become more important in the future.

Release time. A number of union officials reported that they were experiencing some degree of difficulty in securing enough official release time to deal adequately with union business. Their future approaches to dealing with the problem seem likely to involve either the filing of unfair labor practice charges or attempts to negotiate more liberal release-time provisions in the next contract. To date, however, we are not aware of a case in which either of these actions has been initiated.

Performance standards. Problems involving performance standards have been discussed as likely to be the target of union effort in some form. The specific issues mentioned most often are inconsistent application of standards to similar jobs and lack of willingness on the part of management to discuss the rationale used in establishing various standards.

Negotiating costs. A possible problem for the management side is the cost of negotiating. A 1981 FLRA decision requires that management pay travel and per diem expenses for all negotiations. Since many contracts are negotiated on a national basis and involve a relatively large number of participants, the costs could become substantial during protracted negotiations. One instance has been described (OPM 1981) in which the Veteran's Administration reportedly spent at least $463,000 for union negotiators' salaries, travel, and per diem. Some observers suggest that unions, now freed from the constant concern for the financial drain of travel and per diem costs on limited union treasuries, may choose to stretch out negotiations as a means of obtaining management concessions. Others describe this change somewhat differently, referring to it as a way of giving management needed motivation to bargain. Whether this lever can or will be used remains to be seen.[6]

National Versus Local Change

While changes in labor-management relations at the study sites are minimal, change is more visible in the parent agencies and the corresponding national unions. Thus far, the most significant change in federal labor-management relations related to CSRA seems to be the consolidation of bargaining units and a shift in the primary locus of collective bargaining from the local to the national, or a consolidated, level.

Effect of consolidation on federal unions. Since the passage of the Reform Act, the local union at each of the study sites has become part of a consolidated unit. The effect of consolidation has been to remove from the local labor-management relationship the necessity to engage in collective bargaining, except with regard to a narrow set of issues designated as "local issues" by the national level master agreements. The effects on the local union of this shift in the locus of collective bargaining activity are not yet known, since the sites vary in the length of time the local unit has been consolidated and the stage of national level collective bargaining. It appears that one major effect might be to cause the local unions to focus primarily on contract administration and enforcement. The local unions would then earn their keep by representing employees in grievances and arbitrations, and otherwise acting as the protector of employees' rights.

Whether and how the increasing centralization of collective bargaining will affect local union autonomy is not yet known. There are indications from some, but not all, of the sites that the national union is already playing a stronger role in advising and training local union leaders, as well as in formulating general strategy for selecting "test" arbitrations and unfair labor practice charges. To date, however, this involvement has been largely advisory and has not been viewed by local union leaders as an effort by the national to intrude in local affairs.

Effects of consolidation on agency management. Although there are differences among the agencies in this study concerning the nature and degree of change, the elevation of collective bargaining to the agency level appears to have had an impact on agency level labor-management relations. The requirement to bargain with the union on agency policies and procedures has altered the manner in which the agency managers implement their decisions. For some of the agencies, consolidation and agency-level bargaining had already occurred prior to the commencement of the study. In these agencies, it is difficult to determine the effects of this change since, for the most part, the managers and union leaders involved had already incorporated the change and do not associate it with CSRA. For one agency that recently completed negotiating its first master contract, however, the effects are viewed by agency managers and national union leaders as substantial. There is considerable disagreement, particularly among managers, though, about whether these effects will be positive or negative for the agency. Some managers believe that agency-level collective bargaining will be good for the agency and will contribute to overall uniformity and standardization of labor relations consistent with the agency's high priority on uniformity. Others believe that the effects will be negative and will interfere with the ability of local administrators to manage their own installations. Evidence from other agencies where master agreements are already in place suggests that both are possible outcomes.

Consolidation and national-level bargaining, and the subsequent formalization of labor-management relationships, are having varying impacts on the autonomy of local labor-relations offices and management officials. Some of the sites express satisfaction with the degree of guidance they receive from the agency level; but at least one site feels that the agency is insufficiently sensitive to local conditions and does not allow management officials sufficient latitude to carry out their local responsibilities.

Change in labor-management relations: a waterfall effect? It would probably be a mistake to assume, because Title VII of the CSRA has not yet affected local labor-management relations in any marked fashion, that no such effect will be forthcoming. Among the labor-management officials we have interviewed from both union and management, there were two distinct schools of thought on this subject. One view is that the effects of Title VII will continue to be felt mostly at the national level and may never have a notable impact on field installations, except as a result of increasing standardization of collective bargaining agreements. The other view holds that the effects of Title VII will be felt first at the national level and will eventually begin to filter down to the local level in the form of increased national-level union efforts to strengthen local unions, increased formalization of local labor-management relationships, and increased attention by agency policy level managers to improving the labor-relations skills of field managers.

A CONCLUDING NOTE

The interview and questionnaire data we have examined suggest that union membership is not large. Thus, the power of the federal unions in the study sites remains relatively limited, and the number of members is essentially static. In at least some instances, however, the union leadership is gaining sophistication, and significant growth appears possible if the unions can show evidence that they are able to advance worker interests. In the locations having such unions, management is obviously aware that it must make continued strides toward learning to deal with the union in a constructive fashion.

It is particularly important, we believe, for the preceding information with respect to union membership to be kept in perspective.
The fact that a relatively small proportion of the eligible employees
have chosen to join the union is not necessarily a repudiation of the
union. The data suggest to us that the employees' attitudes are more
in the nature of ambivalence, stemming from several factors—the
fact that one need not join the union to be represented, the existence
of relatively placid and generally amicable labor-management relations, and the absence of a significant source of dissatisfaction or
frustration that the employees see themselves as unable to affect.
Should such an issue emerge, we believe that a union with capable
leadership might quickly crystallize such sentiment and mobilize such
support that the union could move from a position of having no
major effect on the organization, as is the case now, to one in which
it would become a formidable adversary.

NOTES

1. The discussion of legislative history is drawn largely from a paper by
   Toni Marzotto, Charles W. Gossett, and Carolyn Ban, *The Dynamics of
   Civil Service Reform: The Case of Labor Management Relations* (1981).
2. Clay's bill was H.R. 13 and Ford's was H.R. 1589.
3. Letter to Hy Krieger, Director, Federal Personnel and Compensation,
   of the General Accounting Office, commenting on the draft GAO report,
   "The Federal Labor Relations Authority: An Overview and Assessment
   of its First Year of Operation." This letter is reproduced in "The Federal
   Labor Relations Authority: Its First Year in Operation," the final report
   by the GAO, April 2, 1980.
4. Those unfamiliar with labor arbitration should note the distinction
   between grievance (or rights) arbitration and interest arbitration. The
   latter refers to arbitration over disputed contractual terms in collective
   bargaining that has reached an impasse. Interest arbitration is allowed
   by Title VII if the FSIP approves its use by the parties. On the other
   hand, Title VII mandates the use of binding arbitration for unsettled
   grievances.
5. Part of the data used in this chapter were analyzed previously and
   were presented in annual reports to the Office of Personnel Management.
   The authors are especially indebted to Stanley E. Seashore, Cortlandt
   Cammann, and Arthur Granville who contributed significantly to the
   labor-management portions of these reports.
6. While this book was in press, "the Supreme Court struck down labor's
   entitlement to travel and per diem for their negotiators, overruling the
   Federal Labor Relations Authority" (*Federal Times,* January 23, 1984,
   p. 2).

BIBLIOGRAPHY

Coleman, Charles J. 1980. "The Civil Service Reform Act of 1978: Its Meaning and Its Roots." *Labor Law Journal* 31, no. 4: 200–206.

Frazier, Henry B., III. 1979. "Labor-Management Relations in the Federal Government," *Labor Law Journal* 30, no. 3: 131–138.

Gershenfeld, Walter J. 1977. "An Introduction to the Scope of Bargaining in the Public Sector," in *Scope of Public Sector Bargaining,* ed. Gershenfeld, Loewenberg, and Ingster. Lexington: D.C. Heath.

Klingner, Donald E. 1980. "Federal Labor Relations After CSRA." *Public Personnel Management* 9, no. 3: 172–83.

Lowman, Rodney L., and Donald F. Parker. 1982. "Change Assumptions of the Civil Service Reform Act," Paper presented at the National Convention, Academy of Management, New York, August.

Marzotto, Toni, Charles W. Gossett, and Carolyn Ban. 1981. "The Dynamics of Civil Service Reform: The Case of Labor Management Relations." Paper presented at the National Meetings, Association for Public Policy Analysis and Management, Washington, D.C.

U.S. Office of Personnel Management. 1980. *Organizational Assessments of the Effects of Civil Service Reform.* First Year Report submitted by the Institute for Social Research. Washington, D.C.: U.S. Office of Personnel Management.

U.S. Office of Personnel Management. 1981. *Organizational Assessments of the Effects of Civil Service Reform.* Second Year Report submitted by the Institute for Social Research. Washington, D.C.: U.S. Office of Personnel Management.

U.S. Office of Personnel Management. 1982. *Organizational Assessments of the Effects of Civil Service Reform.* Third Year Report submitted by the Institute for Social Research. Washington, D.C.: U.S. Office of Personnel Management.

Rehmus, Charles M. 1974. "Labour Relations in the Public Sector in the United States." *International Labour Review* 109, no. 3.

CHAPTER NINE

The Civil Service Reform Act and EEO: The Record to Date

DAVID H. ROSENBLOOM AND CURTIS R. BERRY

The Civil Service Reform Act of 1978 (CSRA) was hailed as the centerpiece of President Carter's efforts to reorganize the federal bureaucracy in order to make it more manageable. President Carter himself was hailed by many as a chief executive fully committed to equal employment opportunity (EEO). Here was a president billed as both a public manager par excellence and the leader of the struggle to eliminate illegal discrimination throughout the nation. If ever the time was opportune for a successful integration of federal personnel management and federal equal employment opportunity, this was it. Yet, achieving results in the EEO field has been difficult and elusive during four decades of evolving federal programs. Reorganization after reorganization and policy modification after modification have seemingly produced only painfully slow changes and the most incremental of results. Even then, it is rarely completely clear whether the EEO programs or other factors are actually responsible for the federal government's improving record. Thus, despite the high expectations generated during the Carter years, the record of EEO under the Civil Service Reform Act should be considered in light of a history of efforts to overcome what often appears to be an intractable problem.

THE FEDERAL EEO "PROBLEM"

The fundamental nature of the federal government's EEO problem has changed over the years.[1] When the first EEO program was introduced in 1941, the main task was to eliminate the overt discrimination in employment that prevented blacks from being hired and promoted within the ranks of the federal service. Racial segregation in the government was commonplace at the time, and blacks were overwhelmingly confined to the government's lower-level jobs. Over the years, overt discrimination was drastically reduced, although not fully eliminated, and blacks gained greater access to federal positions. For blacks, by the 1970s, entry into the federal service was no longer the central problem; rather, advancement within its ranks and employment in the higher-level positions were viewed as the major concerns. Today, for example, the percentage of federal employees who are black is greater than the percentage of blacks in the nation's general workforce, but blacks are still heavily concentrated in the grades below GS–9, and especially in the lowest five grades. For blacks, then, the EEO problem is eliminating barriers to access to the upper grades. But, the overall EEO problem is far more complex.

There is little doubt that, at the outset, the federal EEO program was aimed overwhelmingly at aiding the employment opportunities of blacks. President Franklin D. Roosevelt issued Executive Order 8802 (1941), prohibiting discrimination based on race, color, or national origin in federal employment and defense contracting, partly in response to black leaders' threats to organize a mass march on Washington as a means of showing their displeasure with discrimination in employment and other areas of life. In the 1960s, the EEO program broadened its focus and gave greater attention to the interests of women and Hispanics. Women were brought within the program for the first time in 1967, and, in 1970, a special office to promote the interests of the Spanish-speaking was created. Greater attention has also been paid to Native Americans, Alaskan Natives, Pacific Islanders, and Asian Americans. By the end of the 1970s, federal EEO efforts also encompassed the physically and mentally handicapped, rehabilitated offenders, and veterans.[2]

The extension of the EEO program's emphasis to include these groups has added immensely to the complexity of achieving satisfactory results. The employment problem faced by each group is somewhat different from that of the others. In its ramifications in public personnel management, sexism is different from racism. The social class background of women, generally, is different from that of blacks, Hispanics, Native Americans, Alaskan Natives, and perhaps other groups. Hispanics face distinct language barriers. Native Americans and Alaskan Natives face cultural barriers that are not shared by the majority of women and may exceed those faced by blacks. Indeed, it has been recognized that the employment interests of these groups may be at odds with one another, and separate offices within the EEO program have been established to deal with the special circumstances confronting women and Hispanics.[3] Moreover, the problems faced by the handicapped are radically different from those faced by the various social groups. These differences have sometimes led to serious problems of coordination and a somewhat immobilizing struggle over the use of scarce EEO resources.

Despite these disparities, with the exception of Hispanics, each of the social groups (i.e., racial, ethnic, and gender groups) faces a federal employment situation similar to that of blacks; that is, the percentage of federal employees who are members of each group exceeds their percentage in the general workforce, but they are heavily concentrated in the lower half of the federal grade structure. Hispanics, on the other hand, are not only concentrated in the lower levels, their percentage in the federal workforce is less than in the nation's workforce as a whole. For Hispanics, therefore, the basic problem of entry into the federal service may still remain.

PRIOR EFFORTS TO ACHIEVE EEO

The EEO problem sometimes appears as intractable as it is complex. During the past four decades, several agencies have been used in an effort to obtain more satisfactory advances toward assuring EEO. A brief review of these helps place the contemporary EEO program in an organizational and policy perspective.

1. *The Fair Employment Practice Committee* (1941–46). The FEPC had jurisdiction over both federal and defense-related private employment. It had no enforcement powers, was shifted from one agency to another in 1943, and concentrated its efforts primarily on discrimination in nonfederal employment. It tended to view EEO as a complaint-processing exercise.

2. *The Fair Employment Board* (1948–55). The FEB was organized within the Civil Service Commission (CSC). It retained the complaint orientation developed earlier, but tended to view EEO as requiring "constructive" action as well. Nevertheless, it failed to develop the latter approach to any substantial extent.

3. *The President's Committee on Government Employment Policy* (1955–61). The PCGEP was the first of the EEO agencies to begin to come to grips with the dimensions of the problems faced. It undertook statistical surveys in an effort to ascertain clearly the precise nature of discrimination and considered it necessary to sensitize federal officials to the needs of minorities and to the importance of a successful program. Moreover, it viewed special efforts to recruit, train, and otherwise aid minorities as a fundamental part of EEO.

4. *The President's Committee on EEO* (1961–65). The PCEEO was relatively aggressive in implementing a threefold program: (1) early

"affirmative action," such as special recruitment drives and training efforts; (2) an annual census of minority employment; and (3) a review of agency actions in response to complaints of prohibited discrimination. Perhaps most noteworthy was the PCEEO's approach that, in order to establish EEO in federal employment, it would be necessary for the government and the society to face up to the more general problem of inequality throughout national life.

5. *The Civil Service Commission* (1965–79). In 1965, the EEO program was reorganized (or disorganized)[4] in the Civil Service Commission (CSC), which since 1883 had been the federal government's central personnel agency. The program underwent a number of reorganizations within the CSC, including the establishment of the Office of Federal EEO, in 1969. This office remained the main focal point of federal EEO efforts until 1979, when the program was transferred to the Equal Employment Opportunity Commission (EEOC), as part of the Carter civil service reform.[5] Under the CSC's stewardship, the EEO program became: (1) organizationally fragmented, first through dispersal among the agency's various operating bureaus, and then by the inclusion of a Federal Women's Program and a Spanish-Speaking Program within it; (2) more elaborately developed in its mechanisms for dealing with complaints; and (3) reliant, after 1971, upon the use of affirmative action hiring and promotion goals and timetables, as a means of achieving equal opportunity. The CSC was heavily criticized for its disorganization and unenthusiastic support for EEO, but during its administration of the program, the basic EEO problem shifted from the entry of minorities and women into the federal service to their employment in the upper ranks.

The history of federal EEO efforts has been one of substantial progress in eliminating formal barriers to equal employment opportunity. Formal racial, ethnic, and gender barriers to the employment of individuals and racial segregation have been almost entirely eliminated. Overt, illegal, interpersonal discrimination has also been drastically reduced. Federal managers and employees have become far more sensitive to the requirements of EEO and, consequently, unconscious discrimination has also been diminished. Yet, the federal personnel system still apparently contains systemic discrimination, and it has also failed to overcome the negative impacts on EEO of inequality within the society at large. For instance, the most notable and debilitating example of the persistence of the combination of these two factors has been the government's experience with a general entry career examination. The Federal Service Entrance Examination (FSEE) was used from 1955 to 1974, with a very harsh impact on blacks, and probably other minorities as well. The exam accounted for some 10,000 to 14,000 placements per year in career positions that could lead to advancement to the very top of the General Schedule grade structure. According to some sources, blacks had a passing rate of about 12 percent, compared with 60 percent for whites.[6] After being seriously challenged through litigation, the exam was dropped in favor of a Professional and Administrative Career Examination (PACE).[7] This exam had an even harsher racial bias against blacks and became the object of a great deal of legal maneuvering,[8] which eventually led to its demise. Various federal agencies are now developing selection devices specifically suited to their particular needs. However, when coupled with the merit principle of selection of the best qualified, roughly as denoted by score, and also with societal discrimination that prevents blacks and others from gaining equal access to "merit," exams and other rating procedures can constitute major barriers to resolving aspects of the contemporary EEO problem. To be successful in furthering EEO, therefore, the civil service reform of 1978 would have to change some of the ground rules for entry into the career structure of the federal service, and, with the abandonment of the PACE exam, some change has occurred.

THE REFORM

The Civil Service Reform Act sought to temper the quest for merit with an emphasis on social representation. It declared explicitly for the first time that "it is the policy of the United States . . . to provide . . . a Federal work force reflective of the Nation's diversity" by endeavoring "to achieve a work force from all segments of society." [9] This language signalled an important shift in the focus and language of federal EEO. Earlier, affirmative action had been difficult to implement. It was considered a means of overcoming discrimination rather than a way of creating a socially representative work force per se. To many, it was never clear how discrimination could be eliminated through the use of quotalike devices. They questioned the desirability of a socially representative work force and tended to view it as an erosion of merit principles. However, once the EEO objective is framed in terms of representation, goals or quotas may be highly appropriate. This is especially true if the desire for representation comes to supersede traditional concerns with the "merit system."

Indeed, the reform changed the ground rules here, too. The CSC's handling of the EEO program had been commonly criticized on the ground that the agency was so committed to the merit system, which it was established to implement and refine, that it failed to understand how merit concepts and practices were themselves sometimes a major cause of illegitimate discrimination. The agency had developed an institutional culture that made it a conservative defender of "merit" above all else; although it is perhaps too much to say that the CSC was still fighting the spoilsmen, the agency clearly had failed to understand the political importance and force of the quest for EEO in a representational sense.[10] It is possible to overcome bureaucratic intractability through less drastic means, of course, but one approach to changing the way an agency behaves is to abolish it.[11] This was the route taken by President Carter. The CSC was dismantled and its functions were more or less dispersed among four separate agencies, three of which were created by the reform. The creation of the Office of Personnel Management (OPM), the Merit Systems Protection Board (MSPB), and the Federal Labor Relations Authority (FLRA) are discussed elsewhere in this volume. It is important to note though, that an existing agency, the Equal Employment Opportunity Commission, received primary authority for the federal EEO program. Although this change was an integral part of the reform, it was accomplished through a reorganization plan rather than by the Act itself. At the same time, the Act created a Federal Equal Opportunity Recruitment Program (FEORP) in the OPM. The FEORP is charged with developing approaches for eliminating the underrepresentation of minorities and women in various categories of federal employment. It also has responsibility for evaluating and overseeing the EEO recruitment activities of federal agencies generally.

The transfer of the program to the EEOC held both great potential and substantial risks for federal EEO. The agency had jurisdiction over EEO in state and local employment and in most private employment. It was created in 1965, pursuant to the Civil Rights Act of 1964, and had therefore gained considerable experience in EEO matters. Its powers and jurisdiction were expanded by the EEO Act of 1972. Not having been associated with the development of "merit-oriented" federal personnel policy, the EEOC appeared to have no vested interest in maintaining the status quo where traditional practices presented a barrier to attaining EEO. Especially important, it was not involved in the development of the merit exams having a harsh impact on EEO. Consequently, the EEOC was more likely to oppose their use than was the CSC. It had long been argued that allowing the CSC to implement EEO created a conflict of interest and the EEOC offered a dramatic change in this regard.

On the other hand, the agency had a strikingly poor performance record.[12] In fact, in proposing the transfer, the White House press release of February 23, 1978, remarked that the EEOC "has had management problems in past administrations." In part these accounted for a backlog of over 150,000 cases at various times. The

EEOC was also an internally fractious organization, with a high level of conflict among its black, Hispanic, and nonminority female employees. Moreover, although the EEOC supported affirmative action as a vehicle for achieving EEO, it tended to do so by threatening law suits, which would not be particularly efficacious in the federal sector. This litigious approach to EEO also encouraged a heavy reliance on complaint processing, which since the 1960s had been considered of secondary importance in federal employment, where employment practices can be readily changed by the same government ostensibly seeking to promote EEO. In addition, placing the bulk of EEO functions in one agency, already overworked, was politically risky in a time of general budget cutting and continued civil rights "backlash."

However well the EEOC performs, though, another difficulty of substantial proportions remains. Since EEO is ultimately a personnel function, it must be coordinated with other personnel functions. At one time, the CSC went so far in seeking to integrate EEO into the personnel system that the program had no focus or focal point. Conversely, however, separating EEO from general personnel management means that it must be superimposed upon that system from outside. This is a task that requires a great deal of understanding, subtle political bargaining, and coordination. If it is to be accomplished successfully, the EEO agency not only needs to be skilled, but the legitimacy of its priorities must be accepted by other parties. Thus, OPM must accept the EEOC's interpretation of personnel priorities, as must the MSPB and the FLRA on occasion. Further, OPM and EEOC need to coordinate the recruitment program with other EEO activities—a process that has met with some difficulty. This could be established at the outset only if the political coalition developed in favor of reform held a coherent vision of federal personnel policy. The evidence suggests that this failed to occur, and consequently the politics of enacting reform may ultimately be a barrier to its effective implementation.

IMPLEMENTING REFORM

The Civil Service Reform Act was the most fundamental change in federal personnel administration since the passage of the Civil Service Act of 1883 (Pendleton Act). The Carter administration displayed deft political skill in guiding it through the legislature. Rather than engage in a fundamental debate about the kind of federal personnel administration that was most desirable in contemporary government and politics—what its priorities should be and who would benefit at whose expense—a political coalition was built by promising something to several of the major interest groups associated with federal personnel policy. Thus, political executives and the presidency obtained an agency, the OPM, clearly designed to be responsive to their managerial interests; career employees were promised stronger protection against partisan intrusion into personnel actions by the creation of the MSPB; the FLRA provided labor unions with a less managerially dominated forum for resolving issues associated with federal collective bargaining; and women and minorities were promised a more forceful EEO program under the administration of the EEOC. Each group received much of what it wanted, but inadequate attention may have been paid to the whole enterprise.

A second look at the nature of this coalition and the agencies created suggests that a major accomplishment of the reform was to vest each of the historical federal personnel values in a separate agency,[13] rather than allow them to remain within one agency, such as the CSC. Thus, for the most part, the value of executive leadership was vested in the OPM, that of politically neutral competence in the MSPB, and representativeness was placed in the EEOC. In addition, the more recently developed value of worker participation was placed in the FLRA.[14] However, much of the overall problem faced by the CSC and federal personnel administration over the years has been an inability to maximize all these values at once or to establish priorities among them. Consequently, federal personnel administration has long been characterized by fragmentation and incoherence, and personnel specialists have lacked a clear identity.[15] Although the reform strengthened each of the values, it did not establish the primacy of any one over the others. No vision of a new federal personnel administration was created through the integration of the competing values into a coherent policy unit. Rather, the values were housed separately, and it was assumed that integration would take place through incremental adjustments over the years.

After enactment, however, members of the coalition backing reform demonstrated a lack of support for the package as a whole. For instance, the MSPB was severely underfunded and some of its key positions went unstaffed or temporarily staffed. Key pay arrangements for Senior Executive Service members and employees in grades GS 13–15 were altered. Moreover, conflicts arose among the four major personnel agencies over a wide variety of personnel matters.

Under these conditions the representationist approach to EEO promoted by the CSRA could be effective only if the EEOC were able to gain agreement among the other agencies, especially OPM, that this value should be promoted even where it compromised another personnel value. Thus far, the EEOC has faced a number of problems in this regard.

Despite the transfer of primary responsibility for EEO to the EEOC, much of the former program was vested in the OPM. Especially important is that agency's Office of Affirmative Employment Programs, which includes the FEORP, the Federal Women's Program, the Hispanic Employment Program, Veterans Employment Programs, Minority Programs/Outreach and Upward Mobility Programs, and Selective Placement Programs (for the handicapped, disabled veterans, and rehabilitated offenders). The recruitment program (FEORP) is ". . . designed to eliminate underrepresentation in employment through a process of need assessment and intensive recruitment focused directly at underrepresented groups." [16] Under these programs, OPM reviews agency reports concerning EEO and monitors and evaluates agency activities in this area. In essence, this is the same function that the CSC played with regard to annual agency EEO plans. The major change is that now goals and timetables are used to correct "underrepresentation" rather than simply to implement EEO.

If OPM is fully committed to the value of representation, this approach may work well. However, the agency is intended to be the president's arm for personnel management, and a president's political agenda may or may not stress EEO. Moreover, it may place a heavier emphasis on EEO for some groups, such as veterans, the handicapped, or Hispanics, than for others. In a time of retrenchment, when emphasis is placed on efficient management, OPM may tend to devalue the premium placed on the representationist approach to EEO. In fact, this is precisely what has occurred in two important areas under the Reagan Administration.

First, EEOC and OPM have been unable to agree on a method of funding the EEOC's request to redesign the retrieval capability of the government's Central Personnel Data File (CPDF) as a means of generating further information pertinent to EEO. The gist of the problem was conveniently conveyed in a report by Dr. J. Clay Smith, Jr., Acting Chairman of the EEOC, on October 8, 1981:

> . . . On September 21, 1981, Mr. Devine [Director of OPM] wrote to me advising that while they are prepared from a management point of view to provide CPDF data support service to the Commission, the FY '82 budget reductions directed by OMB [Office of Management and Budget] have caused OPM to reduce the level of resources allocated to the CPDF. He therefore requested that EEOC make whatever arrangements are necessary to allocate to OPM the necessary funds and ceiling required to support our program. We are presently preparing a response to Mr. Devine for the purpose

of advising him of our lack of resources to provide these funds and of our ongoing efforts to obtain the necessary amount from the Office of Management and Budget. OMB, however, has been conducting a study of the CPDF on its own and cannot make any money immediately available to the project at this time.[17]

That this kind of bargaining is common in the federal government should not obscure the basic fact that it becomes all the more necessary as a result of the division of personnel and EEO functions between OPM and the EEOC. Moreover, if EEO were OPM's top objective and if representation were its chief value, it would have been far more likely that the data capability desired by the EEOC would have been previously built into the CPDF system.

Second, after much politicking, the Reagan Administration agreed to abandon use of the PACE exam, which it originally argued was ". . . a fair and cost effective instrument for selecting candidates for the Federal service,"[18] despite its harsh racial impact. However, there is little reason to assume that the demise of the PACE exam will automatically beget greater EEO gains. At present, agencies are making widespread use of "Selective Certification" processes, which, while competitive, may fail to protect against illegal discrimination and political preferences. Moreover, in the absence of a government-wide selection device, EEO suits may have to be brought against each agency individually—a process that may be very costly, time-consuming, and ineffective.

Indeed, OPM has already seemed to express some doubt as to the nature of EEO activities in the postreform period. In its January 1981 "Report to Congress," OPM concluded:

> The relationship between FEORP [Federal Equal Opportunity Recruitment Program] and the affirmative action program administered by the Equal Employment Opportunity Commission must be clarified. OPM, EEOC, and most federal agencies are engaged heavily in activities directed toward those ends. Still, it will take time before it is possible to determine whether these efforts and resources, and the statutory provisions themselves, are appropriate means for meeting the objective of having a Federal work force that represents the diversity of the Nation's population.[19]

THE IMPACT OF REORGANIZATION

Any effort to assess the impact of the civil service reform of 1978 on EEO must take the costs of the reorganization itself into account.

As noted earlier, the case for transferring the EEO program to the EEOC was not unequivocal. Such a move was first seriously considered in the late 1960s,[20] but was not ultimately effectuated until 1979. Among the pitfalls of the reorganization was the likelihood that it would place the EEO program in transition for a year or so at a time when it might otherwise be possible to consolidate the modest gains being made. Indeed, it now appears that the program has seen reduced activity for about *three* years as a result of the transfer. In fiscal 1979, the CSC, realizing that it was being dismantled, paid little attention to EEO. According to Eleanor Holmes Norton, former Chair of the EEOC, upon receiving the program the EEOC took about a year to study and organize it, which accounts for FY 1980.[21] An additional transition year was allotted so that agencies could effectively move away from annual affirmative action reports to a multiyear approach.[22] During this time, the EEOC also sought to develop a more effective complaint system. Under the circumstances, it is reasonable to assume that the full impact of the transfer was not present until FY 1982. By that time, however, the salience of the initial "representationist" approach of the reform had been diminished by the Reagan Administration's priorities for a smaller federal work force. Indeed, evidence suggests that women and minorities have disproportionately borne the burden of reductions-in-force during the Reagan presidency.[23]

Empirical analysis tends to confirm the proposition that the transfer of the EEO program from the CSC to the EEOC placed EEO activities in something of a holding pattern. Table 9.1 presents the changes in average General Schedule grade of various groups in the years from 1976 to 1980. In view of the nature of the federal EEO problem and the Civil Service Reform Act's representational initiative, average grade is a useful summary measure of how various groups are faring in federal employment. As can be seen from the table, for the most part, change during the four-year period has not been dramatic, and there is no consistent pattern regarding amounts or rates of change between 1976 and 1978 as compared to those between 1978 and 1980. Some minority groups, particularly black women, Hispanic women, and Native Americans, did better in the prereform period (1976–78). On the other hand, Asian Americans and Pacific Islanders had greater advances in the early postreform period, and change in the average grade of women remained virtually constant.

Sufficient data are not currently available to determine whether there has been substantial change between 1980 and 1982. However, given the time it has taken to reorganize the program in the EEOC, it is unlikely that whatever changes may have taken place can be attributed to the civil service reform. Moreover, 1981 and 1982

Table 9.1. The Average General Schedule Grade of Various Groups, 1976–80

Group	Year	Average Grade	Change	Percentage Change
Men	1976	9.92		
	1978	10.02	.10	1.008
	1980	10.05	.03	.2994
Women	1976	5.84		
	1978	6.05	.21	3.5958
	1980	6.26	.21	3.3546
Black Men	1976	5.58		
	1978	5.75	.17	3.0465
	1980	5.93	.18	3.1304
Black Women	1976	6.26		
	1978	6.41	.15	2.3961
	1980	6.53	.12	1.872
Hispanic Men	1976	5.23		
	1978	5.48	.25	4.7801
	1980	5.75	.27	4.927
Hispanic Women	1976	6.93		
	1978	7.14	.21	3.0303
	1980	7.28	.14	1.9607
Asian or Pacific Islander Men	1976	10.16		
	1978	10.14	.02	−.19723
	1980	10.24	.14	1.3806
Asian or Pacific Islander Women	1976	6.62		
	1978	6.89	.27	4.0785
	1980	7.16	.27	3.9187
American Indian or Alaskan Men	1976	7.52		
	1978	7.91	.39	5.1861
	1980	8.01	.10	1.2642
American Indian or Alaskan Women	1976	4.79		
	1978	5.08	.29	6.0542
	1980	5.24	.16	3.1496

SOURCE: Office of Personnel Management, "Summary of Full-Time Civilian Employment for Women and Minority Governmentwide, 1970–1980," unpublished, 1981.

witnessed limited hiring and freezes that substantially reduced the possibilities for dramatic EEO progress. According to an OPM "Report to Congress" in 1982, the following developments have occurred:

Black Males

In 1981, black males were fully represented in the Technical and Other categories of the Professional, Administrative, Technical, Clerical, and Other (PATCO) occupational categories, as well as in General Schedule (GS) grades 1, 2, 3, 5, 8, and 9, and in all but two grade groups of the wage pay system, WG 13–15 and WL 12–15.

Black Females

In 1981, black females were fully represented in Administrative occupations, in all grades through GS-10, and in grades WG 1–4, WL 1–4, and WS 1–4.

Hispanic Males

Hispanic men continued to be fully represented in 1981 in the Other category in the PATCO system. There was virtually no change in representation across GS grades for Hispanic men, but some slippage occurred in the higher grades of the wage pay system.

Hispanic Females

Hispanic women continued to be fully represented in Clerical occupations, poorly represented in all grade groups within the wage pay plans, and there was little change across GS grades.

Asian American Males

Asian American males continued to be fully represented in the Professional category in the PATCO system; there was full representation in grades GS 9 and 11–15, and in blue-collar positions, with the exceptions of WL 12–15 and WS 1–9.

Asian American Females

Gains were made in the professional category and in GS 10, where full representation was achieved in 1981. Full representation continued at grades GS 1–7 and GS 9, and in WG 1–4 and WL 1–4.

Native American Males

As in 1980, there was full representation of Native American men in all individual PATCO categories, and in all blue-collar pay plan/

grade levels. The high overall representation of this group is, in large measure, attributable to the high level of Native American representation in the Bureau of Indian Affairs and the Indian Health Service, where provisions of the Indian Preference Act apply.

Native American Females

Native American women were fully represented in all PATCO occupation categories except Other, in all grade levels in the WG pay plan for the first time, and in WL and WS grades 1–9.

White Females

Some progress toward full representation of white females in Professional, Administrative, and Technical occupations was made during 1981. They continued to be fully represented in Clerical occupations. Small gains were made in GS grades 9–15. Representation in blue-collar occupations and grades remained low.[24]

THE FUTURE: RETRENCHMENT AND EEO POLICY

During the latter part of the 1970s, it became apparent that governmental growth at all levels had outpaced the resources available for its support. Many jurisdictions facing fiscal stress, declining tax bases, and taxpayer revolts have been forced to reduce service levels and programs. A major impact of retrenchment on public personnel systems has been the introduction of hiring freezes, reductions-in-force, lay-offs, and the use of attrition as a means of reducing the size of public-sector work forces. Rising federal deficits and cutbacks in federal programs have caused similar strategies of retrenchment to be introduced in the federal government. Retrenchment can have strong negative consequences for the employment of members of minority groups and women. The Office of Personnel Management is cognizant of this and has issued a memorandum to the heads of federal departments and agencies admonishing that:

> In line with the President's commitment to reduce the level of government spending and thereby help restore the vitality of the nation's economy, most of you will be operating under budget restrictions and reduced personnel ceiling levels during the next few years. These conditions mean that recruitment of new Federal employees will be limited. Nevertheless, the Administration expects agencies to pursue all appropriate efforts regarding employment opportunities for the handicapped, veterans, minorities and women, as required by various laws and regulations.[25]

Nevertheless, retrenchment is likely to present new barriers to the achievement of EEO.

Minorities and women are most vulnerable to retrenchment because for the most part they still suffer from the "last hired, first fired syndrome." [26] This problem is compounded by the fact that the agencies that grew most rapidly during the past two decades, when EEO was emphasized, are currently frequently under the greatest pressure for retrenchment. This is likely to diminish the representation of minorities and women in these agencies and detract from the prospects for their advancement upward through the ranks. As competition for dwindling positions and promotions becomes more acute, the systemic biases of the federal merit system will be even more evident. The absence of substantial change in the representation of minorities and women in the federal work force in 1981 may be a precursor of the difficulties EEO will face in the future.

The impact of the EEO Act of 1972 and federal EEO/Affirmative Action programs upon the employment levels of members of minority groups and women during the past decade has been modest at best. Generally, minorities and women continue to be concentrated in lower-level positions that have traditionally been open to them. Faced with the slow pace of change and the period of retrenchment now confronting the public sector, perhaps the time for a fundamental re-evaluation of EEO programs has arrived. At the very least, the following questions should be readdressed: What are the remaining institutional barriers to the hiring and promotion of members of different minority groups and women, and how should these be dealt with in the future? Can the bias of merit exams having a harsh racial impact because of their middle-class orientation be eliminated without destroying the (limited) validity of these selection devices? If so, should these biases be eliminated, or should we be candid in accepting that the federal service, and especially its middle and upper levels, is inherently middle class in the language, values, and skills it utilizes? Realism dictates that, after four decades of EEO, we recognize that a major form of continuing discrimination is based upon social class rather than simply upon race, color, or ethnicity. There is only so much that a federal EEO program can do to counteract the impact of discrimination, inequality, and cumulative disadvantage in the society at large. Reorganization and refurbishment of the current EEO program will not satisfactorily enable members of the lower class to obtain the prerequisites for entrance into the vast majority of middle-class federal positions. In the words of the former President's Committee on EEO, "It is apparent that full equality of employment opportunity requires that we face up to the whole problem of equality itself." [27] For example, there is a limit to what can be accomplished in federal EEO when only 8 percent of the students in schools which are members of NASPAA (the National Association of Schools of Public Affairs and Administration) are black.[28]

Under such conditions, in the absence of a wholly new concept concerning fitness for the federal service, changes in personnel law and EEO programs are likely to serve more to distract our attention from the crux of the problem than to bring about much change in the social composition of the federal workforce.

Perhaps the solution to the representative bureaucracy problem must be considered in long-range terms. Emphasis needs to be placed on assisting members of minority groups to gain the education and communication skills needed to compete in middle-class American society and in the federal bureaucracy. This solution may be more painful and take longer, but it will be less vulnerable to changing political moods and more acceptable to the society at large. Mainstream America has long required, as a price for equality, that immigrants and members of other minority groups predominantly accept its fundamental values in matters of law, politics, employment, and social relationships. In the long run, by instituting differential requirements for minorities seeking employment, governmental policy could inevitably reduce the prospects for members of minority groups of attaining equality in the society at large. In addition, means of compensating for the effects of inequality, such as the use of affirmative action goals and timetables, have had a tendency to polarize the federal work force along racial and gender lines.[29] Adopting a more comprehensive strategy for dealing with cumulative disadvantages might well be less divisive. In sum, contemporary EEO programs and efforts should be continually refined, improved, and adjusted to changing circumstances, but at the same time, far greater governmental efforts must be made to increase the pool of qualified minority candidates for positions in the public service. Only then is the commitment of the Civil Service Reform Act to a socially representative federal work force likely to be realized.

NOTES

1. For the history of EEO efforts in the federal service, see Samuel Krislov, *The Negro in Federal Employment* (Minneapolis: University of Minnesota Press, 1967); and David H. Rosenbloom, *Federal Equal Employment Opportunity* (New York: Praeger, 1977).
2. For a brief description, see Office of Personnel Management, "Office of Affirmative Employment Programs," Pamphlet EM–1, September 1980.

3. Rosenbloom, *Federal EEO*, ch. 1, and pp. 90–94.
4. Ibid., ch. 4.
5. Reorganization Plan No. 1 of 1978.
6. See Rosenbloom, *Federal EEO*, p. 139.
7. Ibid., pp. 138–42; Douglas v. Hampton, 338 F. Supp. 18 (1972); 512 F2d 976 (1975).
8. See *Public Administration Times*, May 15, 1979, pp. 1 ff. According to the General Accounting Office, 58 percent of all whites taking the PACE exam passed, whereas only 12 percent of all blacks did. Some recent aspects of the consent decree are mentioned in Office of Management and Budget, *The Budget of the United States Government, 1983,* Special Analysis J: "Civil Rights Activities," February 1982.
9. P.L. 95–454, Sects. 3, 2301 (b) (1).
10. Rosenbloom, *Federal EEO*, pp. 95–100.
11. See Harold Seidman, *Politics, Position, and Power,* 2d ed. (New York: Oxford University Press, 1975) for an analysis of the political uses of reorganization.
12. See U.S. Commission on Civil Rights, *The Federal Civil Rights Enforcement Effort, 1974* (Washington, D.C.: Commission on Civil Rights, 1975) chap. 5; pp. 643–6; idem, *The Federal Civil Rights Enforcement Effort—1977: To Eliminate Employment Discrimination: A Sequel* (Washington, D.C.: Commission on Civil Rights, 1977), chap. 4.
13. Herbert Kaufman, "Emerging Conflicts in the Doctrines of Public Administration," *American Political Science Review* 50 (December 1956): 1057–73.
14. See Executive Order 10988 (January 17, 1962), 27 *Federal Register* 551, for an explicit statement.
15. See Robert Hampton, "The Basic Question," *Civil Service Journal* 13 (January/March 1973): 2–5.
16. Office of Personnel Management, Pamphlet EM–1, September 1980.
17. J. Clay Smith, "Report to the Civil Rights and Business Community," October 8, 1981, p. 30 (unpublished) (hereafter cited as "Smith Report").
18. Office of Management and Budget, "Special Analysis J," p. 22.
19. Office of Personnel Management, *Report to Congress: Annual Report on Implementation of the Federal Equal Opportunity Recruitment Program,* January 31, 1981, p. 18.
20. Rosenbloom, *Federal EEO*, p. 96.
21. Interview with David H. Rosenbloom, Washington, D.C., March 1979.
22. "Smith Report," p. 30.
23. See *Washington Post,* December 30, 1982, p. A5.
24. Office of Personnel Management, *Report to Congress: Annual Report on the Implementation of the Federal Equal Opportunity Recruitment Program,* January 31, 1982, unpaged.
25. Memorandum from Office of Personnel Management Director Donald J. Devine to Heads of Departments and Independent Establishments, June 5, 1981, p. 1.

26. See Robert N. Roberts, " 'Last-Hired, First-Fired' and Public Employee Layoffs: The Equal Employment Opportunity Dilemma," *Review of Public Personnel Administration* 2 (Fall 1981): 29–48.

27. Quoted in Rosenbloom, *Federal EEO,* p. 69.

28. See Lee Sigelman and Albert Karnig, "Black Education and Bureaucratic Employment," *Social Science Quarterly* 58 (March 1977): 858–63; page 863 cites National Association of Schools of Public Affairs and Administration, *Graduate School Programs in Public Affairs and Public Administration—1974* (Washington, D.C.: NASPAA, 1974).

29. See David H. Rosenbloom, "Federal Equal Employment Opportunity: Is the Polarization Worth the Preference?" *Southern Review of Public Administration* 5 (Spring 1981): 63–72.

III

Civil Service Reform as Public Policy: Can We Judge Success or Failure?

CHAPTER TEN

Civil Service Reform in Comparative Perspective: The United States and Great Britain

David L. Dillman

In the political arena an institution so seemingly dull as the civil service generates a surprising amount of interest and even passion. It is perpetually being condemned, reformed, and condemned. Each successive round of condemnation typically points out a vice contrary to that alleged earlier, and the later reform response is likely in a direction contrary to, or at least distinctly different from, that essayed earlier. Why so much attention to this supposedly anonymous, routine, deadly boring institution?

In short, the answer is that civil service reform is fundamentally a political debate between individuals and groups holding alternative notions of the nature of responsible government. The outcomes of these debates are of crucial significance for establishing a civil service that is politically neutral and yet responsive to executive leadership, accountable and yet capable of initiative, professionally competent and yet representative and sensitive to public ethics. The outcomes of these debates are significant for deciding who rules and to what effect.

As the British civil service entered the 1980s, it found itself in the midst of such a political debate. Much of the condemnation flowed from Prime Minister Margaret Thatcher's war on waste and inefficiency, led by the Prime Minister's advisor on government management, Sir Derek Rayner, the joint managing director of a chain of large department stores. Thatcher and Sir Derek wanted to cut almost 100,000 jobs by 1984 and streamline the service by abolishing the rank of undersecretary and "hiving-off" functions currently performed by the public sector to the private sector, to realize huge savings in civil service expenditures. Yet at the same time, it is not so clear to many observers that the civil service deserves to be attacked, nor is there full agreement that economy and efficiency are the proper criteria to apply to it.

CREATING CIVIL SERVICE SYSTEMS

This effort of the 1980s, of course, is not the first attempt to reform the British civil service. The Northcote-Trevelyan Report of 1853[1] stands as a landmark in the creation of a unified Home Civil Service based on career employment. One lesson of the period from 1853 to 1870 is that reform of the British civil service was not pulled from the proverbial magician's hat, but was the product of a complex assortment of factors that merged into a consensus for reform.[2] It is clear that the reformers were not unified in their purposes or approaches, but that the reform process incorporated a number of different perspectives of what the purposes of reform should be and what a reformed civil service should look like. The Northcote-Trevelyan Report itself was commissioned as the result of Parliament's concern for economy in government, but Sir Stafford Northcote and Sir Charles Trevelyan adapted it to their desire for more efficient administration through neutral, competent officials. Theirs was a political intent to purify a "corrupt" society and further "meritocracy" in politics and education.[3] Some of those who had a hand in implementing the report, notably W. E. Gladstone, were less concerned about economy and efficiency than in using administrative reform to achieve political advantage by bringing together the interests of the aristocracy and the middle class. The emerging middle class saw in the reforms an opportunity for increased access to government and more jobs. Others, like department heads, were more narrowly concerned with the administrative convenience that reform would offer. Each of these perspectives on reform was woven into a fabric of nineteenth century liberal, laissez-faire ideology and ongoing social and economic changes.

The Northcote-Trevelyan period left a deep impression on the character of public administration in Britain. The report's emphasis on selecting politically neutral civil servants of high intellectual and social caliber, who had studied classics at the traditional universities of Oxford and Cambridge, and its role in creating higher and lower classes of the civil service are felt over 100 years later. But because the reform process is a continuous bolt of cloth, these same emphases were the objects of attack when new political and social pressures arrived on the scene. In large measure, then, the creative act in Great Britain was a political attempt to make responsible a public service that was perceived by political and opinion leaders to be irresponsible.

In the same way, the creation of a civil service system in the United States in 1883 was the product of multiple forces: political and social pressures, ideas, and events external to the immediate reform context. Passage of the Pendleton Act[4] was the result of the application of political skills by intensely committed reformers, participation by a wide variety of interest groups, the death of a President, and attempts by both political parties to exploit the reform issue for partisan advantage.

Reform in 1883 was also woven out of a complex variety of motives and interests. The predominant view among students of American administrative history is that reforms, motivated by moral outrage, were intent on purifying political life and public administration. Reformers, in the words of Carl Schurz, were attempting "to restore ability, high character, and true public spirit once more to their legitimate spheres in our public life, and to make active politics once more attractive to men of self-respect and high patriotic aspirations."[5] At the same time, Martin Schiesl persuasively argues that reformers were motivated by a commitment to administrative efficiency.[6] Frank Stewart concludes that it was those reformers who entered the reform movement later, as it began to be drained of its leadership in the 1890s and early 1900s, who were "inclined to stress reform as an instrument to improve the efficiency of the administration as well as a moral force for the purification of politics."[7]

Yet the reformers were political men motivated by more than a moral crusade. For example, it is probably correct that Thomas A. Jenckes, a leading reform advocate and political foe of President Johnson, first introduced his civil service reform bill in 1865 in an attempt to weaken the powers of the President. Furthermore, Ari Hoogenboom's class interpretation lays less stress on the reformers' moral motivation and more on the view that the movement "had resulted primarily from the loss of political power" by the establishment WASPs.[8] Whether the primary motive was morality, efficiency, or power, the reform movement was not intended simply to make technical improvements, "rather it sought fundamental political change."[9]

Congressional motives were perhaps as complex. A few Congressmen were undoubtedly concerned with the moral argument, a few were seeking revenge or redress at being overlooked in the scramble for patronage. Many, maybe most, were troubled by their perceptions of the imminent 1884 election and responded to their political instincts. President Arthur's support for reform apparently proceeded from this source as well as a desire to rid himself of the nightmare of dividing the spoils, rather than from an interest in strengthening presidential leadership. It is clear that the Congress neither expected

nor wanted power to accrue to the President. Although department
heads and appointing officers lost their discretionary appointment
power, indications are that many were willing to give it up in return
for more competent employees. E. L. Godkin, a leader in the civil
service reform movement, notes that reform was not "the result of
clear national policy." [10] It was, one might add, the result of the
coalescing of a number of external pressures, personal and political
motives, and administrative needs into a compromise that momen-
tarily served a variety of purposes.

Passage and implementation of the Pendleton Act planted the seed
for future political concerns. While most observers agree that the
introduction of competitive exams led to a different type of individual
entering the service, there is disagreement over the nature of the
new civil service. Leonard White, for example, argues that the examinations helped replace political and personal favorites with citizens capable of demonstrating their fitness and ability for office—a
thoroughly democratic principle.[11] Carl Russell Fish contends that
examinations resulted in replacing opportunities for "clever, sometimes brilliant, men" with a service that attracted "the steady-going
and unimaginative." [12] Hoogenboom stresses the view that competitive exams resulted in the recruitment of persons of a higher social
status and were thus, by implication, less democratic.[13] Conversely,
Van Riper claims that the reform, given the political and social
conditions of the late nineteenth century, made the service *more*
representative.[14] Whether more or less representative or more or less
democratic, the representative nature of the public service was changed
in a way that left it open to future political questioning.

The character of the civil service was affected in other ways. For
one, more businessmen were brought into the government. Second,
business methods and the new disciplines of economics and statistics
were introduced to government activities. Third, with the prohibition
of assessments, politicians turned for financial support to businessmen
who, in turn, gained political power.[15] And fourth, civil service
protection was pushed to higher and higher levels in the bureaucracy.
Thus, while the civil service perhaps became more efficient, the seeds
were sown for later reformers to ask whether it had grown politically
unresponsive.

REFORM DYNAMICS IN POSTWAR AMERICA

After its creation, the U.S. civil service developed through a series
of incremental victories and defeats. By the end of World War II,
the Civil Service Commission largely had met its basic goals—
selection by examination, tenure for good behavior, and political

neutrality. It had closed the front door to the service; in its enthusiasm to protect personnel from political pressure and provide security, it had also closed the back door. In the late 1950s, Van Riper argued that the civil service system had become overburdened with "red tape, greater procedural controls, more restrictive dismissal procedures, and more and more review and appeals boards—all in the name of justice, security, and fair play for civil employees." [16] This emphasis on "neutral protectionism" and "legalistic complexity" was invigorated following Watergate revelations of raids on the merit system.[17]

Coupled with this trend of increased employee protection—indeed, a reaction to it—has been an increasing politicization of the civil service. Administrations arrive believing that bureaucratic power constitutes a threat to their political goals. The number of political executives is increased, career executives are screened for their loyalty, and "dissenters" are banished. Then, almost simultaneously, efforts to protect career officials from political influence and merit abuse are initiated, which encourage further politicization. It is no wonder that the problem of accommodating both continuity and change has proven to be tenacious.

Events surrounding the creation and work of the Second Hoover Commission (1953–5) illustrate this political dynamic of civil service reform. The Second Hoover Commission was in large part the attempt by a new Republican Administration and Congress to make a bureaucracy that was perceived to be hostile to conservative values and interests more representative of, and responsive to, those values and interests. Diagnosing that the source of the bureaucracy's irresponsibility was the presence of career officials (who, moreover, were Democrats) functioning as policy makers, the Hoover Commission prescribed sharpening the separation between career and noncareer administrators and neutralizing the political and emotional attachments of the permanent bureaucrats in a Senior Civil Service. The Commission believed this remedy would result in an increased number of political appointees with more conservative and business orientations. Unfortunately for supporters of the second Hoover Report,[18] the political environment was no longer fertile ground for reform when the commission reported in 1955.

When Jimmy Carter launched his White House career, he, no less than his predecessors, was concerned about getting control of a powerful federal bureaucracy. He had campaigned on the promise to clean up the "horrible bureaucratic mess in Washington" and to institute "tight, businesslike management and planning techniques" in government.[19] These promises touched a tender spot with a voting public that has indicated through opinion polls since the mid-1960s a decreasing confidence in public administration. Carter came into office with a high degree of mutual distrust and even hostility marking the relationship between bureaucrats and political appointees. The Civil Service Reform Act of 1978, (CSRA) and the Senior Executive Service (SES) particularly, would provide a mechanism to shake up the policy subsystems and make the bureaucracy more responsive to future presidential initiatives.[20] In addition, it was hoped that reform would create an administrative process more on the model of the private sector as a remedy for what was widely perceived as low government productivity.

Indeed, Carter's stated purposes in pushing civil service reform legislation were to increase governmental efficiency, defined as increasing productivity with less inputs while, simultaneously, increasing the protection of employees against political abuse.[21] Yet the clear emphasis of the Carter Administration was on what Civil Service Commission Chairman Alan Campbell termed the "semi-paralysis in administration," the tangle of rules, regulations, and procedures that "impede the ability of top political appointees to select, motivate and manage their staffs." [22] Thus, the Carter reforms were an attempt to re-open the back door of the civil service.

Support for the CSRA and its SES component came from a variety of sources. Senior career staff and line administrators agreed that their work lives were governed by an overly centralized system bound by self-defeating rules.[23] Many career officials with managerial responsibility agreed that the system weakened their ability to do their work by making it impossible to hold employees accountable and to reward outstanding executives or to penalize poor performance. Career officials in the Civil Service Commission (CSC) had been working since the Nixon years on proposals to create a corps of professional, government-wide managers in the federal service and were ready when Carter's staff made inquiries. Thus, much of the substance in the Carter initiative was a product of the bureaucracy itself.[24]

Key roles, of course, were played by Alan Campbell and Jule Sugarman as Chairman and Vice Chairman of the CSC in skillfully developing the support of career employees, Congress, and interest groups. President Carter was himself heavily and directly involved in the effort to generate support within his Cabinet and the Congress. Final legislative success owed much to a favorable political climate and skilled congressional leadership.[25]

In selling the SES to Congress, senior executives, and the public, the Carter Administration stressed the need for better "management." From the Administration's perspective, efficient and effective management had two faces. It would give political managers the tools to secure and reward greater responsiveness and productivity, defined in terms of administration goals, while, at the same time, giving the individual bureaucrat greater material incentives to strive for professional competence.[26]

Yet by no means did all of these actors share common objectives or expectations. As Sugarman points out, civil service reform in 1978 was "a coming together of a great many forces which had previously operated in ignorance of one another. Suddenly a moment seems to arise when all these forces are united and the momentum exists for real change." [27] But such a consensus regarding civil reform is rarely permanent.

It is now clear that many senior civil servants are skeptical of, if not hostile to, key features of the reform. Many officials believe that the SES offers insufficient incentives to retain competent employees, certainly a response to the congressionally imposed pay cap and reduction of performance awards. At the same time, many top officials appear to feel insulted by the bonus system, believing that it suggests that they were not already working hard enough. Performance appraisal is also a source of intense concern among top career officials. A large number of executives do not see a linkage between performance evaluations and pay, awards, or other personnel actions. Many senior administrators believe that the performance appraisal system, along with the loss of appeals rights for removal from the SES for unsatisfactory performance and provisions for greater management flexibility, have politicized the higher civil service, reducing its value as a source of independent judgment.

The result of what is at best only partial implementation of the Senior Executive Service has been a drop in morale, an increase in the retirement rate of senior executives from government, and the creation of a Senior Executive Association (SEA) to represent the interest of SES members. It appears unlikely that the SES will pass its fifth year review by Congress unscathed.

TURBULENCE AND REFORM IN POSTWAR BRITAIN

In Great Britain, the consensus that had developed around the principles established by the Northcote-Trevelyan Report had begun to crumble before the end of the Second World War. In the first place, the changing nature of public administration brought on by the growth in its size, complexity, and functions raised concerns about the power of the civil service and the adequacy of the traditional concept of ministerial responsibility to maintain a responsible bureaucracy. In addition, postwar economic decline, social pessimism and self-criticism, and educational expansion and democratization, resulted in intense pressure upon the civil service to adopt new structures and processes.[28]

The political dynamics that culminated in the creation of the Fulton Committee were a whirlpool of professional, political, and personal motives and values that resulted in conflicting themes of reform. It is clear that much of the academic and popular literature in calling for less secrecy in decision making, more parliamentary oversight, more specialists, better management, and abolition of the class structure, was stressing the themes of openness and representativeness.[29] But because these themes may be mutually contradictory, those charged with implementing change were sometimes bewildered.

Nor were the signals coming from politicians less confusing. While members of Parliament were, on the one hand, attacking civil servants for their lack of initiative and drive, they were, on the other hand, criticizing them for their lack of responsiveness and establishing more detailed accountability through parliamentary committees. At the same time, civil service staff associations wanted to make it easier for their members to move into administrative jobs or to increase their members' status relative to the Administrative Class, while simultaneously protecting their own members from competition from either outside or inside the civil service.

Higher civil servants, too, had a role in initiating reforms. By the time the Fulton Committee was appointed, several changes had been made in administrative organization and practices in the direction that some critics were urging. Yet it is notable that the values pursued by the civil servants were often different than those pursued by the external critics. Those running the machine were often concerned with internal efficiency and keeping the machine well-oiled while protecting the status and character of the Administrative Class and the basic principles of ministerial responsibility. Many external critics, however, were out to provide Ministers with alternative sources of advice and make the Administrative Class more egalitarian.

In 1964, internal and external pressures for change merged with party politics. The Conservative, Sir Alec Douglas-Home—a product of Eton and Cambridge, a believer in the wisdom of the amateur, and a member of a Scottish family whose title dated back fourteen generations—representing the traditional qualities of birth and character, was being challenged by Wilson and Labour, who represented progress through science and management.[30] The Labour Party brought to the 1964 election a deep suspicion of the civil service, distrusting its power to control information and to set the framework in which policy is made. Likewise, Harold Wilson, a man of humble background and an economist by training, promised to increase the number of scientists and economists in the civil service, increase the number of political appointees in the Prime Minister's office, and introduce more scientific management techniques. When Wilson won the debate on the direction Britain should take, the spirit of reform quickly spread through the Government.

In quick succession, between 1965 and 1969, reports were issued from the Mallaby Committee on staffing local government, the Maud Committee on management of local government, the Seebohm Committee on local authority personal social services, and the Redcliffe-Maud Royal Commission on local government structure. Even the Cabinet was a target for reform as Wilson, in 1968, implemented a reorganization scheme. The creation, in 1966, of the Fulton Committee on the Civil Service was part of this reforming activity.

When the Fulton Committee reported in 1968,[31] it was clear that its findings were not much more than a compilation of the current fashionable criticisms and were little affected by its own research and evidence. It is not unreasonable to suggest that the Committee's effort was a political expedient to help Wilson create a reforming image. Clearly, the Committee Report was a product of a larger political debate.

The fundamental and lasting reforms that the Committee hoped to secure were precluded by the ambiguity of its recommendations. The 158 proposals contained something for everyone, with the result that they were often vague or conflicting. For example, creating a more professional service would increase its power vis-à-vis the politicians and conflict with efforts to achieve more political control. While the Committee expected the higher civil service to remain a career service, it also called for increased late entry and more movement in and out of the service. These conflicting proposals are sufficient to indicate the failure of the Committee to consider its goals thoughtfully and to suggest that the last word on civil service reform had not been pronounced.

Despite the ambiguous nature of the Fulton Report, it has a clear emphasis on managerial-technical approaches to achieving a more efficient, professionally competent administration. The Committee found a civil service that was, in their estimation, amateurish, incompetent, and unprofessional. Attempting to apply new standards of performance to the civil service, the Committee adopted the techniques and language of business and quantitative management. Its recommendations to establish "accountable units" of work, reduce the anonymity of administrators, and recruit more technically trained civil service struck at the center of the traditional notion of ministerial responsibility.[32]

The Wilson Government very quickly accepted three key recommendations of the Committee: the creation of a new Civil Service

Department, the establishment of a Civil Service College, and the abolition of classes within the civil service. The politicians' concern to appear to respond to popular demands for reform had been accomplished. As the pressures of more immediate constituent and policy concerns took over, the detailed implementation of the reforms was left to the civil servants.

Whether one accepts the view that the civil service sabotaged the Fulton reforms,[33] or the pluralist interpretation[34] that union and official self-interest, parliamentary-political disinterest in details, and lack of clear guiding principles resulted in only partial implementation, it is true that changes were incremental. For example, steps taken to reform the class structure fell short of the Fulton recommendation to establish a unified grading structure from top to bottom. Because of the incremental nature of the implemented reforms and because reform was part of a larger political context, it is not surprising that a new wave of criticism of the civil service soon began to swell.

The tone and nature of the criticisms, beginning shortly after Fulton reported and continuing into the 1980s, fills one with a sense of déjà vu. In late 1973, a Fabian tract appeared calling for the next step in administrative reform,[35] and through the late 1970s and early 1980s editorial comment, letters to the editors, popular periodicals, and academics began to debate civil service issues.[36] By 1976, Parliament had taken enough notice of the criticisms of the civil service for the House of Commons Expenditure Committee to conduct a review of matters affecting the efficiency and effectiveness of the service.[37] While the external critics are building pressure for new reform, internal critics, ingredients that have proved necessary in the past, are also stimulating change. Civil service unions and higher officials continue to press for changes that will benefit their members and facilitate administrative flexibility and continuity. In part responding to this pressure and in part pursuing her own quest to bring the bureaucracy under greater control, Prime Minister Thatcher abolished the rather short-lived Civil Service Department, in November of 1981. It was merged back into the Treasury Department from whence it had come before the Fulton reforms. What of the future? Perhaps with the proper political push, such as a return of a Labour Government in the mid-1980s, Britain will see the creation of a new committee charged with restoring responsible administration.

LESSONS OF ADMINISTRATIVE REFORM

Although important differences may be noted between British and American reform proposals, the similarities of the reform processes are more striking. Each of the reform efforts noted here has received its impetus from mounting social and intellectual pressures. Changes in administrative structure and practices have been made to make administration compatible with newly predominant social values. Indeed, Dwight Waldo persuasively argues that "administrative devices *are* relative to the economic and social composition and ideological complexion of the societies in which they exist." [38] And the British student of public administration, C. H. Sisson, agrees that administrative techniques and procedures "are essentially not solutions to administrative problems—if indeed such things as purely administrative problems may be said to exist at all—but responses, more or less slow, coming from sources more or less deep in the histories of the countries concerned, to particular political problems of a more or less enduring sort." [39] Thus, although it is true that, in the environment of politics, ideas and analysis are often subordinated to bargained agreement among interest groups, ideas do have consequences.

For example, after World War II, British society was deeply influenced by egalitarian values and a growing belief in science, technology, and management science. Responsive to this new climate, the Fulton Committee applied new standards to the selection, training, and organization of senior civil servants. It recommended the elimination of the Administrative Class in favor of a more open Administrative Group. In the selection and training of top administrators, the Committee believed that more emphasis should be given to relevant subjects such as economics, social science, and management.

In the 19th century in Britain, the rise of a new middle class to positions of social and political predominance led to pressures for a more representative bureaucracy.[40] Similarly, the emergence of a strong labor movement in the postwar years led to demands for a more representative higher civil service. The effort to replace generalists/amateurs with specialists/managers, and Oxbridge educated elites with middle- and working-class graduates of the London School of Economics and red brick universities, was evidence of widespread perceptions of the Administrative Class as unrepresentative of the outlook of the middle class and their political leadership.

In the United States, the postwar years, with the exception of the 1960s, have been characterized by widespread demands for reduced governmental spending and activity and by a pervasive belief that business principles and management techniques are key remedies for problems in government. The ideologically conservative Second Hoover Commission responded to these trends by proposing drastic overall reductions in governmental functions and a corps of career senior civil servants distinctly separated from political executives. This Commission had less a concern for social class representativeness than for the increased representation of conservative business values in the higher civil service.

The 1970s saw the re-emergence of deep distrust in government and the growth of social attitudes that disparage public service and worship the marketplace. In this environment a Senior Executive Service was created to change administrative behavior by stressing monetary incentives and security disincentives and to make the civil service more representative of the managerial attitudes of the Carter Administration. Reformers held up the civil service to a yardstick metered by business performance standards and managerial techniques and found it wanting. Thus, both the Fulton and Carter reforms have emphasized the need for making the higher civil service more representative of the values of the reform leaders and the need for responsiveness to political leadership. Both reforms have stressed managerial competence and market incentives.

Institutional reform of public bureaucracy, therefore, is a response to changing political values and goals. It should be added, however, that to view reform as the well-coordinated pursuit of agreed-on goals would be too simplistic. Civil service reform "is not necessarily a developmental one towards a clearly defined goal known in advance, but a complex matter of acceding to pressures, communicating and discussing ideas, stimulating comments from groups with potential interests, and making judgments within the administrative system about tactics and timing for the introduction of particular changes." [41] Reform, then, is a complex web of *reactions* to changing political values and external events, *responses* to political pressures from groups outside and inside bureaucracy, and *initiatives* by interested groups.

In both the U.S. and Britain, for example, economic pressures have stimulated efforts to reform the civil service. War, scandal, and growth of government are examples of other external factors that have precipitated political demands for administrative change. The reform periods surveyed here also illustrate the pluralist nature of civil service reform. Reform proposals have emerged from the interaction of reform leaders, senior civil servants, interest groups, political parties, legislators, and chief executives. Reform has been the pursuit of many political interests and values. Where consensus fails, proposals for reform are laid on the shelf. Where a favorable consensus is reached, at least some of the proposals are accepted. Disputants then go home, only to return to debate another day.

Thus, finally, British and American reform efforts do suggest that civil service reform is a continuous bolt of cloth. For if history teaches any lessons, it is that, in democratic polities, civil service structures and practices sooner or later will be made to conform to the values of a changing society and the outlook and interests of new leaders.

NOTES

1. Great Britain, *Report on the Organization of the Permanent Civil Service,* c. 1713 (1854).
2. For discussions of the Northcote-Trevelyan Report and its aftermath, see Emmeline W. Cohen, *The Growth of the British Civil Service, 1780–1939* (London: Frank Cass and Co. Ltd., 1965); K. C. Wheare, *The Civil Service in the Constitution* (London: The Athlone Press, 1954); and G. A. Campbell, *The Civil Service in Britain,* 2nd ed. (London: Gerald Duckworth and Co. Ltd., 1965).
3. See Richard A. Chapman and J. R. Greenaway, *The Dynamics of Administrative Reform* (London: Croom Helm Ltd., 1980), ch. 1, for a discussion of the context and tone of the Northcote-Trevelyan Report.
4. 22 *U.S. Statutes,* 403 (1883).
5. Quoted in David Rosenbloom, "Public Personnel Policy in a Political Environment," *Policy Studies Journal* 9 (Winter 1980): 449–50.
6. Martin J. Schiesl, *The Politics of Efficiency* (Berkeley: University of California Press, 1977), passim.
7. Frank Mann Stewart, *The National Civil Service Reform League* (Austin: University of Texas Press, 1929), p. 258.
8. Ari Hoogenboom, *Outlawing the Spoils* (Urbana: University of Illinois Press, 1961), p. 67.
9. Rosenbloom, "Public Personnel Policy," p. 450.
10. Ari Hoogenboom, ed., *Spoilsmen and Reformers* (Chicago: Rand McNally and Company, 1964), p. 50.
11. Leonard D. White, *The Republican Era: 1869–1901* (New York: The MacMillan Company, 1958), pp. 351–2.
12. Carl Russell Fish, *The Civil Service and Patronage* (New York: Longmans, Green, and Co., 1905), p. 233.
13. Ari Hoogenboom, "The Pendleton Act and the Civil Service," *American Historical Review* 64 (1958–9): 312.
14. Paul P. Van Riper, *History of the United States Civil Service* (Evanston, Ill.: Row, Peterson and Company, 1958), pp. 101–111, 538ff.
15. See Hoogenboom, "The Pendleton Act," pp. 316–7, and Matthew Josephson, *The Politicos, 1865–1896* (New York: Harcourt, Brace and Company, 1938), pp. 322–3.
16. Van Riper, *U.S. Civil Service,* p. 529.
17. See Chester A. Newland, "Public Personnel Administration: Legalistic Reform vs. Effectiveness, Efficiency, and Economy," *Public Administration Review* 36, no. 5 (September/October 1976): 529–37.
18. Commission on Organization of the Executive Branch of the Government, *Personnel and Civil Service, A Report to the Congress* (Washington: Government Printing Office, February 1955).

19. Eliot Marshall, "The Efficiency Expert," *The New Republic* 175, nos. 8, 9 (August 21, 28, 1976): 15.

20. U.S., Congress, House, Committee on Post Office and Civil Service, Public Law 95–454, *An Act to Reform the Civil Service Laws*, Committee Print No. 96–1, 96th Cong., 1st sess., 1979. Title IV contains the Senior Executive Service provisions.

21. Alan K. Campbell, "Civil Service Reform as a Remedy for Bureaucratic Ills," in *Making Bureaucracies Work*, ed. Carol H. Weiss and Allen H. Barton (Beverly Hills, CA: Sage Publications, 1979), p. 157; and Jimmy Carter, "Federal Civil Service Reform," Message to Congress, *Weekly Compilation of Presidential Documents* vol. 14, No. 9 (March 2, 1978), p. 444.

22. Alan K. Campbell, "Civil Service Reform: A New Commitment," *Public Administration Review* 38, no. 2 (March/April 1978): 101.

23. See Herbert Kaufman, "The Growth of the Federal Personnel System," in *The Federal Government Service*, 2nd ed., ed. Wallace Sayre (Englewood Cliffs, N.J.: Prentice-Hall, Inc., 1965), pp. 58–59.

24. For early thinking of the CSC staff, see Personnel Management Project, Task Force on Executive Personnel, "Initial Option Paper," July 27, 1977, and Personnel Management Project, *Final Report*, Vol. 2, Appendix 2, "Task Force Report on Senior Executive Service," December 1977.

25. Felix A. Nigro, "The Politics of Civil Service Reform," *Southern Review of Public Administration* 3, no. 2 (September 1979) examines the political dynamics of the bill's passage.

26. For further development of this point see, Frederick C. Thayer, "The President's Management 'Reforms': Theory X Triumphant," (chapter 2, above); and Warren Lasko, "Executive Accountability: Will SES Make a Difference? " *The Bureaucrat* 9, no. 3 (Fall 1980).

27. Jule Sugarman, "What the Administration Wanted," *The Bureaucrat* 7, no. 2 (Summer 1978): 8.

28. For a more detailed discussion see V. Subramanian, "The Fulton Report: A Sociological Background Analysis," *Administration* 18 (Summer 1970); and Anthony Sampson, *Anatomy of Britain* (London: Hodder and Stoughton Ltd., 1962), especially pp. 637–8.

29. For examples of this literature see Hugh Thomas, ed., *The Establishment* (London: Anthony Blond Ltd., 1959); Brian Chapman, *British Government Observed* (George Allen and Unwin Ltd., 1963); Peter Shore, *Entitled to Know* (London: Macgibbon and Kee Ltd., 1966) and Michael Shanks, *The Stagnant Society* (Harmondsworth, England: Penguin, 1964).

30. See Robert Presthus, "Decline of the Generalist Myth," *Public Administration Review* 24 (December 1964): 211–6.

31. Great Britain, Committee on the Civil Service, *The Civil Service* Cmnd. 3638, Vols. 1–5 (June 1968).

32. For a discussion of this view, see "Editorial: Reforming the Bureaucracy," *Public Administration* 46 (Winter 1968): 374; and Lord Plowden and Sir Robert Hall, "The Supremacy of Politics," *The Political Quarterly* 39 (October/December 1968): 368.

33. See Peter Kellner and Lord Crowther-Hunt, *The Civil Servants* (London: Macdonald General Books, 1980) for this position.

34. See Chapman and Greenaway, *Dynamics of Administrative Reform*, chs. 3, 4, for a pluralist view.

35. John Garrett and Robert Sheldon, *Administrative Reform: The Next Step*, Fabian Tract 428 (London: Fabian Society, 1973).

36. For example, David Lipsey, "Who's in Charge in Whitehall? " *New Society* 52 (April 24, 1980): 155–7; G. Cunningham, "Myths and Mandarins," *New Statesman* 94 (September 23, 1977): 387–8; and Michael Meacher, "Men who Block the Corridors of Power," *The Guardian* (June 14, 1979): 16.

37. Great Britain, Eleventh Report from the Expenditure Committee, *The Civil Service*, Vols. 1–3, 1977.

38. Dwight Waldo, "Development of Theory of Democratic Administration," *American Political Science Review* 46 (March 1952): 91.

39. C. H. Sisson, *The Spirit of British Administration* (London: Faber and Faber Ltd., 1959), p. 117.

40. See Donald J. Kingsley, *Representative Bureaucracy* (Yellow Springs, Ohio: Antioch Press, 1944) for the presentation of this argument.

41. Chapman and Greenaway, *The Dymanics of Administrative Reform*, p. 183.

Chapter Eleven

Civil Service Reform in the Context of Presidential Transitions

GREGORY H. GAERTNER AND KAREN N. GAERTNER

INTRODUCTION

The period following the presidential election of November 1980 was one of re-evaluation for many agencies of government. A period of uncertainty, followed by new emphases and priorities for many agencies, new ways of doing business, and reduced resources with which business could be done have all to varying degrees left their marks on government agencies.

The Civil Service Reform Act of 1978 (CSRA), has, to this point, played a relatively minor direct role in these changes. As we will show in this chapter, however, the implementation of the Reform Act has been affected, in some ways dramatically, by the reformulation of the appropriate role of the federal government that accompanied the 1980 election, and by the context of federal agencies coping with this reformulation. In this chapter we present case studies of two federal agencies in the period between late 1980 and early 1982 as they struggle with the joint tasks of implementation of civil service reform and presidential transition.

Presidential transitions create two dilemmas in government agencies. The first is that centralization, formalization, timidity, and decreased communication are frequently observed during episodes of stressful change in organizations; these responses, however, are easily

The research reported here was supported by the U.S. Office of Personnel Management (Contract #OPM–23–80). More complete discussions of the research carried out under this contract are available in our annual reports. *Organizational Assessments of Civil Service Reform*, 1980, 1981, and 1982.

misperceived as resistance to change by new agency leadership, which is likely to respond with increasing efforts at control, thus further increasing dysfunctional organizational reactions. Second, in the context of stressful change, issues that formerly were dealt with easily in the organization become difficult to handle in the atmosphere of formalization, centralization, and distrust that the change and reactions to it foster. Thus, the organization is faced with more problems, but a decreased capacity to handle them.

We will argue that civil service reform was caught squarely in these two paradoxes of stressful change. The experiences of two federal agencies in dealing with the dual issues of transition and civil service reform will be analyzed at the policy and operational levels. We will begin by proposing a theory of transition reactions at the agency level in terms of the two dilemmas described above. We then give a brief description of the agencies and their respective pretransition approaches to implementing civil service reform. We then describe how, at the level of policy, the new leaderships interpreted and altered these pre-transition stances. Finally, we describe the reactions of operational level personnel to the transition: in one agency, because change was traumatic, much of the agency's initial push for civil service reform has been blunted. In the other agency, where change was less stressful, reform efforts seem actually to have been aided by the transition, after a period of initial confusion and uncertainty. Thus, in the short term, transition seemed to upset the continuity and focus of reform. In the longer term, the effects of transition depended on how reactions to transition in terms of the two paradoxes were managed.

A Theory of the Effects of Transition

We have argued elsewhere (Gaertner, Gaertner, and Devine 1983) that transition presents a contradiction between organizational and democratic theory. Organizations are ill equipped to deal constructively with the jarring discontinuities of drastic changes in leadership and priorities occasioned by political transition.

Contradictions between democratic and organizational theory arise in two different contexts. The first can be called the dilemma of responsiveness versus rigidity. Democratic theory generally supposes that the ability of a new President to enact the policy preferences expressed by the electorate is not severely limited by inflexibility of executive branch agencies. Organizational theory, however, points out the rather stringent limits on the malleability and speed of organizations in coping with change.

In part, some of the difficulty of organizational change is caused by organizational reactions to the change stimulus. Increases in rigidity of structure, task orientation, coordination, and control are observed in organizations undergoing stressful change (Hall and Mansfield 1971; Fleishman, Harris, and Burtt 1955; Meridith 1966). Centralization of authority (Hermann 1963) and formalization of standards and procedures (Staw, Sankelands, and Dutton 1981) have likewise been noted as characteristic organizational responses to change. Ironically, most of these features make the organization less able to deal with the turbulence or uncertainty (Lawrence and Lorsch 1967). As communication channels break down, especially between the top of the organization and its operational levels, hierarchic channels of information and direction lose their capacity to inform and direct (Hermann 1963). Turnover, absenteeism, timidity, and outright resistance make the organization seem increasingly unreliable to those who are supposed to control and direct it, leading to increased effort at control, which can, in turn, increase rigidity and unresponsiveness.

The second dilemma is both more subtle and more familiar—the contradiction between continuity and change. The classic studies of transition by Henry (1960) and Heclo (1977) have noted the programmatic discontinuities associated mainly with party turnover transitions. Internal to the agency, this contradiction seems to have a slightly different form. While democratic theory posits that responses to the new electoral mandate should supercede the ongoing commitments of executive branch agencies (save those rooted in law), many organization theorists have pointed out that it is precisely by establishing ongoing commitments externally and internally that organizations maintain a legitimate domain of activity and reasonable understandings for getting work done. As these are disturbed by the events of transition, routine problems become aggravated. Externally this may mean that previously friendly relations with congressional members or committees, or other agencies, or private groups, revert to arm's length as new leadership reassesses its choices of allies and adversaries. Internally, this can mean that previously agreed-upon programmatic or administrative mechanisms become doubtful guides to action as the new leadership establishes new mechanisms or reaffirms old ones. The shifting fates of various budget and management control systems in government (the Planning-Programming-Budgeting System [PPBS], Management by Objectives [MBO], zero-based budgeting) provide a case in point. As a result, previously routine problems become more difficult to resolve when both the ends and the means of policy implementation and administration are called into question.

Further, the two dilemmas interact in important ways. As distrust and fear increase, previously established work relations within the organization become problematic. Agency effectiveness in either retaining old directions or establishing new ones is decreased, and work relations that might support a more productive atmosphere in the agency are inhibited. The self-oriented actions of individuals within organizations in crisis do little to foster supportive or even adversarial relations with new leadership—instead, the tendency might be toward individual self-protection and decreased organizational commitment.

At the agency level, the two dilemmas can mean increasing numbers of problems to solve at the same time that there is decreased capacity to solve them. Obviously, both of these contradictions gain force and focus depending on how the new mandate is interpreted, and how the reactions to transition are managed

In a basic sense, these contradictions suggest that the conditions for an effective democratic regime that responds quickly to shifting electoral mandates are not the conditions that support effective operation of the large organizations designed to implement that mandate. To be sure, the contradiction is most forceful when the transition represents an extreme departure from established ways of doing business in agencies. The data reviewed below suggest that, at least in one of the agencies under study, the 1980 elections presented just such a departure.

For the remainder of this chapter we will show that, in the agencies we studied, the Civil Service Reform Act provides a stark example of an ongoing, but not well-established, policy caught in the tug of these two dilemmas. Before doing so, however, we should describe these agencies in greater detail.

DATA AND METHODS

Our discussion is based on data collected as part of a five-year study of the effects of civil service reform, conducted for the Office of Personnel Management (OPM). Two federal agencies, the Environmental Protection Agency (EPA) and the Mine Safety and Health Administration (MSHA), volunteered sites for the study. In EPA, the agency's headquarters and a large regional installation were selected; the MSHA sites include the agency's headquarters and two regional installations.

In many respects MSHA and EPA are similar. Both are regulatory agencies of the executive branch having missions that include the regulation of the behavior of firms in the private sector. Moreover, both are governed by specific enabling legislation, frequently mandating certain regulatory activities to be accomplished by certain dates. Both agencies have been supported and criticized not only for their firm adherence to these activities and deadlines, but also for deviations from their legislative mandates.

Yet the two agencies are also rather different. MSHA is far older and is currently a bureau within the Department of Labor, while EPA is an independent agency of relatively recent origin. Moreover, MSHA is far smaller in budget and personnel, and the agency's activities are more local in their effects. Consequently, EPA has had more public attention generally, especially during electoral campaigns. Because of these differences, detailed comparison of the two agencies' experiences is perilous. In the analysis to follow, it seems preferable to treat them as separate cases, illustrative of the variety of responses to organizational change during a presidential transition.

The main data sources include questionnaires administered at the sites in 1980, 1981, and 1982, interviews conducted with a variety of site personnel during these years, and examination of published and archival documents.

For EPA's regional office and our three MSHA sites, we collected questionnaire data in the late summer of 1980, and again in March of 1982. Thus, our first fieldings are clearly pretransition while our second fieldings occurred in the midst of transition-related events. These fieldings represent total enumerations of permanent, general schedule employees, full-time or part-time, at the sites, with response rates of well over 80 percent at each site.

We collected two waves of questionnaire data at EPA headquarters—once in May 1981, and a second time in April 1982. Thus, both waves are in the midst of the transition, although undergoing different phases of the unfolding events. Response rates at EPA's headquarters are about 60 percent in the two fieldings.

Our second major data source is the set of interviews we have conducted with unit managers, Senior Executive Service (SES) incumbents, and key resource people throughout the course of the study. These interviews (about 300) have been spaced relatively evenly through the study period, beginning in April 1980 and running through August 1982.

The third major data source is the documents we have collected from the press and from internal intra-agency and interagency communications.

PRETRANSITION AGENCY VIEWS ON CIVIL SERVICE REFORM

At the level of policy, the intentions and hopes of the outgoing leadership in the two agencies provide a useful baseline from which to begin our analysis.

In EPA, one explicit aim of the implementation planners was to produce a system that might serve any new set of managers, regardless of partisan affiliation or management style. EPA's chief administrative officer, in an interview in August 1980, said, "We need to create a system which services new managers immediately, or they will simply throw it out. Whether [the system] can do this will be its litmus test." By January 1981, the most important architects of the performance appraisal system had left the agency, and the system would face its litmus test, perhaps sooner than its planners would have preferred.

Part of the planners' dismay could be traced to the short time that the system was in operation before facing this major test. They were painfully aware of the new attitudes required on the part of both supervisors and subordinates to make the system operate in its intended fashion. This system required supervisors to sit down with their subordinates and agree on goals and measures of their attainment and, in the process, unearth and resolve differences between them on these goals and measures. This was also a system in which performance standards would provide, in concert with the zero-based budget review and the internal review and concurrence procedures, the primary ways of agreeing upon and tracking agency and individual goals and their accomplishment. Finally, performance appraisal was to be an occasion for managers at all levels to select and reward their high performers, to send unmistakable signals to poorer performers, and to halt the drain of good young managers to the private sector.

The Department of Labor's approach to reform was broadly similar. The Department's guiding philosophy was to use the performance standards and appraisal functions as means to integrate their Management-by-Objectives and budget processes. The vision at the policy level in the Department was broad and integrative, viewing CSRA not as a mandated personnel system, but rather as a management tool of considerable scope and prominence.

MSHA, although a bureau in the Department of Labor, did not entirely accept this view of the reforms, at least at first. It should be noted here that MSHA, having moved from the Department of the Interior into Labor shortly before the passage of the Reform Act, was in a state of double transition.

The leaders of MSHA at this time were long-time federal employees. According to several people who were involved, the motivation of MSHA's top management was to implement the law, but not to disrupt MSHA any more than necessary, given that the agency had already gone through such a large change from the Department of the Interior to the Department of Labor. In one person's words,

"Without undermining the law, we wanted to make this as easy as possible." Management's first priority was to let the agency do its work. As a result, while they were in favor of the Act, they did not see the need to reinterpret the Department's system in any substantial way to address pressing agency problems, nor did they generate much internal enthusiasm for the Act.

As we will explore below, this minimal disruption strategy of implementation ironically sowed the seeds for a climate supportive of reform at the policy level after transition.

In summary, Reform Act implementation planners at EPA and the Department of Labor had interpreted the performance contracting and appraisal elements of the Reform Act as central integrative mechanisms that would provide focus and opportunities for key managerial processes. These goals for the system would not be attained overnight, or even in the first cycle of the system's operation. The inculcation of supportive attitudes would require careful nurturance and consistent guidance, reinforcement, and correction, probably over several runs of the system. Most planners felt that the presidential transition, occurring before even one full performance appraisal cycle had been completed, would likely disrupt this careful cultivation process.

REFORM IN TRANSITION: POLICY

The Reform Act was uniquely vulnerable during the transition, particularly in its performance appraisal, merit pay, and SES provisions. These provisions labored under two somewhat contradictory disadvantages. First, the reforms were not a new initiative, nor did they figure prominently in the electoral campaigns. Thus, in a sense, they were old news. Second, the reforms were not yet institutionalized in government. We can elaborate on each of these weaknesses in turn, concentrating on the policy level for the moment.

Many of the provisions of the Act had not yet been implemented as of November 1980—the first payouts under Merit Pay would not be conducted government-wide until November 1981. This notwithstanding, the Act was no longer a novel experiment in the management of the federal sector—it was, now, simply the law. As one EPA official put it: "People around here don't talk about the Reform Act anymore. Reforms are now the old system, and if you ask about civil service reform, people won't know what you're talking about." Another official who had served under the previous administration noted: "It will probably be several months before the new people know what the Civil Service Reform Act is." These comments do not reflect an indifference to CSRA or to the law in principle—rather the agency and its programs, procedures, and people were all equally unknown to the new leadership, CSRA included. A prominent official in the Department of Labor echoed this sentiment: "The Reform Act has lost a lot of momentum." Another noted: "The CSRA is a victim of bad timing—the transition and all makes it difficult to keep up the effort."

To the extent that it was noted at all, civil service reform was slightly suspect. As an initiative of the outgoing administration, the new leadership was unlikely to embrace it enthusiastically. Moreover, the Reform Act as it was being implemented in EPA and the Department of Labor was out of step with the philosophies of the new leadership in both agencies and with the general thrust of personnel management under the Reagan Administration. As one of EPA's new political appointees put it: "I sometimes think that [the outgoing leadership] was more concerned with process than product." The new Administrator felt, in the words of one highly placed official, "that the agency had not been managed at all in the past, and now it would be. Her task was to be 180 degrees opposite of [the outgoing agency leadership]. The agency had, in the past, attempted to set an example in administering the federal government. In this administration, EPA would not be an exemplary agency—it would be a well run agency." In the view of the new leadership, the outgoing group had been strong on innovation and weak on followthrough; their task was to return to bottom-line, "old-fashioned" management, emphasizing centralized planning and direction, accountability, and results less than the management process itself.

In sum, in EPA, the Reform Act was not the new system, but rather the existing one. To the extent that the reforms were seen as new at all, they were seen as an administrative tool of the previous leadership, with whom a decisive break was sought generally. Moreover, their decentralized orientation was in scant accord with the centralized results-oriented style of the new leadership.

While we have far less detailed information regarding the reforms in the Department of Labor, it was clear that they were not to retain a central role in work planning and coordination. In place of an emphasis on management would be an emphasis on the attainment of key policy objectives of the new Secretary.

It is important to note that these stances by the new leadership of EPA and the Department of Labor were consistent with the early signals coming from the Office of Personnel Management. Early statements from the new Director, charting a course toward "bedrock personnel management," gave little encouragement for innovative applications of civil service reform, at least in the eyes of respondents in EPA and the Department of Labor.

In summary, at the policy level, transition changed the thrust of civil service reform from center stage to supporting cast, in EPA and in the Department of Labor, partly because of signals issuing from the Office of Personnel Management. Several features of the Reform Act, however, made the transition to a supporting mechanism difficult.

First and foremost, although by this time the legislation was nearly two years old, the merit pay and performance appraisal provisions had not yet been utilized throughout government; moreover, the SES had yet to face its sternest test, a party turnover transition. Several things followed from this.

First, the system had few viable traditions to support the regulations and laws that bore on it directly. Neither supervisors nor subordinates nor policy makers had experience with it in any detail, and the system had no track record to validate its promise. Further, the system had few viable internal champions—most of the policy-level personnel supporting it in EPA in the early implementation period had been political appointees in the outgoing administration. While a few influential supporters of the original reform implementation remained in the Department of Labor, they read the signals from their leadership and OPM as discouraging innovative applications of reform to managerial practice. Finally, particularly given the constraints of the merit pay implementation of 1981, there was little or no groundswell of support for merit pay or performance appraisal, and much disappointment with the recent history of the SES.

Thus, the transition came at an awkward period for the Reform Act. The new leadership in the agencies saw it as the old system, the law, to be obeyed but requiring no special support and, if anything, some suspicion as a holdover of policies they were determined not to continue. As we explore presently, to career employees it was the new system, and by no means a popular one, auguring more danger than opportunity and, in the context of major change and uncertainty, not particularly deserving of support or attention. We can now turn to a more detailed examination of reactions to transition in the two agencies and how these related to the implementation of civil service reform.

AGENCIES IN TRANSITION

Transition can be said to begin with the presidential election and to end with the installation of the key political appointees making up the new agency leadership. In this respect, transition appears as an event bounded in time and effect. However, if we define the transition's end as the point at which the new leadership has been able to forge a workable external and internal consensus in support of its new priorities and programs, the boundries of transition become far more blurred. In one of the agencies under study, it was not yet complete in early 1983. Moreover, transition can be seen to have been a very different experience in the two agencies. We begin by tracing themes and events associated with transition in the two agencies. We will then review questionnaire and interview evidence bearing on the effects of transition.

Transition in MSHA

The first important characteristic of transition in MSHA was the lack of new political leadership for nearly a year following the election. The reasons for delay are far from clear—there was apparently some difficulty in finding a qualified nominee willing to accept the position of Assistant Secretary. By the summer of 1981, a qualified nominee did emerge, but his confirmation was delayed until late October, coinciding with a second disruptive event for the agency. One of the provisions of the supplemental appropriations enacted by Congress in November 1981 in lieu of an FY 1982 budget removed authorization for the inspection of some noncoal mines from MSHA's mission. This implied that the inspectors responsible for these activities would have to be separated from the agency. An emergency furlough, followed by a furlough under reduction-in-force (RIF) procedures commenced, and, when the March 1982 resolution included the same removal provision, the RIF began in earnest.

Because of the arcane RIF procedures in force in the federal government, although the change in mission involved only 20 percent of MSHA's inspection obligation, virtually all of MSHA's field operations were affected. While 260 employees of MSHA's 3,000 total field employees were eventually separated, one personnel officer in MSHA estimated that three times that many changed jobs as a result of the RIF. By the time the last RIF was begun in April 1982, the Assistant Secretary had also initiated a reorganization. This reorganization, a common practice during a change in leadership, was the third major factor in MSHA's transition.

The reorganization did not involve the separation of any personnel, although closing some small regional offices and physically relocating some affected employees was required. However, the timing of the reorganization coincided with the RIF, creating confusion, misunderstanding, and chaos in some regional offices. The confusion of the RIF and reorganization, although not directly a function of transition, was so great that field employees cannot distinguish among the events, and even those at headquarters refer to the episode as the "RIF-reorganization."

In sum, there were three critical aspects of the transition period at MSHA; the lack of political leadership for nearly a year after the election, the RIF required by the loss of authority to inspect certain mines, and the reorganization, particularly in the field activities.

Transition in EPA

Questionnaire and interview evidence suggests that the change of leadership in EPA has had much more profound effects than in MSHA. Several reasons seem to stand out in the events of the transition period.

First, regulatory reform in general, and EPA in particular, had been focal in the presidential campaign of 1980. To be sure, the general area of regulatory reform had been gaining momentum even prior to 1980 with respect to EPA (Gaertner and Ramnarayan 1983), and there was substantial support within EPA for reform in agency policy. However, the persistence of the issue of regulatory reform in the context of declining support for the consensus favoring environmental regulation made agency personnel wary of the Reagan Administration (see chap. 12).

Second, press reports on the new Administrator of the agency gave the impression that there were more direct threats posed to the jobs of top career managers. Rumors of quotes attributed to the Administrator-designee predicting a massive restaffing of top career posts, of a "hit list" of SES incumbents closely associated with previous Administrators, and of close ties between the Administrator-designee and powerful business-oriented forces in the new Administration all made agency employees uneasy.

The confirmation of the new Administrator might have been expected to, and in some areas did, dispel much of this uncertainty as new directions could be charted. The outlines of the new leadership's priorities began to take shape: protection of the environment coupled with regulatory reform, increased efficiency, delegation to the states, and a less adversarial stance for the agency (according to the Administrator's speech to agency employees in May 1981). The atmosphere of distrust and uncertainty changed only little overall, however, and the reasons for this constitute some of the other signal characteristics of the transition in EPA.

While many of the key political positions were filled quickly, several were not. Further, two key appointees resigned. The earliest political appointee to resign was rumored to have left because he relied too heavily on career officials. His resignation fueled the feelings that the new Administrator had no use for career civil servants. Perhaps most important, it gave agency personnel the feeling that transition was not yet over. This feeling was exacerbated by the continuing fights over the FY 1982 and FY 1983 agency budgets, as well as the continuing drumbeat of hostile press and environmentalist comment. The nature of the new order of business was not yet clear to most personnel, and the SES in particular had little sense of their place in the new directions.

This latter ambiguity was heightened by the centralization and decrease in communication that frequently accompanies stressful organizational change. The decline in communication between the political and career staffs left many managers feeling they were in limbo, without direction about programs they were administering. Their ability to work effectively was, they felt, thwarted by the lack of information, coordination, or response from the top.

The plight of the regional office typified the predicament SES managers faced. Our interviews (November 1981) indicate that during this period many regional office managers felt they were working in an informational vacuum. Not only was the region not receiving direction from headquarters, managers were unable to get responses to many of their requests. Not surprisingly, we encountered a tense, guarded, suspicious atmosphere, and rumors about EPA's fate were rampant.

People felt so far removed from organizational decision making that the only alternative seemed to be to guard one's own position. As Schein (1965) suggests, in the absence of an internal climate of support and freedom from threat, external threats undermine good communication, reduce flexibility, and encourage self-protection rather than concern for the organization as a whole. This individual response, of course, only served to aggravate the organizational problem, and it made the SES appear to be intransigent and therefore another obstacle to overcome from the perspective of top management. This self-reinforcing cycle of mutual uncertainty and distrust continued, unabated, until early 1982. Then, between January and June, several events seemed to break this cycle.

First, the Administrator issued a memo in which she stated that there would be no involuntary reductions in personnel in FY 1982, and, she hoped, in FY 1983. Second, and shortly thereafter, several key political appointments were confirmed. Third, well-respected EPA career officials were chosen for sensitive policy posts, signaling some trust in the career bureaucracy.

Finally, it became apparent that there would not be large numbers of geographical SES transfers. One respondent close to the Administrator noted that the new leadership had moved, "perhaps ten or twelve people," and even the most hostile observers could name few more than this. While we have no wish to minimize the hardships to some of these SES incumbents, or to negate the effects of the rumors of forced transfers, the fact remains that the widespread transfers and dismissals of SES personnel envisioned by many did not occur.

This carries the narrative up to the close of our formal data collection efforts in EPA, in June 1982. As the events culminating in the Administrator's resignation in March 1983 suggest, however, transition and redirection in the agency remained problematic well into 1983. While we can draw no definitive connection between the various resignations in the agency and the evidence reviewed here and below, it is apparent that, by March 1983, there was little support for the Administrator either in the agency or elsewhere. We argue below that this lack of support carried over to some of the Reform Act provisions that had been sponsored by the Administrator.

To give some sense of the relative magnitude of reaction in the two agencies, we can present some evidence gathered from questionnaires distributed in the five study sites in the two agencies. Table 11.1 reports the proportions of our total samples of employees, first overall and then by sites, agreeing with each of a set of questions having mainly to do with the effects of changes in leadership and with the cutbacks and budget difficulties of the previous year.

The first three items taken together seem to support the general view that the transition was more difficult in EPA than MSHA. They also suggest that comparisons of regional to headquarters units in the two agencies yield opposite results. In EPA the feelings of lessened personal and mission commitment are more frequent in the regional office than in headquarters; in MSHA, the regional units do not differ much from headquarters personnel in their reactions. We will return to this point.

Since the first two items reported here seem to tap general reactions, at a personal and organizational level, to the change in agency leadership, we have correlated them with the other items reported in this table and the next for the sample as a whole. We feel safe in reporting the overall correlations because, although the levels of agreement with each statement frequently differ by site and agency, the correlations generally do not. For example, the correlations between personal and organizational commitment are just about the same in the five sites, although the proportions agreeing differ significantly across sites and agencies.

The next four items in the table measure various ways in which the changes in agency priorities were expected—or perhaps welcomed—by employees at the sites. While overall, between one-fifth and one-half of the sampled employees are willing to be critical of past agency performance, depending on the measure, this criticism

Table 11.1 Extent of Organizational Change, Spring 1982

	% "Agree" or "Strongly Agree"						Pearson Correlation	
	Overall	EPA Headquarters	EPA Region	MSHA Headquarters	MSHA Region A	MSHA Region B	Expected Efficiency	Personal Commitment
Commitment and Mission Agreement								
1. I am less committed to this agency as a place to work now than I was a year ago.	49.8*	54.1	61.5	39.8	36.9	36.5	-.32	—
2. I believe this agency will become more efficient under the new administration.	12.3	12.8	10.1	18.8	8.9	10.5	—	-.32
3. I am less committed to this agency's new goals than I was to its old goals.	41.2*	48.2	58.5	23.8	25.4	15.1	-.37	.61
Foreshadowing								
4. In the past, regulations put out by this agency have been too complex to enforce efficiently.	31.6*	34.6	35.5	20.5	37.9	18.7	.11	.15
5. Changes in this agency's mission were likely to occur regardless of who was in the White House.	24.3	—	24.0	21.3	29.9	22.0	.29	-.02
6. Resources have been wasted in this agency in the last 4 or 5 years.	45.2*	—	52.2	41.7	37.6	41.6	.12	.22
7. In the past 4 or 5 years this agency has lacked a sense of direction.	21.8	—	17.9	22.6	30.0	18.4	.07	.12
Uncertainty								
8. At this point the effect of budget cuts for FY 82 is unclear.	50.1*	—	26.3	60.1	69.1	69.2	.17	-.08
9. I'm not getting the information I need in order to do my job.	27.9*	31.2	32.7	21.3	23.2	21.5	-.22	.29

Table 11.1. Extent of Organizational Change, Spring 1982

	Overall	EPA Headquarters	EPA Region	MSHA Headquarters	MSHA Region A	MSHA Region B	Pearson Correlation† Expected Efficiency	Personal Commitment
			% "Agree" or "Strongly Agree"					
Awareness								
10. I have not felt any effects of the Presidential transition in my job.	14.8*	15.4	9.3	15.3	17.6	22.3	.39	-.24
11. I am doing pretty much the same work now as I was a year ago.	61.7*	53.6	53.2	58.9	84.0	84.3	.11	-.10
Budget Effects								
12. The uncertainty regarding budget cuts has made it difficult to get down to work.	69.7	71.9	69.0	67.1	66.4	72.6	-.36	.26
13. Index of Resource redirection.‡	52.2*	45.2	72.6	45.3	42.9	33.3	-.28	.24
14. I expect to be RIFed in the next few months.	9.3*	—	4.6	8.8	15.5	16.9	-.09	.10
Other Effects								
15. Some of our best people here left the agency in the last year.	74.6*	78.3	86.7	68.3	62.9	49.4	-.30	.27
16. The new administration does not trust high-level career civil servants in the agency.	68.1*	81.3	76.0	39.6	48.8	40.0	-.36	.28

NOTE: Questions were asked in a Likert-type format using a five-point response scale ranging from (1) strongly disagree to (5) strongly agree.
* Differences between agencies statistically significant, $p \leq .05$ (Chi-Square test, 1 degree of freedom).
† Correlations $\geq .15$ are statistically significant, $p \leq .05$.
‡ Index composed of responses to the following items (coefficient alpha = .78)
Using the scale (1 = funding increase; 2 = no change in funding; 3 = a small decrease; 4 = moderate decrease; 5 = large decrease) what do you think will happen to the funding for each of the following items: (1) contract and consultant funds for my unit; (2) support facilities such as duplicating and typewriters at this installation; (3) clerical and other support services at this installation; (4) training and development funds in the agency; (5) travel funds in the agency.

is not closely associated with the recent lessening of personal commitment nor optimism about the agency's future performance. In general, those who are critical of the agency's past performance are as likely as those defending its recent actions to feel personally disillusioned and to feel pessimistic about increases in efficiency. In two of the four items, however, EPA's employees were more likely than MSHA's to be critical of past agency performance, regulatory complexity, and waste, suggesting support among some of EPA's employees for the reorientations of the new Administration.

In the chronology of EPA's transition, it appeared that one of the first reactions to change in leadership was uncertainty. Items 8 and 9 presented in the table suggest that, as of 1982, uncertainty was still widespread, particularly in EPA.

We also argued in previous sections that the impact of the presidential transition was likely to be greater at EPA than MSHA because of the magnitude of the proposed changes and the public awareness of, and interest in, these changes. The next two items in table 11.1 support this contention. EPA employees are less likely to agree that they have been unaffected by the transition (items 10 and 11) than MSHA employees.

One of the key issues throughout the transition has been budgetary change sought by the new Administration. The next three items address this, and we note that MSHA employees indicate more problems with uncertainty (item 12) and RIF potential (item 14) than EPA's employees. These concerns about budget cuts were not only widespread, but damaging to expectations and personal commitment as well (correlations of $-.28$ and $.24$, respectively).

Loss of good people and feelings of distrust by the new Administration in top-level career employees seem nearly as damaging to personal commitment and expectations of greater efficiency as the uncertainty and fears of resource losses (items 15 and 16). Moreover, particularly in EPA, they are more widespread. More than 80 percent of EPA employees, and more than 60 percent in MSHA, think that some of their best people have left the agency in the last year. Nearly 80 percent of EPA employees, compared with 40 percent in MSHA, agree that, "the new administration does not trust high-level career civil servants in the agency."

Another way to understand the changes in these agencies is to compare the responses to some questions asked in 1980 to the corresponding responses in 1982. These data are presented in table 11.2. While the attribution of change in an item to the change in leadership is perilous, our confidence in the interpretation is increased if the variable is closely correlated with one of our two summary measures, efficiency improvement or personal commitment.

Table 11.2. Changes in Selected Variables Over Time

		% "Agree" and "Strongly Agree" (except as noted)						Pearson Correlations‡	
	Year†	Overall	EPA Headquarters	EPA Region	MSHA Headquarters	MSHA Region A	MSHA Region B	Efficiency Expectation	Personal Commitment
Performance									
1. Overall this agency is effective in accomplishing its objectives.	82	44.8*	22.2	33.8	69.6	73.0	73.3	.29	-.41
	80	58.8*	38.1	52.3	77.3	79.0	71.0		
2. The goals of my work unit are almost always met.	82	83.8*	79.1	80.7	91.2	91.4	85.3	.05	-.18
	80	80.5*	77.6	77.4	86.2	85.4	78.4		
Communications and Participation									
3. I can communicate well with my supervisor.	82	73.5	74.8	70.4	75.4	76.4	70.1	.03	-.19
	80	78.7	81.7	76.5	82.5	77.7	70.4		
4. I am able to communicate well with others in my work unit.	82	94.0	95.0	94.8	92.2	92.4	93.5	-.01	-.03
	80	93.4	93.6	93.9	93.1	93.0	92.2		
5. Scale on relationship with supervisor.**	82	32.4*	32.3	26.6	38.2	38.0	30.4	.11	-.29
	80	39.1*	32.6	36.1	50.5	47.7	30.0		
6. I trust my supervisor to keep my interests in mind when she/he makes decisions.	82	53.3*	50.3	51.1	56.3	58.9	57.1	.08	-.25
	80	57.8*	52.0	56.3	66.5	62.7	55.4		
7. When decisions affecting me are made in this agency, I am given the chance to express my ideas.	82	34.2*	25.8	33.3	46.8	38.2	41.0	.25	-.30
	80	44.1*	34.0	44.6	58.3	43.0	55.0		
Satisfaction (% "A little" or "very" satisfied)									
8. (with) Job overall.	82	61.4*	55.8	57.4	65.2	74.4	68.6	.14	-.40
	80	68.3*	61.6	65.6	71.6	75.7	78.0		
9. (with) Job security.	82	34.2	39.5	30.1	36.3	30.1	28.0	.25	-.21
	80	63.5*	54.5	76.5	76.5	67.4	77.3		

10. (with) Feeling of accomplishment from job.	82	55.6*	49.1	45.8	65.0	68.6	71.0	.21	-.41
	80	64.2*	56.4	60.2	70.0	75.3	68.1		
11. Quality of working life scale.††	82	37.3*	33.9	31.7	43.2	46.0	42.6	.16	-.35
	80	47.5*	38.3	43.2	59.2	55.1	55.5		
Attitudes Toward Hierarchy									
12. A good management system is one that makes the agency responsive to the current Administration's priorities.	82	51.9*	49.6	48.9	54.7	65.7	44.9	.29	-.16
	80	61.0*	56.5	57.9	80.7	64.3	76.5		
13. People in this agency are sometimes penalized because of their personal political views.	82	33.7*	57.0	31.0	12.8	17.4	6.8	-.28	.27
	80	14.1*	26.4	12.2	5.5	8.8	6.7		

NOTE: Questions were asked in a Likert-type format using a five-point response scale ranging from (1) strongly disagree to (5) strongly agree.

* Differences between agencies statistically significant, $p \leq .05$ (Chi-Square test, 1 degree of freedom).

† EPA-headquarters "1980" data are from spring of 1981, not summer of 1980. All 1982 data are from the same time period.

‡ Correlations $\geq .15$ are statistically significant, $p \leq .05$.

** This index is the average of responses to seven variables:

I trust my supervisor to keep my interests in mind when he/she makes decisions.
I respect my supervisor's judgment on most issues.
My supervisor often lets me know how well he/she thinks I am performing my job.
I can communicate well with my supervisor.
My supervisor encourages me to give my best effort.
My supervisor shows me how to improve my performance.
My supervisor lets me know what is expected of me.

Cronbach's alpha for the scale is $\geq .85$ in both years.

Figures shown are percent with mean score ≥ 4.0.

†† This scale is the average of responses to the questions:

When decisions affecting me are made in this agency, I am given the chance to express my ideas.
My job is one where a lot of other people can be affected by how well the work gets done.
My job requires me to do many different things at work using a variety of skills and talents.
My job gives me considerable opportunity for independence and freedom in how I do the work.
All things considered, I am satisfied with my job.

Cronbach's alpha is $\geq .70$ in both years.

Figures shown are percent with mean score ≥ 4.0.

One of the sharpest drops comparing the 1980 and 1982 data is in employee perceptions of overall agency effectiveness. In 1980, nearly 60 percent of employees agreed that overall, "this agency is effective in accomplishing its objectives." This overall figure concealed a significant difference between the agencies—only 45 percent of EPA employees thought the agency effective compared with 77 percent of MSHA employees. These proportions drop precipitously in EPA by 1982, and a little in MSHA. Moreover, the belief that the agency is effective is linked to belief that the agency will become more efficient ($r = .29$) as well as decreased personal commitment to the agency ($r = -.41$). This cynicism does not extend to the work group level where, if anything, respondents see effectiveness to have increased. Feelings of work group effectiveness, moreover, are not closely associated with either summary variable. While EPA's employees are less likely than MSHA employees to see their *work groups* as generally meeting their goals, the difference between the agencies is far less than when *agency* performance is the reference.

While communications with supervisors and with co-workers have not deteriorated sharply (items 3 and 4), there is a small drop in trust of supervisors and the quality of relations with them (items 6 and 5, respectively). Respondents are less inclined to indicate trust in supervisors in 1982 than 1980, but the difference is small (about 5 percent). There is also a small drop in the index of quality of supervisory relations between 1982 and 1980. Both of these variables are associated with the level of personal commitment (r's $= -.29$ and $-.25$).

Level of participation in decision making (item 7) has declined more drastically in both agencies, about equally. Since participation is associated with both personal commitment ($r = -.30$) and efficiency expectations ($r = .25$), we are inclined to attribute this drop to the events surrounding the transition.

From the next set of variables, we see that satisfaction with most aspects of jobs has decreased in both agencies. Overall job satisfaction has decreased in both agencies (about 7 percent). This overall level of satisfaction is rather closely associated with personal commitment to the agency ($r = -.40$).

Satisfaction with accomplishment and job security have declined, the latter substantially, in all the sites. The drop in feelings of accomplishment is steeper in EPA, while the drop in job security is more pronounced in MSHA. This overall drop in satisfaction with job security, from 69 percent to half of that, 34 percent, is mute testament to the changing conditions of federal work. Both it and feelings of accomplishment are associated with expected organizational efficiency and personal commitment. Interestingly, feelings of accomplishment are more closely linked to personal commitment than job security (r = .41 and .21, respectively). This reinforces what we have heard so often in interviews, that the public service ethic is a primary motivator for federal government employment.

The scale devised to measure overall quality of work life (item 11) drops during the period by about 10 percent. The drop is steeper in MSHA, narrowing the difference between the agencies.

Probably as a result of all this, attitudes toward top management have worsened considerably in both agencies, generally more so in EPA (items 12, 13). Employees in both agencies are less inclined to find responsiveness a characteristic of a good management system. Interestingly, the drop is much sharper in MSHA. The likelihood of agreement that "people in this agency are sometimes penalized because of their personal political views" has more than doubled overall in all sites but one. However, this proportion was never large in MSHA and still is not large (overall, in MSHA, 13 percent agree); in EPA the proportion is rather large, 47 percent in 1982.

Several summary impressions emerge from the examination of the two tables. First, nearly all of the predicted reactions to change do emerge. Lessened personal commitment; disruption of established patterns of participation, influence, and communication; perceived centralization of authority in top management; decreases in general and in specific aspects of job satisfaction; and felt decreases in organizational effectiveness are all clearly in evidence. Interestingly, the quality of relations with top management or "the agency" declines far more than those at the work group or supervisor-subordinate levels. This suggests a possible reaction of increased group cohesion in response to the threat of profound change (Homans 1950).

Second, reaction to the transition is rather more extreme in EPA than in MSHA, although the latter is not unaffected. In EPA the largest effects seem associated with reorientation to work and mission. In MSHA the impact has been less at an organizational level and more on the social fabric of the agency.

Third, neither of the agencies would seem to provide fallow ground for the implementation of a major new personnel reform. Employees were generally fearful for their jobs and distrustful of many of the new initiatives of the new leadership, particularly in EPA. Second, as we have noted above, neither agency's new leadership was particularly committed to the Reform Act.

REFORM IN TRANSITION: OPERATIONAL LEVEL REACTIONS

Interview and questionnaire evidence suggest that, at the operational level as well as the policy level, reform was caught up in transition in two ways. First, the provisions of the Act were not especially important to most agency employees and managers in the context of agency transition difficulties explored above. Second, and because of this, such activities as creating meaningful standards, using them to track progress, and removing roadblocks to progress received relatively little attention. As a result, attitudes toward the reforms are more negative, we suspect, than they might have been had they been implemented under more stable circumstances. We can discuss these points in turn.

Interview data suggest that reform was not a major concern for agency employees during the transition period. The case of one high-level EPA official is instructive. In October 1980, he told us that performance appraisal "is an occasion for many things—among them me telling some people that I don't like their work." In October 1981, this same official said, "No, with all the mess in the agency I didn't try to change any ratings" to force a lower distribution. He went on, "I just didn't have the heart." In MSHA, similar comments were in evidence. Several supervisors pointed out that, without knowing what mines they were going to inspect, with what people, and at which level of resources, it was difficult to take performance standards seriously.

To be sure, it is unlikely, given the results of our findings in chapter 5, to argue that, without transition, performance appraisal and merit pay would have been popular systems. However, the data in table 11.3 suggest that the circumstances of transition did affect attitudes toward the system directly and indirectly.

Table 11.3 presents correlations between several variables used above to describe the organizational changes in the agencies and several indicators of CSRA implementation.

Variables in the first two columns measure, respectively, approval of merit pay implementation and overall acceptance of merit pay. The former is measured by responses to the question: "All in all, I approve of the way this agency is implementing merit pay"; the latter by responses to: "If I had my way, I would not be in merit pay." We have a similar measure for acceptance of the SES: "I would not join the SES if given the option." (The latter two questions were asked only of GS 13–15's; their scales have been reversed for presentation in the table so that high scores on the variables indicate *acceptance* of merit pay and SES). The fourth column is a summary measure of approval of performance appraisal: "The performance evaluation in 1981 was better than the old system (pre-CSRA) overall." There follows a scale measuring the usefulness of performance standards. We have also presented two summary measures of behavior directed toward performance tracking. The first (column 6) measures

Table 11.3. Correlations of Reactions to Transition with Attitudes toward Reform Act

	Approval of merit pay[1] implementation	Acceptance of merit pay[2]	Acceptance of SES[3]	Approval of performance[4] appraisal	Usefulness of performance[5] standards	Autonomous effort on[6] standards	Supervisory-related effort[7] on standards
I'm not getting the information I need to do my job.	-.17*	-.09	.10*	-.05*	-.14*	.00	-.03
I have not felt any effects of the presidential transition on my job.	.00	-.08	-.04	-.06	.17*	.03	.07
The new administration does not trust high-level career civil servants in this agency.	-.15*	-.08	-.03	-.08	-.17*	-.13*	-.15*
Index of resource redirection (see table 11.1, and text).	-.09	-.11*	.03	-.11*	-.07	.05	-.02
I am less committed to this agency as a place to work than I was last year.	-.15*	-.13*	.07	-.09*	-.22*	-.14*	-.17*
I believe this agency will be more efficient under the new administration.	.24*	.20*	.04	.15*	.30*	.04	.14*

* Significant at .05 or less.
1. Responses to the question: "All in all, I approve of the way in which this agency is implementing merit pay."
2. Responses to the question: "If I had my way I would not be in merit pay." (Scale reversed in computing correlations.)
3. Responses to the question: "I would *not* join the SES if given the option." (Scale reversed in computing correlations.)
4. Responses to the question: "The performance evaluation in 1981 was better than the old system (pre-CSRA) overall."
5. Responses to the scale created from the following set of items:
   a. Writing my current performance standards helped me identify my own training needs.
   b. My performance standards have helped me understand my supervisor's job.
   c. My performance standards have helped me manage my time more effectively.
   d. Performance standards protect me from arbitrary actions by my supervisor.
   e. My performance standards have helped me maintain continuity in my work during the past year.
   f. Writing performance standards has helped me plan my work for the year.
   g. Writing performance standards has helped me coordinate my work with others' work.
   Scale alpha = .75

Table 11.3. Correlations of Reactions to Transition with Attitudes toward Reform Act

6. Responses to the scale created from the following set of items:
   To what extent did you do each of the following things during the past year with respect to your standards?
   a. Focus on the quantifiable parts of my job.
   b. Document my work.
   c. Focus effort on the part for which I have standards.
   d. Set work priorities.
   Responses included: (1) to a very little extent, (2) to a small extent, (3) to a moderate extent, (4) to a large extent, (5) to a very great extent.
   Scale alpha = .70
7. Responses to the scale created from the following set of items:
   To what extent did you emphasize each of the following things during the past year with respect to your standards.
   a. Meet with my supervisor to review progress on my standards.
   b. Seek guidance from my supervisor on writing good standards.
   c. Change my standards during the year if necessary.
   Responses as in no. 6.
Scale alpha = .68.

the amount of emphasis placed by employees on behavior related to standards that could be pursued without the involvement of supervisors (emphasis on quantifiable parts of jobs, on documenting work, on focusing on work covered by standards, and on setting work priorities). The second measure (column 7) deals with work behaviors where supervisory involvement is required (seeking guidance from supervisors, reviewing progress on standards, and changing standards during the year, if necessary). We can discuss the associations of the change variables with these measures in order.

Overall disapproval of merit pay implementation in the two agencies is moderately associated with lack of information (especially in EPA) and feeling that the new leadership distrusts career managers, as well as overall lessened commitment and skepticism regarding the efficiency of the agency under the new administration. Personal acceptance of merit pay is negatively associated with personal commitment, and with mission agreement as well. The pattern of these relations suggests that the personal and organizational alienation resulting from the change in leadership spills over into attitudes toward merit pay.

It is perhaps surprising that attitudes toward transition do *not* apparently affect willingness to join the SES. Interview data (and available questionnaire material) from SES members certainly suggest that the transition has been disruptive, at least in EPA. We can only guess that this question, directed not to the SES but to the feeder group, GS 13–15 employees, cannot distinguish between incumbency in the SES per se and in the *position* designated as SES. Apparently, regardless of feelings about transition, these employees are sufficiently ambitious to take on both the benefits and problems of the SES.

It is in the usefulness of performance standards that change has its most profound effects. The scale measures the rated helpfulness of standards to time management, work planning and coordination, identifying training needs, protection from arbitrary actions by supervisors, and the like. It is associated with all but one measure of organizational change—usefulness dwindles with uncertainty, feelings of distrust, lessened personal commitment, and skepticism of changes in leadership. Since usefulness of standards is critical, as chapter 5 suggests, this finding becomes of crucial importance.

This association is even stronger when measured at an organizational level. For the twenty one division-sized units at EPA (at headquarters and region) for which we had data, we calculated the mean values of the standards' usefulness scale and the mean values of the questions on whether the respondent believes the agency will become more efficient under the new administration. Among EPA employees, this correlation is .31; among units it is .61. It is perhaps reasonable that the usefulness of standards should be more an organizational than a personal phenomenon, since usefulness is frequently defined with reference to co-workers. That units which have had difficulty, for various reasons, in reacting to the change in leadership also do not find standards useful (more strong, organizationally than individually) likewise seems reasonable. It also reflects the pervasiveness of reactions to change.

Effort and emphasis devoted to standards, whether autonomous or involving interaction with the supervisor, is likewise weakly but significantly associated with measures of organizational change, mainly through feelings of distrust and lessened personal commitment.

This measure, too, is more responsive to change at the subunit level than at the individual level. Unit means on the variable measuring lack of information are substantially associated with unit means on autonomous standards behavior ($r = .36$), although no association is found at the individual level.

The data on the whole support the following interpretation. Changes associated with transition have some direct effect on attitudes toward general provisions of the Reform Act. Far larger and more important, however, are the associations between transition reactions and the usefulness of standards and the tracking of performance against them. As we argue in chapter 5, performance tracking and usefulness of standards are closely associated with acceptance of the system; thus the indirect effects of transition on discouraging attention to performance standards may be more damaging to the system than the spillover of general alienation into the overall evaluation of these provisions.

SUMMARY

We began this chapter by positing two conflicts between responsive government and effective agency operation during political transition. The first is between responsiveness and rigidity—as new political leadership enters an agency, the more decisive its intended break with the past, the more self-protective the reactions of career employees are likely to be. The results—centralization, decrease in communications, hostility, resentment, and uncertainty—are likely to convince political leadership that more direct control and more decisive change are required, provoking still further hostility and resentment.

The second conflict is between continuity and change—as old mechanisms and relationships become problematic, previously routine problems become more difficult to handle. The interaction of these two suggests that the agency will have increasingly large numbers of problems to solve, new ones as well as old, with a decreased capacity to solve them.

The evidence reviewed suggests that, at both policy and operational levels, civil service reform was caught squarely in these two dilemmas. At the policy level, career personnel familiar with both the novelty of the reform and the original reform implementers' intentions were unwilling to put these concerns forcefully to the new leadership. For its part, the new leadership saw reform as an old system, not particularly deserving of support or encouragement, and if anything a suspect holdover from previous administrations and practices. Thus, at a policy level, civil service reform was neither new nor institutionalized, but rather a vulnerable mix having neither the patina of novelty nor a track record and entrenched supporters.

At the operational level, compared with RIF's, transfers, budget cuts, and perceived assaults on the agencies' historical missions, performance standards and performance appraisal were not particularly noteworthy. Performance standards in these circumstances were not seen as terribly useful, and the ongoing tracking of performance against them suffered. Ironically, because of this, performance appraisals became far more difficult than they would have been in the presence of clear signals of support from policy levels and ongoing attention to standards—and reactions, both to standards and to appraisal, more negative. The result, as noted in many of our interviews, was that civil service reform lost much of its thrust and momentum, though, ironicallly, no one clearly intended that it should.

Discussion and Postscript

Civil service reform was and remains a potential major change in the way the federal government handles matters of personnel and policy, and it deserves study in its own right. The implications of this analysis, however, can be applied to many other innovations in federal management as well. Several general conclusions emerge.

First, although the formulation and implementation of strategic decisions in organizations frequently takes between three and five years (Mintzberg, Raisinghani, and Theoret 1976), this time horizon seems much too long for innovation in the federal section, given the increasing frequency of one-term presidencies. While the mandated three-year lag between passage of the Reform Act and the first implementation of merit pay makes good organizational sense, its political sense is more problematic.

Second, without entrenched support in the agencies or in any agency in government, there was little leverage with which to regain momentum as implementation of the reforms proceeded. The role of "fixer" advocated in Bardach (1977) seems not to have been filled in the case of reform. Ironically, the CSRA itself played a part in this, since its SES provisions were seen to have substantially reduced the protections afforded some who might have played this role. In fact, the institution of a senior executive cadre, which had been advocated by Heclo (1977) to reduce the turmoil of transition, was itself impeded by transition.

We can conclude, however, with a more optimistic postscript. In MSHA, where the original implementation had as far as possible minimized the effects (both positive and negative) of reform, there is some evidence, at least at the policy level, that the agency is now ready to grapple with the difficult problems of meaningful appraisal and standards-creation and the use of these in work planning and execution. In part, this new awareness was made possible by the retention of several key people associated with implementation who saw the need for more serious attention to reform. In a sense, for them, transition provided the opportunity to begin implementation again without having to defend past practices. It is also substantially aided by a relatively low reservoir of distrust and disillusionment stemming from the transition. Extensive training and discussion on how to use the new performance-management systems is now under way in the agency. Whether it will succeed, and whether MSHA's experience is generalizable to other agencies, remain to be seen.

REFERENCES

Bardach, Eugene. 1977. *The Implementation Game.* Cambridge, Mass: MIT Press.

Fleishman, E., E. Harris, and A. Burtt. 1955. "Leadership and Supervision in Industry: An Evaluation of a Supervisory Training Program." Columbus: Ohio State University, Bureau of Education Research.

Gaertner, Gregory H., Karen N. Gaertner, and Irene Devine. 1983. "Federal Agencies in the Context of Transition: A Contrast between Democratic and Organizational Theories." *Public Administration Review,* 43(5): 421–432.

Gaertner, G. H., and Ramnarayan, S. 1983. "Organizational Effectiveness: An Alternative Perspective." *Academy of Management Review* 8(1): 97–107.

Hall, Douglas T., and Roger Mansfield. 1971. "Organizational and Individual Response to External Stress." *Administrative Science Quarterly* 16(3): 533–47.

Heclo, Hugh. 1977. *A Government of Strangers.* Washington, D.C.: Brookings Institution.

Henry, Laurin. 1960. *Presidential Transitions.* Washington, D.C.: Brookings Institution.

Hermann, Charles F. 1963. "Some Consequences of Crisis Which Limit the Viability of Organization." *Administrative Science Quarterly* 8(1): 61–82.

Homans, G. C. 1950. *The Human Group.* New York: Harcourt-Brace, Inc.

Lawrence, P., and J. Lorsch. 1967. *Organization and Environment.* Boston: Division of Research, Harvard Business School.

Meredith, David. 1966. "The Impact of Office Automation on Supervisory Behavior." Ph.D. dissertation, Boston: Massachusetts Institute of Technology, unpublished.

Mintzberg, H., Raisinghani, D., and Theoret, A. 1976. "The Structure of Unstructured Decision Processes." *Administrative Science Quarterly* 21: 246–75.

Schein, Edgar H. 1965. *Organizational Psychology.* Englewood Cliffs, N.J.: Prentice-Hall.

Staw, B., L. E. Sankelands, and J. E. Dutton. 1981. "Threat-Rigidity Effects in Organizational Behavior." *Administrative Science Quarterly* 26:501–24.

CHAPTER TWELVE

Implementing the
Civil Service Reform Act
in a Time of Turbulence

MARK A. ABRAMSON AND RICHARD E. SCHMIDT

INTRODUCTION

A major task for those evaluating the Civil Service Reform Act of 1978 (CSRA) is to understand the environment in which it was implemented. It was implemented in a time of great change and turbulence in the government. In relation to this volume, it is important to note that CSRA was implemented in an era of "retrenchment" or "cutback management" at the federal level of government. This broad environment, we argue, has conditioned the atmosphere in which the Act has been implemented. We have identified the following environmental variables which, we feel, directly influenced the implementation of CSRA:

- Relative political consensus on specific federal functions
- Attitude of noncareer appointees toward the career civil service
- Degree of turbulence in the agency and program

The above variables are not directly related to CSRA itself, but CSRA was created during a time of major shifts in some of the variables. Noncareer appointees changed, political consensus shifted, and environmental turbulence increased. Many of the variables are interactive.

It is in the context of the above environmental variables and a time of cutback management that the impact of civil service reform must be examined. Based on conversations with Senior Executive Service (SES) members across the government, the distinction between CSRA and the environment appears to become blurred. CSRA did not cause the many changes that have taken place during the past several years, but many people's perception of CSRA has been directly affected by those changes. With an understanding of environmental variables, one can better understand the implementation of CSRA and begin to assess the impact of CSRA and the Senior Executive Service on government. When making judgments on the impact of CSRA, it is important to understand the time period in which it was implemented.

This chapter brings together two popular topics: cutback management and civil service reform. While both have been occurring simultaneously, they have seldom been looked at together.[1] In examining their interrelationships, one can ask what impact a cutback management environment had on the implementation of the Civil Service Reform Act. The relationship between the two, as discussed in this paper, is presented in Approach 1, in figure 12.1. Approach 2, examining the impact of CSRA tools in implementing cutback management, is another subject and will not be discussed in this paper.

UNDERSTANDING THE ENVIRONMENT IN WHICH CIVIL SERVICE REFORM OPERATES

We have selected three key variables to assist us in understanding the environments in which CSRA was implemented. Each is discussed below.

Environmental Variable No. 1: Political Consensus

As stated earlier, the nation is now in the midst of a major political debate on the nature and appropriateness of federal roles in many areas.[2] Table 12.1 divides the government into two groups of agencies: one with a high degree of consensus on the federal role and the other with a low degree of consensus.

The first group of agencies includes the Departments of State, Defense, and Treasury. Although debate goes on over specific policies in these agencies, there is little debate over either the existence of these organizations or their federal roles. A consensus on the federal role can be said to exist. One may disagree with the specific policies of the State Department, but one agrees that the Department is fulfilling an important federal function—the conduct of international relations. A similar argument applies to both the Departments of Defense and Treasury. While there is debate over specific policies, agreement exists on the appropriateness of the federal function and the credibility of the organization.

Fig 12.1 Alternative Approaches to Examining the Relationship Between Civil Service Reform and "Cutback Management"

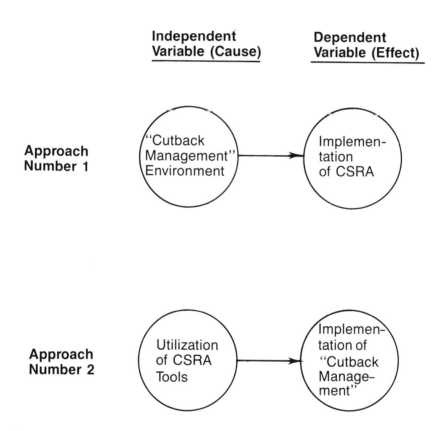

Table 12.1. Degree of Consensus on Federal Role

Degree of Consensus on Federal Role and Agency Mission	Agency
High	Examples: State Defense Treasury Justice HHS/NIH Weather Service National Bureau of Standards Agriculture (parts) U.S. Geological Service Bureau of the Census Implication: There is a strong commitment to making these agencies work well; atmosphere is highly conducive to CSRA activities.
Low	Examples: Energy (parts) Environmental Protection Agency Education Federal Trade Commission Legal Services Corporation Office of Economic Opportunity (1973) Implication: There is a tendency for these agencies to become almost paralyzed and cease functioning effectively; agencies may be reorganized out of existence and their function or mission reassigned to new organizations; little chance for CSRA to have any positive impact; environment unconducive to civil service reform activities.

In another set of agencies, there is less consensus over the appropriateness of their federal roles. The Departments of Energy and Education are now the most prominent of these agencies. Agencies in which there is major disagreement over the appropriateness of the federal role face two possible futures—they are either abolished or placed in an environment that is often characterized by "cutbacks" but little "management." Recent years have witnessed examples of federal agencies being phased out. In 1973, the Office of Economic Opportunity (OEO) was abolished and its functions and staff reassigned to several Departments. In 1982, the Community Services Administration—the historical legacy of OEO—was abolished. In 1980, the Law Enforcement Assistance Administration closed down. All these agencies had lost political support for their federal missions. In many respects, abolishing an agency that has lost political support for its federal mission is the preferred solution. At least, then, the debate over the appropriate federal role for the agency is resolved. Other organizations in similar situations are not so lucky.

Most organizations caught in such political battles are not abolished. Instead, they continue in a turbulent environment while the political debate takes place. Frequently, the political debate paralyzes the functioning of the agency. This appears to be happening in the case of the Departments of Energy and Education. The most troublesome aspect of this paralysis is the lack of any conflict resolution mechanism. The debate goes on and on; the agencies continue in limbo.

There are many negative consequences in such situations. All employees, whether in the public or private sector, like to think that what they do is worthwhile. When told constantly that what they do is not worthwhile, their morale will sink. As morale sinks, people start to leave the organization. Often the best people leave. In commenting on the departure of a recent cabinet official, the *Washington Post* stated: "He did succeed in encouraging most of its [the agency's] ablest people to find employment elsewhere."

In addition to those who leave voluntarily, reductions-in-force (RIFs) often follow as a consequence of the political debate over appropriateness of federal function. While it is clearly legitimate for the executive branch to propose major budget reductions and to use RIFs to accomplish reductions, RIFs can occur as a result of stalemate over the appropriations process. Many of the RIF decisions were caused indirectly by congressional inaction rather than directly by enactment of final appropriations bills. Living with uncertainty, therefore, has become a way of life in many federal agencies. Agencies live from one continuing resolution to another. Orderly planning for either cutbacks, stability, or even growth becomes difficult or impossible.

What about civil service reform in such an environment? We now believe that the impact of civil service reform has been different in different types of agencies. In agencies in which consensus, and hence stability, exists, there is evidence that civil service reform has had some positive impact. Parts of the Department of Health and Human Services fall into this category.[3] The key explanatory variable is the conduciveness of the environment and the receptivity to management innovations, such as those stemming from CSRA. In agencies facing a lack of consensus over the appropriateness of their function, such management approaches as CSRA receive low priority. Emphasis is often placed on retrenchment and changing the direction of the program. Management devotes little time to trying to improve program performance. The very existence of programs is called into question, not a program's effectiveness or efficiency. The attempt to use civil service reform to improve performance appears to be more common in those agencies in which high performance is desired, and civil service reform is viewed as a tool to bringing about that high performance.

Environmental Variable No. 2: Attitude of Noncareer Appointees

Table 12.2 presents the relationship between political consensus and the attitudes of agency noncareer leadership. This table builds upon the prior discussion of political consensus by adding another key variable—political leadership. As a consequence of adding another variable, we now have four distinct situations—each of which has different implications for CSRA implementation.

Box 1 of table 12.2 lists agencies in which political leadership is supportive of career servants and political consensus exists on the appropriateness of the agency's federal role. This is the preferred position of most federal agencies. In this situation, civil service reform stands a good chance of succeeding and flourishing. As noted above,

Table 12.2. Implication of Noncareer Attitudes and Political Consensus on Implementation of Civil Service Reform Act Activities

Political Consensus on Federal Function	Attitude of Noncareer Appointees Toward Career Civil Servants	
	Supportive	*Less Supportive*
High Consensus	1 *Examples:* State Defense Treasury HHS/NIH OEO (under Shriver) *Implication:* Environment conducive to successful implementation of CSRA.	2 *Examples:* Parts of Interior Parts of Labor *Implication:* Successful implementation of CSRA less likely.
Moderate to Low Consensus	3 *Examples:* HHS/HRSA HHS/FDA OEO (under Carlucci) *Implication:* Successful implementation of CSRA difficult; success of implementation highly dependent on leadership qualities of agency head.	4 *Examples:* Energy Education EPA OEO (under Phillips) *Implication:* Environment hostile to effective CSRA implementation; little incentive to use CSRA as management tool.

evidence is beginning to accumulate that civil service reform is succeeding—to some extent—in these environments.

Successful implementation of civil service reform becomes more problematic in boxes 2 and 3. In both situations, an agency's noncareer leaders need to be supportive of career employees and career systems. In many respects, civil service reform is clearly oriented to career employees. It is a time-consuming system to make operative. A supportive environment is needed to implement it and use it to its greatest advantage. While an agency in the situation of Box 3 clearly faces problems, these problems can be overcome by astute and committed agency leadership, but the "noise" in the environment stemming from the political debate over the federal function can drown any impact from civil service reform activities.

Finally, agencies in the situation of Box 4 are in dire straits. This is the environment in which cutback management is most likely to occur. Given the lack of supportive noncareer leadership and substantial political disagreement on the appropriateness of federal role, civil service reform activities tend simply to become irrelevant in the day-to-day functioning of an agency. An agency deep in the midst of cutbacks is also likely to experience an environment hostile to effective implementation of civil service reform. There is some evidence that this occurred in some federal agencies during the implementation of civil service reform.

Environmental Variable No. 3: Amount of Turbulence in the Environment

Table 12.3 presents the interactive relationship between the attitude of noncareer appointees and the degree of turbulence in the environment. To a large extent, the degree of turbulence in the environment is a reflection of the amount of political consensus concerning the appropriateness of an agency's federal role. When low consensus is prevalent, turbulence is likely to follow.

Turbulence, however, can also occur in agencies that have a high degree of consensus over the appropriateness of the federal role. Specifically, turbulence can be defined as consisting of any of the following events: (1) major budget reductions resulting in RIFs; (2) rapid turnover of agency heads or among key noncareer appointees; (3) departure of many key career staff; (4) major reorganizations, either internally or involving a merger with another organization; (5) major shift in policy direction, resulting in changes in the way the organization operates; (6) addition of new functions, not previously carried out by the organization; or (7) subtraction of a previous agency function, necessitating a redefinition of the agency mission.

Table 12.3. Implication of Noncareer Attitudes and Environmental Turbulence on Implementation of Civil Service Reform Act Activities

Degree of Turbulence in Environment	Attitude of Noncareer Appointees Toward Career Civil Servants	
	Supportive	Less Supportive
Low Turbulence	1 *Examples:* State Defense Treasury HHS/NIH *Implication:* The Civil Service Reform Act was premised on this environment; given this environment, CSRA likely to be implemented successfully.	2 *Examples:* Parts of Interior Parts of Labor *Implication:* Successful implementation of CSRA less likely.
High Turbulence	3 *Examples:* HHS/ADAMHA HHS/HDS *Implication:* High level of "noise" in environment makes CSRA very difficult to implement successfully; agency head leadership essential.	4 *Examples:* Energy EPA Education *Implication:* CSRA activities became almost impossible to implement successfully; CSRA activities likely to recieve low priority and little attention.

Any of the above either singly or in combination can cause major turbulence. The last several years have witnessed many agencies thrust into highly turbulent environments.

Weathering the storm of turbulence requires astute agency leadership. Agency morale can either be stablized or made worse by the attitude expressed by the agency's noncareer leadership. Given a supportive environment, civil service reform stands a clear chance of succeeding. In the case of high turbulence, the need for a supportive environment is even greater. Without such support, implementation of CSRA activities becomes very difficult. To a large extent, the concept of civil service reform is based on normal times.

CONCLUSION

In sum, it is our argument that an agency's environment does make a difference in the implementation of civil service reform. To a large extent, the environment of retrenchment can be viewed as an independent variable affecting the quality of civil service reform implementation. Based on this analysis, we argue:

- In part, civil service reform is a victim of the era of retrenchment. In such times, management processes—such as CSRA—take second place to the job of cutting back and surviving.
- There are several key factors in an organization's climate that can create either a conducive or nonconducive environment in which to implement CSRA. Several characteristics of retrenchment make it nonconducive to CSRA activities.

It is only with an understanding of this environment that one can begin to evaluate the impact of the Civil Service Reform Act on federal management. If the Act did not live up to expectations, it is the task of the evaluator not only to document whether the expectation was achieved or not, but also to begin to explore the reasons why the Act did or did not succeed. It is our argument that the management environment within federal agencies must also be assessed while evaluating the impact of the Civil Service Reform Act of 1978.

NOTES

1. An important exception is Patricia W. Ingraham and Charles J. Barrilleaux, "Motivating Government Managers for Retrenchment: Some Possible Lessons from the Senior Executive Service." *Public Administration Review* (September/October 1983): 393–402. An earlier version of this paper was presented at the Annual Meeting of the American Political Science Association, September 1–4, 1982, Denver, Colorado.
2. For a more detailed discussion on the impact of public consensus on federal programs, see Richard E. Schmidt and Mark A. Abramson, "Politics and Performance: What Does It Mean for Civil Servants?" *Public Administration Review* (March/April 1983): 155–60.
3. For a discussion of the Department of Health and Human Services experience, see chap. 6, "Evaluating the Civil Service Reform Act of 1978: The Experience of the U.S. Department of Health and Human Services."

CHAPTER THIRTEEN

Epilogue to
"The President's Management
'Reforms': Theory X Triumphant"

FREDERICK C. THAYER

Among books and articles I have published, "The President's Management 'Reforms': Theory X Triumphant" was unusual in terms of immediate responses from present and former career administrators. Without exception, the letter writers endorsed my critique of the "reform" legislation, saying they were happy to see someone raising questions about a proposal that had gathered widespread bipartisan political support, and also had been endorsed virtually across the board by academics who study administration. It is not a matter of great joy to conclude that my original analysis and predictions have stood up rather well, nor do I relish making the observation that those who are dedicated to "Theory X" management show little or no interest in the empirical research which indicates, as it has from the start, that practitioners greatly dislike this "reform". Sadly, the broader world view associated with "Theory X" is so embedded in our culture that even academics who profess their dedication to seeking the truth simply turn away from such evidence.

In looking back, having now had the opportunity to listen to explanations from some of those most involved in pushing through the "reform," I cannot choose between the two most likely explanations for the "reform's" most glaring and obvious contradiction. President Carter and his "reformers" may have intentionally deceived everyone by highlighting their desire to protect whistleblowers, knowing full well that the "reform" was designed to do precisely the opposite. The glaring contradiction was quite obvious. Career administrators were to be threatened with adverse actions if they did not perform up to the levels prescribed by superiors, but the President also insisted that reform would provide much greater protection for whistleblowers. I pointed out that administrators would be less likely to disagree with their bosses, and that "protection" for whistleblowers probably would be ineffective or meaningless. A twenty-year administrator recently resigned from the Office of Merit Systems Review and Studies, a part of the Merit Systems Protection Board, because he had "absolutely nothing to do, week after week, month after month." After consulting two doctors about his growing anxiety over the lack of meaningful work, he decided to look for new work in business, in Florida. So much for one of the loudest claims put forth by those who gave us civil service reform (*Pittsburgh Press*, April 20, 1983. From the Washington Post Service).

Alternatively, the "reformers" may have been so swept up in the chaotic policy jungle of Washington that they simply overlooked basic contradictions in a legislative effort that was far too hasty in terms of the subject's importance. If the civil service is to be "reformed" once each century, speed limits are in order. Unfortunately, "reform" was singled out as something the Carterites could win in haste, and it is much more important to collect votes in Congress than to think through the items being voted on. Because the "reform" effort also was connected with extensive reorganization of government management functions, especially including the new Office of Personnel Management, "reform" got caught up in searches for personal prestige and promotion. When people are selling themselves as much or more than the actual legislation, others are bound to suffer; today's victims are the civil servants.

I was remiss in failing to notice from the beginning that the bonus provisions for members of the Senior Executive Service (SES) would be inherently unworkable. Not only is there no easily available yardstick for making such determinations (nor are profits a wholly valid measure in the private sector), but it should have been obvious that having to secure large additional bonus appropriations every year would turn out to be politically impossible. Inevitably, then, the rationale for the SES self-destructed in short order. If government is going to designate some of its administrators as truly outstanding (the broad criterion for SES membership in the first place), then all of them, or virtually all of them, are logically worthy of bonuses. Once the extra money was limited to a small percentage of SES members, the effect was to label publicly most SES members as only "mediocre."

In trying to take the broadest possible view, I have concluded that the deeper causes of civil service "reform" lie in some combination of the following:

1. Only a few years ago, governments at all levels were immersed in the search for higher "productivity." Having found it impossible to measure what administrators actually turn out, the effort shifted to attempts to measure the administrators themselves. If the search for productivity was not well thought out, the "reformers" failed to note that reliance upon performance appraisal systems was bound not to work.

2. The changing nature of political campaigns, together with a slumping economy, have spawned, rather quietly but very quickly, a new form of spoils system. Electioneering is not only more expensive than ever, but it now employs very large numbers of people skilled in information systems, computer technology, and policy analysis. These people look to their bosses for help when those bosses win elections, and "reform" offers more hope for lateral entry into the career service. Indeed, it may now make more sense for those with advanced degrees in such fields to attach themselves to political candidates than to apply for civil service jobs. Understandably, well-trained people seek promising careers. The tragedy is that, through the use of such heinous devices as quotas ("grading on a curve"), other careers must be ruined to make room.

3. Merit is the only form of discrimination that remains legitimate. Because legislation now rules out discrimination on such grounds as race, sex, religion, and age, care must be taken to show in writing that all adverse actions are based upon incompetence. In this sense, civil service "reform" is a somewhat natural follow-up to the civil rights legislation of the 1960s. Because the underlying organizational premise is that any subordinate is, by definition, less competent than the boss, the former cannot prove the boss's evaluation is incorrect. It is worth noting that if the merit approach is put into full operation, and if all equal employment and affirmative action provisions are fully implemented, we will be left with a new underclass that will be known as the "incorrigibly stupid."

I do not know if any of the "reformers" were conscious of the likely connection between their efforts and the trends outlined above. On the other hand, no cause-effect relationship can be proved beyond question; yet every decision must be based upon a presumed relationship. Any decision (cause) tests the hypothesis that the desired effect (objective) will be achieved, as Martin Landau has noted. If decisions, therefore, are experiments, all conclusions are speculative. My speculation is as reasonable as anyone else's.

Finally, the advocates and critics of civil service "reform" have shed yet more light upon one of the oldest controversies in the field of public administration. Textbooks routinely proclaim that policy and administration are inseparable, at least in the sense that career administrators not only *are* involved in the shaping of policy decisions, but *should be* so involved. In a curious way, the advocates and critics agree that the "reform" fully lives up to this textbook norm. But, do they really agree after all?

Nobody had more to do with bringing civil service "reform" to fruition than Alan Campbell, a former dean of the Maxwell School at Syracuse University, probably the most renowned school in the field. Over and over again, he argued that the "reform" epitomizes the symbiosis of policy and administration, because it is designed to insure that administrators will indeed become more and more "accountable" and "responsible" for acting in complete accordance with policy directives. James Sundquist, on the other hand, has observed that civil service "reform" politicizes administration more than ever, because administrators now know that, whatever the "neutral competence" that justifies their status, they are expected to express complete loyalty to the objectives of their policy-making (political) superiors.

If Campbell is proud that policy and administration must now be more closely aligned than ever, Sundquist mourns the demise of the administrator's function, or even duty, to disagree with political bosses. If Campbell is happy that *obedience* is now enshrined as the cardinal principle of the civil service, Sundquist regrets a speeding up of the march toward the Weberian "ideal." Regrettably, Campbell's view is more strongly grounded in political and constitutional theory. Stripped to essentials, American "democracy" varies not a whit from other modern systems; "Theory X" is indeed triumphant.

CHAPTER FOURTEEN

Civil Service Reform, Then and Now: A Sojourner's Outlook

DAVID T. STANLEY

When the editors used the word "sojourner" in their suggested title for this piece, they may not have recalled that the word means someone who dwells in a place as a temporary resident or a stranger, and that I have been dwelling in and around problems of the federal civil service since 1938. It has been a long sojourn.

During the symposium at Binghamton, which is the basis for this volume, my remarks were intended to answer the question: Was civil service reform necessary? My answer was that civil service reform is *always* necessary. A subsidiary but perhaps more important question is: Reform in what degree? That is, how radical the change, how incremental? This suggests other questions: Suppose nothing had been done? Would there have been a disaster, or perhaps merely occasional ups and downs?

David Dillman has noted that politics is an enduring part of the reform process. A summary of major presidential action in the last fifty years clarifies the impact of presidential politics on the civil service system in the United States, and the extent to which changes have occurred in the past.

When Franklin Roosevelt was President, he expanded the bureaucracy dramatically, primarily on a merit basis, bringing into the civil service thousands of employees newly appointed to do the work of the New Deal. His Administration started or strengthened personnel offices in the various departments and agencies. He appointed an able, competent Civil Service Commission and approved the Veterans Preference Act.

President Truman continued the Roosevelt policies. Most of the staff work was done in his own office under Donald Dawson, who, oddly enough, handled political patronage as well as career service personnel matters. This practice was one of many that later led to calls for reform.

President Eisenhower campaigned to "clean up the mess in Washington." Though he also expressed his confidence in the public service and his appreciation of the work being done, many of his cabinet appointees showed a distrust of the career service. In fact, Eisenhower's executive staff prepared a plan for undermining the civil service with patronage politics. On the other hand, he appointed a high-calibre Civil Service Commission, and the changeover from Korean wartime emergency personnel methods to more normal processes was accomplished with some efficiency. In addition, the Eisenhower Administration sponsored a significant advance in fringe benefits for federal employees and established statutory authority for employee training.

President Kennedy was a believer in a competent civil service, although his administration, like others before and after his, was characterized by some partisan incursions into the merit system. As other Presidents before him had left their marks on the civil service system, Kennedy left his in the Pay Comparability Act, which attempted to link federal salary levels to those in the private sector.

President Lyndon Johnson had a firm political grasp of his administration, and civil service, as before, was both supported and invaded by the political necessities of the time. Johnson, however, was better organized about recruiting political executives for presidential appointments than most previous administrations. Again, partisan politics and merit were mixed because this task was performed for him by John Macy, who was also Chairman of the U.S. Civil Service Commission.

President Nixon presided over a massive effort to assure White House control of departments and agencies by placing loyal Nixon sympathizers in key jobs. The Nixon Administration was noted for ethical slippage and busy political commissars. Merit suffered further, and the Civil Service Commission members themselves were a bit tarnished. Gerald Ford's Administration, although engaging in some cleanup work, generally continued to encourage the growing politicization of some key career posts.

Finally, Jimmy Carter, in his campaign, made much of the fact that he was a Washington outsider and that there was a lot wrong with the bureaucracy. He complained that it was difficult to fire the "duds" in the government, and he put great and possibly excessive emphasis on reorganization. The keystone of his efforts was the Civil Service Reform Act of 1978.

WHAT HAS GONE RIGHT AND GONE WRONG?

The preceding chapters have outlined the many experiences of various aspects of the reform and of the implementation process in several agencies. The continuing effect of politics has been noted. Is it possible to sum up the pluses and minuses of the Civil Service Reform Act of 1978? Mine is a subjective and impressionistic summary. However, it is based upon considerable familiarity with the growing literature on federal civil service reform, and on staff work and meetings of the Panel on the Public Service (formerly the Panel on Civil Service Reform) of the National Academy of Public Administration. In weighing these impressions, bear in mind that the Reagan Administration came to power not long after the Civil Service Reform Act went into full effect. This new set of presidential politics and policies involved radical alterations in existing philosophies of government, as well as wholesale turnover in the upper layers of the federal service. Once again, therefore, a President has shaped the civil service by his tenure. But what of civil service reform specifically?

The Good News

To begin a recital of what has gone right with civil service reform, it is clear that the initial establishment of the Office of Personnel Management (OPM), the Merit Systems Protection Board (MSPB), including the Office of Special Counsel, and the Federal Labor Relations Authority (FLRA), proceeded in a businesslike and competent way. Although MSPB and FLRA were handicapped by inadequate office space and staff, they undertook their missions professionally and competently. Indeed, the Merit Systems Protection Board made very impressive progress in cleaning up the large backlog of undecided appeal cases it inherited from the U.S. Civil Service Commission.

Second, the Senior Executive Service (SES) was established, and most of the eligible employees joined. Bonus systems were put in place and administered, despite the unfamiliarity of federal officials with that method of compensation. There was a variation in quality of work rewarded, but in a variety of agencies the bonuses were regarded as well-deserved. There was widespread participation by both management and employees in setting standards of performance and in developing the new performance appraisal plans required by the Act. In many agencies, careful planning and action began on executive development programs.

Under the research and experimentation title of the law, new departures in pay administration are meeting with some success in Navy activities in California. Unfortunately, this is the only instance of use of this authority.

The Bad News

There is a longer list of things that have gone wrong, or at least things that are cause for worry. Heading the list is the fact that the establishment of the Senior Executive Service has not had the positive motivational effect that was hoped for. On the contrary, the average member of the SES is profoundly disaffected. This is the result primarily of unrealized expectations fostered by the Civil Service Reform Act. Senior executives were more vulnerable to being transferred or even downgraded if their services or style were not acceptable to their superiors. In return for this greater risk, they were to be eligible for departmental bonuses and for Meritorious or Distinguished "rank" awards, with large cash payments attached. In some departments the bonuses were poorly administered. Throughout the government, the bonuses were subjected to a percentage limitation lower than that permitted in the legislation. Clearly the executives have some reason to complain of bad faith on this matter.

As Abramson, Schmidt, and Baxter have pointed out in chapter 6, other reasons for their disaffection are not directly traceable to the CSRA. These include the drumfire of criticism directed toward "the bureaucracy," and hence, presumably, to its leadership. Further, senior executives were long prevented from getting pay increases by the pay cap, which froze thousands at the same salary level. Many federal senior executives were also disappointed or angry because of what they considered the poor quality of the political leaders appointed by both the Carter Administration and the Reagan Administration. All these factors, plus the discomfort and insecurity resulting from the political party transition, contributed to an escalating bitterness.

In relation to other government managers, the Gaertners have noted that the merit pay provisions for executives in grades 13 to 15, though conscientiously administered in most of the departments that moved promptly on this matter, sometimes resulted in smaller pay increases for those executives eligible for merit pay than they would have received had they stayed out of the merit pay category. This is partly the result of the small amounts of money appropriated for the merit pay provisions. It now appears that legislating a system of merit pay without loosening up the federal pay structure was an error in mathematics and logic.

The labor relations title of the Act is another area in which results have been disappointing. The Federal Labor Relations Authority has had difficulty disposing of its caseload, particularly a rapidly growing mass of unfair labor practice complaints. Because the law provided that the unions need not pay for such proceedings, an incentive was created for aggrieved employees and their representatives to select this means of remedying complaints. There are complaints about excessive negotiation time and consideration of relatively trivial matters. Of course, this might have been expected because collective bargaining in the federal government does not deal with pay and benefits, but only with conditions of work.

Disappointment was also felt by those who were led by President Carter and others to believe that it would be easier to downgrade, reassign, or dismiss inadequately performing employees under the new law. It is difficult to draw meaningful statistical conclusions from the small number of formal cases of this type that are processed. Nevertheless, the complaints one hears about this indicate that there has been little change; that is, employees who are performing below standard are able to hold onto their jobs because of a combination of use of appeal provisions, the strength of labor organizations that help them with their grievances, and the general reluctance of managerial officials to spend a lot of time on such matters.

The performance of the Office of the Special Counsel within the Merit Systems Protection Board has been inadequate, although the Act itself cannot be blamed for this. The Carter Administration ended without obtaining a Special Counsel confirmed by the Senate. The Acting Special Counsel, and those with whom that official was supposed to work most closely, the members of the Merit Systems Protection Board, had significant policy disagreements; indeed, they went to court over them and over control of resources for the Office of the Special Counsel. This situation has been corrected by the Reagan Administration, but time has been lost. The new Special Counsel has an onerous task in establishing the credibility of the office, in rebuilding a demoralized and somewhat less qualified staff than would be desired, and in moving the office caseload.

Finally, the general administration budget cuts of the Reagan Administration were severe blows to all three of the agencies created by the Civil Service Reform Act. The Federal Labor Relations Authority and the Merit Systems Protection Board both furloughed employees and curtailed travel and hearing schedules. The Office of Personnel Management furloughed employees, made some budget-saving reorganizations, and threatened to abolish the government's primary executive training institution, the Federal Executive Institute. This organization was saved from extinction only by pressures from Congress and from its alumni.

TRYING TO LOOK AHEAD

All these disappointments, plus others not mentioned, command more attention than things that are proceeding smoothly. While it is necessary to emphasize that important public work is still being accomplished throughout the government, much of it with care and competence by people who are reasonably satisfied and leading reasonably comfortable lives, there *is* cause for concern. In planning for the future, it will again be necessary to correct a number of major problems. First, the media, political leaders, and interested scholars must encourage positive attitudes toward public service as a vital instrument in the functioning of our society. Second, federal pay and benefits must be adequate in comparison to those of other employers. The need to economize is granted, and jobs may be abolished if necessary; but every effort must be made to compensate adequately the employees who remain. Third, political leadership must be repeatedly reminded to do a good job of personnel management within the area of political appointments. The political party that controls the executive branch of the government is certainly entitled to install policy-making officials of its own persuasion, but care must be exercised to assure the selection of officials who are competent both as managers and as informed persons in the fields in which they will be working.

In conclusion, I would ask: What would have happened if the Civil Service Reform Act had not been passed? There would have been a continuation of encroachments on the merit system with less opportunity for persons disadvantaged by these events to appeal or complain. Labor relations would have been in an even worse state than they are at present, and the pay situation would have been no better. Again, it is necessary to repeat that many of the problems of reform are not directly attributable to the Civil Service Reform Act itself, but to bad administration or to inadequate political leadership.

There is a need to correct these problems, as well as problems of personnel management, because a government whose quality of performance continues to slip is a danger to the nation that it leads. Civil service reform is still new and needs many adjustments. It is difficult to say how, when, and to what effect the Act will be amended. There is, however, a need for a constant effort to administer government more equitably and more logically.

CHAPTER FIFTEEN

Civil Service Reform and Public Policy: Do We Know How To Judge Success or Failure?

PATRICIA W. INGRAHAM

In our introduction to this book, we wrote, "Given the Civil Service Reform Act's comprehensive nature and its internal conflict, we can anticipate dramatically different perceptions of success or failure and different reactions to the reform's overall effectiveness." Certainly the various preceding chapters demonstrate the lack of consensus regarding the overall outcomes of CSRA. The years since its passage have seen other widely varying assessments of the Act's strengths and weaknesses. Alan Campbell, who early on proclaimed the policy's success, now wonders if there must be a "truce" between politicians and bureaucrats if success is to be attained.[1]

Failure to resolve the old politics-administration dichotomy, however, is not the Act's only perceived failure. Others have been attributed to incomplete implementation, to incorrect design, to political and environmental instability, to budgetary cutbacks that placed reform in a tenuous organizational position, and to failure to convince the career civil servants most affected by the legislation that the changes it proposed were in their best interests. Some of these problems are specific to CSRA and can be attributed to unique characteristics of that policy. Others, however, mirror "failures" of other public policies as well. They are caused by characteristics of the American public-policy process that make evaluating the success or failure of *any* public policy difficult. Lest our judgment of civil service reform be too harsh, therefore, it is useful to place its experience within the larger context of the public-policy process in the United States.

CIVIL SERVICE REFORM AS PUBLIC POLICY

The most widely used frameworks for the description and analysis of public policy make two basic assumptions:

1. It is a *process;* policies evolve and develop as they proceed through the stages of the process.

2. It is *dynamic;* public policies constantly change—describing and assessing their impact is critically related to time.

In relation to these points, Hugh Heclo has written: "Dynamic changes in public policy seem so overwhelming that both actors and scholars are often left digging in barren ground as the show inexorably moves on." [2]

In attempts to impose some order on the very diffuse activities and actions that create public policy and allow it to develop, Charles Jones and others have proposed a process model of policy which suggests not only that it is dynamic, but that it is cyclical.[3] A brief description of a modified version of the Jones model, and examples of its application to civil service reform, illustrate not only the complexity of the process, but the potential for policy distortion that it contains.

Policy Design

The process of public policy design is a composite of several key activities: correct problem definition, selection of causal theories that correctly link problem and desired outcome, choice of correct solution, choice of correct policy tools, and correct targeting of policy activities. These are ideal components, however, and the gap between the model and the real process may be a large one. A brief discussion of policy design's principal activities demonstrates how and why the necessary linkages may not be made.

Correct problem identification. This is the bottom line in any correct or "good" policy design. On its face, problem identification appears to be relatively straightforward. In fact, however, the enormous complexity of contemporary public problems is awesome. Virtually all are multicausal; most are not amenable to quick or easy solution; many take career bureaucrats, elected officials, and concerned citizens alike to the limits of knowledge and experience. Further, public problems may be defined by political activities or objectives. David Dillman notes that in relation to civil service reform, the problem-definition process is cyclical and continuous: "Where consensus fails, proposals for reform are laid on the shelf. When a favorable consensus is reached, at least some of the proposals are accepted. Disputants then go home, only to return to debate another day" (chap. 10).

Specifically in relation to the Civil Service Reform Act of 1978, it is worth noting again that problem definition took place on at least two levels. One of those was objective and experiential and emerged in part from the Personnel Management Project, and especially from those career civil servants who participated in its task forces. The other, however, was firmly rooted in popular opinion, and echoed in political rhetoric: bureaucrats were inefficient, unproductive, and an unnecessarily large drain on national resources. To be sure, the language in which the Personnel Management Project described problems was more measured; nonetheless, acceptance of the other definition was widespread. In addition, because the Act was to be a comprehensive reform, the problems it proposed to attack were legion. The process of deleting some and including others altered the nature of policy definition from the very beginning. The lack of clarity of some problem statements and program objectives had a tremendous impact on the ability to implement the reforms, once they passed. The labor-management title is one glaring example.

Correct causal theory and policy tools. Closely related to our ability to define public problems accurately is our ability to construct their solutions. The need for correct theories of causality suggests the need to understand the precise causes of the problem we wish to attack and the specific individual or institutional characteristics that must be altered if we are to achieve the change we desire. Choosing the correct policy tools refers to the ability to devise public courses of action that will cause the change and lead to the desired ends. Furthermore, it assumes that we *know* what the correct solution is.

Most attempts at policy assessment and analysis demonstrate potential pitfalls in this process.[4] Many public problems, for example, are caused by, or related to, megaevents or processes. Combatting poverty and unemployment at a time of general economic stress is one example of having a limited number of policy tools with which to attack very widespread and pervasive problems. Educational problems present another type of difficulty in choice of policy tools: the policy activities required for a particular remedy may not be at the disposal of the policy makers who desire change. Federal officials control some elements of education policy; state and local officials, however, are the key to any real change that will occur.

Finally, the range of possible actions available to policy makers may be painfully narrow. Existing laws and regulations have locked policy makers into certain patterns and activities; whatever change is to occur must come at the margins. Civil service reform is a good example of this problem. Changes were proposed, some of them major. But the basic institutions and principles remain. Even in a comprehensive reform, we did not scrap what existed. We altered it slightly and built upon it. In doing so, the framers of the legislation borrowed heavily from academic theory and from experience in the private sector. In many cases, the techniques, or policy tools, they chose to effect the desired changes had never been tested—or evaluated—in a public setting. The Senior Executive Service (SES) provides an excellent example of wholesale transfer of private motivational techniques to the public sector. The same is true of performance evaluation. Given the substantial problems currently being encountered by both, the wisdom of assuming transferability is not now so clear.

Identifying the correct target. To identify the correct target for policy activities is not only properly to identify who, or what, needs to be changed, but to limit policy activities to the group or institution with that need.[5] Again, many of the problems encountered in this regard can be traced to the nature of the political process from which our public policies emerge. The same activities that cause problem definition to become diffuse and less specific also build into the policy additional targets for assistance. We are confronted, therefore, with the reality of such policies as the Comprehensive Employment Training Act, which did indeed provide some assistance to the poor and the chronically unemployed. It also, however, provided employment to middle-class students with master's degrees who were having a bit of difficulty finding employment. Given such a wide range of targets, how does the analyst determine success or failure? And in what terms?

Consistency and consensus. Two additional qualities are important to the overall design of public policies. The first of these is consistency: specifically, internal consistency. All the elements of the design— the problem statement, the causal theories, the proposed solutions— should be consistent and not contradictory, either with respect to policy activities or with respect to potential outcomes. American public policies have historically been plagued by problems of internal inconsistencies. We wish to do too much. In the name of comprehensiveness, we include in the same program or policy elements that will have opposing effects, or mutually cancelling effects. Given this fact, some public policies may actually work against their own chances for achieving success. It is also important to note that often the need for political consensus not only creates inconsistencies, but effectively blurs them into an undecipherable whole.

Consensus is important among the elected officials who create legislation and provide public funds, among the career civil servants who will be responsible for carrying out program activities, and among those groups or institutions that a policy proposes to change. In the absence of such consensus, the policy may be subverted or effectively ignored and, despite its formal presence on the books, may have minimal impact.

In relation to the application of these components of design to CSRA, two points should be noted. First, whatever the actual intent of the reform, career civil servants were considered to be part of the problem. As such, they became targets of many of the policy's activities. Fred Thayer and other critics argue that this is the reason that the reform emphasized coercion and control. Others, such as Campbell, have argued that the intent of the design was to allow civil servants to follow their natural bent: to be more productive and efficient in the public service. Civil servants, in this view, were not the targets of change, but would be among the beneficiaries of change. Whether targets or beneficiaries, the tension is obvious. Civil servants were in some way related to the problems—and possibly were responsible for them—but were also critical to problem solution. Given the manner in which the reform was sold, many careerists perceived themselves not only as targets of policy action, but as targets of *punitive* policy action.[6] Despite that, they were expected to be cooperative participants in the reform efforts.

Second, CSRA contained major inconsistencies and, in fact, institutionalized some of them. Rosenbloom and Berry provide excellent examples, in chapter 9. There are many other inconsistencies within the SES, and within the provisions for, and implementation of, protection of whistleblowers. Because CSRA was comprehensive, it was inevitable that some internal tensions should exist. However, in the name of pleasing as many interests as possible, the legislation contained inconsistencies among the various titles, *within* some of the titles (such as the provisions for SES, equal employment opportunity, and labor management relations), and even in the manner in which the reform was sold to the public and to Congress, as well as to the career bureaucracy who had to make it work.

PROVISION OF RESOURCES

Providing adequate resources to carry out policy objectives is the responsibility of the legislature and of the executive, and they maintain continuous policy influence through control of resources. The resources they can provide include money, organizational support, and expertise. As in policy design, however, there is ample opportunity, in determining resource need and providing the required amounts, to create considerable policy distortion. Though there is rarely ill intent, the explanations for distortion at this stage of policy design and development are varied. First, there is a very real possibility that those who guard the purse strings simply do not know what level of financial support is necessary to achieve a policy's success. This is particularly true if the precise problem, or the correct solution, is unclear and if the proposed policy is, in effect, a stab in the dark. Though this sounds somewhat preposterous, it often occurs, particularly when technologically complex policies and social policies and programs are involved.

Second, although the amount of financial support provided may have been appropriate for the original policy, it may be inadequate for the policy that emerges from legislative—or legislative-executive—compromise. A classic example of this policy problem was the Model Cities program in the late 1960s. Model Cities was originally designed and funded as an experiment for 20 cities, but emerged from compromises between Congress and the Department of Housing and Urban Development serving—with the same amount of financial support—125 cities. The implications of such policy changes for ultimate success or failure are clear: whatever rationale there was in the original policy is effectively thwarted. The analyst is left with the problem of determining what the policy is supposed to accomplish in these new circumstances, as well as the problem of determining what difference it makes.

The final element to be considered is that the provision of resources, too, is political. Congress or other legislative bodies may provide only the bare minimum required to buy off dissent or dissatisfaction. In chapter 3, Carolyn Ban outlines specific instances of such actions in relation to CSRA.

The other critical resources are primarily bureaucratic. The organization in which the program is placed is assumed to have the capacity and expertise to translate legislative policy to street policy. The match between policy scope and administrative resources is critical. Another important element is having sufficient control over the resources designated for a policy to be able to use them for carrying out that policy and not for some other purpose. This, of course, speaks to the problem of guaranteeing bureaucratic responsiveness to legislative and executive directives.

Finally, with respect to resources, it is important to consider the question of expertise. National, state, and local bureaucracies are the repositories of the required administrative and program expertise. Yet, to the extent that the problem and/or program has not been clearly defined prior to reaching the bureaucracy, bureaucratic expertise is dissipated by a continuing process of problem definition. In addition, there are some policy areas in which we consciously tax our bureaucratic resources. In environmental policy, for example, initial objectives and expectations have exceeded bureaucratic capacity.

Many of these potential hazards have, in fact, been realized in CSRA. If a policy must have adequate financial and organizational resources to succeed, the expectations for CSRA should have been lowered early on. As several chapters in this book make clear, some titles of the Act never received adequate resources. The Federal Labor Relations Board, the Merit Systems Protection Board, and others were inhibited from the beginning by inadequate staff, inadequate office space, lack of political support, and the failure to appoint key political leadership.

In other cases, such as the Senior Executive Service, though financial resources may have initially been adequate, congressional action within the first six months of program operation altered their supply. Other, less tangible, resources such as sabbatical leaves, additional career development monies, and the like were either not forthcoming or extremely limited. The extremely limited amounts of money available for other provisions, such as merit pay, reinforce the lesson. From the very beginning, the ability of CSRA to carry out its objectives was limited by lack of resources.

POLICY IMPLEMENTATION

Implementation Strategy

Closely related to the issues of resources are those of implementation. Besides the provisions of adequate financial and organizational resources, it is necessary that an appropriate strategy for their use be in place. Implementation strategies vary; they may be centralized or decentralized, they may be long-term or short-term, they may be objective-oriented, or, like revenue sharing programs, they may be open-ended and flexible. Underlying the decision to utilize any of these strategies is the critical issue of control. To the extent that a program is decentralized, open-ended, or process-oriented, rather than objective-oriented, the ability to control its outcomes is diminished. Thus, for example, when the federal government provides funds for a program, but turns program design and administration over to the state or local governments, the federal government does not really control the program but is reduced to serving a monitoring function. The same is true when one agency takes the lead responsibility for a program but decentralizes choice of administrative strategy to other agencies. The continuing rationale for decentralization and flexibility is their potential for enhancing innovation and better tailoring of solution to problem. Though this may in fact occur, the tradeoff for that flexibility is a decreased ability to specify accurately the program's goals and objectives and, therefore, to assess its success or failure.

Environmental and organizational stability

Whatever the implementation strategy adopted for a particular program or policy, the need for full implementation is clear. This implies several things. First, if a program is to be fully implemented, organizational and financial resources should remain stable, or at least continue at adequate levels. To the extent that original objectives remain in place, but financial resources are cut, the program will necessarily be judged a partial failure. Similarly, a policy implemented by an agency whose internal stability is jeopardized or whose future is unclear, will probably not be fully implemented.

The common element in both of these problems is that of continuing political and environmental support. Public policies are constantly vulnerable to political shifts and changes (as, indeed, our system of government demands they should be). Many of the resources critical to a policy's success are externally controlled. Again, the issue of control becomes central. A policy with a long-term implementation strategy may be nipped in the bud by congressional elections or a presidential transition. Further, congressional decisions relating either to total resources available, or to the number of persons or units eligible to compete for those resources, can dramatically alter the nature of a public policy. As with the example of the Model Cities program, an experimental program may well become something entirely different. In summary, then, if program assessment is to proceed with some degree of accuracy, there should be enough political and organizational stability to permit a program to move through the implementation process with continuing consensus about its value, about the level of resources it requires for success, and about its desired outcomes. In the presence of these conditions, the task of an evaluator or analyst is greatly simplified.

In relation to CSRA, chapter 3 and the chapters in section two indicate that its implementation strategy was long-term and decentralized. This strategy guaranteed differing outcomes in different agencies, since there would be varying levels of commitment to the reforms from agency to agency. In addition, because the early directors of the implementation effort recognized the long time required for institutionalization of comprehensive reform, their strategy did not anticipate or promise short-term payoffs. Given long-term stability and political support, such a strategy makes a good deal of sense. In the presence of turmoil and dwindling political support, however, its costs are high. If support is decreased, continued inability to demonstrate positive effects of reform efforts is sure to diminish support even further.

The experience of specific agencies with the reform package is also a complicating factor. Again, the chapters in Section Two demonstrate the wide range of patterns that exist. In Health and Human Services, for example, commitment to the reform was strong. The agency itself funded one of the few long range, and continuing, evaluations of CSRA. As a case study in utilizing evaluation to inform the decision-making process, that evaluation stands as one of the successes of the reform. At the other end of the spectrum, Gregory and Karen Gaertner (see chapter 11) detail the approach of the Mine Safety and Health Administration. Officials responsible for reform implementation in that agency consciously chose to downplay the importance of civil service reform. As one MSHA official said, "Without undermining the law, we wanted to make this as easy as possible." The impact of decentralization is compounded when one considers the differences between headquarters and regional or area agencies. In explaining some of their findings, for example, the Gaertners note that, "comparisons of regional to headquarters units in the two agencies yield opposite results." The same could well be true if different agencies or bureaus within the same department were the units of analysis.

The presidential election in 1980, the subsequent dismissal of old political appointees, and the naming of new ones, introduced another source of variation in the implementation of the Act. In some agencies, where the implementation had begun to take hold, reform activities were viewed as the "old" way of doing things. In other agencies, where implementation was not so advanced, the intent of the reform was not clear to the incoming appointees. In all cases, the reform appears to have received a lower priority and a redesigned implementation strategy at mid-point.

As the previous comments suggest, the Civil Service Reform Act of 1978 was not implemented in an environment that was even minimally stable. The first indication of the real instability occurred in the first year of its history, when Congress reduced both the total dollars available for SES bonuses and the number of SES members who could compete for them. The major disruption, however, was the election of Ronald Reagan and the immediate round of budgetary and organizational reductions that he initiated.

It is important to note that Reagan, as had many presidents before him, campaigned against big government and bureaucrats. This did little to enhance the relationship between him, or his political appointees, and career civil servants.

Quite aside from the political transition, reform efforts were dealt a serious blow by budgetary cutbacks and the reductions in force effected in many agencies. Whatever positive impact the reforms may have had were frequently lost or obfuscated by the trauma of the larger instability. Further, these combined forces made manifest one of the unanticipated consequences of the reform: members of the Senior Executive Service, already disenchanted by the perceived breach of faith in relation to the bonuses and merit awards, chose to leave government rather than to stay to fight another day.[7] For many, the *coup de grace* was the lack of concern on the part of the Reagan Administration and its appointees with managing what was left after the budget cuts and reductions in force had occurred. A reform, one primary objective of which was improved management, had become the stepchild of an administration to whom management was not important.

POLICY EVALUATION

The final element in a developmental model of public policy is the evaluation process. In an ideal model, there are at least three major points to consider.

Integrated evaluation stragegy. To assess program performance accurately, the evaluation activities should be considered concurrently with program design. Appropriate baseline data should be gathered prior to program start up, and evaluation should be closely involved in any change or redesign that takes place in program goals and objectives. The evaluation strategy, obviously, should match the implementation strategy to the maximum extent possible. If the program is to be decentralized, for example, there should be evaluation resources and receptivity to the evaluation process at the level of service delivery. Further, the evaluation activities should be viewed as important by those who fund the program, by those who deliver services, and by those who are the program's recipients.

Adequate and stable resources. Just as adequate financial and organizational support is critical to effective program implementation, so too is it necessary to evaluation. Good evaluation is time-consuming and often costly. It requires a high level of staff expertise and specialized training.

There is also a need for continuing organizational support of evaluation activities and findings. Evaluation can be a threatening activity; to the extent that findings are critical or not supportive of program efforts, it is easy to downgrade the emphasis evaluation receives. Finally, since evaluation activities often do not produce the tangible results of those activities more directly concerned with service delivery or client relations, in times of organizational stress or reduction, evaluation activities and staff are often the first to go.

Timeliness of assessment. Though the statement is somewhat tautological, change takes time. Different kinds of policies and different kinds of changes require dramatically different time spans to become effective and institutionalized. Further, it is important to note that change is disruptive, painful, and often resisted. Evaluation activities that occur too early in the life of a policy, therefore, may tap only the dissatisfaction at leaving the status quo, and may miss improvements or increased satisfaction, which may occur later in the process. There is no single and absolutely appropriate time at which to evaluate; much depends on the nature of the policy and the changes it proposes. In the ideal situation, however, evaluation is ongoing, so that, while the initial disruption is documented, the gradual changing and eventual institutionalization of the change is noted and evaluated as well.

One final note: the evaluation stage of the public policy model necessarily implies a clear idea of what policy success would look like. Conclusive evaluation determines the match between what a program or policy is *supposed* to accomplish and what it does, in fact, achieve. No matter which level of evaluation activity is chosen, it is necesary to specify program or policy objectives, along with performance measures for the activities directed toward them. Again, an apparently simple task becomes difficult in the public environment. The politics of public policies often cause policy objectives to be couched in grand, symbolic terms; that is, to "improve the quality of urban life," or "to make the streets safe." The number of specific interpretations such broad statements allow is enormous. In chapter 6, Abramson, Schmidt, and Baxter provide one concrete example of the problems this causes for evaluation: "We are left," they write, "with alternative propositions as to what was supposed to change as a result of the Act. . . . [during Phase I inteviews] we were told:

- By the Office of Management and Budget, that improvement would be reflected in the number of bureaucrats fired [not through reduction in force, but fired];
- By OPM, that improvement would be reflected in the actual improvement in performance of government programs and services, although they had no means to judge such changes.

Evaluation of CSRA has been significantly hampered by the lack of consensus about measures of success or failure. Other factors have also been important, however. As events seemed to overtake development and implementation of the Act, so too did they alter efforts to evaluate its impacts. Initially, the Office of Personnel Management had established an office for evaluation activities and a staff devoted to evaluation of CSRA. Under the supervision of that staff, Phases One and Two of the Federal Employee Attitude Survey ((FEAS) were designed and executed,[8] long-range organizational assessments were contracted for,[9] and numerous smaller-scale evaluation activities were begun. The Reagan Administration did not retain this priority for evaluation, In fact, the evaluation staff was decimated and most evaluation work terminated. In other actions, Reagan appointees terminated research grants and demonstration projects and eliminated proposed conferences and research related to productivity and the development of productivity measures. Though it initially appeared that FEAS III would be axed as well, it was administered, in a briefer form, in 1983. Only one of the organizational assessment contracts survived into its fourth year, again in reduced form.

Under other auspices, the study at the Department of Health and Human Services, partially reported here in chapter 6, continues. There have been numerous academic analyses of the impact of CSRA and its various components. Most of them, unfortunately, present findings from a single time point. The only organization that continues to evaluate systematically some aspects of the reform throughout government is the General Accounting Office.

Although more limited policy evaluation efforts do continue, few are under the auspices of the Office of Personnel Management, and virtually none (the Health and Human Services study is the obvious exception) are being conducted for the purpose of informing the decision-making process. The ability to track the various effects of CSRA and to examine those effects in a variety of settings is severely diminished. In the final analysis, our assessment of CSRA must consist of fitting together disparate pieces. The early capacity for thorough and ongoing research, for innovative research, and for experimental projects no longer exists.

CONCLUSION: CIVIL SERVICE REFORM: SUCCESS OR FAILURE?

As the preceding section suggests, assessing policy success or failure is no easy task. Charles Jones notes in the closing chapter of his textbook that, ". . . it should be apparent that one seldom has a sense of closure in studying the policy process . . . public problems aren't comprehensively or universally 'solved.' " [10] Reaching a similar conclusion, Ingram and Mann write: "The fate of policies cannot be separated from the course of politics. . . . Reasonable policy demand

and agreement on realizable goals . . . are an important condition of policy success." [11]

Our own summary of the match between a model for policy success and the experience of CSRA underlines the problem: to understand policy impact, we must understand policy process. To understand process, however, can often be an exercise in analytic defeat. If we do not know *what* a policy is supposed to do, or *how* it is supposed to do it, we are ill advised to examine overall impact. Understanding this process makes clear why so few policies are viewed as undisputed successes. There are too many obstacles to overcome as a policy grows and develops. The Civil Service Reform Act encountered nearly all of them; it was only sporadically successful in overcoming the major ones. In this regard, CSRA is not unique. Also in this regard, CSRA is, on its face, a nearly classic case study of policy failure. Is that, however, an adequate assessment?

We would argue that it *is* an accurate assessment, but that it is only one part of a larger whole. The public policy process *has* distorted this policy, and has changed both what it intended to do and what it did. But what does that mean? Five years after its enactment, it is clear that the Civil Service Reform Act has not achieved most of what it apparently was intended to do. There are many areas of policy activity in which CSRA, for all its human and economic costs, simply hasn't made much difference one way or the other. Increased protection for whistleblowers, improved labor-management relations, and progress in affirmative action are all examples of this nonprogress. Other policy activities, such as decentralization of examining and early retirement options, have been subject to such changing emphasis that it is nearly impossible to tell if they are working or not. Still others, such as performance evaluation, require long time periods to become institutionalized and to begin to have the desired effects. It is too early to tell if they are effective.

On the other hand, some aspects of CSRA have had very negative, unanticipated consequences. The splintering of responsibilities among angecies, which Ban, and Rosenbloom and Berry chronicle, is one such example. The profound disaffection of many members of the Senior Executive Service is another. An increased exit rate of the best managers in the career service does not bode well for increased productivity or effectiveness. Closely related to this is the dissatisfaction of merit pay managers. If the most experienced managers leave, and the waters are poisoned for the next managerial echelon as well, negative policy consequences are both immediate and long-term.

Finally, the gap between the grand promises of civil service reform and the limited reality exacerbated a problem it was intended to remedy. Framers of the legislation promised a policy that would enhance government productivity and effectiveness by increasing political direction and control, but also by creating greater managerial commitment and competence. If both are to occur simultaneously, two conditions must be present. As Abramson and Schmidt note (chap. 12), there must be a consensus about the proper role of government and the proper scope of public policy activities. Equally important, as Dillman notes (chap. 10), is a mutual trust between those elected officials who have the power to change government's role and policy scope and the career civil servants who can make it happen. Absent those conditions, the policy cycle Jones describes becomes, not a self-correcting device, but a vehicle for increasing dissatisfaction with governmental processes and institutions. We would argue that the election of Ronald Reagan effectively destabilized the policy consensus surrounding many federal agencies. The tendency of that Administration and its appointees to continue to "bash the bureaucrat" heightened the atmosphere of distrust between political appointee and careerist. Finally, the Reagan Administration's concern with cutting back was not balanced by a commitment to effective management of what was left. This caused many career managers to question the value of their public service.

In describing the Reagan transition, the Gaertners accurately pinpoint a tension between orgranizational theory and democratic theory. Political change is often short-term, bureaucratic change is not. Yet the political system and the personnel system have been viewed as compatible, simply because each served as an effective counterbalance to the other. Kaufman, Dillman, and others have described previous efforts at reform as exercises in value equilibrium.[12] As one set of values becomes ascendant, others recede, or become less important. But the machinery of government does not grind to a halt, because there is continued consensus about the purpose and function of government and about the value of an objective career service.

In our view, the juxtaposition of a reform widely viewed as punitive, of an administration bent on cutting back government at whatever cost, and of a continuing view of the career civil servant as public policy problem is more than just the story of another public policy of limited effectiveness. A government that does not value management eventually becomes a government that cannot manage. A government that does not understand that government managers can be problem solvers and not problems is a government that squanders necessary resources. A government that notes past policy failures but does not learn from them becomes a government that cannot solve important problems. Civil service reform speaks to all of these issues;

to treat its lessons as isolated, or unique to personnel management, would be a grave error.

NOTES

1. Alan Campbell, "The Bureaucrats and Politicians Need A Treaty," *Washington Post,* January 16, 1983, p. A8.
2. Hugh Heclo, "Policy Dynamics," in *The Dynamics of Public Policy: A Comparative Analysis,* ed. Richard Rose (Beverly Hills, Cal.: Sage, 1976), p. 237.
3. Charles Jones, *An Introduction to the Study of Public Policy,* 2nd ed. (North Scituate, Mass.: Duxbury, 1977), especially chaps. 1 and 2. See also Thomas Dye, *Understanding Public Policy,* 4th ed. (Englewood Cliffs, N.J.: Prentice-Hall, 1981).
4. See, for example, Helen Ingram and Dean Mann, eds. *Why Policies Succeed or Fail* (Beverly Hills, Cal.: Sage, 1980); Kurt Finsterbusch and Annabelle Bender Motz, *Social Research for Policy Decisions* (Belmont, Cal.: Wadsworth, 1980); and Joseph Wholey, *Evaluation and Effective Public Management* (Boston: Little, Brown, 1983); and David Nachmias, *Public Policy Evaluation* (New York: St. Martins, 1979).
5. See, for example, Richard I. Hofferbert, "Differential Program Impact as a Function of Target Need: Or Why Some Good Policies Often Seem to Fail," *Policy Studies Review* (November 1982): 279–92.
6. See Patricia W. Ingraham and Peter W. Colby, "Politics and Government Management: the Case of the Senior Executive Service," *Policy Studies Journal* (December 1982): 304–317.
7. See, for example, Paul Taylor, "Civil Service Turns 100, Burdened by Stereotypes," *Washington Post,* January 16, 1983, p. A1.
8. U.S. Office of Personnel Management, *Federal Employee Attitude Survey, Phase I,* (Washington, D.C.: GPO, 1980); *Federal Employee Attitude Survey, Phase II,* (Washington, D.C.: GPO, 1982).
9. Organizational assessment contracts were awarded to three universities: Case Western Reserve (funded for four years), University of Michigan (funded for three years), and University of California at Irvine (funded for two years).
10. Charles Jones, *Study of Public Policy,* p. 211.
11. Ingram and Mann, *Why Policies Succeed or Fail,* p. 27.
12. See Herbert Kaufman, "Administrative Decentralization and Political Power," in *Current Issues in Public Administration,* ed. Frederick Lane (New York: St. Martins, 1978); and David Dillman, "The Politics of Civil Service Reform: The Search for Responsible Administration in Great Britain and the United States" (Ph.D. diss., University of Massachusetts at Amherst, 1982) from which chap. 10 of this book is excerpted.

APPENDIX

THE CIVIL SERVICE REFORM ACT OF 1978
PUBLIC LAW 95–454

Public Law 95–454
95th Congress

An Act

To reform the civil service laws.

Be it enacted by the Senate and House of Representatives of the United States of America in Congress assembled,

Oct. 13, 1978
[S. 2640]

SHORT TITLE

SECTION 1. This Act may be cited as the "Civil Service Reform Act of 1978".

Civil Service
Reform Act of
1978.
5 USC 1101 note.

TABLE OF CONTENTS

SEC. 2. The table of contents is as follows:

FINDINGS AND STATEMENT OF PURPOSE

5 USC 1101 note.

SEC. 3. It is the policy of the United States that—

(1) in order to provide the people of the United States with a competent, honest, and productive Federal work force reflective of the Nation's diversity, and to improve the quality of public service, Federal personnel management should be implemented consistent with merit system principles and free from prohibited personnel practices;

(2) the merit system principles which shall govern in the competitive service and in the executive branch of the Federal Government should be expressly stated to furnish guidance to Federal agencies in carrying out their responsibilities in administering the public business, and prohibited personnel practices should be statutorily defined to enable Federal employees to avoid conduct which undermines the merit system principles and the integrity of the merit system;

(3) Federal employees should receive appropriate protection through increasing the authority and powers of the Merit Systems Protection Board in processing hearings and appeals affecting Federal employees;

(4) the authority and power of the Special Counsel should be increased so that the Special Counsel may investigate allegations involving prohibited personnel practices and reprisals against Federal employees for the lawful disclosure of certain information and may file complaints against agency officials and employees who engage in such conduct;

(5) the function of filling positions and other personnel functions in the competitive service and in the executive branch should

be delegated in appropriate cases to the agencies to expedite processing appointments and other personnel actions, with the control and oversight of this delegation being maintained by the Office of Personnel Management to protect against prohibited personnel practices and the use of unsound management practices by the agencies;

"(6) a Senior Executive Service should be established to provide the flexibility needed by agencies to recruit and retain the highly competent and qualified executives needed to provide more effective management of agencies and their functions, and the more expeditious administration of the public business;

"(7) in appropriate instances, pay increases should be based on quality of performance rather than length of service;

"(8) research programs and demonstration projects should be authorized to permit Federal agencies to experiment, subject to congressional oversight, with new and different personnel management concepts in controlled situations to achieve more efficient management of the Government's human resources and greater productivity in the delivery of service to the public;

"(9) the training program of the Government should include retraining of employees for positions in other agencies to avoid separations during reductions in force and the loss to the Government of the knowledge and experience that these employees possess; and

"(10) the right of Federal employees to organize, bargain collectively, and participate through labor organizations in decisions which affect them, with full regard for the public interest and the effective conduct of public business, should be specifically recognized in statute.

TITLE I—MERIT SYSTEM PRINCIPLES

MERIT SYSTEM PRINCIPLES; PROHIBITED PERSONNEL PRACTICES

SEC. 101. (a) Title 5, United States Code, is amended by inserting after chapter 21 the following new chapter:

"CHAPTER 23—MERIT SYSTEM PRINCIPLES

"Sec.
"2301. Merit system principles.
"2302. Prohibited personnel practices.
"2303. Prohibited personnel practices in the Federal Bureau of Investigation.
"2304. Responsibility of the General Accounting Office.
"2305. Coordination with certain other provisions of law.

"§ 2301. Merit system principles   5 USC 2301.

"(a) This section shall apply to—
"(1) an Executive agency;
"(2) the Administrative Office of the United States Courts; and
"(3) the Government Printing Office.

"(b) Federal personnel management should be implemented consistent with the following merit system principles:

"(1) Recruitment should be from qualified individuals from appropriate sources in an endeavor to achieve a work force from all segments of society, and selection and advancement should be determined solely on the basis of relative ability, knowledge, and skills, after fair and open competition which assures that all receive equal opportunity.

"(2) All employees and applicants for employment should receive fair and equitable treatment in all aspects of personnel management without regard to political affiliation, race, color, religion, national origin, sex, marital status, age, or handicapping condition, and with proper regard for their privacy and constitutional rights.

"(3) Equal pay should be provided for work of equal value, with appropriate consideration of both national and local rates paid by employers in the private sector, and appropriate incentives and recognition should be provided for excellence in performance.

"(4) All employees should maintain high standards of integrity, conduct, and concern for the public interest.

"(5) The Federal work force should be used efficiently and effectively.

"(6) Employees should be retained on the basis of the adequacy of their performance, inadequate performance should be corrected, and employees should be separated who cannot or will not improve their performance to meet required standards.

"(7) Employees should be provided effective education and training in cases in which such education and training would result in better organizational and individual performance.

"(8) Employees should be—

"(A) protected against arbitrary action, personal favoritism, or coercion for partisan political purposes, and

"(B) prohibited from using their official authority or influence for the purpose of interfering with or affecting the result of an election or a nomination for election.

"(9) Employees should be protected against reprisal for the lawful disclosure of information which the employees reasonably believe evidences—

"(A) a violation of any law, rule. or regulation, or

"(B) mismanagement, a gross waste of funds, an abuse of authority, or a substantial and specific danger to public health or safety.

"(c) In administering the provisions of this chapter—

Infra.

"(1) with respect to any agency (as defined in section 2302(a) (2) (C) of this title), the President shall, pursuant to the authority otherwise available under this title, take any action, including the issuance of rules, regulations, or directives; and

"(2) with respect to any entity in the executive branch which is not such an agency or part of such an agency, the head of such entity shall, pursuant to authority otherwise available, take any action, including the issuance of rules, regulations, or directives; which is consistent with the provisions of this title and which the President or the head, as the case may be, determines is necessary to ensure that personnel management is based on and embodies the merit system principles.

5 USC 2302.
Definitions.

"§ 2302. Prohibited personnel practices

"(a) (1) For the purpose of this title, 'prohibited personnel practice' means any action described in subsection (b) of this section.

"(2) For the purpose of this section—

"(A) 'personnel action' means—

"(i) an appointment;

"(ii) a promotion;

"(iii) an action under chapter 75 of this title or other disciplinary or corrective action;

"(iv) a detail, transfer, or reassignment;

"(v) a reinstatement;

"(vi) a restoration;

"(vii) a reemployment;

"(viii) a performance evaluation under chapter 43 of this title;

"(ix) a decision concerning pay, benefits, or awards, or concerning education or training if the education or training may reasonably be expected to lead to an appointment, promotion, performance evaluation, or other action described in this subparagraph; and

"(x) any other significant change in duties or responsibilities which is inconsistent with the employee's salary or grade level;

with respect to an employee in, or applicant for, a covered position in an agency;

"(B) 'covered position' means any position in the competitive service, a career appointee position in the Senior Executive Service, or a position in the excepted service, but does not include—

"(i) a position which is excepted from the competitive service because of its confidential, policy-determining, policy-making, or policy-advocating character; or

"(ii) any position excluded from the coverage of this section by the President based on a determination by the President that it is necessary and warranted by conditions of good administration.

"(C) 'agency' means an Executive agency, the Administrative Office of the United States Courts, and the Government Printing Office, but does not include—

"(i) a Government corporation;

"(ii) the Federal Bureau of Investigation, the Central Intelligence Agency, the Defense Intelligence Agency, the National Security Agency, and, as determined by the President, any Executive agency or unit thereof the principal function of which is the conduct of foreign intelligence or counterintelligence activities; or

"(iii) the General Accounting Office.

"(b) Any employee who has authority to take, direct others to take, recommend, or approve any personnel action, shall not, with respect to such authority—

"(1) discriminate for or against any employee or applicant for employment—

"(A) on the basis of race, color, religion, sex, or national origin, as prohibited under section 717 of the Civil Rights Act of 1964 (42 U.S.C. 2000e–16);

"(B) on the basis of age, as prohibited under sections 12 and 15 of the Age Discrimination in Employment Act of 1967 (29 U.S.C. 631, 633a);

"(C) on the basis of sex, as prohibited under section 6(d) of the Fair Labor Standards Act of 1938 (29 U.S.C. 206(d));

"(D) on the basis of handicapping condition, as prohibited under section 501 of the Rehabilitation Act of 1973 (29 U.S.C. 791); or

"(E) on the basis of marital status or political affiliation, as prohibited under any law, rule, or regulation;

"(2) solicit or consider any recommendation or statement, oral or written, with respect to any individual who requests or is under consideration for any personnel action unless such recommendation or statement is based on the personal knowledge or records of the person furnishing it and consists of—

"(A) an evaluation of the work performance, ability, aptitude, or general qualifications of such individual; or

"(B) an evaluation of the character, loyalty, or suitability of such individual;

"(3) coerce the political activity of any person (including the providing of any political contribution or service), or take any action against any employee or applicant for employment as a reprisal for the refusal of any person to engage in such political activity;

"(4) deceive or willfully obstruct any person with respect to such person's right to compete for employment;

"(5) influence any person to withdraw from competition for any position for the purpose of improving or injuring the prospects of any other person for employment;

"(6) grant any preference or advantage not authorized by law, rule, or regulation to any employee or applicant for employment (including defining the scope or manner of competition or the requirements for any position) for the purpose of improving or injuring the prospects of any particular person for employment;

5 USC 3110.

"(7) appoint, employ, promote, advance, or advocate for appointment, employment, promotion, or advancement, in or to a civilian position any individual who is a relative (as defined in section 3110(a)(3) of this title) of such employee if such position is in the agency in which such employee is serving as a public official (as defined in section 3110(a)(2) of this title) or over which such employee exercises jurisdiction or control as such an official;

"(8) take or fail to take a personnel action with respect to any employee or applicant for employment as a reprisal for—

"(A) a disclosure of information by an employee or applicant which the employee or applicant reasonably believes evidences—

"(i) a violation of any law, rule, or regulation, or

"(ii) mismanagement, a gross waste of funds, an abuse of authority, or a substantial and specific danger to public health or safety,

if such disclosure is not specifically prohibited by law and if such information is not specifically required by Executive order to be kept secret in the interest of national defense or the conduct of foreign affairs; or

"(B) a disclosure to the Special Counsel of the Merit Systems Protection Board, or to the Inspector General of an agency or another employee designated by the head of the agency to receive such disclosures, of information which the employee or applicant reasonably believes evidences—

"(i) a violation of any law, rule, or regulation, or

"(ii) mismanagement, a gross waste of funds, an abuse of authority, or a substantial and specific danger to public health or safety;

"(9) take or fail to take any personnel action against any employee or applicant for employment as a reprisal for the exercise of any appeal right granted by any law, rule, or regulation;

"(10) discriminate for or against any employee or applicant for employment on the basis of conduct which does not adversely affect the performance of the employee or applicant or the performance of others; except that nothing in this paragraph shall prohibit an agency from taking into account in determining suitability or fitness any conviction of the employee or applicant for any crime under the laws of any State, of the District of Columbia, or of the United States; or

"(11) take or fail to take any other personnel action if the taking of or failure to take such action violates any law, rule, or regulation implementing, or directly concerning, the merit system principles contained in section 2301 of this title.

This subsection shall not be construed to authorize the withholding of information from the Congress or the taking of any personnel action against an employee who discloses information to the Congress.

"(c) The head of each agency shall be responsible for the prevention of prohibited personnel practices, for the compliance with and enforcement of applicable civil service laws, rules, and regulations, and other aspects of personnel management. Any individual to whom the head of an agency delegates authority for personnel management, or for any aspect thereof, shall be similarly responsible within the limits of the delegation.

"(d) This section shall not be construed to extinguish or lessen any effort to achieve equal employment opportunity through affirmative action or any right or remedy available to any employee or applicant for employment in the civil service under—

"(1) section 717 of the Civil Rights Act of 1964 (42 U.S.C. 2000e–16), prohibiting discrimination on the basis of race, color, religion, sex, or national origin;

"(2) sections 12 and 15 of the Age Discrimination in Employment Act of 1967 (29 U.S.C. 631, 633a), prohibiting discrimination on the basis of age;

"(3) under section 6(d) of the Fair Labor Standards Act of 1938 (29 U.S.C. 206(d)), prohibiting discrimination on the basis of sex;

"(4) section 501 of the Rehabilitation Act of 1973 (29 U.S.C. 791), prohibiting discrimination on the basis of handicapping condition; or

"(5) the provisions of any law, rule, or regulation prohibiting discrimination on the basis of marital status or political affiliation.

"**2303. Prohibited personnel practices in the Federal Bureau of Investigation**   5 USC 2303.

"(a) Any employee of the Federal Bureau of Investigation who has authority to take, direct others to take, recommend, or approve any personnel action, shall not, with respect to such authority, take or fail to take a personnel action with respect to any employee of the Bureau as a reprisal for a disclosure of information by the employee to the Attorney General (or an employee designated by the Attorney General for such purpose) which the employee or applicant reasonably believes evidences—

"(1) a violation of any law, rule, or regulation, or

"(2) mismanagement, a gross waste of funds, an abuse of authority, or a substantial and specific danger to public health or safety.

For the purpose of this subsection, 'personnel action' means any action described in clauses (i) through (x) of section 2302(a)(2)(A) of this   "Personnel action."

title with respect to an employee in, or applicant for, a position in the Bureau (other than a position of a confidential, policy-determining, policymaking, or policy-advocating character).

Regulations.

"(b) The Attorney General shall prescribe regulations to ensure that such a personnel action shall not be taken against an employee of the Bureau as a reprisal for any disclosure of information described in subsection (a) of this section.

Presidential enforcement.
Post, p. 1125.
5 USC 2304.

"(c) The President shall provide for the enforcement of this section in a manner consistent with the provisions of section 1206 of this title.

"§ 2304. Responsibility of the General Accounting Office

"(a) If requested by either House of the Congress (or any committee thereof), or if considered necessary by the Comptroller General, the General Accounting Office shall conduct audits and reviews to assure compliance with the laws, rules, and regulations governing employment in the executive branch and in the competitive service and to assess the effectiveness and soundness of Federal personnel management.

Report to President and Congress.

"(b) the General Accounting Office shall prepare and submit an annual report to the President and the Congress on the activities of the Merit Systems Protection Board and the Office of Personnel Management. The report shall include a description of—

"(1) significant actions taken by the Board to carry out its functions under this title; and

"(2) significant actions of the Office of Personnel Management, including an analysis of whether or not the actions of the Office are in accord with merit system principles and free from prohibited personnel practices.

5 USC 2305.

"§ 2305. Coordination with certain other provisions of law

"No provision of this chapter, or action taken under this chapter, shall be construed to impair the authorities and responsibilities set forth in section 102 of the National Security Act of 1947 (61 Stat. 495; 50 U.S.C. 403), the Central Intelligence Agency Act of 1949 (63 Stat. 208; 50 U.S.C. 403a and following), the Act entitled 'An Act to provide certain administrative authorities for the National Security Agency, and for other purposes', approved May 29, 1959 (73 Stat. 63; 50 U.S.C. 402 note), and the Act entitled 'An Act to amend the Internal Security Act of 1950', approved March 26, 1964 (78 Stat. 168; 50 U.S.C. 831–835).".

(b)(1) The table of chapters for part III of title 5, United States Code, is amended by adding after the item relating to chapter 21 the following new item:

"23. Merit system principles_____ 2301".

(2) Section 7153 of title 5, United States Code, is amended—

(A) by striking out **"Physical handicap"** in the catchline and inserting in lieu thereof **"Handicapping condition"**; and

(B) by striking out "physical handicap" each place it appears in the text and inserting in lieu thereof "handicapping condition".

TITLE II—CIVIL SERVICE FUNCTIONS: PERFORMANCE APPRAISAL; ADVERSE ACTIONS

OFFICE OF PERSONNEL MANAGEMENT

SEC. 201. (a) Chapter 11 of title 5, United States Code, is amended to read as follows:

"CHAPTER 11—OFFICE OF PERSONNEL MANAGEMENT

"§ 1101. Office of Personnel Management   5 USC 1101.

"The Office of Personnel Management is an independent establishment in the executive branch. The Office shall have an official seal, which shall be judicially noticed, and shall have its principal office in the District of Columbia, and may have field offices in other appropriate locations.

"§ 1102. Director; Deputy Director; Associate Directors   5 USC 1102.

"(a) There is at the head of the Office of Personnel Management a Director of the Office of Personnel Management appointed by the President, by and with the advice and consent of the Senate. The term of office of any individual appointed as Director shall be 4 years.

"(b) There is in the Office a Deputy Director of the Office of Personnel Management appointed by the President, by and with the advice and consent of the Senate. The Deputy Director shall perform such functions as the Director may from time to time prescribe and shall act as Director during the absence or disability of the Director or when the office of Director is vacant.

"(c) No individual shall, while serving as Director or Deputy Director, serve in any other office or position in the Government of the United States except as otherwise provided by law or at the direction of the President. The Director and Deputy Director shall not recommend any individual for appointment to any position (other than Deputy Director of the Office) which requires the advice and consent of the Senate.

"(d) There may be within the Office of Personnel Management not more than 5 Associate Directors, as determined from time to time by the Director. Each Associate Director shall be appointed by the Director.

"§ 1103. Functions of the Director   5 USC 1103.

"(a) The following functions are vested in the Director of the Office of Personnel Management, and shall be performed by the Director, or subject to section 1104 of this title, by such employees of the Office as the Director designates:

  "(1) securing accuracy, uniformity, and justice in the functions of the Office;

  "(2) appointing individuals to be employed by the Office;

  "(3) directing and supervising employees of the Office, distributing business among employees and organizational units of the Office, and directing the internal management of the Office;

  "(4) directing the preparation of requests for appropriations for the Office and the use and expenditure of funds by the Office;

  "(5) executing, administering, and enforcing—

     "(A) the civil service rules and regulations of the President and the Office and the laws governing the civil service; and

     "(B) the other activities of the Office including retirement and classification activities;

except with respect to functions for which the Merit Systems Protection Board or the Special Counsel is primarily responsible;

"(6) reviewing the operations under chapter 87 of this title;

"(7) aiding the President, as the President may request, in preparing such civil service rules as the President prescribes, and otherwise advising the President on actions which may be taken to promote an efficient civil service and a systematic application of the merit system principles, including recommending policies relating to the selection, promotion, transfer, performance, pay, conditions of service, tenure, and separation of employees; and

"(8) conducting, or otherwise providing for the conduct of, studies and research under chapter 47 of this title into methods of assuring improvements in personnel management.

Notice of propsed rules or regulations. Publication in Federal Register. 5 USC 553.

"(b)(1) The Director shall publish in the Federal Register general notice of any rule or regulation which is proposed by the Office and the application of which does not apply solely to the Office or its employees. Any such notice shall include the matter required under section 553(b) (1), (2), and (3) of this title.

"(2) The Director shall take steps to ensure that—

"(A) any proposed rule or regulation to which paragraph (1) of this subsection applies is posted in offices of Federal agencies maintaining copies of the Federal personnel regulations; and

"(B) to the extent the Director determines appropriate and practical, exclusive representatives of employees affected by such proposed rule or regulation and interested members of the public are notified of such proposed rule or regulation.

"(3) Paragraphs (1) and (2) of this subsection shall not apply to any proposed rule or regulation which is temporary in nature and which is necessary to be implemented expeditiously as a result of an emergency.

5 USC 1104.

"§ 1104. Delegation of authority for personnel management

"(a) Subject to subsection (b)(3) of this section—

"(1) the President may delegate, in whole or in part, authority for personnel management functions, including authority for competitive examinations, to the Director of the Office of Personnel Management; and

"(2) the Director may delegate, in whole or in part, any function vested in or delegated to the Director, including authority for competitive examinations (except competitive examinations for administrative law judges appointed under section 3105 of this title), to the heads of agencies in the executive branch and other agencies employing persons in the competitive service;

except that the Director may not delegate authority for competitive examinations with respect to positions that have requirements which are common to agencies in the Federal Government, other than in exceptional cases in which the interests of economy and efficiency require such delegation and in which such delegation will not weaken the application of the merit system principles.

Standards.

"(b)(1) The Office shall establish standards which shall apply to the activities of the Office or any other agency under authority delegated under subsection (a) of this section.

Oversight program.

"(2) The Office shall establish and maintain an oversight program to ensure that activities under any authority delegated under subsection (a) of this section are in accordance with the merit system principles and the standards established under paragraph (1) of this subsection.

"(3) Nothing in subsection (a) of this section shall be construed as affecting the responsibility of the Director to prescribe regulations and to ensure compliance with the civil service laws, rules, and regulations.

"(c) If the Office makes a written finding, on the basis of information obtained under the program established under subsection (b)(2) of this section or otherwise, that any action taken by an agency pursuant to authority delegated under subsection (a)(2) of this section is contrary to any law, rule, or regulation, or is contrary to any standard established under subsection (b)(1) of this section, the agency involved shall take any corrective action the Office may require.

"§ 1105. Administrative procedure

5 USC 1105.

"Subject to section 1103(b) of this title, in the exercise of the functions assigned under this chapter, the Director shall be subject to subsections (b), (c), and (d) of section 553 of this title, notwithstanding subsection (a) of such section 553.".

5 USC 553.

(b)(1) Section 5313 of title 5, United States Code, is amended by inserting at the end thereof the following new paragraph:

"(24) Director of the Office of Personnel Management.".

(2) Section 5314 of such title is amended by inserting at the end thereof the following new paragraph:

5 USC 5314.

"(68) Deputy Director of the Office of Personnel Management.".

(3) Section 5316 of such title is amended by inserting after paragraph (121) the following:

5 USC 5316.

"(122) Associate Directors of the Office of Personnel Management (5).".

(c)(1) The heading of part II of title 5, United States Code is amended by striking out "**THE UNITED STATES CIVIL SERVICE COMMISSION**" and inserting in lieu thereof "**CIVIL SERVICE FUNCTIONS AND RESPONSIBILITIES**".

(2) The item relating to chapter 11 in the table of chapters for part II of such title is amended by striking out "**Organization**" and inserting in lieu thereof "**Office of Personnel Management**".

MERIT SYSTEMS PROTECTION BOARD AND SPECIAL COUNSEL

SEC. 202. (a) Title 5, United States Code, is amended by inserting after chapter 11 the following new chapter:

"CHAPTER 12—MERIT SYSTEMS PROTECTION BOARD AND SPECIAL COUNSEL

"§ 1201. Appointment of members of the Merit Systems Protection Board

5 USC 1201.

"The Merit Systems Protection Board is composed of 3 members appointed by the President, by and with the advice and consent of the Senate, not more than 2 of whom may be adherents of the same political party. The Chairman and members of the Board shall be individuals who, by demonstrated ability, background, training, or experience are especially qualified to carry out the functions of the Board. No member of the Board may hold another office or position in the Government of the United States, except as otherwise provided by law or at the direction of the President. The Board shall have an official seal which shall be judicially noticed. The Board shall have its principal office in the District of Columbia and may have field offices in other appropriate locations.

5 USC 1202.

"§ 1202. Term of office, filling vacancies; removal

"(a) The term of office of each member of the Merit Systems Protection Board is 7 years.

"(b) A member appointed to fill a vacancy occurring before the end of a term of office of his predecessor serves for the remainder of that term. Any appointment to fill a vacancy is subject to the requirements of section 1201 of this title.

"(c) Any member appointed for a 7-year term may not be reappointed to any following term but may continue to serve beyond the expiration of the term until a successor is appointed and has qualified, except that such member may not continue to serve for more than one year after the date on which the term of the member would otherwise expire under this section.

"(d) Any member may be removed by the President only for inefficiency, neglect of duty, or malfeasance in office.

5 USC 1203.

"§ 1203. Chairman; Vice Chairman

"(a) The President shall from time to time, appoint, by and with the advice and consent of the Senate, one of the members of the Merit Systems Protection Board as the Chairman of the Board. The Chairman is the chief executive and administrative officer of the Board.

"(b) The President shall from time to time designate one of the members of the Board as Vice Chairman of the Board. During the absence or disability of the Chairman, or when the office of Chairman is vacant, the Vice Chairman shall perform the functions vested in the Chairman.

"(c) During the absence or disability of both the Chairman and Vice Chairman, or when the offices of Chairman and Vice Chairman are vacant, the remaining Board member shall perform the functions vested in the Chairman.

5 USC 1204.

"§ 1204. Special Counsel; appointment and removal

"The Special Counsel of the Merit Systems Protection Board shall be appointed by the President from attorneys, by and with the advice and consent of the Senate, for a term of 5 years. A Special Counsel appointed to fill a vacancy occurring before the end of a term of office of his predecessor serves for the remainder of the term. The Special Counsel may be removed by the President only for inefficiency, neglect of duty, or malfeasance in office.

5 USC 1205.

"§ 1205. Powers and functions of the Merit Systems Protection Board and Special Counsel

"(a) The Merit Systems Protection Board shall—

"(1) hear, adjudicate, or provide for the hearing or adjudication, of all matters within the jurisdiction of the Board under this title, section 2023 of title 38, or any other law, rule, or regulation, and, subject to otherwise applicable provisions of law, take final action on any such matter;

"(2) order any Federal agency or employee to comply with any order or decision issued by the Board under the authority granted under paragraph (1) of this subsection and enforce compliance with any such order;

"(3) conduct, from time to time, special studies relating to the civil service and to other merit systems in the executive branch, and report to the President and to the Congress as to whether the public interest in a civil service free of prohibited personnel practices is being adequately protected; and

"(4) review, as provided in subsection (e) of this section, rules and regulations of the Office of Personnel Management.

"(b)(1) Any member of the Merit Systems Protection Board, the Special Counsel, any administrative law judge appointed by the Board under section 3105 of this title, and any employee of the Board designated by the Board may administer oaths, examine witnesses, take depositions, and receive evidence.   5 USC 3105.

"(2) Any member of the Board, the Special Counsel, and any administrative law judge appointed by the Board under section 3105 of this title may—

"(A) issue subpenas requiring the attendance and testimony   Subpenas. of witnesses and the production of documentary or other evidence from any place in the United States or any territory or possession thereof, the Commonwealth of Puerto Rico, or the District of Columbia; and

"(B) order the taking of depositions and order responses to written interrogatories.

"(3) Witnesses (whether appearing voluntarily or under subpena)   Witnesses. shall be paid the same fee and mileage allowances which are paid subpenaed witnesses in the courts of the United States.

"(c) In the case of contumacy or failure to obey a subpena issued under subsection (b)(2) of this section, the United States district court for the judicial district in which the person to whom the subpena is addressed resides or is served may issue an order requiring such person to appear at any designated place to testify or to produce documentary or other evidence. Any failure to obey the order of the court may be punished by the court as a contempt thereof.

"(d)(1) In any proceeding under subsection (a)(1) of this section, any member of the Board may request from the Director of the Office of Personnel Management an advisory opinion concerning the interpretation of any rule, regulation, or other policy directive promulgated by the Office of Personnel Management.

"(2) In enforcing compliance with any order under subsection (a)(2) of this section, the Board may order that any employee charged with complying with such order, other than an employee appointed by the President by and with the advice and consent of the Senate, shall not be entitled to receive payment for service as an employee during any period that the order has not been complied with. The Board shall certify to the Comptroller General of the United States that such an order has been issued and no payment shall be made out of the Treasury of the United States for any service specified in such order.

"(3) In carrying out any study under subsection (a)(3) of this section, the Board shall make such inquiries as may be necessary and, unless otherwise prohibited by law, shall have access to personnel records or information collected by the Office and may require additional reports from other agencies as needed.

Ante, p. 1119.

"(e)(1) At any time after the effective date of any rule or regulation issued by the Director in carrying out functions under section 1103 of this title, the Board shall review any provision of such rule or regulation—

"(A) on its own motion;

"(B) on the granting by the Board, in its sole discretion, of any petition for such review filed with the Board by any interested person, after consideration of the petition by the Board; or

"(C) on the filing of a written complaint by the Special Counsel requesting such review.

"(2) In reviewing any provision of any rule or regulation pursuant to this subsection the Board shall declare such provision—

Ante, p. 1114.

"(A) invalid on its face, if the Board determines that such provision would, if implemented by any agency, on its face, require any employee to violate section 2302(b) of this title; or

"(B) invalidly implemented by any agency, if the Board determines that such provision, as it has been implemented by the agency through any personnel action taken by the agency or through any policy adopted by the agency in conformity with such provision, has required any employee to violate section 2302(b) of this title.

"(3)(A) The Director of the Office of Personnel Management, and the head of any agency implementing any provision of any rule or regulation under review pursuant to this subsection, shall have the right to participate in such review.

"(B) Any review conducted by the Board pursuant to this subsection shall be limited to determining—

"(i) the validity on its face of the provision under review; and

"(ii) whether the provision under review has been validly implemented.

"(C) The Board shall require any agency—

"(i) to cease compliance with any provisions of any rule or regulation which the Board declares under this subsection to be invalid on its face; and

"(ii) to correct any invalid implementation by the agency of any provision of any rule or regulation which the Board declares under this subsection to have been invalidly implemented by the agency.

"(f) The Board may delegate the performance of any of its administrative functions under this title to any employee of the Board.

Regulations.

Publication in
Federal Register.

"(g) The Board shall have the authority to prescribe such regulations as may be necessary for the performance of its functions. The Board shall not issue advisory opinions. All regulations of the Board shall be published in the Federal Register.

"(h) Except as provided in section 518 of title 28, relating to litigation before the Supreme Court, attorneys designated by the Chairman of the Board may appear for the Board, and represent the Board, in any civil action brought in connection with any function carried out by the Board pursuant to this title or as otherwise authorized by law.

"(i) The Chairman of the Board may appoint such personnel as may be necessary to perform the functions of the Board. Any appointment made under this subsection shall comply with the provisions of this title, except that such appointment shall not be subject to the approval or supervision of the Office of Personnel Management or the Executive Office of the President (other than approval required under

5 USC 3324.
Post, p. 1161.

section 3324 or subchapter VIII of chapter 33 of this title).

"(j) The Board shall prepare and submit to the President, and, at the same time, to the appropriate committees of Congress, an annual budget of the expenses and other items relating to the Board which shall, as revised, be included as a separate item in the budget required to be transmitted to the Congress under section 201 of the Budget and Accounting Act, 1921 (31 U.S.C. 11).

"(k) The Board shall submit to the President, and, at the same time, to each House of the Congress, any legislative recommendations of the Board relating to any of its functions under this title.

Recommendations, submittal to President and Congress.

"§ 1206. Authority and responsibilities of the Special Counsel

"(a)(1) The Special Counsel shall receive any allegation of a prohibited personnel practice and shall investigate the allegation to the extent necessary to determine whether there are reasonable grounds to believe that a prohibited personnel practice has occurred, exists, or is to be taken.

"(2) If the Special Counsel terminates any investigation under paragraph (1) of this subsection, the Special Counsel shall prepare and transmit to any person on whose allegation the investigation was initiated a written statement notifying the person of the termination of the investigation and the reasons therefor.

"(3) In addition to authority granted under paragraph (1) of this subsection, the Special Counsel may, in the absence of an allegation, conduct an investigation for the purpose of determining whether there are reasonable grounds to believe that a prohibited personnel practice has occurred, exists, or is to be taken.

"(b)(1) In any case involving—

"(A) any disclosure of information by an employee or applicant for employment which the employee or applicant reasonably believes evidences—

"(i) a violation of any law, rule, or regulation; or

"(ii) mismanagement, a gross waste of funds, an abuse of authority, or a substantial and specific danger to public health or safety;

if the disclosure is not specifically prohibited by law and if the information is not specifically required by Executive order to be kept secret in the interest of national defense or the conduct of foreign affairs; or

"(B) a disclosure by an employee or applicant for employment to the Special Counsel of the Merit Systems Protection Board, or to the Inspector General of an agency or another employee designated by the head of the agency to receive such disclosures of information which the employee or applicant reasonably believes evidences—

"(i) a violation of any law, rule, or regulation; or

"(ii) mismanagement, a gross waste of funds, an abuse of authority, or a substantial and specific danger to public health or safety;

the identity of the employee or applicant may not be disclosed without the consent of the employee or applicant during any investigation under subsection (a) of this section or under paragraph (3) of this subsection, unless the Special Counsel determines that the disclosure of the identity of the employee or applicant is necessary in order to carry out the functions of the Special Counsel.

"(2) Whenever the Special Counsel receives information of the type described in paragraph (1) of this subsection, the Special Counsel shall promptly transmit such information to the appropriate agency head.

"(3)(A) In the case of information received by the Special Counsel under paragraph (1) of this section, if, after such review as the Special Counsel determines practicable (but not later than 15 days after the receipt of the information), the Special Counsel determines that there is a substantial likelihood that the information discloses a violation of any law, rule, or regulation, or mismanagement, gross waste of funds, abuse of authority, or substantial and specific danger to the public health or safety, the Special Counsel may, to the extent provided in subparagraph (B) of this paragraph, require the head of the agency to—

Investigation. "(i) conduct an investigation of the information and any related matters transmitted by the Special Counsel to the head of the agency; and

Written report. "(ii) submit a written report setting forth the findings of the head of the agency within 60 days after the date on which the information is transmitted to the head of the agency or within any longer period of time agreed to in writing by the Special Counsel.

"(B) The Special Counsel may require an agency head to conduct an investigation and submit a written report under subparagraph (A) of this paragraph only if the information was transmitted to the Special Counsel by—

"(i) any employee or former employee or applicant for employment in the agency which the information concerns; or

"(ii) any employee who obtained the information in connection with the performance of the employee's duties and responsibilities.

"(4) Any report required under paragraph (3)(A) of this subsection shall be reviewed and signed by the head of the agency and shall include—

"(A) a summary of the information with respect to which the investigation was initiated;

"(B) a description of the conduct of the investigation;

"(C) a summary of any evidence obtained from the investigation;

"(D) a listing of any violation or apparent violation of any law, rule, or regulation; and

"(E) a description of any corrective action taken or planned as a result of the investigation, such as—

"(i) changes in agency rules, regulations, or practices;

"(ii) the restoration of any aggrieved employee;

"(iii) disciplinary action against any employee; and

"(iv) referral to the Attorney General of any evidence of a criminal violation.

"(5)(A) Any such report shall be submitted to the Congress, to the President, and to the Special Counsel for transmittal to the complainant. Whenever the Special Counsel does not receive the report of the agency head within the time prescribed in paragraph (3)(A)(ii) of this subsection, the Special Counsel may transmit a copy of the information which was transmitted to the agency head to the President and to the Congress together with a statement noting the failure of the head of the agency to file the required report.

"(B) In any case in which evidence of a criminal violation obtained by an agency in an investigation under paragraph (3) of this subsection is referred to the Attorney General—

"(i) the report shall not be transmitted to the complainant; and "(ii) the agency shall notify the Office of Personnel Management and the Office of Management and Budget of the referral.

"(6) Upon receipt of any report of the head of any agency required under paragraph (3)(A)(ii) of this subsection, the Special Counsel shall review the report and determine whether—

"(A) the findings of the head of the agency appear reasonable; and

"(B) the agency's report under paragraph (3)(A)(ii) of this subsection contains the information required under paragraph (4) of this subsection.

"(7) Whenever the Special Counsel transmits any information to the head of the agency under paragraph (2) of this subsection but does not require an investigation under paragraph (3) of this subsection, the head of the agency shall, within a reasonable time after the information was transmitted, inform the Special Counsel, in writing, of what action has been or is to be taken and when such action will be completed. The Special Counsel shall inform the complainant of the report of the agency head.

"(8) Except as specifically authorized under this subsection, the provisions of this subsection shall not be considered to authorize disclosure of any information by any agency or any person which is—

"(A) specifically prohibited from disclosure by any other provision of law; or

"(B) specifically required by Executive order to be kept secret in the interest of national defense or the conduct of foreign affairs.

"(9) In any case under subsection (b)(1)(B) of this section involving foreign intelligence or counterintelligence information the disclosure of which is specifically prohibited by law or by Executive order, the Special Counsel shall transmit such information to the Permanent Select Committee on Intelligence of the House of Representatives and the Select Committee on Intelligence of the Senate.

Information. transmittal to congressional committees.

"(c)(1)(A) If, in connection with any investigation under this section, the Special Counsel determines that there are reasonable grounds to believe that a prohibited personnel practice has occurred, exists, or is to be taken which requires corrective action, the Special Counsel shall report the determination together with any findings or recommendations to the Board, the agency involved, and to the Office, and may report the determination, findings, and recommendations to the President. The Special Counsel may include in the report recommendations as to what corrective action should be taken.

"(B) If, after a reasonable period, the agency has not taken the corrective action recommended, the Special Counsel may request the Board to consider the matter. The Board may order such corrective action as the Board considers appropriate, after opportunity for comment by the agency concerned and the Office of Personnel Management.

"(2)(A) If, in connection with any investigation under this section, the Special Counsel determines that there is reasonable cause to believe that a criminal violation by an employee has occurred, the Special Counsel shall report the determination to the Attorney General and to the head of the agency involved, and shall submit a copy of the report to the Director of the Office of Personnel Management and the Director of the Office of Management and Budget.

"(B) In any case in which the Special Counsel determines that there are reasonable grounds to believe that a prohibited personnel practice has occurred, exists, or is to be taken, the Special Counsel may proceed with any investigation or proceeding instituted under this section notwithstanding that the alleged violation has been reported to the Attorney General.

"(3) If, in connection with any investigation under this section, the Special Counsel determines that there is reasonable cause to believe that any violation of any law, rule, or regulation has occurred which is not referred to in paragraph (1) or (2) of this subsection, the violation shall be reported to the head of the agency involved. The Special Counsel shall require, within 30 days of the receipt of the report by the agency, a certification by the head of the agency which states—

"(A) that the head of the agency has personally reviewed the report; and

"(B) what action has been, or is to be, taken, and when the action will be completed.

Public list.

"(d) The Special Counsel shall maintain and make available to the public a list of noncriminal matters referred to heads of agencies under subsections (b)(3)(A) and (c)(3) of this section, together with—

Reports.

"(1) reports by the heads of agencies under subsection (b)(3) (A) of this section, in the case of matters referred under subsection (b); and

Certifications.

"(2) certifications by heads of agencies under subsection (c) (3), in the case of matters referred under subsection (c).

The Special Counsel shall take steps to ensure that any such public list does not contain any information the disclosure of which is prohibited by law or by Executive order requiring that information be kept secret in the interest of national defense or the conduct of foreign affairs.

"(e)(1) In addition to the authority otherwise provided in this section, the Special Counsel shall, except as provided in paragraph (2) of this subsection, conduct an investigation of any allegation concerning—

5 USC 7321.

"(A) political activity prohibited under subchapter III of chapter 73 of this title, relating to political activities by Federal employees;

"(B) political activity prohibited under chapter 15 of this title, relating to political activities by certain State and local officers and employees;

5 USC 552.

"(C) arbitrary or capricious withholding of information prohibited under section 552 of this title, except that the Special Counsel shall make no investigation under this subsection of any withholding of foreign intelligence or counterintelligence information the disclosure of which is specifically prohibited by law or by Executive order;

"(D) activities prohibited by any civil service law, rule, or regulation, including any activity relating to political intrusion in personnel decisionmaking; and

"(E) involvement by any employee in any prohibited discrimination found by any court or appropriate administrative authority to have occurred in the course of any personnel action.

"(2) The Special Counsel shall make no investigation of any allegation of any prohibited activity referred to in paragraph (1)(D) or (1)(E) of this subsection if the Special Counsel determines that the allegation may be resolved more appropriately under an administrative appeals procedure.

"(f) During any investigation initiated under this section, no disciplinary action shall be taken against any employee for any alleged prohibited activity under investigation or for any related activity without the approval of the Special Counsel.

"(g)(1) Except as provided in paragraph (2) of this subsection, if the Special Counsel determines that disciplinary action should be taken against any employee—

"(A) after any investigation under this section, or

"(B) on the basis of any knowing and willful refusal or failure by an employee to comply with an order of the Merit Systems Protection Board,

the Special Counsel shall prepare a written complaint against the employee containing his determination, together with a statement of supporting facts, and present the complaint and statement to the employee and the Merit Systems Protection Board in accordance with section 1207 of this title.

"(2) In the case of an employee in a confidential, policy-making, policy-determining, or policy-advocating position appointed by the President, by and with the advice and consent of the Senate (other than an individual in the Foreign Service of the United States), the complaint and statement referred to in paragraph (1) of this subsection, together with any response by the employee, shall be presented to the President for appropriate action in lieu of being presented under section 1207 of this title.

"(h) If the Special Counsel believes there is a pattern of prohibited personnel practices and such practices involve matters which are not otherwise appealable to the Board under section 7701 of this title, the Special Counsel may seek corrective action by filing a written complaint with the Board against the agency or employee involved and the Board shall order such corrective action as the Board determines necessary.   *Post,* p. 1138.

"(i) The Special Counsel may as a matter of right intervene or otherwise participate in any proceeding before the Merit Systems Protection Board, except that the Special Counsel shall comply with the rules of the Board and the Special Counsel shall not have any right of judicial review in connection with such intervention.

"(j)(1) The Special Counsel may appoint the legal, administrative, and support personnel necessary to perform the functions of the Special Counsel.

"(2) Any appointment made under this subsection shall comply with the provisions of this title, except that such appointment shall not be subject to the approval or supervision of the Office of Personnel Management or the Executive Office of the President (other than approval required under section 3324 or subchapter VIII of chapter 33 of this title).   5 USC 3324.
                                                                    Post, p. 1161.

"(k) The Special Counsel may prescribe regulations relating to the   Regulations.
receipt and investigation of matters under the jurisdiction of the Special Counsel. Such regulations shall be published in the Federal   Publication in
Register.   Federal Register.

"(l) The Special Counsel shall not issue any advisory opinion concerning any law, rule, or regulation (other than an advisory opinion concerning chapter 15 or subchapter III of chapter 73 of this title).   5 USC 1501 *et*
                                                                    seq., 7321.

"(m) The Special Counsel shall submit an annual report to the Congress on the activities of the Special Counsel, including the number,   Report to
types, and disposition of allegations of prohibited personnel practices   Congress.
filed with it, investigations conducted by it, and actions initiated by it before the Board, as well as a description of the recommendations and reports made by it to other agencies pursuant to this section, and the actions taken by the agencies as a result of the reports or recom-

mendations. The report required by this subsection shall include whatever recommendations for legislation or other action by Congress the Special Counsel may deem appropriate.

5 USC 1207.

"§ 1207. Hearings and decisions on complaints filed by the Special Counsel

"(a) Any employee against whom a complaint has been presented to the Merit Systems Protection Board under section 1206(g) of this title is entitled to—

"(1) a reasonable time to answer orally and in writing and to furnish affidavits and other documentary evidence in support of the answer;

"(2) be represented by an attorney or other representative;

"(3) a hearing before the Board or an administrative law judge

5 USC 3105.

appointed under section 3105 of this title and designated by the Board;

"(4) have a transcript kept of any hearing under paragraph (3) of this subsection; and

"(5) a written decision and reasons therefor at the earliest practicable date, including a copy of any final order imposing disciplinary action.

Final order.

"(b) A final order of the Board may impose disciplinary action consisting of removal, reduction in grade, debarment from Federal employment for a period not to exceed 5 years, suspension, reprimand, or an assessment of a civil penalty not to exceed $1,000.

"(c) There may be no administrative appeal from an order of the Board. An employee subject to a final order imposing disciplinary action under this section may obtain judicial review of the order in the United States court of appeals for the judicial circuit in which the employee resides or is employed at the time of the action.

"(d) In the case of any State or local officer or employee under

5 USC 1501 et seq.

chapter 15 of this title, the Board shall consider the case in accordance with the provisions of such chapter.

5 USC 1208.

"§ 1208. Stays of certain personnel actions

"(a)(1) The Special Counsel may request any member of the Merit Systems Protection Board to order a stay of any personnel action for 15 calendar days if the Special Counsel determines that there are reasonable grounds to believe that the personnel action was taken, or is to be taken, as a result of a prohibited personnel practice.

"(2) Any member of the Board requested by the Special Counsel to order a stay under paragraph (1) of this subsection shall order such stay unless the member determines that, under the facts and circumstances involved, such a stay would not be appropriate.

"(3) Unless denied under paragraph (2) of this subsection, any stay under this subsection shall be granted within 3 calendar days (excluding Saturdays, Sundays, and legal holidays) after the date of the request for the stay by the Special Counsel.

"(b) Any member of the Board may, on the request of the Special Counsel, extend the period of any stay ordered under subsection (a) of this section for a period of not more than 30 calendar days.

"(c) The Board may extend the period of any stay granted under subsection (a) of this section for any period which the Board considers appropriate, but only if the Board concurs in the determination of the Special Counsel under such subsection, after an opportunity is provided for oral or written comment by the Special Counsel and the agency involved.

"§ 1209. Information

5 USC 1209.

"(a) Notwithstanding any other provision of law or any rule, regulation or policy directive, any member of the Board, or any employee of the Board designated by the Board, may transmit to the Congress on the request of any committee or subcommittee thereof, by report, testimony, or otherwise, information and views on functions, responsibilities, or other matters relating to the Board, without review, clearance, or approval by any other administrative authority.

"(b) The Board shall submit an annual report to the President and the Congress on its activities, which shall include a description of significant actions taken by the Board to carry out its functions under this title. The report shall also review the significant actions of the Office of Personnel Management, including an analysis of whether the actions of the Office of Personnel Management are in accord with merit system principles and free from prohibited personnel practices.".

Report to President and Congress. 5 USC 1201 note.

(b) Any term of office of any member of the Merit Systems Protection Board serving on the effective date of this Act shall continue in effect until the term would expire under section 1102 of title 5, United States Code, as in effect immediately before the effective date of this Act, and upon expiration of the term, appointments to such office shall be made under sections 1201 and 1202 of title 5, United States Code (as added by this section).

(c)(1) Section 5314(17) of title 5, United States Code, is amended by striking out "Chairman of the United States Civil Service Commission" and inserting in lieu thereof "Chairman of the Merit Systems Protection Board".

(2) Section 5315(66) of such title is amended by striking out "Members, United States Civil Service Commission" and inserting in lieu thereof "Members, Merit Systems Protection Board".

5 USC 5315.

(3) Section 5315 of such title is further amended by adding at the end thereof the following new paragraph:

"(123) Special Counsel of the Merit Systems Protection Board.".

(4) Paragraph (99) of section 5316 of such title is hereby repealed.

5 USC 5316.

(d) The table of chapters for part II of title 5, United States Code, is amended by inserting after the item relating to chapter 11 the following new item:

"12. Merit Systems Protection Board and Special Counsel_____ 1201".

PERFORMANCE APPRAISAL

SEC. 203. (a) Chapter 43 of title 5, United States Code, is amended to read as follows:

"CHAPTER 43—PERFORMANCE APPRAISAL

"SUBCHAPTER I—GENERAL PROVISIONS

"Sec.
"4301. Definitions.
"4302. Establishment of performance appraisal systems.
"4303. Actions based on unacceptable performance.
"4304. Responsibilities of Office of Personnel Management.
"4305. Regulations.

"§ 4301. Definitions

5 USC 4301.

"For the purpose of this subchapter—
    "(1) 'agency' means—
        "(A) an Executive agency;

"(B) the Administrative Office of the United States Courts;
and
"(C) the Government Printing Office;
but does not include—
"(i) a Government corporation;
"(ii) the Central Intelligence Agency, the Defense Intelligence Agency, the National Security Agency, or any Executive agency or unit thereof which is designated by the President and the principal function of which is the conduct of foreign intelligence or counterintelligence activities; or
"(iii) the General Accounting Office;
"(2) 'employee' means an individual employed in or under an agency, but does not include—
"(A) an employee outside the United States who is paid in accordance with local native prevailing wage rates for the area in which employed;
"(B) an individual in the Foreign Service of the United States;
"(C) a physician, dentist, nurse, or other employee in the Department of Medicine and Surgery, Veterans' Administration whose pay is fixed under chapter 73 of title 38;
"(D) an administrative law judge appointed under section 3105 of this title;
"(E) an individual in the Senior Executive Service;
"(F) an individual appointed by the President; or
"(G) an individual occupying a position not in the competitive service excluded from coverage of this subchapter by regulations of the Office of Personnel Management; and
"(3) 'unacceptable performance' means performance of an employee which fails to meet established performance standards in one or more critical elements of such employee's position.

38 USC 4101 *et seq.*

5 USC 4302.

"**§ 4302. Establishment of performance appraisal systems**
"(a) Each agency shall develop one or more performance appraisal systems which—
"(1) provide for periodic appraisals of job performance of employees;
"(2) encourage employee participation in establishing performance standards; and
"(3) use the results of performance appraisals as a basis for training, rewarding, reassigning, promoting, reducing in grade, retaining, and removing employees;
"(b) Under regulations which the Office of Personnel Management shall prescribe, each performance appraisal system shall provide for—
"(1) establishing performance standards which will, to the maximum extent feasible, permit the accurate evaluation of job performance on the basis of objective criteria (which may include the extent of courtesy demonstrated to the public) related to the job in question for each employee or position under the system;
"(2) as soon as practicable, but not later than October 1, 1981, with respect to initial appraisal periods, and thereafter at the beginning of each following appraisal period, communicating to each employee the performance standards and the critical elements of the employee's position;
"(3) evaluating each employee during the appraisal period on such standards;

"(4) recognizing and rewarding employees whose performance so warrants;

"(5) assisting employees in improving unacceptable performance; and

"(6) reassigning, reducing in grade, or removing employees who continue to have unacceptable performance but only after an opportunity to demonstrate acceptable performance.

"§ 4303. Actions based on unacceptable performance

5 USC 4303.

"(a) Subject to the provisions of this section, an agency may reduce in grade or remove an employee for unacceptable performance.

Removal or reduction in grade.

"(b)(1) An employee whose reduction in grade or removal is proposed under this section is entitled to—

"(A) 30 days' advance written notice of the proposed action which identifies—

Notice.

"(i) specific instances of unacceptable performance by the employee on which the proposed action is based; and

"(ii) the critical elements of the employee's position involved in each instance of unacceptable performance;

"(B) be represented by an attorney or other representative;

Representation.

"(C) a reasonable time to answer orally and in writing; and

"(D) a written decision which—

Written decision.

"(i) in the case of a reduction in grade or removal under this section, specifies the instances of unacceptable performance by the employee on which the reduction in grade or removal is based, and

"(ii) unless proposed by the head of the agency, has been concurred in by an employee who is in a higher position than the employee who proposed the action.

"(2) An agency may, under regulations prescribed by the head of such agency, extend the notice period under subsection (b)(1)(A) of this section for not more than 30 days. An agency may extend the notice period for more than 30 days only in accordance with regulations issued by the Office of Personnel Management.

Extension of notice.

"(c) The decision to retain, reduce in grade, or remove an employee—

"(1) shall be made within 30 days after the date of expiration of the notice period, and

"(2) in the case of a reduction in grade or removal, may be based only on those instances of unacceptable performance by the employee—

"(A) which occurred during the 1-year period ending on the date of the notice under subsection (b)(1)(A) of this section in connection with the decision; and

"(B) for which the notice and other requirements of this section are complied with.

"(d) If, because of performance improvement by the employee during the notice period, the employee is not reduced in grade or removed, and the employee's performance continues to be acceptable for 1 year from the date of the advance written notice provided under subsection (b)(1)(A) of this section, any entry or other notation of the unacceptable performance for which the action was proposed under this section shall be removed from any agency record relating to the employee.

"(e) Any employee who is a preference eligible or is in the competitive service and who has been reduced in grade or removed under this section is entitled to appeal the action to the Merit Systems Protection Board under section 7701 of this title.

Post, p. 1138.

"(f) This section does not apply to—

"(1) the reduction to the grade previously held of a supervisor or manager who has not completed the probationary period under 5 USC 3321. section 3321(a)(2) of this title,

"(2) the reduction in grade or removal of an employee in the competitive service who is serving a probationary or trial period under an initial appointment or who has not completed 1 year of current continuous employment under other than a temporary appointment limited to 1 year or less, or

"(3) the reduction in grade or removal of an employee in the excepted service who has not completed 1 year of current continuous employment in the same or similar positions.

5 USC 4304.

Technical assistance.

Review of performance appraisal system.

"§ 4304. Responsibilities of the Office of Personnel Management

"(a) The Office of Personnel Management shall make technical assistance available to agencies in the development of performance appraisal systems.

"(b)(1) The Office shall review each performance appraisal system developed by any agency under this section and determine whether the performance appraisal system meets the requirements of this subchapter.

"(2) The Comptroller General shall from time to time review on a selected basis performance appraisal systems established under this subchapter to determine the extent to which any such system meets the requirements of this subchapter and shall periodically report its findings to the Office and to the Congress.

"(3) If the Office determines that a system does not meet the requirements of this subchapter (including regulations prescribed under section 4305), the Office shall direct the agency to implement an appropriate system or to correct operations under the system, and any such agency shall take any action so required.

5 USC 4305.

"§ 4305. Regulations

"The Office of Personnel Management may prescribe regulations to carry out the purpose of this subchapter.".

(b) The item relating to chapter 43 in the chapter analysis for part III of title 5, United States Code, is amended by striking out "Performance Rating" and inserting in lieu thereof "Performance Appraisal".

ADVERSE ACTIONS

SEC. 204. (a) Chapter 75 of title 5, United States Code, is amended by striking out subchapters I, II, and III and inserting in lieu thereof the following:

"SUBCHAPTER I—SUSPENSION FOR 14 DAYS OR LESS

5 USC 7501.

"§ 7501. Definitions

"For the purpose of this subchapter—

"(1) 'employee' means an individual in the competitive service who is not serving a probationary or trial period under an initial appointment or who has completed 1 year of current continuous employment in the same or similar positions under other than a temporary appointment limited to 1 year or less; and

"(2) 'suspension' means the placing of an employee, for disciplinary reasons, in a temporary status without duties and pay.

"§ 7502. Actions covered

"This subchapter applies to a suspension for 14 days or less, but does not apply to a suspension under section 7521 or 7532 of this title or any action initiated under section 1206 of this title.

5 USC 7502.
Post, p. 1137.
5 USC 7532.
Ante, p. 1125.

"§ 7503. Cause and procedure

"(a) Under regulations prescribed by the Office of Personnel Management, an employee may be suspended for 14 days or less for such cause as will promote the efficiency of the service (including discourteous conduct to the public confirmed by an immediate supervisor's report of four such instances within any one-year period or any other pattern of discourteous conduct).

"(b) An employee against whom a suspension for 14 days or less is proposed is entitled to—

"(1) an advance written notice stating the specific reasons for the proposed action;

Notice.

"(2) a reasonable time to answer orally and in writing and to furnish affidavits and other documentary evidence in support of the answer;

"(3) be represented by an attorney or other representative; and

Representation.

"(4) a written decision and the specific reasons therefor at the earliest practicable date.

"(c) Copies of the notice of proposed action, the answer of the employee if written, a summary thereof if made orally, the notice of decision and reasons therefor, and any order effecting the suspension, together with any supporting material, shall be maintained by the agency and shall be furnished to the Merit Systems Protection Board upon its request and to the employee affected upon the employee's request.

Availability of information.

"§ 7504. Regulations

"The Office of Personnel Management may prescribe regulations to carry out the purpose of this subchapter.

5 USC 7504.

"SUBCHAPTER II—REMOVAL, SUSPENSION FOR MORE THAN 14 DAYS, REDUCTION IN GRADE OR PAY, OR FURLOUGH FOR 30 DAYS OR LESS

"§ 7511. Definitions; application

"(a) For the purpose of this subchapter—

"(1) 'employee' means—

"(A) an individual in the competitive service who is not serving a probationary or trial period under an initial appointment or who has completed 1 year of current continuous employment under other than a temporary appointment limited to 1 year or less; and

"(B) a preference eligible in an Executive agency in the excepted service, and a preference eligible in the United States Postal Service or the Postal Rate Commission, who has completed 1 year of current continuous service in the same or similar positions;

"(2) 'suspension' has the meaning as set forth in section 7501(2) of this title;

"(3) 'grade' means a level of classification under a position classification system;

5 USC 7511.

Ante, p. 1134.

"(4) 'pay' means the rate of basic pay fixed by law or administrative action for the position held by an employee; and

"(5) 'furlough' means the placing of an employee in a temporary status without duties and pay because of lack of work or funds or other nondisciplinary reasons.

"(b) This subchapter does not apply to an employee—

"(1) whose appointment is made by and with the advice and consent of the Senate;

"(2) whose position has been determined to be of a confidential, policy-determining, policy-making or policy-advocating character by—

"(A) the Office of Personnel Management for a position that it has excepted from the competitive service; or

"(B) the President or the head of an agency for a position which is excepted from the competitive service by statute.

"(c) The Office may provide for the application of this subchapter to any position or group of positions excepted from the competitive service by regulation of the Office.

5 USC 7512.

"§ 7512. Actions covered

"This subchapter applies to—

"(1) a removal;

"(2) a suspension for more than 14 days;

"(3) a reduction in grade;

"(4) a reduction in pay; and

"(5) a furlough of 30 days or less;

but does not apply to—

5 USC 7532.
5 USC 3502.

"(A) a suspension or removal under section 7532 of this title,

"(B) a reduction-in-force action under section 3502 of this title,

"(C) the reduction in grade of a supervisor or manager who has not completed the probationary period under section 3321(a)

Post, p. 1146.

(2) of this title if such reduction is to the grade held immediately before becoming such a supervisor or manager,

Ante, p. 1133.

"(D) a reduction in grade or removal under section 4303 of this title, or

Ante, p. 1125,
Post, p. 1137.
5 USC 7513.

"(E) an action initiated under section 1206 or 7521 of this title.

"§ 7513. Cause and procedure

"(a) Under regulations prescribed by the Office of Personnel Management, an agency may take an action covered by this subchapter against an employee only for such cause as will promote the efficiency of the service.

"(b) An employee against whom an action is proposed is entitled to—

Notice.

"(1) at least 30 days' advance written notice, unless there is reasonable cause to believe the employee has committed a crime for which a sentence of imprisonment may be imposed, stating the specific reasons for the proposed action;

"(2) a reasonable time, but not less than 7 days, to answer orally and in writing and to furnish affidavits and other documentary evidence in support of the answer;

Representation.

"(3) be represented by an attorney or other representative; and

"(4) a written decision and the specific reasons therefor at the earliest practicable date.

Hearing.

"(c) An agency may provide, by regulation, for a hearing which may be in lieu of or in addition to the opportunity to answer provided under subsection (b)(2) of this section.

"(d) An employee against whom an action is taken under this section is entitled to appeal to the Merit Systems Protection Board under section 7701 of this title.

"(e) Copies of the notice of proposed action, the answer of the employee when written, a summary thereof when made orally, the notice of decision and reasons therefor, and any order effecting an action covered by this subchapter, together with any supporting material, shall be maintained by the agency and shall be furnished to the Board upon its request and to the employee affected upon the employee's request.

Post, p. 1138.
Availability of information.

"§ 7514. Regulations

5 USC 7514.

"The Office of Personnel Management may prescribe regulations to carry out the purpose of this subchapter, except as it concerns any matter with respect to which the Merit Systems Protection Board may prescribe regulations.".

"SUBCHAPTER III—ADMINISTRATIVE LAW JUDGES

"§ 7521. Actions against administrative law judges

5 USC 7521.

"(a) An action may be taken against an administrative law judge appointed under section 3105 of this title by the agency in which the administrative law judge is employed only for good cause established and determined by the Merit Systems Protection Board on the record after opportunity for hearing before the Board.

5 USC 3105.

"(b) The actions covered by this section are—
"(1) a removal;
"(2) a suspension;
"(3) a reduction in grade;
"(4) a reduction in pay; and
"(5) a furlough of 30 days or less;
but do not include—
"(A) a suspension or removal under section 7532 of this title;
"(B) a reduction-in-force action under section 3502 of this title; or
"(C) any action initiated under section 1206 of this title.".

5 USC 7532.
5 USC 3502.
Ante, p. 1125.

(b) So much of the analysis for chapter 75 of title 5, United States Code, as precedes the items relating to subchapter IV is amended to read as follows:

"CHAPTER 75—ADVERSE ACTIONS

"SUBCHAPTER III—ADMINISTRATIVE LAW JUDGES

"7521. Actions against administrative law judges.".

APPEALS

SEC. 205. Chapter 77 of title 5, United States Code, is amended to read as follows:

"CHAPTER 77—APPEALS

"Sec.
"7701. Appellate procedures.
"7702. Actions involving discrimination.
"7703. Judicial review of decisions of the Merit Systems Protection Board.

5 USC 1138.

"§ 7701. Appellate procedures

"(a) An employee, or applicant for employment, may submit an appeal to the Merit Systems Protection Board from any action which is appealable to the Board under any law, rule, or regulation. An appellant shall have the right—

Hearing.
Representation.

"(1) to a hearing for which a transcript will be kept; and

"(2) to be represented by an attorney or other representative. Appeals shall be processed in accordance with regulations prescribed by the Board.

"(b) The Board may hear any case appealed to it or may refer the case to an administrative law judge appointed under section 3105 of this title or other employee of the Board designated by the Board to hear such cases, except that in any case involving a removal from the service, the case shall be heard by the Board, an employee experienced in hearing appeals, or an administrative law judge. The Board, administrative law judge, or other employee (as the case may be) shall make a decision after receipt of the written representations of the parties to the appeal and after opportunity for a hearing under subsection (a) (1) of this section. A copy of the decision shall be furnished to each party to the appeal and to the Office of Personnel Management.

5 USC 3105.

Copies of
decisions.

"(c)(1) Subject to paragraph (2) of this subsection, the decision of the agency shall be sustained under subsection (b) only if the agency's decision—

Ante, p. 1133.

"(A) in the case of an action based on unacceptable performance described in section 4303 of this title, is supported by substantial evidence, or

"(B) in any other case, is supported by a preponderance of the evidence.

"(2) Notwithstanding paragraph (1), the agency's decision may not be sustained under subsection (b) of this section if the employee or applicant for employment—

"(A) shows harmful error in the application of the agency's procedures in arriving at such decision;

Ante, p. 1114.

"(B) shows that the decision was based on any prohibited personnel practice described in section 2302(b) of this title; or

"(C) shows that the decision was not in accordance with law.

"(d)(1) In any case in which—

"(A) the interpretation or application of any civil service law, rule, or regulation, under the jurisdiction of the Office of Personnel Management is at issue in any proceeding under this section; and

"(B) the Director of the Office of Personnel Management is of the opinion that an erroneous decision would have a substantial impact on any civil service law, rule, or regulation under the jurisdiction of the Office;

the Director may as a matter of right intervene or otherwise participate in that proceeding before the Board. If the Director exercises his right to participate in a proceeding before the Board, he shall do so as early in the proceeding as practicable. Nothing in this title shall be construed to permit the Office to interfere with the independent decisionmaking of the Merit Systems Protection Board.

"(2) The Board shall promptly notify the Director whenever the interpretation of any civil service law, rule, or regulation under the jurisdiction of the Office is at issue in any proceeding under this section.

Notification.

"(e)(1) Except as provided in section 7702 of this title, any decision under subsection (b) of this section shall be final unless—

Decisions.

"(A) a party to the appeal or the Director petitions the Board for review within 30 days after the receipt of the decision; or

"(B) the Board reopens and reconsiders a case on its own motion.

The Board, for good cause shown, may extend the 30-day period referred to in subparagraph (A) of this paragraph. One member of the Board may grant a petition or otherwise direct that a decision be reviewed by the full Board. The preceding sentence shall not apply if, by law, a decision of an administration law judge is required to be acted upon by the Board.

"(2) The Director may petition the Board for a review under paragraph (1) of this subsection only if the Director is of the opinion that the decision is erroneous and will have a substantial impact on any civil service law, rule, or regulation under the jurisdiction of the Office.

Petition for review.

"(f) The Board, or an administrative law judge or other employee of the Board designated to hear a case, may—

"(1) consolidate appeals filed by two or more appellants, or

"(2) join two or more appeals filed by the same appellant and hear and decide them concurrently,

if the deciding official or officials hearing the cases are of the opinion that the action could result in the appeals' being processed more expeditiously and would not adversely affect any party.

"(g)(1) Except as provided in paragraph (2) of this subsection, the Board, or an administrative law judge or other employee of the Board designated to hear a case, may require payment by the agency involved of reasonable attorney fees incurred by an employee or applicant for employment if the employee or applicant is the prevailing party and the Board, administrative law judge, or other employee, as the case may be, determines that payment by the agency is warranted in the interest of justice, including any case in which a prohibited personnel practice was engaged in by the agency or any case in which the agency's action was clearly without merit.

"(2) If an employee or applicant for employment is the prevailing party and the decision is based on a finding of discrimination prohibited under section 2302(b)(1) of this title, the payment of attorney fees shall be in accordance with the standards prescribed under section 706(k) of the Civil Rights Act of 1964 (42 U.S.C. 2000e–5(k)).

Ante. p. 1114.

"(h) The Board may, by regulation, provide for one or more alternative methods for settling matters subject to the appellate jurisdiction of the Board which shall be applicable at the election of an applicant for employment or of an employee who is not in a unit for which a labor organization is accorded exclusive recognition, and shall be in lieu of other procedures provided for under this section. A decision under such a method shall be final, unless the Board reopens and reconsiders a case at the request of the Office of Personnel Management under subsection (d) of this section.

"(i)(1) Upon the submission of any appeal to the Board under this section, the Board, through reference to such categories of cases, or other means, as it determines appropriate, shall establish and announce publicly the date by which it intends to complete action on the matter. Such date shall assure expeditious consideration of the appeal, consistent with the interests of fairness and other priorities of the Board. If the Board fails to complete action on the appeal by the announced date, and the expected delay will exceed 30 days, the Board shall publicly announce the new date by which it intends to complete action on the appeal.

Report to
Congress.

"(2) Not later than March 1 of each year, the Board shall submit to the Congress a report describing the number of appeals submitted to it during the preceding calendar year, the number of appeals on which it completed action during that year, and the number of instances during that year in which it failed to conclude a proceeding by the date originally announced, together with an explanation of the reasons therefor.

"(3) The Board shall by rule indicate any other category of significant Board action which the Board determines should be subject to the provisions of this subsection.

"(4) It shall be the duty of the Board, an administrative law judge, or employee designated by the Board to hear any proceeding under this section to expedite to the extent practicable that proceeding.

Regulations.

"(j) The Board may prescribe regulations to carry out the purpose of this section.

5 USC 7702.

"§ 7702. Actions involving discrimination

"(a)(1) Notwithstanding any other provision of law, and except as provided in paragraph (2) of this subsection, in the case of any employee or applicant for employment who—

"(A) has been effected by an action which the employee or applicant may appeal to the Merit Systems Protection Board, and

"(B) alleges that a basis for the action was discrimination prohibited by—

"(i) section 717 of the Civil Rights Act of 1964 (42 U.S.C. 2000e–16c),

"(ii) section 6(d) of the Fair Labor Standards Act of 1938 (29 U.S.C. 206(d)),

"(iii) section 501 of the Rehabilitation Act of 1973 (29 U.S.C. 791),

"(iv) sections 12 and 15 of the Age Discrimination in Employment Act of 1967 (29 U.S.C. 631, 633a), or

"(v) any rule, regulation, or policy directive prescribed under any provision of law described in clauses (i) through (iv) of this subparagraph,

the Board shall, within 120 days of the filing of the appeal, decide both the issue of discrimination and the appealable action in accordance with the Board's appellate procedures under section 7701 of this title and this section.

"(2) In any matter before an agency which involves—

"(A) any action described in paragraph (1)(A) of this subsection; and

"(B) any issue of discrimination prohibited under any provision of law described in paragraph (1)(B) of this subsection;

the agency shall resolve such matter within 120 days. The decision of the agency in any such matter shall be a judicially reviewable action unless the employee appeals the matter to the Board under paragraph (1) of this subsection.

"(3) Any decision of the Board under paragraph (1) of this subsection shall be a judicially reviewable action as of—

"(A) the date of issuance of the decision if the employee or applicant does not file a petition with the Equal Employment Opportunity Commission under subsection (b)(1) of this section, or

"(B) the date the Commission determines not to consider the decision under subsection (b)(2) of this section.

"(b)(1) An employee or applicant may, within 30 days after notice of the decision of the Board under subsection (a)(1) of this section, petition the Commission to consider the decision.

"(2) The Commission shall, within 30 days after the date of the petition, determine whether to consider the decision. A determination of the Commission not to consider the decision may not be used as evidence with respect to any issue of discrimination in any judicial proceeding concerning that issue.

"(3) If the Commission makes a determination to consider the decision, the Commission shall, within 60 days after the date of the determination, consider the entire record of the proceedings of the Board and, on the basis of the evidentiary record before the Board, as supplemented under paragraph (4) of this subsection, either—

"(A) concur in the decision of the Board; or

"(B) issue in writing another decision which differs from the decision of the Board to the extent that the Commission finds that, as a matter of law—

"(i) the decision of the Board constitutes an incorrect interpretation of any provision of any law, rule, regulation, or policy directive referred to in subsection (a)(1)(B) of this section, or

"(ii) the decision involving such provision is not supported by the evidence in the record as a whole.

"(4) In considering any decision of the Board under this subsection, the Commission may refer the case to the Board, or provide on its own, for the taking (within such period as permits the Commission to make a decision within the 60-day period prescribed under this subsection) of additional evidence to the extent it considers necessary to supplement the record.

"(5)(A) If the Commission concurs pursuant to paragraph (3)(A) of this subsection in the decision of the Board, the decision of the Board shall be a judicially reviewable action.

"(B) If the Commission issues any decision under paragraph (3)(B) of this subsection, the Commission shall immediately refer the matter to the Board.

"(c) Within 30 days after receipt by the Board of the decision of the Commission under subsection (b)(5)(B) of this section, the Board shall consider the decision and—

"(1) concur and adopt in whole the decision of the Commission; or

"(2) to the extent that the Board finds that, as a matter of law, (A) the Commission decision constitutes an incorrect interpretation of any provision of any civil service law, rule, regulation or policy directive, or (B) the Commission decision involving such provision is not supported by the evidence in the record as a whole—

"(i) reaffirm the initial decision of the Board; or

"(ii) reaffirm the initial decision of the Board with such revisions as it determines appropriate.

If the Board takes the action provided under paragraph (1), the decision of the Board shall be a judicially reviewable action.

"(d)(1) If the Board takes any action under subsection (c)(2) of this section, the matter shall be immediately certified to a special panel described in paragraph (6) of this subsection. Upon certification, the Board shall, within 5 days (excluding Saturdays, Sundays, and holidays), transmit to the special panel the administrative record in the proceeding, including—

"(A) the factual record compiled under this section,

"(B) the decisions issued by the Board and the Commission under this section, and

"(C) any transcript of oral arguments made, or legal briefs filed, before the Board or the Commission.

"(2)(A) The special panel shall, within 45 days after a matter has been certified to it, review the administrative record transmitted to it and, on the basis of the record, decide the issues in dispute and issue a final decision which shall be a judicially reviewable action.

"(B) The special panel shall give due deference to the respective expertise of the Board and Commission in making its decision.

"(3) The special panel shall refer its decision under paragraph (2) of this subsection to the Board and the Board shall order any agency to take any action appropriate to carry out the decision.

"(4) The special panel shall permit the employee or applicant who brought the complaint and the employing agency to appear before the panel to present oral arguments and to present written arguments with respect to the matter.

"(5) Upon application by the employee or applicant, the Commission may issue such interim relief as it determines appropriate to mitigate any exceptional hardship the employee or applicant might otherwise incur as a result of the certification of any matter under this subsection, except that the Commission may not stay, or order any agency to review on an interim basis, the action referred to in subsection (a)(1) of this section.

Special panel.   "(6)(A) Each time the Board takes any action under subsection (c)(2) of this section, a special panel shall be convened which shall consist of—

"(i) an individual appointed by the President, by and with the advice and consent of the Senate, to serve for a term of 6 years as chairman of the special panel each time it is convened;

"(ii) one member of the Board designated by the Chairman of the Board each time a panel is convened; and

"(iii) one member of the Commission designated by the Chairman of the Commission each time a panel is convened.

The chairman of the special panel may be removed by the President only for inefficiency, neglect of duty, or malfeasance in office.

5 USC 5332 note.   "(B) The chairman is entitled to pay at a rate equal to the maximum annual rate of basic pay payable under the General Schedule for each day he is engaged in the performance of official business on the work of the special panel.

Administrative   "(C) The Board and the Commission shall provide such adminis-
assistance.   trative assistance to the special panel as may be necessary and, to the extent practicable, shall equally divide the costs of providing the administrative assistance.

"(e)(1) Notwithstanding any other provision of law, if at any time after—

"(A) the 120th day following the filing of any matter described in subsection (a)(2) of this section with an agency, there is no judicially reviewable action under this section or an appeal under paragraph (2) of this subsection;

"(B) the 120th day following the filing of an appeal with the Board under subsection (a)(1) of this section, there is no judicially reviewable action (unless such action is not as the result of the filing of a petition by the employee under subsection (b)(1) of this section); or

"(C) the 180th day following the filing of a petition with the Equal Employment Opportunity Commission under subsection (b)(1) of this title, there is no final agency action under subsection (b), (c), or (d) of this section;

an employee shall be entitled to file a civil action to the same extent and in the same manner as provided in section 717(c) of the Civil Rights Act of 1964 (42 U.S.C. 2000e-16(c)), section 15(c) of the Age Discrimination in Employment Act of 1967 (29 U.S.C. 633a(c)), or section 16(b) of the Fair Labor Standards Act of 1938 (29 U.S.C. 216(d)).

"(2) If, at any time after the 120th day following the filing of any matter described in subsection (a)(2) of this section with an agency, there is no judicially reviewable action, the employee may appeal the matter to the Board under subsection (a)(1) of this section.

"(3) Nothing in this section shall be construed to affect the right to trial de novo under any provision of law described in subsection (a)(1) of this section after a judicially reviewable action, including the decision of an agency under subsection (a)(2) of this section.

"(f) In any case in which an employee is required to file any action, appeal, or petition under this section and the employee timely files the action, appeal, or petition with an agency other than the agency with which the action, appeal, or petition is to be filed, the employee shall be treated as having timely filed the action, appeal, or petition as of the date it is filed with the proper agency.

"§ 7703. Judicial review of decisions of the Merit Systems Protection Board

5 USC 7703.

"(a)(1) Any employee or applicant for employment adversely affected or aggrieved by a final order or decision of the Merit Systems Protection Board may obtain judicial review of the order or decision.

"(2) The Board shall be the named respondent in any proceeding brought pursuant to this subsection, unless the employee or applicant for employment seeks review of a final order or decision issued by the Board under section 7701. In review of a final order or decision issued under section 7701, the agency responsible for taking the action appealed to the Board shall be the named respondent.

"(b)(1) Except as provided in paragraph (2) of this subsection, a petition to review a final order or final decision of the Board shall be filed in the Court of Claims or a United States court of appeals as provided in chapters 91 and 158, respectively, of title 28. Notwithstanding any other provision of law, any petition for review must be filed within 30 days after the date the petitioner received notice of the final order or decision of the Board.

28 USC 1491 et seq., 2341 et seq.

"(2) Cases of discrimination subject to the provisions of section 7702 of this title shall be filed under section 717(c) of the Civil Rights Act of 1964 (42 U.S.C. 2000e-16(c)), section 15(c) of the Age Discrimination in Employment Act of 1967 (29 U.S.C. 633a(c)), and section 16(b) of the Fair Labor Standards Act of 1938, as amended (29 U.S.C. 216(b)), as applicable. Notwithstanding any other provision of law, any such case filed under any such section must be filed within 30 days after the date the individual filing the case received notice of the judicially reviewable action under such section 7702.

"(c) In any case filed in the United States Court of Claims or a United States court of appeals, the court shall review the record and hold unlawful and set aside any agency action, findings, or conclusions found to be—

"(1) arbitrary, capricious, an abuse of discretion, or otherwise not in accordance with law;

"(2) obtained without procedures required by law, rule, or regulation having been followed; or

"(3) unsupported by substantial evidence;

except that in the case of discrimination brought under any section referred to in subsection (b)(2) of this section, the employee or applicant shall have the right to have the facts subject to trial de novo by the reviewing court.

Petition.

"(d) The Director of the Office of Personnel Management may obtain review of any final order or decision of the Board by filing a petition for judicial review in the United States Court of Appeals for the District of Columbia if the Director determines, in his discretion, that the Board erred in interpreting a civil service law, rule, or regulation affecting personnel management and that the Board's decision will have a substantial impact on a civil service law, rule, regulation, or policy directive. If the Director did not intervene in a matter before the Board, the Director may not petition for review of a Board decision under this section unless the Director first petitions the Board for a reconsideration of its decision, and such petition is denied. In addition to the named respondent, the Board and all other parties to the proceedings before the Board shall have the right to appear in the proceeding before the Court of Appeals. The granting of the petition for judicial review shall be at the discretion of the Court of Appeals.".

TECHNICAL AND CONFORMING AMENDMENTS

SEC. 206. Section 2342 of title 28, United States Code, is amended—

(1) by striking out "and" at the end of paragraph (4),

(2) by striking out the period at the end of paragraph (5) and inserting in lieu thereof "; and", and

(3) by adding at the end thereof the following new paragraph:

"(6) all final orders of the Merit Systems Protection Board

Ante, p. 1143.   except as provided for in section 7703(b) of title 5.".

TITLE III—STAFFING

VOLUNTEER SERVICE

SEC. 301. (a) Chapter 31 of title 5, United States Code, is amended by adding at the end thereof the following new section:

5 USC 3111.
"Student."

"§ 3111. Acceptance of volunteer service

"(a) For the purpose of this section, 'student' means an individual who is enrolled, not less than half-time, in a high school, trade school, technical or vocational institute, junior college, college, university, or comparable recognized educational institution. An individual who is a student is deemed not to have ceased to be a student during an interim between school years if the interim is not more than 5 months and if such individual shows to the satisfaction of the Office of Personnel Management that the individual has a bona fide intention of continuing to pursue a course of study or training in the same or different educational institution during the school semester (or other period into which the school year is divided) immediately after the interim.

"(b) Notwithstanding section 3679(b) of the Revised Statutes (31 U.S.C. 665(b)), the head of an agency may accept, subject to regulations issued by the Office, voluntary service for the United States if the service—

"(1) is performed by a student, with the permission of the institution at which the student is enrolled, as part of an agency program established for the purpose of providing educational experiences for the student:

"(2) is to be uncompensated; and

"(3) will not be used to displace any employee.

"(c) Any student who provides voluntary service under subsection (b) of this section shall not be considered a Federal employee for any purpose other than for purposes of chapter 81 of this title (relating to compensation for injury) and sections 2671 through 2680 of title 28 (relating to tort claims).".   5 USC 810 *et seq.*

(b) The analysis of chapter 31 of title 5, United States Code, is amended by adding at the end thereof the following new item:

"3111. Acceptance of volunteer service.".

INTERPRETING ASSISTANTS FOR DEAF EMPLOYEES

SEC. 302. (a) Section 3102 of title 5, United States Code, is amended—

(1) by redesignating paragraph (4) of subsection (a) as paragraph (5), by striking out "and" at the end of paragraph (3), and inserting after paragraph (3) the following new paragraph (4):

"(4) 'deaf employee' means an individual employed by an agency who, in accordance with regulations prescribed by the head of the agency, establishes to the satisfaction of the appropriate authority of the agency concerned that the employee has a hearing impairment, either permanent or temporary, so severe or disabling that the employment of an interpreting assistant or assistants for the employee is necessary or desirable to enable such employee to perform the work of the employee; and ":   "Deaf employee."

(2) in subsection (b), by inserting "and interpreting assistant or assistants for a deaf employee" after "or assistants for a blind employee", and amending the last sentence to read as follows: "A reading assistant or an interpreting assistant, other than the one employed or assigned under subsection (d) of this section, may receive pay for services performed by the assistant by and from the blind or deaf employee or a nonprofit organization, without regard to section 209 of title 18.";

(3) in subsection (c), by inserting "or deaf" after "blind"; and

(4) by inserting at the end thereof the following new subsection:

"(d) The head of each agency may also employ or assign, subject to section 209 of title 18 and to the provisions of this title governing appointment and chapter 51 and subchapter III of chapter 53 of this title governing classification and pay, such reading assistants for blind employees and such interpreting assistants for deaf employees as may be necessary to enable such employees to perform their work.".   5 USC 5101 *et seq.*, 5331.

(b)(1) The analysis of chapter 31 of title 5, United States Code, is amended by striking out the item relating to section 3102 and inserting in lieu thereof the following:

"3102. Employment of reading assistants for blind employees and interpreting assistants for deaf employees.".

(2) The heading for section 3102 of title 5, United States Code, is amended to read as follows:

"§ 3102. Employment of reading assistants for blind employees and interpreting assistants for deaf employees".

(c) Section 410(b)(1) of title 39, United States Code, is amended by inserting after "open meetings)" a comma and "3102 (employment of reading assistants for blind employees and interpreting assistants for deaf employees),".

PROBATIONARY PERIOD

Sec. 303. (a) Section 3321 of title 5, United States Code, is amended to read as follows:

"§ 3321. Competitive service; probationary period

"(a) The President may take such action, including the issuance of rules, regulations, and directives, as shall provide as nearly as conditions of good administration warrant for a period of probation—

"(1) before an appointment in the competitive service becomes final; and

"(2) before initial appointment as a supervisor or manager becomes final.

"(b) An individual—

"(1) who has been transferred, assigned, or promoted from a position to a supervisory or managerial position, and

"(2) who does not satisfactorily complete the probationary period under subsection (a)(2) of this section,

shall be returned to a position of no lower grade and pay than the position from which the individual was transferred, assigned, or promoted. Nothing in this section prohibits an agency from taking an action against an individual serving a probationary period under subsection (a)(2) of this section for cause unrelated to supervisory or managerial performance.

"(c) Subsections (a) and (b) of this section shall not apply with respect to appointments in the Senior Executive Service.".

(b) The item in the analysis for chapter 33 of title 5, United States Code, is amended to read as follows:

"3321. Competitive service; probationary period.".

TRAINING

Sec. 304. Section 4103 of title 5, United States Code, is amended by inserting "(a)" before "In order to increase" and by adding at the end thereof the following new subsection:

"(b)(1) Notwithstanding any other provision of this chapter, an agency may train any employee of the agency to prepare the employee for placement in another agency if the head of the agency determines that the employee will otherwise be separated under conditions which would entitle the employee to severance pay under section 5595 of this title.

"(2) Before undertaking any training under this subsection, the head of the agency shall obtain verification from the Office of Personnel Management that there exists a reasonable expectation of placement in another agency.

"(3) In selecting an employee for training under this subsection, the head of the agency shall consider—

"(A) the extent to which the current skills, knowledge, and abilities of the employee may be utilized in the new position;

"(B) the employee's capability to learn skills and acquire knowledge and abilities needed in the new position; and

"(C) the benefits to the Government which would result from retaining the employee in the Federal service.".

TRAVEL, TRANSPORTATION, AND SUBSISTENCE

SEC. 305. Section 5723(d) of title 5, United States Code, is amended by striking out "not".

RETIREMENT

SEC. 306. Section 8336(d)(2) of title 5, United States Code, is amended to read as follows:

"(2) voluntarily, during a period when the agency in which the employee is serving is undergoing a major reorganization, a major reduction in force, or a major transfer of function, as determined by the Office of Personnel Management, and the employee is serving in a geographic area designated by the Office;".

VETERANS AND PREFERENCE ELIGIBLES

SEC. 307. (a) Effective beginning October 1, 1980, section 2108 of title 5, United States Code, is amended—

(1) by striking out "and" at the end of paragraph (2);

(2) by inserting in paragraph (3) after "means" the following: ", except as provided in paragraph (4) of this section";

(3) by striking out the period at the end of paragraph (3) and inserting in lieu thereof a semicolon; and

(4) by adding at the end thereof the following new paragraphs:

"(4) except for the purposes of chapters 43 and 75 of this title, 'preference eligible' does not include a retired member of the armed forces unless—

"(A) the individual is a disabled veteran; or

"(B) the individual retired below the rank of major or its equivalent; and

"(5) 'retired member of the armed forces' means a member or former member of the armed forces who is entitled, under statute, to retired, retirement, or retainer pay on account of service as a member.".

5 USC 4301 *et seq.*, 7501 *et seq.*

"Retired member of the Armed Forces."

(b)(1) Chapter 31 of title 5, United States Code, is amended by adding at the end thereof the following new section:

"§ 3112. Disabled veterans; noncompetitive appointment

5 USC 3112.

"Under such regulations as the Office of Personnel Management shall prescribe, an agency may make a noncompetitive appointment leading to conversion to career or career-conditional employment of a disabled veteran who has a compensable service-connected disability of 30 percent or more."

(2) The Director of the Office of Personnel Management shall include in the reports required by section 2014(d) of title 38, United States Code, the same type of information regarding the use of the

38 USC 2014 note.

authority provided in section 3112 of title 5, United States Code (as added by paragraph (1) of this subsection), as is required by such section 2014 with respect to the use of the authority to make veterans readjustment appointments.

(3) The analysis of chapter 31 of title 5, United States Code, is amended by adding at the end thereof the following new item:

"3112. Disabled veterans; noncompetitive appointment.".

(c) Section 3312 of title 5, United States Code, is amended—
(1) by inserting "(a)" before "In"; and
(2) by adding at the end thereof the following new subsection:

5 USC 2108.

"(b) If an examining agency determines that, on the basis of evidence before it, a preference eligible under section 2108(3)(C) of this title who has a compensable service-connected disability of 30 percent or more is not able to fulfill the physical requirements of the position, the examining agency shall notify the Office of the determination and, at the same time, the examining agency shall notify the preference eligible of the reasons for the determination and of the right to respond, within 15 days of the date of the notification, to the Office. The Office shall require a demonstration by the appointing authority that the notification was timely sent to the preference eligible's last known address and shall, before the selection of any other person for the position, make a final determination on the physical ability of the preference eligible to perform the duties of the position, taking into account any additional information provided in any such response. When the Office has completed its review of the proposed disqualification on the basis of physical disability, it shall send its findings to the appointing authority and the preference eligible. The appointing authority shall comply with the findings of the Office. The functions of the Office under this subsection may not be delegated.".

(d) Section 3318(b) of title 5, United States Code, is amended to read as follows:

"(b)(1) If an appointing authority proposes to pass over a preference eligible on a certificate in order to select an individual who is not a preference eligible, such authority shall file written reasons with the Office for passing over the preference eligible. The Office shall make the reasons presented by the appointing authority part of the record of the preference eligible and may require the submission of more detailed information from the appointing authority in support of the passing over of the preference eligible. The Office shall determine the sufficiency or insufficiency of the reasons submitted by the appointing authority, taking into account any response received from the preference eligible under paragraph (2) of this subsection. When the Office has completed its review of the proposed passover, it shall send its findings to the appointing authority and to the preference eligible. The appointing authority shall comply with the findings of the Office.

"(2) In the case of a preference eligible described in section 2108(3) (C) of this title who has a compensable service-connected disability of 30 percent or more, the appointing authority shall at the same time it notifies the Office under paragraph (1) of this subsection, notify the preference eligible of the proposed passover, of the reasons therefor, and of his right to respond to such reasons to the Office within 15 days of the date of such notification. The Office shall, before completing its review under paragraph (1) of this subsection, require a demonstration by the appointing authority that the passover notification was timely sent to the preference eligible's last known address.

"(3) A preference eligible not described in paragraph (2) of this subsection, or his representative, shall be entitled, on request, to a copy of—

"(A) the reasons submitted by the appointing authority in support of the proposed passover, and

"(B) the findings of the Office.

"(4) In the case of a preference eligible described in paragraph (2) of this subsection, the functions of the Office under this subsection may not be delegated.".

(e) Section 3502 of title 5, United States Code, is amended by striking out subsection (b) and inserting in lieu thereof the following new subsections:

"(b) A preference eligible described in section 2108(3)(C) of this title who has a compensable service-connected disability of 30 percent or more and whose performance has not been rated unacceptable under a performance appraisal system implemented under chapter 43 of this title is entitled to be retained in preference to other preference eligibles.   5 USC 2108.

"(c) An employee who is entitled to retention preference and whose performance has not been rated unacceptable under a performance appraisal system implemented under chapter 43 of this title is entitled to be retained in preference to other competing employees.".   5 USC 4301 et seq.

(f) Section 3503 of title 5, United States Code, is amended by striking out in subsection (a) and (b) "each preference eligible employee" and inserting in lieu thereof "each competing employee" both places it appears.

(g) Section 3504 of title 5, United States Code, is amended—

(1) by inserting "(a)" before "In"; and

(2) by adding at the end thereof the following new subsection:

"(b) If an examining agency determines that, on the basis of evidence before it, a preference eligible described in section 2108(3)(C) of this title who has a compensable service-connected disability of 30 percent or more is not able to fulfill the physical requirements of the position, the examining agency shall notify the Office of the determination and, at the same time, the examining agency shall notify the preference eligible of the reasons for the determination and of the right to respond, within 15 days of the date of the notification, to the Office. The Office shall require a demonstration by the appointing authority that the notification was timely sent to the preference eligible's last known address and shall, before the selection of any other person for the position, make a final determination on the physical ability of the preference eligible to perform the duties of the position, taking into account any additional information provided in the response. When the Office has completed its review of the proposed disqualification on the basis of physical disability, it shall send its findings to the appointing authority and the preference eligible. The appointing authority shall comply with the findings of the Office. The functions of the Office under this subsection may not be delegated.".

(h)(1) Section 3319 of chapter 33 of title 5, United States Code, is repealed.   Repeal.

(2) The analysis for chapter 33 of title 5, United States Code, is amended by striking out the item relating to section 3319.

DUAL PAY FOR RETIRED MEMBERS OF THE UNIFORMED SERVICES

SEC. 308. (a) Section 5532 of title 5, United States Code, relating to retired officers of the uniformed services, is amended by redesignating subsections (c) and (d) as subsections (d) and (e) and by inserting after subsection (b) the following:

"(c)(1) If any member or former member of a uniformed service is receiving retired or retainer pay and is employed in a position the annual rate of basic pay for which, when combined with the member's annual rate of retired or retainer pay (reduced as provided under subsection (b) of this section), exceeds the rate of basic pay then currently paid for level V of the Executive Schedule, such member's retired or retainer pay shall be reduced by an amount computed under paragraph (2) of this subsection. The amounts of the reductions shall be deposited to the general fund of the Treasury of the United States.

5 USC 5316 note.

"(2) The amount of each reduction under paragraph (1) of this subsection allocable for any pay period in connection with employment in a position shall be equal to the retired or retainer pay allocable to the pay period (reduced as provided under subsection (b) of this section), except that the amount of the reduction may not result in—

"(A) the amount of retired or retainer pay allocable to the pay period after being reduced, when combined with the basic pay for the employment during the pay period, being at a rate less than the rate of basic pay then currently paid for level V of the Executive Schedule; or

"(B) the amount of retired pay or retainer pay being reduced to an amount less than the amount deducted from the retired or retainer pay as a result of participation in any survivor's benefits in connection with the retired or retainer pay or veterans insurance programs.".

(b) Section 5531 of title 5, United States Code is amended—

(1) by striking out paragraph (1) and inserting in lieu thereof the following:

"(1) 'member' has the meaning given such term by section 101 (23) of title 37;";

(2) by striking out the period at the end of paragraph (2) and inserting in lieu thereof "; and"; and

(3) by adding at the end thereof the following new paragraph:

"Retired or
retainer pay."
5 USC 8311.

"(3) 'retired or retainer pay' means retired pay, as defined in section 8311(3) of this title, determined without regard to subparagraphs (B) through (D) of such section 8311(3); except that such term does not include an annuity payable to an eligible beneficiary of a member or former member of a uniformed service under chapter 73 of title 10.".

10 USC 1431 et
seq.

(c) Section 5532(d) of title 5, United States Code, as amended by subsection (a), is amended—

(1) by striking out "subsection (b) of";

(2) by striking out "or retirement" each place it appears and inserting in lieu thereof "or retainer";

(3) by striking out "a retired officer of a regular component of a uniformed service" and inserting in lieu thereof "a member or former member of a uniformed service who is receiving retired or retainer pay"; and

(4) in paragraph (1), by striking out "whose retirement was" and inserting in lieu thereof "whose retired or retainer pay is computed, in whole or in part,".

(d) Section 5532(e) of title 5, United States Code, as amended by subsection (a), is amended to read as follows:

Ante, p. 1111.

"(e) The Office of Personnel Management may, during the 5-year period after the effective date of the Civil Service Reform Act of 1978 authorize exceptions to the restrictions in subsections (a), (b), and (c) of this section only when necessary to meet special or emergency employment needs which result from a severe shortage of well qualified candidates in positions of medical officers which otherwise cannot be readily met. An exception granted by the office with respect to any individual shall terminate upon a break in service of 3 days or more.".

(e) Section 5532(b) of title 5, United States Code, is amended by striking out "or retirement" each place it appears and inserting in lieu thereof "or retainer".

(f)(1) The heading for section 5532 of title 5, United States Code, is amended to read as follows:

"§ 5532. Employment of retired members of the uniformed services; reduction in retired or retainer pay".

(2) The item relating to section 5532 in the table of sections for chapter 55 of title 5, United States Code, is amended to read as follows:

"5532. Employment of retired members of the uniformed services; reduction in retired or retainer pay.".

(g)(1) Except as provided in paragraph (2) of this subsection, the amendments made by this section shall apply only with respect to pay periods beginning after the effective date of this Act and only with respect to members of the uniformed services who first receive retired or retainer pay (as defined in section 5531(3) of title 5, United States Code (as amended by this section)), after the effective date of this Act.   5 USC 5532 note.

(2) Such amendments shall not apply to any individual employed in a position on the date of the enactment of this Act so long as the individual continues to hold any such position (disregarding any break in service of 3 days or less) if the individual, on that date, would have been entitled to retired or retainer pay but for the fact the individual does not satisfy any applicable age requirement.

(3) The provisions of section 5532 of title 5, United States Code, as in effect immediately before the effective date of this Act, shall apply with respect to any retired officer of a regular component of the uniformed services who is receiving retired pay on or before such date, or any individual to whom paragraph (2) applies, in the same manner and to the same extent as if the preceding subsections of this section had not been enacted.

CIVIL SERVICE EMPLOYMENT INFORMATION

Sec. 309. (a) Chapter 33 of title 5, United States Code, is amended by adding at the end thereof the following new section:

"§ 3327. Civil service employment information   5 USC 3327.

"(a) The Office of Personnel Management shall provide that information concerning opportunities to participate in competitive examinations conducted by, or under authority delegated by, the Office of Personnel Management shall be made available to the employment offices of the United States Employment Service.

"(b) Subject to such regulations as the Office may issue, each agency shall promptly notify the Office and the employment offices of the United States Employment Service of—

"(1) each vacant position in the agency which is in the competitive service or the Senior Executive Service and for which the agency seeks applications from persons outside the Federal service, and

"(2) the period during which applications will be accepted. As used in this subsection, 'agency' means an agency as defined in section 5102(a)(1) of this title other than an agency all the positions in which are excepted by statute from the competitive service.".   "Agency."
5 USC 5102.

(b) The table of sections for chapter 33 of title 5, United States Code, is amended by inserting after the item relating to section 3326 the following new item:

"3327. Civil service employment information."

MINORITY RECRUITMENT PROGRAM

SEC. 310. Section 7151 of title 5, United States Code, is amended—
    (1) by striking out the section heading and inserting in lieu thereof the following:

"§ 7151. Antidiscrimination policy; minority recruitment program";

    (2) by inserting after such section heading the following new subsection:

"(a) For the purpose of this section—

"Underrepresentation."

"(1) 'underrepresentation' means a situation in which the number of members of a minority group designation (determined by the Equal Employment Opportunity Commission in consultation with the Office of Personnel Management, on the basis of the policy set forth in subsection (b) of this section) within a category of civil service employment constitutes a lower percentage of the total number of employees within the employment category than the percentage that the minority constituted within the labor force of the United States, as determined under the most recent decennial or mid-decade census, or current population survey, under title 13, and

"Category of civil service employment."

"(2) 'category of civil service employment' means—
    "(A) each grade of the General Schedule described in section 5104 of this title;
    "(B) each position subject to subchapter IV of chapter 53 of this title;
    "(C) such occupational, professional, or other groupings (including occupational series) within the categories established under subparagraphs (A) and (B) of this paragraph as the Office determines appropriate.";
(3) by inserting "(b)" before "It is the policy"; and
(4) by adding at the end thereof the following new subsection:

"(c) Not later than 180 days after the date of the enactment of the

Ante, p. 1111.

Civil Service Reform Act of 1978, the Office of Personnel Management shall, by regulation, implement a minority recruitment program which shall provide, to the maximum extent practicable—

"(1) that each Executive agency conduct a continuing program for the recruitment of members of minorities for positions in the agency to carry out the policy set forth in subsection (b) in a manner designed to eliminate underrepresentation of minorities in the various categories of civil service employment within the Federal service, with special efforts directed at recruiting in minority communities, in educational institutions, and from other sources from which minorities can be recruited; and

"(2) that the Office conduct a continuing program of—
    "(A) assistance to agencies in carrying out programs under paragraph (1) of this subsection, and
    "(B) evaluation and oversight and such recruitment programs to determine their effectiveness in eliminating such minority underrepresentation.

"(d) Not later than 60 days after the date of the enactment of the Civil Service Reform Act of 1978, the Equal Employment Opportunity Commission shall—
Ante, p. 1111.

"(1) establish the guidelines proposed to be used in carrying out the program required under subsection (c) of this section; and
Proposed guidelines.

"(2) make determinations of underrepresentation which are proposed to be used initially under such program; and
Determinations.

"(3) transmit to the Executive agencies involved, to the Office of Personnel Management, and to the Congress the determinations made under paragraph (2) of this subsection.
Transmittal to Executive agencies.

"(e) Not later than January 31 of each year, the Office shall prepare and transmit to each House of the Congress a report on the activities of the Office and of Executive agencies under subsection (c) of this section, including the affirmative action plans submitted under section 717 of the Civil Rights Act of 1964 (42 U.S.C. 2000e–16), the personnel data file maintained by the Office of Personnel Management, and any other data necessary to evaluate the effectiveness of the program for each category of civil service employment and for each minority group designation, for the preceding fiscal year, together with recommendations for administrative or legislative action the Office considers appropriate.".
Report to Congress.

TEMPORARY EMPLOYMENT LIMITATION

SEC. 311. (a) The total number of civilian employees in the executive branch, on September 30, 1979, on September 30, 1980, and on September 30, 1981, shall not exceed the number of such employees on September 30, 1977.
5 USC 3101 note.

(b)(1) For the purpose of this section, "civilian employees in the executive branch" means all civilian employees within the executive branch of the Government (other than in the United States Postal Service or the Postal Rate Commission), whether employed on a full-time, part-time, or intermittent basis and whether employed on a direct hire or indirect hire basis.
"Civilian employees in the executive branch."

(2)(A) Such term does not include individuals participating in special employment programs established for students and disadvantaged youth.

(B) The total number of individuals participating in such programs shall not at any time exceed 60,000.

(c) In applying the limitation of subsection (a)—

(1) part-time civilian employees in excess of the number of part-time civilian employees in the executive branch employed on September 30, 1977, may be counted as a fraction which is determined by dividing 40 hours into the average number of hours of such employees' regularly scheduled workweek; and

(2) the number of civilian employees in the executive branch on September 30, 1977, shall be determined on the basis of the number of such employees as set forth in the Monthly Report of Civilian Employment published by the Civil Service Commission.

(d)(1) The provisions of this section shall not apply during a time of war or during a period of national emergency declared by the Congress or the President.

(2)(A) Subject to the limitation of subparagraph (B) of this paragraph, the President may authorize employment of civilian employees in excess of the limitation of subsection (a) if he deems that such action is necessary in the public interest.

(B) The President may not, under this paragraph, increase the maximum number of civilian employees in the executive branch by more than the percentage increase of the population of the United States since September 30, 1978, as estimated by the Bureau of the Census.

(e) The President shall provide that no increase occurs in the procurement of personal services by contract by reason of the enactment of this section except in cases in which it is to the financial advantage of the Government to do so.

Regulations.

(f) The President shall prescribe regulations to carry out the purposes of this section.

Termination.

(g) The provisions of this section shall terminate on January 31, 1981.

TITLE IV—SENIOR EXECUTIVE SERVICE

GENERAL PROVISIONS

Sec. 401. (a) Chapter 21 of title 5, United States Code, is amended by inserting after section 2101 the following new section:

5 USC 2101a.

"§ 2101a. The Senior Executive Service

Post, p. 1156.

"The 'Senior Executive Service' consists of Senior Executive Service positions (as defined in section 3132(a)(2) of this title).".

(b) Section 2102(a)(1) of title 5, United States Code, is amended—

(1) by striking out "and" at the end of subparagraph (A);
(2) by adding "and" at the end of subparagraph (B); and
(3) by adding at the end thereof the following new subparagraph:

"(C) positions in the Senior Executive Service;".

(c) Section 2103(a) of title 5, United States Code, is amended by inserting before the period at the end thereof the following: "or the Senior Executive Service".

Ante, p. 1147.

(d) Section 2108(5) of title 5, United States Code (as amended in section 307 of this Act), is further amended—

(1) by striking out the period at the end thereof and inserting in lieu thereof a semicolon; and
(2) by adding at the end thereof the following:

"but does not include applicants for, or members of, the Senior Executive Service.".

(e) The analysis for chapter 21 of title 5, United States Code, is amended by inserting after the item relating to section 2101 the following new item:

"2101a. The Senior Executive Service.".

AUTHORITY FOR EMPLOYMENT

Sec. 402. (a) Chapter 31 of title 5, United States Code, is amended

Ante, p. 1147.

by inserting after section 3112 (as added by section 307(b) of this Act), the following new subchapter:

"SUBCHAPTER II—THE SENIOR EXECUTIVE SERVICE

5 USC 3131.

"§ 3131. The Senior Executive Service

"It is the purpose of this subchapter to establish a Senior Executive Service to ensure that the executive management of the Government of the United States is responsive to the needs, policies, and goals of the Nation and otherwise is of the highest quality. The Senior Executive Service shall be administered so as to—

"(1) provide for a compensation system, including salaries, benefits, and incentives, and for other conditions of employment, designed to attract and retain highly competent senior executives;

"(2) ensure that compensation, retention, and tenure are contingent on executive success which is measured on the basis of individual and organizational performance (including such factors as improvements in efficiency, productivity, quality of work or service, cost efficiency, and timeliness of performance and success in meeting equal employment opportunity goals) :

"(3) assure that senior executives are accountable and responsible for the effectiveness and productivity of employees under them :

"(4) recognize exceptional accomplishment;

"(5) enable the head of an agency to reassign senior executives to best accomplish the agency's mission;

"(6) provide for severance pay, early retirement, and placement assistance for senior executives who are removed from the Senior Executive Service for nondisciplinary reasons;

"(7) protect senior executives from arbitrary or capricious actions;

"(8) provide for program continuity and policy advocacy in the management of public programs;

"(9) maintain a merit personnel system free of prohibited personnel practices;

"(10) ensure accountability for honest, economical, and efficent Government;

"(11) ensure compliance with all applicable civil service laws, rules, and regulations, including those related to equal employment opportunity, political activity, and conflicts of interest;

"(12) provide for the initial and continuing systematic development of highly competent senior executives;

"(13) provide for an executive system which is guided by the public interest and free from improper political interference: and

"(14) appoint career executives to fill Senior Executive Service positions to the extent practicable, consistent with the effective and efficient implementation of agency policies and responsibilities.

"§ 3132. Definitions and exclusions

5 USC 3132.

"(a) For the purpose of this subchapter—

"(1) 'agency' means an Executive agency, except a Government corporation and the General Accounting Office, but does not include—

"(A) any agency or unit thereof excluded from coverage by the President under subsection (c) of this section: or

"(B) the Federal Bureau of Investigation, the Central Intelligence Agency, the Defense Intelligence Agency, the National Security Agency, as determined by the President, an Executive agency, or unit thereof, whose principal function is the conduct of foreign intelligence or counterintelligence activities;

5 USC 5332 note.

5 USC 5315, 5316.

"(2) 'Senior Executive Service position' means any position in an agency which is in GS-16, 17, or 18 of the General Schedule or in level IV or V of the Executive Schedule, or an equivalent position, which is not required to be filled by an appointment by the President by and with the advice and consent of the Senate, and in which an employee—

"(A) directs the work of an organizational unit;

"(B) is held accountable for the success of one or more specific programs or projects;

"(C) monitors progress toward organizational goals and periodically evaluates and makes appropriate adjustments to such goals;

"(D) supervises the work of employees other than personal assistants; or

"(E) otherwise exercises important policy-making, policy-determining, or other executive functions;

but does not include—

"(i) any position in the Foreign Service of the United States;

"(ii) an administrative law judge position under section 3105 of this title; or

"(iii) any position in the Drug Enforcement Administration which is excluded from the competitive service under section 201 of the Crime Control Act of 1976 (5 U.S.C. 5108 note; 90 Stat. 2425);

28 USC 509 note.

"(3) 'senior executive' means a member of the Senior Executive Service;

"(4) 'career appointee' means an individual in a Senior Executive Service position whose appointment to the position or previous appointment to another Senior Executive Service position was based on approval by the Office of Personnel Management of the executive qualifications of such individual;

"(5) 'limited term appointee' means an individual appointed under a nonrenewable appointment for a term of 3 years or less to a Senior Executive Service position the duties of which will expire at the end of such term;

"(6) 'limited emergency appointee' means an individual appointed under a nonrenewable appointment, not to exceed 18 months, to a Senior Executive Service position established to meet a bona fide, unanticipated, urgent need;

"(7) 'noncareer appointee' means an individual in a Senior Executive Service position who is not a career appointee, a limited term appointee, or a limited emergency appointee;

"(8) 'career reserved position' means a position which is required to be filled by a career appointee and which is designated under subsection (b) of this section; and

"(9) 'general position' means any position, other than a career reserved position, which may be filled by either a career appointee, noncareer appointee, limited emergency appointee, or limited term appointee.

Criteria and regulations.

"(b)(1) For the purpose of paragraph (8) of subsection (a) of this section, the Office shall prescribe the criteria and regulations governing the designation of career reserved positions. The criteria and regulations shall provide that a position shall be designated as a career reserved position only if the filling of the position by a career appointee is necessary to ensure impartiality, or the public's confidence in the impartiality, of the Government. The head of each agency shall be responsible for designating career reserved positions in such agency in accordance with such criteria and regulations.

"(2) The Office shall periodically review general positions to determine whether the positions should be designated as career reserved. If the Office determines that any such position should be so designated, it shall order the agency to make the designation. Review.

"(3) Notwithstanding the provisions of any other law, any position to be designated as a Senior Executive Service position (except a position in the Executive Office of the President) which—

"(A) is under the Executive Schedule, or for which the rate of basic pay is determined by reference to the Executive Schedule, and 5 USC 5312.

"(B) on the day before the date of the enactment of the Civil Service Reform Act of 1978 was specifically required under section 2102 of this title or otherwise required by law to be in the competitive service, Ante, p. 1111.

shall be designated as a career reserved position if the position entails direct responsibility to the public for the management or operation of particular government programs or functions.

"(4) Not later than March 1 of each year, the head of each agency shall publish in the Federal Register a list of positions in the agency which were career reserved positions during the preceding calendar year. Publication in Federal Register.

"(c) An agency may file an application with the Office setting forth reasons why it, or a unit thereof, should be excluded from the coverage of this subchapter. The Office shall— Application for exclusion coverage.

"(1) review the application and stated reasons,

"(2) undertake a review to determine whether the agency or unit should be excluded from the coverage of this subchapter, and

"(3) upon completion of its review, recommend to the President whether the agency or unit should be excluded from the coverage of this subchapter.

If the Office recommends that an agency or unit thereof be excluded from the coverage of this subchapter, the President may, on written determination, make the exclusion for the period determined by the President to be appropriate.

"(d) Any agency or unit which is excluded from coverage under subsection (c) of this section shall make a sustained effort to bring its personnel system into conformity with the Senior Executive Service to the extent practicable.

"(e) The Office may at any time recommend to the President that any exclusion previously granted to an agency or unit thereof under subsection (c) of this section be revoked. Upon recommendation of the Office, the President may revoke, by written determination, any exclusion made under subsection (c) of this section. Exclusion or revocation.

"(f) If—

"(1) any agency is excluded under subsection (c) of this section, or

"(2) any exclusion is revoked under subsection (e) of this section,

the Office shall, within 30 days after the action, transmit to the Congress written notice of the exclusion or revocation. Report to Congress.

5 USC 3133.

"§ 3133. Authorization of positions; authority for appointment

"(a) During each even-numbered calendar year, each agency shall—

"(1) examine its needs for Senior Executive Service positions for each of the 2 fiscal years beginning after such calendar year; and

Written request to OPM.

"(2) submit to the Office of Personnel Management a written request for a specific number of Senior Executive Service positions for each of such fiscal years.

"(b) Each agency request submitted under subsection (a) of this section shall—

"(1) be based on the anticipated type and extent of program activities and budget requests of the agency for each of the 2 fiscal years involved, and such other factors as may be prescribed from time to time by the Office; and

"(2) identify, by position title, positions which are proposed to be designated as or removed from designation as career reserved positions, and set forth justifications for such proposed actions.

"(c) The Office of Personnel Management, in consultation with the Office of Management and Budget, shall review the request of each agency and shall authorize, for each of the 2 fiscal years covered by requests required under subsection (a) of this section, a specific number of Senior Executive Service positions for each agency.

"(d)(1) The Office of Personnel Management may, on a written request of an agency or on its own initiative, make an adjustment in the number of positions authorized for any agency. Each agency request under this paragraph shall be submitted in such form, and shall be based on such factors, as the Office shall prescribe.

"(2) The total number of positions in the Senior Executive Service may not at any time during any fiscal year exceed 105 percent of the total number of positions authorized under subsection (c) of this section for such fiscal year.

"(e)(1) Not later than July 1, 1979, and from time to time thereafter as the Director of the Office of Personnel Management finds appropriate, the Director shall establish, by rule issued in accordance with section 1103(b) of this title, the number of positions out of the total number of positions in the Senior Executive Service, as authorized by this section or section 413 of the Civil Service Reform Act of

Post, p. 1175.

1978, which are to be career reserved positions. Except as provided in paragraph (2) of this subsection, the number of positions required by this subsection to be career reserved positions shall not be less than the number of the positions then in the Senior Executive Service which before the date of such Act, were authorized to be filled only through competitive civil service examination.

"(2) The Director may, by rule, designate a number of career reserved positions which is less than the number required by paragraph (1) of this subsection only if the Director determines such lesser number necessary in order to designate as general positions one or more positions (other than positions described in section 3132(b)(3) of this title) which—

"(A) involve policymaking responsibilities which require the advocacy or management of programs of the President and support of controversial aspects of such programs;

"(B) involve significant participation in the major political policies of the President; or

"(C) require the senior executives in the positions to serve as personal assistants of, or advisers to, Presidential appointees.

The Director shall provide a full explanation for his determination in each case.

"§ 3134. Limitations on noncareer and limited appointments

5 USC 3134.

"(a) During each calendar year, each agency shall—

"(1) examine its needs for employment of noncareer appointees for the fiscal year beginning in the following year; and

"(2) submit to the Office of Personnel Management, in accordance with regulations prescribed by the Office, a written request for authority to employ a specific number of noncareer appointees for such fiscal year.

"(b) The number of noncareer appointees in each agency shall be determined annually by the Office on the basis of demonstrated need of the agency. The total number of noncareer appointees in all agencies may not exceed 10 percent of the total number of Senior Executive Service positions in all agencies.

"(c) Subject to the 10 percent limitation of subsection (b) of this section, the Office may adjust the number of noncareer positions authorized for any agency under subsection (b) of this section if emergency needs arise that were not anticipated when the original authorizations were made.

"(d) The number of Senior Executive Service positions in any agency which are filled by noncareer appointees may not at any time exceed the greater of—

"(1) 25 percent of the total number of Senior Executive Service positions in the agency; or

"(2) the number of positions in the agency which were filled on the date of the enactment of the Civil Service Reform Act of 1978 by—

"(A) noncareer executive assignments under subpart F of part 305 of title 5, Code of Federal Regulations, as in effect on such date, or

5 CFR 305.101 *et seq.*

"(B) appointments to level IV or V of the Executive Schedule which were not required on such date to be made by and with the advice and consent of the Senate.

5 USC 5315, 5316.

This subsection shall not apply in the case of any agency having fewer than 4 Senior Executive Service positions.

"(e) The total number of limited emergency appointees and limited term appointees in all agencies may not exceed 5 percent of the total number of Senior Executive Service positions in all agencies.

"§ 3135. Biennial report

5 USC 3135.

"(a) The Office of Personnel Management shall submit to each House of the Congress, at the time the budget is submitted by the President to the Congress during each odd-numbered calendar year, a report on the Senior Executive Service. The report shall include—

Report to Congress.

"(1) the number of Senior Executive Service positions authorized for the then current fiscal year, in the aggregate and by agency, and the projected number of Senior Executive Service positions to be authorized for the next two fiscal years, in the aggregate and by agency;

"(2) the authorized number of career appointees and noncareer appointees, in the aggregate and by agency, for the then current fiscal year;

"(3) the position titles and descriptions of Senior Executive Service positions designated for the then current fiscal year;

"(4) a description of each exclusion in effect under section 3132(c) of this title during the preceding fiscal year;

"(5) the number of career appointees, limited term appointees, limited emergency appointees, and noncareer appointees, in the aggregate and by agency, employed during the preceding fiscal year;

"(6) the percentage of senior executives at each pay rate, in the aggregate and by agency, employed at the end of the preceding fiscal year;

"(7) the distribution and amount of performance awards, in the aggregate and by agency, paid during the preceding fiscal year;

"(8) the estimated number of career reserved positions which, during the two fiscal years following the then current fiscal year, will become general positions and the estimated number of general positions which during such two fiscal years, will become career reserved positions; and

"(9) such other information regarding the Senior Executive Service as the Office considers appropriate.

Report to Congress.

"(b) The Office of Personnel Management shall submit to each House of the Congress, at the time the budget is submitted to the Congress during each even-numbered calendar year, an interim report showing changes in matters required to be reported under subsection (a) of this section.

5 USC 3136.

"**§ 3136. Regulations**

"The Office of Personnel Management shall prescribe regulations to carry out the purpose of this subchapter.".

(b) Section 3109 of title 5, United States Code, is amended by inserting at the end thereof the following new subsection:

"(c) Positions in the Senior Executive Service may not be filled under the authority of subsection (b) of this section.".

(c) The analysis for chapter 31 of title 5, United States Code, is amended—

(1) by striking out the heading for chapter 31 and inserting in lieu thereof the following:

"CHAPTER 31—AUTHORITY FOR EMPLOYMENT

"SUBCHAPTER I—EMPLOYMENT AUTHORITIES";

and

(2) by inserting at the end thereof the following:

"SUBCHAPTER II—THE SENIOR EXECUTIVE SERVICE

"Sec.
"3131. The Senior Executive Service.
"3132. Definitions and exclusions.
"3133. Authorization of positions; authority for appointment.
"3134. Limitations on noncareer and limited appointments.
"3135. Biennial report.
"3136. Regulations.".

EXAMINATION, CERTIFICATION, AND APPOINTMENT

Sec. 403. (a) Chapter 33 of title 5, United States Code, is amended by adding at the end thereof the following new subchapter:

"SUBCHAPTER VIII—APPOINTMENT, REASSIGNMENT, TRANSFER, AND DEVELOPMENT IN THE SENIOR EXECUTIVE SERVICE

"§ 3391. Definitions

"For the purpose of this subchapter, 'agency', 'Senior Executive Service position', 'senior executive', 'career appointee', 'limited term appointee', 'limited emergency appointee', 'noncareer appointee', and 'general position' have the meanings set forth in section 3132(a) of this title.

5 USC 3391.

"§ 3392. General appointment provisions

"(a) Qualification standards shall be established by the head of each agency for each Senior Executive Service position in the agency—

"(1) in accordance with requirements established by the Office of Personnel Management, with respect to standards for career reserved positions, and

"(2) after consultation with the Office, with respect to standards for general positions.

"(b) Not more than 30 percent of the Senior Executive Service positions authorized under section 3133 of this title may at any time be filled by individuals who did not have 5 years of current continuous service in the civil service immediately preceding their initial appointment to the Senior Executive Service, unless the President certifies to the Congress that the limitation would hinder the efficiency of the Government. In applying the preceding sentence, any break in service of 3 days or less shall be disregarded.

"(c) If a career appointee is appointed by the President, by and with the advice and consent of the Senate, to a civilian position in the executive branch which is not in the Senior Executive Service, and the rate of basic pay payable for which is equal to or greater than the rate payable for level V of the Executive Schedule, the career appointee may elect (at such time and in such manner as the Office may prescribe) to continue to have the provisions of this title relating to basic pay, performance awards, awarding of ranks, severance pay, leave, and retirement apply as if the career appointee remained in the Senior Executive Service position from which he was appointed. Such provisions shall apply in lieu of the provisions which would otherwise apply—

"(1) to the extent provided under regulations prescribed by the Office, and

"(2) so long as the appointee continues to serve under such Presidential appointment.

"(d) Appointment or removal of a person to or from any Senior Executive Service position in an independent regulatory commission shall not be subject, directly or indirectly, to review or approval by any officer or entity within the Executive Office of the President.

5 USC 3392.
Qualification standards, establishment.

Ante, p. 1158.

5 USC 5316.

"§ 3393. Career appointments

"(a) Each agency shall establish a recruitment program, in accordance with guidelines which shall be issued by the Office of Personnel

5 USC 3393.
Recruitment program.

Management, which provides for recruitment of career appointees
from—
"(1) all groups of qualified individuals within the civil service;
or
"(2) all groups of qualified individuals whether or not within
the civil service.

Executive resources boards, establishment. "(b) Each agency shall establish one or more executive resources
boards, as appropriate, the members of which shall be appointed by
the head of the agency from among employees of the agency. The
boards shall, in accordance with merit staffing requirements established
by the Office, conduct the merit staffing process for career appointees,
including—
"(1) reviewing the executive qualifications of each candidate
for a position to be filled by a career appointee; and
"(2) making written recommendations to the appropriate
appointing authority concerning such candidates.

Review boards, establishment. "(c)(1) The Office shall establish one or more qualifications review
boards, as appropriate. It is the function of the boards to certify the
executive qualifications of candidates for initial appointment as
career appointees in accordance with regulations prescribed by the
Office. Of the members of each board more than one-half shall be
appointed from among career appointees. Appointments to such boards
shall be made on a non-partisan basis, the sole selection criterion being
the professional knowledge of public management and knowledge of
the appropriate occupational fields of the intended appointee.

Career appointees, criteria. "(2) The Office shall, in consultation with the various qualification
review boards, prescribe criteria for establishing executive qualifica-
tions for appointment of career appointees. The criteria shall provide
for—
"(A) consideration of demonstrated executive experience;
"(B) consideration of successful participation in a career executive development program which is approved by the Office; and
"(C) sufficient flexibility to allow for the appointment of
individuals who have special or unique qualities which indicate a
likelihood of executive success and who would not otherwise be
eligible for appointment.

Probationary period requirement. "(d) An individual's initial appointment as a career appointee shall
become final only after the individual has served a 1-year probationary
period as a career appointee.
"(e) Each career appointee shall meet the executive qualifications of
the position to which appointed, as determined in writing by the
appointing authority.

Publication in Federal Register. "(f) The title of each career reserved position shall be published in
the Federal Register.

5 USC 3394. ## "§ 3394. Noncareer and limited appointments

"(a) Each noncareer appointee, limited term appointee, and limited
emergency appointee shall meet the qualifications of the position to
which appointed, as determined in writing by the appointing authority.
"(b) An individual may not be appointed as a limited term appointee
or as a limited emergency appointee without the prior approval of the
exercise of such appointing authority by the Office of Personnel
Management.

"**§ 3395. Reassignment and transfer within the Senior Executive** 5 USC 3395.
Service

"(a)(1) A career appointee in an agency—

"(A) may, subject to paragraph (2) of this subsection, be reassigned to any Senior Executive Service position in the same agency for which the appointee is qualified; and

"(B) may transfer to a Senior Executive Service position in another agency for which the appointee is qualified, with the approval of the agency to which the appointee transfers.

"(2) A career appointee may be reassigned to any Senior Executive Service position only if the career appointee receives a written notice of the reassignment at least 15 days in advance of such reassignment.

"(b)(1) Notwithstanding section 3394(b) of this title, a limited emergency appointee may be reassigned to another Senior Executive Service position in the same agency established to meet a bona fide, unanticipated, urgent need, except that the appointee may not serve in one or more positions in such agency under such appointment in excess of 18 months.

"(2) Notwithstanding section 3394(b) of this title, a limited term appointee may be reassigned to another Senior Executive Service position in the same agency the duties of which will expire at the end of a term of 3 years or less, except that the appointee may not serve in one or more positions in the agency under such appointment in excess of 3 years.

"(c) A limited term appointee or a limited emergency appointee may not be appointed to, or continue to hold, a position under such an appointment if, within the preceding 48 months, the individual has served more than 36 months, in the aggregate, under any combination of such types of appointment.

"(d) A noncareer appointee in an agency—

"(1) may be reassigned to any general position in the agency for which the appointee is qualified; and

"(2) may transfer to a general position in another agency with the approval of the agency to which the appointee transfers.

"(e)(1) Except as provided in paragraph (2) of this subsection, a career appointee in an agency may not be involuntarily reassigned—

"(A) within 120 days after an appointment of the head of the agency; or

"(B) within 120 days after the appointment in the agency of the career appointee's most immediate supervisor who—

"(i) is a noncareer appointee; and

"(ii) has the authority to reassign the career appointee.

"(2) Paragraph (1) of this subsection does not apply with respect to—

"(A) any reassignment under section 4314(b)(3) of this title; *Post,* p. 1169.
or

"(B) any disciplinary action initiated before an appointment referred to in paragraph (1) of this subsection.

"**§ 3396. Development for and within the Senior Executive Service** 5 USC 3396.

"(a) The Office of Personnel Management shall establish programs for the systematic development of candidates for the Senior Executive Service and for the continuing development of senior executives, or require agencies to establish such programs which meet criteria prescribed by the Office.

"(b) The Office shall assist agencies in the establishment of programs required under subsection (a) of this section and shall monitor the implementation of the programs. If the Office finds that any agency's program under subsection (a) of this section is not in compliance with the criteria prescribed under such subsection, it shall require the agency to take such corrective action as may be necessary to bring the program into compliance with the criteria.

Sabbatical grant.

"(c)(1) The head of an agency may grant a sabbatical to any career appointee for not to exceed 11 months in order to permit the appointee to engage in study or uncompensated work experience which will contribute to the appointee's development and effectiveness. A sabbatical shall not result in loss of, or reduction in, pay, leave to which the career appointee is otherwise entitled, credit for time or service, or performance or efficiency rating. The head of the agency may authorize in

5 USC 5701.

accordance with chapter 57 of this title such travel expenses (including per diem allowances) as the head of the agency may determine to be essential for the study or experience.

Exclusions.

"(2) A sabbatical under this subsection may not be granted to any career appointee—
"(A) more than once in any 10-year period;
"(B) unless the appointee has completed 7 years of service—
"(i) in one or more positions in the Senior Executive Service;
"(ii) in one or more other positions in the civil service the level of duties and responsibilities of which are equivalent to the level of duties and responsibilities of positions in the Senior Executive Service; or
"(iii) in any combination of such positions, except that not less than 2 years of such 7 years of service must be in the Senior Executive Service; and
"(C) if the appointee is eligible for voluntary retirement with a right to an immediate annuity under section 8336 of this title.
Any period of assignment under section 3373 of this title, relating to assignments of employees to State and local governments, shall not be considered a period of service for the purpose of subparagraph (B) of this paragraph.

Condition for acceptance.

"(3)(A) Any career appointee in an agency may be granted a sabbatical under this subsection only if the appointee agrees, as a condition of accepting the sabbatical, to serve in the civil service upon the completion of the sabbatical for a period of 2 consecutive years.

"(B) Each agreement required under subparagraph (A) of this paragraph shall provide that in the event the career appointee fails to carry out the agreement (except for good and sufficient reason as determined by the head of the agency who granted the sabbatical) the appointee shall be liable to the United States for payment of all expenses (including salary) of the sabbatical. The amount shall be treated as a debt due the United States.

"(d) The Office shall encourage and assist individuals to improve their skills and increase their contribution by service in a variety of agencies as well as by accepting temporary placements in State or local governments or in the private sector.

5 USC 3397.

"§ 3397. Regulations

"The Office of Personnel Management shall prescribe regulations to carry out the purpose of this subchapter.".

(b) The analysis for chapter 33 of title 5, United States Code, is amended by inserting after the item relating to section 3385 the following:

"SUBCHAPTER VIII—APPOINTMENT, REASSIGNMENT, TRANSFER, AND DEVELOPMENT IN THE SENIOR EXECUTIVE SERVICE

"Sec.
"3391. Definitions.
"3392. General appointment provisions.
"3393. Career appointments.
"3394. Noncareer and limited appointments.
"3395. Reassignment and transfer within the Senior Executive Service.
"3396. Development for and within the Senior Executive Service.
"3397. Regulations.".

RETENTION PREFERENCE

SEC. 404. (a) Section 3501(b) of title 5, United States Code, is amended by striking out the period at the end thereof and inserting in lieu thereof: "or to a member of the Senior Executive Service.".

(b) Chapter 35 of title 5, United States Code, is amended by adding at the end thereof the following new subchapter:

"SUBCHAPTER V—REMOVAL, REINSTATEMENT, AND GUARANTEED PLACEMENT IN THE SENIOR EXECUTIVE SERVICE

"§ 3591. Definitions   5 USC 3591.

"For the purpose of this subchapter, 'agency', 'Senior Executive Service position', 'senior executive', 'career appointee', 'limited term appointee', 'limited emergency appointee', 'noncareer appointee', and 'general position' have the meanings set forth in section 3132(a) of this title.   Ante, p. 1155.

"§ 3592. Removal from the Senior Executive Service   5 USC 3592.

"(a) Except as provided in subsection (b) of this section, a career appointee may be removed from the Senior Executive Service to a civil service position outside of the Senior Executive Service—

"(1) during the 1-year period of probation under section 3393 (d) of this title, or   Ante, p. 1161.

"(2) at any time for less than fully successful executive performance as determined under subchapter II of chapter 43 of this title,   Post, p. 1167.

except that in the case of a removal under paragraph (2) of this subsection the career appointee shall, at least 15 days before the removal, be entitled, upon request, to an informal hearing before an official designated by the Merit Systems Protection Board at which the career appointee may appear and present arguments, but such hearing shall not give the career appointee the right to initiate an action with the Board under section 7701 of this title, nor need the removal action be   Ante, p. 1138.
delayed as a result of the granting of such hearing.

"(b)(1) Except as provided in paragraph (2) of this subsection, a career appointee in an agency may not be involuntarily removed—

"(A) within 120 days after an appointment of the head of the agency; or

"(B) within 120 days after the appointment in the agency of the career appointee's most immediate supervisor who—

"(i) is a noncareer appointee; and

"(ii) has the authority to remove the career appointee.

"(2) Paragraph (1) of this subsection does not apply with respect to—

Post, p. 1169.

"(A) any removal under section 4314(b)(3) of this title; or

"(B) any disciplinary action initiated before an appointment referred to in paragraph (1) of this subsection.

"(c) A limited emergency appointee, limited term appointee, or noncareer appointee may be removed from the service at any time.

"§ 3593. Reinstatement in the Senior Executive Service

"(a) A former career appointee may be reinstated, without regard to section 3393 (b) and (c) of this title, to any Senior Executive Service position for which the appointee is qualified if—

Ante, p. 1162.

"(1) the appointee has successfully completed the probationary period established under section 3393(d) of this title; and

"(2) the appointee left the Senior Executive Service for reasons other than misconduct, neglect of duty, malfeasance, or less than fully successful executive performance as determined under subchapter II of chapter 43 of this title.

Post, p. 1167.

Ante, p. 1154.

"(b) A career appointee who is appointed by the President to any civil service position outside the Senior Executive Service and who leaves the position for reasons other than misconduct, neglect of duty, or malfeasance shall be entitled to be placed in the Senior Executive Service if the appointee applies to the Office of Personnel Management within 90 days after separation from the Presidential appointment.

5 USC 3594.

"§ 3594. Guaranteed placement in other personnel systems

"(a) A career appointee who was appointed from a civil service position held under a career or career-conditional appointment (or an appointment of equivalent tenure, as determined by the Office of Personnel Management) and who, for reasons other than misconduct, neglect of duty, or malfeasance, is removed from the Senior Executive Service during the probationary period under section 3393(d) of this

Ante, p. 1162.

title, shall be entitled to be placed in a civil service position (other than a Senior Executive Service position) in any agency.

"(b) A career appointee—

"(1) who has completed the probationary period under section 3393(d) of this title; and

"(2) who is removed from the Senior Executive Service for less than fully successful executive performance as determined under subchapter II of chapter 43 of this title;

shall be entitled to be placed in a civil service position (other than a Senior Executive Service position) in any agency.

"(c)(1) For purposes of subsections (a) and (b) of this section—

"(A) the position in which any career appointee is placed under such subsections shall be a continuing position at GS-15 or above

5 USC 5332 note.

of the General Schedule, or an equivalent position, and, in the case of a career appointee referred to in subsection (a) of this section, the career appointee shall be entitled to an appointment of a tenure equivalent to the tenure of the appointment held in the position from which the career appointee was appointed;

"(B) any career appointee placed under subsection (a) or (b) of this section shall be entitled to receive basic pay at the highest of—

"(i) the rate of basic pay in effect for the position in which placed;

"(ii) the rate of basic pay in effect at the time of the placement for the position the career appointee held in the civil service immediately before being appointed to the Senior Executive Service; or

"(iii) the rate of basic pay in effect for the career appointee immediately before being placed under subsection (a) or (b) of this section; and

"(C) the placement of any career appointee under subsection (a) or (b) of this section may not be made to a position which would cause the separation or reduction in grade of any other employee.

"(2) An employee who is receiving basic pay under paragraph (1) (B) (ii) or (iii) of this subsection is entitled to have the basic pay rate of the employee increased by 50 percent of the amount of each increase in the maximum rate of basic pay for the grade of the position in which the employee is placed under subsection (a) or (b) of this section until the rate is equal to the rate in effect under paragraph (1)(B)(i) of this subsection for the position in which the employee is placed.

"§ 3595. Regulations

5 USC 3595.

"The Office of Personnel Management shall prescribe regulations to carry out the purpose of this subchapter.".

(c) The chapter analysis for chapter 35 of title 5, United States Code, is amended by inserting the following new item:

"SUBCHAPTER V—REMOVAL, REINSTATEMENT, AND GUARANTEED PLACEMENT IN THE SENIOR EXECUTIVE SERVICE

"Sec.
"3591. Definitions.
"3592. Removal from the Senior Executive Service.
"3593. Reinstatement in the Senior Executive Service.
"3594. Guaranteed placement in other personnel systems.
"3595. Regulations.".

PERFORMANCE RATING

SEC. 405. (a) Chapter 43 of title 5, United States Code, is amended by adding at the end thereof the following:

"SUBCHAPTER II—PERFORMANCE APPRAISAL IN THE SENIOR EXECUTIVE SERVICE

"§ 4311. Definitions

5 USC 4311.

"For the purpose of this subchapter, 'agency', 'senior executive', and 'career appointee' have the meanings set forth in section 3132(a) of this title.

"§ 4312. Senior Executive Service performance appraisal systems

5 USC 4312.

"(a) Each agency shall, in accordance with standards established by the Office of Personnel Management, develop one or more performance appraisal systems designed to—

"(1) permit the accurate evaluation of performance in any position on the basis of criteria which are related to the position and which specify the critical elements of the position;

"(2) provide for systematic appraisals of performance of senior executives;

"(3) encourage excellence in performance by senior executives; and

"(4) provide a basis for making eligibility determinations for retention in the Senior Executive Service and for Senior Executive Service performance awards.

"(b) Each performance appraisal system established by an agency under subsection (a) of this section shall provide—

"(1) that, on or before the beginning of each rating period, performance requirements for each senior executive in the agency are established in consultation with the senior executive and communicated to the senior executive;

"(2) that written appraisals of performance are based on the individual and organizational performance requirements established for the rating period involved; and

"(3) that each senior executive in the agency is provided a copy of the appraisal and rating under section 4314 of this title and is given an opportunity to respond in writing and have the rating reviewed by an employee in a higher executive level in the agency before the rating becomes final.

"(c)(1) The Office shall review each agency's performance appraisal system under this section, and determine whether the agency performance appraisal system meets the requirements of this subchapter.

"(2) The Comptroller General shall from time to time review performance appraisal systems under this section to determine the extent to which any such system meets the requirements under this subchapter and shall periodically report its findings to the Office and to each House of the Congress.

Report to OPM and Congress.

"(3) If the Office determines that an agency performance appraisal system does not meet the requirements under this subchapter (including regulations prescribed under section 4315), the agency shall take such corrective action as may be required by the Office.

"(d) A senior executive may not appeal any appraisal and rating under any performance appraisal system under this section.

5 USC 4313.

"§ 4313. Criteria for performance appraisals

"Appraisals of performance in the Senior Executive Service shall be based on both individual and organizational performance, taking into account such factors as—

"(1) improvements in efficiency, productivity, and quality of work or service, including any significant reduction in paperwork;

"(2) cost efficiency;

"(3) timeliness of performance;

"(4) other indications of the effectiveness, productivity, and performance quality of the employees for whom the senior executive is responsible; and

"(5) meeting affirmative action goals and achievement of equal employment opportunity requirements.

"§ 4314. Ratings for performance appraisals

5 USC 4314.

"(a) Each performance appraisal system shall provide for annual summary ratings of levels of performance as follows:

"(1) one or more fully successful levels,

"(2) a minimally satisfactory level, and

"(3) an unsatisfactory level.

"(b) Each performance appraisal system shall provide that—

"(1) any appraisal and any rating under such system—

"(A) are made only after review and evaluation by a performance review board established under subsection (c) of this section;

"(B) are conducted at least annually, subject to the limitation of subsection (c)(3) of this section;

"(C) in the case of a career appointee, may not be made within 120 days after the beginning of a new Presidential administration; and

"(D) are based on performance during a performance appraisal period the duration of which shall be determined under guidelines established by the Office of Personnel Management, but which may be terminated in any case in which the agency making an appraisal determines that an adequate basis exists on which to appraise and rate the senior executive's performance;

"(2) any career appointee receiving a rating at any of the fully successful levels under subsection (a)(1) of this section may be given a performance award under section 5384 of this title:

Post, p. 1172.

"(3) any senior executive receiving an unsatisfactory rating under subsection (a)(3) of this section shall be reassigned or transferred within the Senior Executive Service, or removed from the Senior Executive Service, but any senior executive who receives 2 unsatisfactory ratings in any period of 5 consecutive years shall be removed from the Senior Executive Service; and

"(4) any senior executive who twice in any period of 3 consecutive years receives less than fully successful ratings shall be removed from the Senior Executive Service.

"(c)(1) Each agency shall establish, in accordance with regulations prescribed by the Office, one or more performance review boards, as appropriate. It is the function of the boards to make recommendations to the appropriate appointing authority of the agency relating to the performance of senior executives in the agency.

Performance review boards. Establishment.

"(2) The supervising official of the senior executive shall provide to the performance review board, an initial appraisal of the senior executive's performance. Before making any recommendation with respect to the senior executive, the board shall review any response by the senior executive to the initial appraisal and conduct such further review as the board finds necessary.

"(3) Performance appraisals under this subchapter with respect to any senior executive shall be made by the appointing authority only after considering the recommendations by the performance review board with respect to such senior executive under paragraph (1) of this subsection.

"(4) Members of performance review boards shall be appointed in such a manner as to assure consistency, stability, and objectivity in performance appraisal. Notice of the appointment of an individual to serve as a member shall be published in the Federal Register.

Membership.

Publication in Federal Register.

"(5) In the case of an appraisal of a career appointee, more than one-half of the members of the performance review board shall consist of career appointees. The requirement of the preceding sentence shall not apply in any case in which the Office determines that there exists an insufficient number of career appointees available to comply with the requirement.

Report to
Congress.
Ante, p. 1159.

"(d) The Office shall include in each report submitted to each House of the Congress under section 3135 of this title a report of—

"(1) the performance of any performance review board established under this section,

Ante, p. 1165.

"(2) the number of individuals removed from the Senior Executive Service under subchapter V of chapter 35 of this title for less than fully successful executive performance, and

Post, p. 1172.

"(3) the number of performance awards under section 5384 of this title.

5 USC 4315.

"§ 4315. Regulations

"The Office of Personnel Management shall prescribe regulations to carry out the purpose of this subchapter.".

(b) The analysis for chapter 43 of title 5, United States Code, is amended by inserting at the end thereof the following:

"SUBCHAPTER II—PERFORMANCE APPRAISAL IN THE
SENIOR EXECUTIVE SERVICE
"Sec.
"4311. Definitions.
"4312. Senior Executive Service performance appraisal systems.
"4313. Criteria for performance appraisals.
"4314. Ratings for performance appraisals.
"4315. Regulations.".

AWARDING OF RANKS

SEC. 406. (a) Chapter 45 of title 5, United States Code, is amended by adding at the end thereof the following new section:

5 USC 4507.
Definitions.

"§ 4507. Awarding of ranks in the Senior Executive Service

"(a) For the purpose of this section, 'agency', 'senior executive', and 'career appointee' have the meanings set forth in section 3132(a) of this title.

Recommenda-
tions.

"(b) Each agency shall submit annually to the Office recommendations of career appointees in the agency to be awarded the rank of Meritorious Executive or Distinguished Executive. The recommendations may take into account the individual's performance over a period of years. The Office shall review such recommendations and provide to the President recommendations as to which of the agency recommended appointees should receive such rank.

"(c) During any fiscal year, the President may, subject to subsection (d) of this section, award to any career appointee recommended by the Office the rank of—

"(1) Meritorious Executive, for sustained accomplishment, or

"(2) Distinguished Executive, for sustained extraordinary accomplishment.

A career appointee awarded a rank under paragraph (1) or (2) of this subsection shall not be entitled to be awarded that rank during the following 4 fiscal years.

"(d) During any fiscal year—

"(1) the number of career appointees awarded the rank of Meritorious Executive may not exceed 5 percent of the Senior Executive Service; and

"(2) the number of career appointees awarded the rank of

Distinguished Executive may not exceed 1 percent of the Senior Executive Service.

"(e)(1) Receipt by a career appointee of the rank of Meritorious Executive entitles such individual to a lump-sum payment of $10,000, which shall be in addition to the basic pay paid under section 5382 of this title or any award paid under section 5384 of this title.

"(2) Receipt by a career appointee of the rank of Distinguished Executive entitles the individual to a lump-sum payment of $20,000, which shall be in addition to the basic pay paid under section 5382 of this title or any award paid under section 5384 of this title.".

(b) The analysis for chapter 45 of title 5, United States Code, is amended by adding at the end thereof the following new item:

"4507. Awarding of Ranks in the Senior Executive Service.".

PAY RATES AND SYSTEMS

SEC. 407. (a) Chapter 53 of title 5, United States Code, is amended by adding at the end thereof the following new subchapter:

"SUBCHAPTER VIII—PAY FOR THE SENIOR EXECUTIVE SERVICE

"§ 5381. Definitions

5 USC 5381.

"For the purpose of this subchapter, 'agency', 'Senior Executive Service position', and 'senior executive' have the meanings set forth in section 3132(a) of this title.

Ante, p. 1155.

"§ 5382. Establishment and adjustment of rates of pay for the Senior Executive Service

5 USC 5382.

"(a) There shall be 5 or more rates of basic pay for the Senior Executive Service, and each senior executive shall be paid at one of the rates. The rates of basic pay shall be initially established and thereafter adjusted by the President subject to subsection (b) of this section.

"(b) In setting rates of basic pay, the lowest rate for the Senior Executive Service shall not be less than the minimum rate of basic pay payable for GS-16 of the General Schedule and the highest rate shall not exceed the rate for level IV of the Executive Schedule. The payment of the rates shall not be subject to the pay limitation of section 5308 or 5373 of this title.

5 USC 5315.

5 USC 5308, 5373.

"(c) Subject to subsection (b) of this section, effective at the beginning of the first applicable pay period commencing on or after the first day of the month in which an adjustment takes effect under section 5305 of this title in the rates of pay under the General Schedule, each rate of basic pay for the Senior Executive Service shall be adjusted by an amount determined by the President to be appropriate. The adjusted rates of basic pay for the Senior Executive Service shall be included in the report transmitted to the Congress by the President under section 5305 (a)(3) or (c)(1) of this title.

5 USC 5305.

"(d) The rates of basic pay that are established and adjusted under this section shall be printed in the Federal Register and shall supersede any prior rates of basic pay for the Senior Executive Service.

Publication in Federal Register.
5 USC 5383.

"§ 5383. Setting individual senior executive pay

"(a) Each appointing authority shall determine, in accordance with criteria established by the Office of Personnel Management, which of the rates established under section 5382 of this title shall be paid to each senior executive under such appointing authority.

Ante, p. 1170.

"(b) In no event may the aggregate amount paid to a senior executive during any fiscal year under sections 4507, 5382, and 5384 of this title exceed the annual rate payable for positions at level I of the Executive Schedule in effect at the end of such fiscal year.

5 USC 5312.

"(c) Except for any pay adjustment under section 5382 of this title, the rate of basic pay for any senior executive may not be adjusted more than once during any 12-month period.

"(d) The rate of basic pay for any career appointee may be reduced from any rate of basic pay to any lower rate of basic pay only if the career appointee receives a written notice of the reduction at least 15 days in advance of the reduction.

5 USC 5384.

"§ 5384. Performance awards in the Senior Executive Service

"(a)(1) To encourage excellence in performance by career appointees, performance awards shall be paid to career appointees in accordance with the provisions of this section.

"(2) Such awards shall be paid in a lump sum and shall be in addition to the basic pay paid under section 5382 of this title or any award paid under section 4507 of this title.

Ante, p. 1170.

"(b)(1) No performance award under this section shall be paid to any career appointee whose performance was determined to be less than fully successful at the time of the appointee's most recent performance appraisal and rating under subchapter II of chapter 43 of this title.

Ante, p. 1167.

"(2) The amount of a performance award under this section shall be determined by the agency head but may not exceed 20 percent of the career appointee's rate of basic pay.

"(3) The number of career appointees in any agency paid performance awards under this section during any fiscal year may not exceed 50 percent of the number of Senior Executive Service positions in such agency. This paragraph shall not apply in the case of any agency which has less than 4 Senior Executive Service positions.

"(c) Performance awards paid by any agency under this section shall be based on recommendations by performance review boards established by such agency under section 4314 of this title.

Ante, p. 1169.

"(d) The Office of Personnel Management may issue guidance to agencies concerning the proportion of Senior Executive Service salary expenses that may be appropriately applied to payment of performance awards and the distribution of awards.

5 USC 5385.

"§ 5385. Regulations

"The Office of Personnel Management shall prescribe regulations to carry out the purpose of this subchapter.".

5 USC 5301.

(b) The analysis of chapter 53 of title 5, United States Code, is amended by adding at the end thereof the following new items:

"SUBCHAPTER VIII—PAY FOR THE SENIOR EXECUTIVE SERVICE

"Sec.
"5381. Definitions.
"5382. Establishment and adjustment of rates of pay for the Senior Executive Service.
"5383. Setting individual senior executive pay.
"5384. Performance awards in the Senior Executive Service.
"5385. Regulations.".

PAY ADMINISTRATION

SEC. 408. (a) Chapter 55 of the title 5, United States Code, is amended—
    (1) by inserting "other than an employee or individual excluded by section 5541(2)(xvi) of this section" immediately before the period at the end of section 5504(a)(B);   5 USC 5541.
5 USC 5504.
    (2) by amending section 5541(2) by striking out "or" after clause (xiv), by striking out the period after clause (xv) and inserting "; or" in lieu thereof, and by adding the following clause at the end thereof:
    "(xvi) member of the Senior Executive Service.";
  and
    (3) by inserting "other than a member of the Senior Executive Service" after "employee" in section 5595(a)(2)(i).   5 USC 5595.
  (b)(1) Section 5311 of title 5, United States Code, is amended by   5 USC 5311.
inserting ", other than Senior Executive Service positions," after "positions".
  (2) Section 5331(b) of title 5, United States Code, is amended by   5 USC 5331.
inserting ", other than Senior Executive Service positions," after "positions".

TRAVEL, TRANSPORTATION, AND SUBSISTENCE

SEC. 409. (a) Section 5723(a)(1) of title 5, United States Code, is   5 USC 5723.
amended by striking out "; and" and inserting in lieu thereof "or of a new appointee to the Senior Executive Service; and".
  (b) Subchapter IV of chapter 57 of title 5, United States Code, is amended by adding at the end thereof the following new section:

"§ 5752. Travel expenses of Senior Executive Service candidates   5 USC 5752.

  "Employing agencies may pay candidates for Senior Executive Service positions travel expenses incurred incident to preemployment interviews requested by the employing agency.".
  (c) The analysis for chapter 57 of title 5, United States Code, is amended by inserting after the item relating to section 5751 the following new item:

"5752. Travel expenses of Senior Executive Service candidates.".

LEAVE

SEC. 410. Section 6304 of title 5, United States Code, is amended—   5 USC 6304.
    (1) in subsection (a), by striking out "and (e)" and inserting in lieu thereof "(e), and (f)"; and
    (2) by adding at the end thereof the following new subsection:
  "(f) Annual leave accrued by an individual while serving in a position in the Senior Executive Service shall not be subject to the limitation on accumulation otherwise imposed by this section.".

DISCIPLINARY ACTIONS

SEC. 411. Chapter 75 of title 5, United States Code, is amended—
    (1) by inserting the following in the chapter analysis after subchapter IV:

"SUBCHAPTER V—SENIOR EXECUTIVE SERVICE

"Sec.
"7541. Definitions.
"7542. Actions covered.
"7543. Cause and procedure.";

and

(2) by adding the following after subchapter IV:

"SUBCHAPTER V—SENIOR EXECUTIVE SERVICE

5 USC 7541.

"§ 7541. Definitions

"For the purpose of this subchapter—

"(1) 'employee' means a career appointee in the Senior Executive Service who—

Ante, p. 1161.

"(A) has completed the probationary period prescribed under section 3393(d) of this title; or

"(B) was covered by the provisions of subchapter II of this chapter immediately before appointment to the Senior Executive Service; and

Ante, p. 1134.

"(2) 'suspension' has the meaning set forth in section 7501(2) of this title.

5 USC 7542.

"§ 7542. Actions covered

"This subchapter applies to a removal from the civil service or suspension for more than 14 days, but does not apply to an action initiated under section 1206 of this title, to a suspension or removal under section 7532 of this title, or to a removal under section 3592 of this title.

Ante, p. 1125.

5 USC 7543.

"§ 7543. Cause and procedure

"(a) Under regulations prescribed by the Office of Personnel Management, an agency may take an action covered by this subchapter against an employee only for such cause as will promote the efficiency of the service.

"(b) An employee against whom an action covered by this subchapter is proposed is entitled to—

"(1) at least 30 days' advance written notice, unless there is reasonable cause to believe that the employee has committed a crime for which a sentence of imprisonment can be imposed, stating specific reasons for the proposed action;

"(2) a reasonable time, but not less than 7 days, to answer orally and in writing and to furnish affidavits and other documentary evidence in support of the answer;

"(3) be represented by an attorney or other representative; and

"(4) a written decision and specific reasons therefor at the earliest practicable date.

Hearing.

"(c) An agency may provide, by regulation, for a hearing which may be in lieu of or in addition to the opportunity to answer provided under subsection (b)(2) of this section.

Appeals.

"(d) An employee against whom an action is taken under this section is entitled to appeal to the Merit Systems Protection Board under section 7701 of this title.

Ante, p. 1128.
Record maintenance.

"(e) Copies of the notice of proposed action, the answer of the employee when written, and a summary thereof when made orally, the notice of decision and reasons therefor, and any order effecting an action covered by this subchapter, together with any supporting material, shall be maintained by the agency and shall be furnished to the Merit Systems Protection Board upon its request and to the employee affected upon the employee's request.".

RETIREMENT

SEC. 412. (a) Section 8336 of title 5, United States Code, is amended by redesignating subsection (h) as subsection (i) and inserting immediately after subsection (g) the following new subsection:

"(h) A member of the Senior Executive Service who is removed from the Senior Executive Service for less than fully successful executive performance (as determined under subchapter II of chapter 43 of this title) after completing 25 years of service or after becoming 50 years of age and completing 20 years of service is entitled to an annuity.". *Ante*, p. 1167.

(b) Section 8339(h) of title 5, United States Code, is amended by striking out "section 8336(d)" and inserting in lieu thereof "section 8336 (d) or (h)".

CONVERSION TO THE SENIOR EXECUTIVE SERVICE

SEC. 413. (a) For the purpose of this section, "agency", "Senior Executive Service position", "career appointee", "career reserved position", "limited term appointee", "noncareer appointee", and "general position" have the meanings set forth in section 3132(a) of title 5, United States Code (as added by this title), and "Senior Executive Service" has the meaning set forth in section 2101a of such title 5 (as added by this title). 5 USC 3133 note.
Ante, p. 1151.
Ante, p. 1154.

(b)(1) Under the guidance of the Office of Personnel Management, each agency shall—

(A) designate those positions which it considers should be Senior Executive Service positions and designate which of those positions it considers should be career reserved positions; and

(B) submit to the Office a written request for—

(i) a specific number of Senior Executive Service positions; and

(ii) authority to employ a specific number of noncareer appointees.

(2) The Office of Personnel Management shall review the designations and requests of each agency under paragraph (1) of this subsection, and shall establish interim authorizations in accordance with sections 3133 and 3134 of title 5, United States Code (as added by this Act), and shall publish the titles of the authorized positions in the Federal Register. Publication in Federal Register.
Ante, pp. 1158, 1159.

(c)(1) Each employee serving in a position at the time it is designated as a Senior Executive Service position under subsection (b) of this section shall elect to—

(A) decline conversion and be appointed to a position under such employee's current type of appointment and pay system, retaining the grade, seniority, and other rights and benefits associated with such type of appointment and pay system; or

(B) accept conversion and be appointed to a Senior Executive Service position in accordance with the provisions of subsections (d), (e), (f), (g), and (h) of this section.

The appointment of an employee in an agency because of an election under subparagraph (A) of this paragraph shall not result in the separation or reduction in grade of any other employee in such agency.

Notice.

(2) Any employee in a position which has been designated a Senior Executive Service position under this section shall be notified in writing of such designation, the election required under paragraph (1) of this subsection, and the provisions of subsections (d), (e), (f), (g), and (h) of this section. The employee shall be given 90 days from the date of such notification to make the election under paragraph (1) of this subsection.

(d) Each employee who has elected to accept conversion to a Senior Executive Service position under subsection (c)(1)(B) of this section and who is serving under—

 (1) a career or career-conditional appointment; or

 (2) a similar type of appointment in an excepted service position, as determined by the Office;

in a position which is designated as a Senior Executive Service position shall be appointed as a career appointee to such Senior Executive Service position without regard to section 3393(b)–(e) of title 5, United States Code (as added by this title).

Ante, p. 1161.

(e) Each employee who has elected conversion to a Senior Executive Service position under subsection (c)(1)(B) of this section and who is serving under an excepted appointment in a position which is not designated a career reserved position in the Senior Executive Service, but is—

 (1) a position in Schedule C of subpart C of part 213 of title 5, Code of Federal Regulations;

 (2) a position filled by noncareer executive assignment under subpart F of part 305 of title 5, Code of Federal Regulations; or

 (3) a position in the Executive Schedule under subchapter II of chapter 53 of title 5, United States Code, other than a career Executive Schedule position;

5 USC 5311.

shall be appointed as a noncareer appointee to a Senior Executive Service position.

(f) Each employee who has elected conversion to a Senior Executive Service position under subsection (c)(1)(B) of this section, who is serving in a position described in paragraph (1), (2), or (3) of subsection (e) of this section, and whose position is designated as a career reserved position under subsection (b) of this section shall be appointed as a noncareer appointee to an appropriate general position in the Senior Executive Service or shall be separated.

(g) Each employee who has elected conversion to a Senior Executive Service position under subsection (c)(1)(B) of this section, who is serving in a position described in paragraph (1), (2), or (3) of subsection (e) of this section, and whose position is designated as a Senior Executive Service position and who has reinstatement eligibility to a position in the competitive service, may, on request to the Office, be appointed as a career appointee to a Senior Executive Service position.

Publication in
Federal Register.

The name of, and basis for reinstatement eligibility for, each employee appointed as a career appointee under this subsection shall be published in the Federal Register.

(h) Each employee who has elected conversion to a Senior Executive Service position under subsection (c)(1)(B) of this section and who is serving under a limited executive assignment under subpart F of part 305 of title 5, Code of Federal Regulations, shall—

 (1) be appointed as a limited term appointee to a Senior Execu-

tive Service position if the position then held by such employee
will terminate within 3 years of the date of such appointment;

(2) be appointed as a noncareer appointee to a Senior Executive Service position if the position then held by such employee is
designated as a general position; or

(3) be appointed as a noncareer appointee to a general position
if the position then held by such employee is designated as a career
reserved position.

(i) The rate of basic pay for any employee appointed to a Senior
Executive Service position under this section shall be greater than or
equal to the rate of basic pay payable for the position held by such
employee at the time of such appointment.

(j) Any employee who is aggrieved by any action by any agency
under this section is entitled to appeal to the Merit Systems Protection
Board under section 7701 of title 5, United States Code (as added by   *Ante,* p. 1128.
this title). An agency shall take any corrective action which the Board
orders in its decision on an appeal under this subsection.

(k) The Office shall prescribe regulations to carry out the purpose of   Regulations.
this section.

LIMITATIONS ON EXECUTIVE POSITIONS

SEC. 414. (a)(1)(A) The following provisions of section 5108 of
title 5, United States Code, relating to special authority to place positions at GS-16, 17, and 18 of the General Schedule, are hereby repealed:

(i) paragraphs (2), (4) through (11), and (13) through (16)
of subsection (c), and

(ii) subsections (d) through (g).

(B) Notwithstanding any other provision of law (other than section   5 USC 5108 note.
5108 of such title 5), the authority granted to an agency (as defined in
section 5102(a)(1) of such title 5) under any such provision to place
one or more positions in GS-16, 17, or 18 of the General Schedule, is
hereby terminated.

(C) Subsection (a) of section 5108 of title 5, United States Code, is
amended to read as follows:

"(a) The Director of the Office of Personnel Management may establish, and from time to time revise, the maximum numbers of positions
(not to exceed an aggregate of 10,777) which may at any one time be
placed in—

"(i) GS-16, 17, and 18; and

"(ii) the Senior Executive Service, in accordance with section
3133 of this title.   *Ante,* p. 1158.
A position may be placed in GS-16, 17, or 18, only by action of the
Director of the Office of Personnel Management. The authority of the
Director under this subsection shall be carried out by the President in
the case of positions proposed to be placed in GS-16, 17, and 18 in the
Federal Bureau of Investigation.".

(D) Subsection (c) of section 5108 of title 5, United States Code, is
amended—

(i) by redesignating paragraph (3) as paragraph (2) and by
inserting "and" at the end thereof; and

(ii) by redesignating paragraph (12) as paragraph (3) and by
striking out the semicolon at the end and inserting in lieu thereof
a period.

(2)(A) Notwithstanding any other provision of law (other than   5 USC 3104 note.
section 3104 of title 5, United States Code), the authority granted to

an agency (as defined in section 5102(a)(1) of such title 5) to establish scientific or professional positions outside of the General Schedule is hereby terminated.

(B) Section 3104 of title 5, United States Code, is amended by striking out subsections (a) and (b) and inserting in lieu thereof the following:

"(a)(1) The Director of the Office of Personnel Management may establish, and from time to time revise, the maximum number of scientific or professional positions (not to exceed 517) for carrying out research and development functions which require the services of specially qualified personnel which may be established outside of the General Schedule. Any such position may be established only by action of the Director.

"(2) The provisions of paragraph (1) of this subsection shall not apply to any Senior Executive Service position (as defined in section 3132(a) of this title).

Ante, p. 1155.

"(3) In addition to the number of positions authorized by paragraph (1) of this subsection, the Librarian of Congress may establish, without regard to the second sentence of paragraph (1) of this subsection, not more than 8 scientific or professional positions to carry out the research and development functions of the Library of Congress which require the services of specially qualified personnel.".

(C) Subsection (c) of such section 3104 is amended—
(i) by striking out "(c)" and inserting in lieu thereof "(b)"; and
(ii) by striking out "to establish and fix the pay of positions under this section and section 5361 of this title" and inserting in lieu thereof "to fix under section 5361 of this title the pay for positions established under this section".

5 USC 3104, 5108 notes.

(3)(A) The provisions of paragraphs (1) and (2) of this subsection shall not apply with respect to any position so long as the individual occupying such position on the day before the date of the enactment of this Act continues to occupy such position.

(B) The Director—
(i) in establishing under section 5108 of title 5, United States Code, the maximum number of positions which may be placed in GS-16, 17, and 18 of the General Schedule, and
(ii) in establishing under section 3104 of such title 5 the maximum number of scientific or professional positions which may be established,
shall take into account positions to which subparagraph (A) of this paragraph applies.

(b)(1) Section 5311 of title 5, United States Code, is amended by inserting "(a)" before "The Executive Schedule," and by adding at the end thereof the following new subsection:

Publication in the Federal Register.

"(b)(1) Not later than 180 days after the date of the enactment of the Civil Service Reform Act of 1978, the Director shall determine the number and classification of executive level positions in existence in the executive branch on that date of enactment, and shall publish the determination in the Federal Register. Effective beginning on the date of the publication, the number of executive level positions within the executive branch may not exceed the number published under this subsection.

"Executive level position."

"(2) For the purpose of this subsection, 'executive level position' means—

"(A) any office or position in the civil service the rate of pay for which is equal to or greater than the rate of basic pay payable for positions under section 5316 of this title, or

"(B) any such office or position the rate of pay for which may be fixed by administrative action at a rate equal to or greater than the rate of basic pay payable for positions under section 5316 of this title;

but does not include any Senior Executive Service position, as defined in section 3132(a) of this title.".

5 USC 5316.

(2) The President shall transmit to the Congress by January 1, 1980, a plan for authorizing executive level positions in the executive branch which shall include the maximum number of executive level positions necessary by level and a justification for the positions.

5 USC 3132.
Presidential transmittal to Congress.
5 USC 5311 note.

EFFECTIVE DATE; CONGRESSIONAL REVIEW

SEC. 415. (a)(1) The provisions of this title, other than sections 413 and 414(a), shall take effect 9 months after the date of the enactment of this Act.

5 USC 3131 note.

(2) The provisions of section 413 of this title shall take effect on the date of the enactment of this Act.

(3) The provisions of section 414(a) of this title shall take effect 180 days after the date of the enactment of this Act.

(b)(1) The amendments made by sections 401 through 412 of this title shall continue to have effect unless, during the first period of 60 calendar days of continuous session of the Congress beginning after 5 years after the effective date of such amendments, a concurrent resolution is introduced and adopted by the Congress disapproving the continuation of the Senior Executive Service. Such amendments shall cease to have effect on the first day of the first fiscal year beginning after the date of the adoption of such concurrent resolution.

(2) The continuity of a session is broken only by an adjournment of the Congress sine die, and the days on which either House is not in session because of an adjournment of more than 3 days to a day certain are excluded in the computation of the 60-day period.

(3) The provisions of subsections (d), (e), (f), (g), (h), (i), (j), and (k) of section 5305 of title 5, United States Code, shall apply with respect to any concurrent resolution referred to in paragraph (1) of this subsection, except that for the purpose of this paragraph the reference in such subsection (e) to 10 calendar days shall be considered a reference to 30 calendar days.

(4) During the 5-year period referred to in paragraph (1) of this subsection, the Director of the Office of Personnel Management shall include in each report required under section 3135 of title 5, United States Code (as added by this title) an evaluation of the effectiveness of the Senior Executive Service and the manner in which such Service is administered.

TITLE V—MERIT PAY

PAY FOR PERFORMANCE

SEC. 501. Part III of title 5, United States Code, is amended by inserting after chapter 53 the following new chapter:

"CHAPTER 54—MERIT PAY AND CASH AWARDS

"§ 5401. Purpose

"(a) It is the purpose of this chapter to provide for—

"(1) a merit pay system which shall—

"(A) within available funds, recognize and reward quality performance by varying merit pay adjustments;

"(B) use performance appraisals as the basis for determining merit pay adjustments;

"(C) within available funds, provide for training to improve objectivity and fairness in the evaluation of performance; and

"(D) regulate the costs of merit pay by establishing appropriate control techniques; and

"(2) a cash award program which shall provide cash awards for superior accomplishment and special service.

"(b)(1) Except as provided in paragraph (2) of this subsection, this chapter shall apply to any supervisor or management official (as defined in paragraphs (10) and (11) of section 7103 of this title, respectively) who is in a position which is in GS-13, 14, or 15 of the General Schedule described in section 5104 of this title.

5 USC 7103.

Exclusions.

"(2)(A) Upon application under subparagraph (C) of this paragraph, the President may, in writing, exclude an agency or any unit of an agency from the application of this chapter if the President considers such exclusion to be required as a result of conditions arising from—

"(i) the recent establishment of the agency or unit, or the implementation of a new program,

"(ii) an emergency situation, or

"(iii) any other situation or circumstance.

Presidential reports transmitted to Congress.

"(B) Any exclusion under this paragraph shall not take effect earlier than 30 calendar days after the President transmits to each House of the Congress a report describing the agency or unit to be excluded and the reasons therefor.

Filing of applications.

"(C) An application for exclusion under this paragraph of an agency or any unit of an agency shall be filed by the head of the agency with the Office of Personnel Management, and shall set forth reasons why the agency or unit should be excluded from this chapter. The Office shall review the application and reasons, undertake such other review as it considers appropriate to determine whether the agency or unit should be excluded from the coverage of this chapter, and upon completion of its review, recommend to the President whether the agency or unit should be so excluded.

"(D) Any agency or unit which is excluded pursuant to this paragraph shall, insofar as practicable, make a sustained effort to eliminate the conditions on which the exclusion is based.

Review.

"(E) The Office shall periodically review any exclusion from coverage and may at any time recommend to the President that an exclusion under this paragraph be revoked. The President may at any time revoke, in writing, any exclusion under this paragraph.

"§ 5402. Merit pay system

Establishment.

"(a) In accordance with the purpose set forth in section 5401(a)(1) of this title, the Office of Personnel Management shall establish a merit pay system which shall provide for a range of basic pay for each grade to which the system applies, which range shall be limited by the minimum and maximum rates of basic pay payable for each grade under chapter 53 of this title.

5 USC 5301.

"(b)(1) Under regulations prescribed by the Office, the head of each agency may provide for increases within the range of basic pay for any employee covered by the merit pay system.

"(2) Determinations to provide pay increases under this subsection—

"(A) may take into account individual performance and organizational accomplishment, and

"(B) shall be based on factors such as—

"(i) any improvement in efficiency, productivity, and quality of work or service, including any significant reduction in paperwork;

"(ii) cost efficiency;

"(iii) timeliness of performance; and

"(iv) other indications of the effectiveness, productivity, and quality of performance of the employees for whom the employee is responsible;

"(C) shall be subject to review only in accordance with and to the extent provided by procedures established by the head of the agency; and

"(D) shall be made in accordance with regulations issued by the Office which relate to the distribution of increases authorized under this subsection.

"(3) For any fiscal year, the head of any agency may exercise authority under paragraph (1) of this subsection only to the extent of the funds available for the purpose of this subsection.

"(4) The funds available for the purpose of this subsection to the head of any agency for any fiscal year shall be determined before the beginning of the fiscal year by the Office on the basis of the amount estimated by the Office to be necessary to reflect—

"(A) within-grade step increases and quality step increases which would have been paid under subchapter III of chapter 53 of this title during the fiscal year to the employees of the agency covered by the merit pay system if the employees were not so covered; and

5 USC 5331.

"(B) adjustments under section 5305 of this title which would have been paid under such subchapter during the fiscal year to such employees if the employees were not so covered, less an amount reflecting the adjustment under subsection (c)(1) of this section in rates of basic pay payable to the employees for the fiscal year.

5 USC 5305.

"(c)(1) Effective at the beginning of the first applicable pay period commencing on or after the first day of the month in which an adjustment takes effect under section 5305 of this title, the rate of basic pay for any position under this chapter shall be adjusted by an amount equal to the greater of—

Effective date.

"(A) one-half of the percentage of the adjustment in the annual rate of pay which corresponds to the percentage generally applicable to positions not covered by the merit pay system in the same grade as the position ; or

"(B) such greater amount of such percentage of such adjustment in the annual rate of pay as may be determined by the Office.

"(2) Any employee whose position is brought under the merit pay system shall, so long as the employee continues to occupy the position, be entitled to receive basic pay at a rate of basic pay not less than the rate the employee was receiving when the position was brought under the merit pay system, plus any subsequent adjustment under paragraph (1) of this subsection.

"(3) No employee to whom this chapter applies may be paid less than the minimum rate of basic pay of the grade of the employee's position.

"(d) Under regulations prescribed by the Office, the benefit of advancement through the range of basic pay for a grade shall be preserved for any employee covered by the merit pay system whose continuous service is interrupted in the public interest by service with the armed forces, or by service in essential non-Government civilian employment during a period of war or national emergency.

5 USC 5941.

"(e) For the purpose of section 5941 of this title, rates of basic pay of employees covered by the merit pay system shall be considered rates of basic pay fixed by statute.

"§ 5403. Cash award program

"(a) The head of any agency may pay a cash award to, and incur necessary expenses for the honorary recognition of, any employee covered by the merit pay system who—

"(1) by the employee's suggestion, invention, superior accomplishment, or other personal effort, contributes to the efficiency, economy, or other improvement of Government operations or achieves a significant reduction in paperwork; or

"(2) performs a special act or service in the public interest in connection with or related to the employee's Federal employment.

Presidential cash awards.

"(b) The President may pay a cash award to, and incur necessary expenses for the honorary recognition of, any employee covered by the merit pay system who—

"(1) by the employee's suggestion, invention, superior accomplishment, or other personal effort, contributes to the efficiency, economy, or other improvement of Government operations or achieves a significant reduction in paperwork; or

"(2) performs an exceptionally meritorious special act or service in the public interest in connection with or related to the employee's Federal employment.

A Presidential cash award may be in addition to an agency cash award under subsection (a) of this section.

"(c) A cash award to any employee under this section is in addition to the basic pay of the employee under section 5402 of this title. Acceptance of a cash award under this section constitutes an agreement that the use by the Government of any idea, method, or device for which the award is made does not form the basis of any claim of any nature against the Government by the employee accepting the award, or the employee's heirs or assigns.

Payment of awards.

"(d) A cash award to, and expenses for the honorary recognition of, any employee covered by the merit pay system may be paid from the fund or appropriation available to the activity primarily benefiting, or the various activities benefiting, from the suggestion, invention, superior accomplishment, or other meritorious effort of the employee. The head of the agency concerned shall determine the amount to be contributed by each activity to any agency cash award under subsection (a) of this section. The President shall determine the amount to be contributed by each activity to a Presidential award under subsection (b) of this section.

"(e)(1) Except as provided in paragraph (2) of this subsection, a cash award under this section may not exceed $10,000.   Limitation.

"(2) If the head of an agency certifies to the Office of Personnel Management that the suggestion, invention, superior accomplishment, or other meritorious effort of an employee for which a cash award is proposed is highly exceptional and unusually outstanding, a cash award in excess of $10,000 but not in excess of $25,000 may be awarded to the employee on the approval of the Office.

"(f) The President or the head of an agency may pay a cash award under this section notwithstanding the death or separation from the service of an employee, if the suggestion, invention, superior accomplishment, or other meritorious effort of the employee for which the award is proposed was made or performed while the employee was covered by the merit pay system.

"§ 5404. Report

"The Office of Personnel Management shall include in each annual report required by section 1308(a) of this title a report on the operation of the merit pay system and the cash award program established under this chapter. The report shall include—   5 USC 1308.

"(1) an analysis of the cost and effectiveness of the merit pay system and the cash award program; and

"(2) a statement of the agencies and units excluded from the coverage of this chapter under section 5401(b)(2) of this title, the reasons for which each exclusion was made, and whether the exclusion continues to be warranted.

"§ 5405. Regulations

"The Office of Personnel Management shall prescribe regulations to carry out the purpose of this chapter.".

INCENTIVE AWARDS AMENDMENTS

SEC. 502. (a) Section 4503(1) of title 5, United States Code, is amended by inserting after "operations" the following: "or achieves a significant reduction in paperwork".

(b) Section 4504(1) of title 5, United States Code, is amended by inserting after "operations" the following: "or achieves a significant reduction in paperwork".

TECHNICAL AND CONFORMING AMENDMENTS

SEC. 503. (a) Section 4501(2)(A) of title 5, United States Code, is amended by striking out "; and" and inserting in lieu thereof ", but does not include an employee covered by the merit pay system established under section 5402 of this title; and".

(b) Section 4502(a) of title 5, United States Code, is amended by striking out "$5,000" and inserting in lieu thereof "$10,000".

(c) Section 4502(b) of title 5, United States Code, is amended—

(1) by striking out "Civil Service Commission" and inserting in lieu thereof "Office of Personnel Management";

(2) by striking out "$5,000" and inserting in lieu thereof "$10,000"; and

(3) by striking out "the Commission" and inserting in lieu thereof "the Office".

(d) Section 4506 of title 5, United States Code, is amended by striking out "Civil Service Commission may" and inserting in lieu thereof "Office of Personnel Management shall".

(e) The second sentence of section 5332(a) of title 5, United States Code, is amended by inserting after "applies" the following: ", except an employee covered by the merit pay system established under section 5402 of this title,".

(f) Section 5334 of title 5, United States Code (as amended in section 801(a)(3)(G) of this Act), is amended—

(1) in paragraph (2) of subsection (c), by inserting ", or for an employee appointed to a position covered by the merit pay system established under section 5402 of this title, any dollar amount," after "step"; and

(2) by adding at the end thereof the following new subsection:

"(f) In the case of an employee covered by the merit pay system established under section 5402 of this title, all references in this section to 'two steps' or 'two step-increases' shall be deemed to mean 6 percent.".

(g) Section 5335(e) of title 5, United States Code, is amended by inserting after "individual" the following: "covered by the merit pay system established under section 5402 of this title, or,".

(h) Section 5336(c) of title 5, United States Code, is amended by inserting after "individual" the following: "covered by the merit pay system established under section 5402 of this title, or,".

(i) The table of chapters for part III of title 5, United States Code, is amended by inserting after the item relating to chapter 53 the following new item:

"54. Merit Pay and Cash Awards_____ **5401".**

EFFECTIVE DATE

5 USC 5401 note.   SEC. 504. (a) The provisions of this title shall take effect on the first day of the first applicable pay period which begins on or after October 1, 1981, except that such provisions may take effect with respect to any category or categories of positions before such day to the extent prescribed by the Director of the Office of Personnel Management.

5 USC 5404 note.   (b) The Director of the Office of Personnel Management shall include in the first report required under section 5404 of title 5, United States Code (as added by this title), information with respect to the progress and cost of the implementation of the merit pay system and the cash award program established under chapter 54 of such title (as added by this title).

TITLE VI—RESEARCH, DEMONSTRATION, AND OTHER PROGRAMS

RESEARCH PROGRAMS AND DEMONSTRATION PROJECTS

SEC. 601. (a) Part III of title 5, United States Code, is amended by adding at the end of subpart C thereof the following new chapter:

"CHAPTER 47—PERSONNEL RESEARCH PROGRAMS AND DEMONSTRATION PROJECTS

"§ 4701. Definitions

"(a) For the purpose of this chapter—

"(1) 'agency' means an Executive agency, the Administrative Office of the United States Courts, and the Government Printing Office, but does not include—

"(A) a Government corporation;

"(B) the Federal Bureau of Investigation, the Central Intelligence Agency, the Defense Intelligence Agency, the National Security Agency, and, as determined by the President, any Executive agency or unit thereof which is designated by the President and which has as its principal function the conduct of foreign intelligence or counterintelligence activities; or

"(C) the General Accounting Office;

"(2) 'employee' means an individual employed in or under an agency;

"(3) 'eligible' means an individual who has qualified for appointment in an agency and whose name has been entered on the appropriate register or list of eligibles;

"(4) 'demonstration project' means a project conducted by the Office of Personnel Management, or under its supervision, to determine whether a specified change in personnel management policies or procedures would result in improved Federal personnel management; and

"(5) 'research program' means a planned study of the manner in which public management policies and systems are operating, the effects of those policies and systems, the possibilities for change, and comparisons among policies and systems.

"(b) This subchapter shall not apply to any position in the Drug Enforcement Administration which is excluded from the competitive service under section 201 of the Crime Control Act of 1976 (5 U.S.C. 5108 note; 90 Stat. 2425).

"§ 4702. Research programs

"The Office of Personnel Management shall—

"(1) establish and maintain (and assist in the establishment and maintenance of) research programs to study improved methods and technologies in Federal personnel management;

"(2) evaluate the research programs established under paragraph (1) of this section;

"(3) establish and maintain a program for the collection and public dissemination of information relating to personnel management research and for encouraging and facilitating the exchange of information among interested persons and entities; and

"(4) carry out the preceding functions directly or through agreement or contract.

"§ 4703. Demonstration projects

"(a) Except as provided in this section, the Office of Personnel Management may, directly or through agreement or contract with one or more agencies and other public and private organizations, conduct and evaluate demonstration projects. Subject to the provisions of this section, the conducting of demonstration projects shall not be limited by any lack of specific authority under this title to take the action contemplated, or by any provision of this title or any rule or regulation prescribed under this title which is inconsistent with the action, including any law or regulation relating to—

"(1) the methods of establishing qualification requirements for, recruitment for, and appointment to positions;

"(2) the methods of classifying positions and compensating employees;

"(3) the methods of assigning, reassigning, or promoting employees;

"(4) the methods of disciplining employees;

"(5) the methods of providing incentives to employees, including the provision of group or individual incentive bonuses or pay;

"(6) the hours of work per day or per week;

"(7) the methods of involving employees, labor organizations, and employee organizations in personnel decisions; and

"(8) the methods of reducing overall agency staff and grade levels.

"(b) Before conducting or entering into any agreement or contract to conduct a demonstration project, the Office shall—

"(1) develop a plan for such project which identifies—

"(A) the purposes of the project;

"(B) the types of employees or eligibles, categorized by occupational series, grade, or organizational unit;

"(C) the number of employees or eligibles to be included, in the aggregate and by category;

"(D) the methodology;

"(E) the duration;

"(F) the training to be provided;

"(G) the anticipated costs;

"(H) the methodology and criteria for evaluation;

"(I) a specific description of any aspect of the project for which there is a lack of specific authority; and

"(J) a specific citation to any provision of law, rule, or regulation which, if not waived under this section, would prohibit the conducting of the project, or any part of the project as proposed;

"(2) publish the plan in the Federal Register;

"(3) submit the plan so published to public hearing;

"(4) provide notification of the proposed project, at least 180 days in advance of the date any project proposed under this section is to take effect—

"(A) to employees who are likely to be affected by the project; and

"(B) to each House of the Congress;

"(5) obtain approval from each agency involved of the final version of the plan; and

Plan
development.

Publication in
Federal Register.
Hearing.
Notification.

"(6) provide each House of the Congress with a report at least 90 days in advance of the date the project is to take effect setting forth the final version of the plan as so approved.

"(c) No demonstration project under this section may provide for a waiver of—

"(1) any provision of chapter 63 or subpart G of this title;

"(2)(A) any provision of law referred to in section 2302(b)(1) of this title; or

"(B) any provision of law implementing any provision of law referred to in section 2302(b)(1) of this title by—

"(i) providing for equal employment opportunity through affirmative action; or

"(ii) providing any right or remedy available to any employee or applicant for employment in the civil service;

"(3) any provision of chapter 15 or subchapter III of chapter 73 of this title;

"(4) any rule or regulation prescribed under any provision of law referred to in paragraph (1), (2), or (3) of this subsection; or

"(5) any provision of chapter 23 of this title, or any rule or regulation prescribed under this title, if such waiver is inconsistent with any merit system principle or any provision thereof relating to prohibited personnel practices.

"(d)(1) Each demonstration project shall—

"(A) involve not more than 5,000 individuals other than individuals in any control groups necessary to validate the results of the project; and

"(B) terminate before the end of the 5-year period beginning on the date on which the project takes effect, except that the project may continue beyond the date to the extent necessary to validate the results of the project.

"(2) Not more than 10 active demonstration projects may be in effect at any time.

"(e) Subject to the terms of any written agreement or contract between the Office and an agency, a demonstration project involving the agency may be terminated by the Office, or the agency, if either determines that the project creates a substantial hardship on, or is not in the best interests of, the public, the Federal Government, employees, or eligibles.

"(f) Employees within a unit with respect to which a labor organization is accorded exclusive recognition under chapter 71 of this title shall not be included within any project under subsection (a) of this section—

"(1) if the project would violate a collective bargaining agreement (as defined in section 7103(8) of this title) between the agency and the labor organization, unless there is another written agreement with respect to the project between the agency and the organization permitting the inclusion; or

"(2) if the project is not covered by such a collective bargaining agreement, until there has been consultation or negotiation, as appropriate, by the agency with the labor organization.

"(g) Employees within any unit with respect to which a labor organization has not been accorded exclusive recognition under Chapter 71 of this title shall not be included within any project under subsection (a) of this section unless there has been agency consultation regarding the project with the employees in the unit.

Margin notes:

Report to Congress.

5 USC 6301, 8101.
Ante, p. 1114.

5 USC 1501.
5 USC 7321.

Ante, p. 1113.

Termination.

Post, p. 1191.

Post, p. 1192.

Evaluations.

"(h) The Office shall provide for an evaluation of the results of each demonstration project and its impact on improving public management.

"(i) Upon request of the Director of the Office of Personnel Management, agencies shall cooperate with and assist the Office, to the extent practicable, in any evaluation undertaken under subsection (h) of this section and provide the Office with requested information and reports relating to the conducting of demonstration projects in their respective agencies.

"§ 4704. Allocation of funds

"Funds appropriated to the Office of Personnel Management for the purpose of this chapter may be allocated by the Office to any agency conducting demonstration projects or assisting the Office in conducting such projects. Funds so allocated shall remain available for such period as may be specified in appropriation Acts. No contract shall be entered into under this chapter unless the contract has been provided for in advance in appropriation Acts.

"§ 4705. Reports

5 USC 1308.

"The Office of Personnel Management shall include in the annual report required by section 1308(a) of this title a summary of research programs and demonstration projects conducted during the year covered by the report, the effect of the programs and projects on improving public management and increasing Government efficiency, and recommendations of policies and procedures which will improve such management and efficiency.

"§ 4706. Regulations

"The Office of Personnel Management shall prescribe regulations to carry out the purpose of this chapter.".

(b) The table of chapters for part III of title 5, United States Code, is amended by inserting after the item relating to chapter 45 the following new item:

"47. Personnel Research Programs and Demonstration Projects......... 4701".

INTERGOVERNMENTAL PERSONNEL ACT AMENDMENTS

SEC. 602. (a) Section 208 of the Intergovernmental Personnel Act of 1970 (42 U.S.C. 4728) is amended—

(1) by striking out the section heading and inserting in lieu thereof the following:

"TRANSFER OF FUNCTIONS AND ADMINISTRATION OF MERIT POLICIES";

(2) by redesignating subsections (b), (c), (d), (e), and (f) as subsections (c), (d), (e), (f), and (g), respectively, and by inserting after subsection (a) the following new subsection:

"(b) In accordance with regulations of the Office of Personnel Management, Federal agencies may require as a condition of participation in assistance programs, systems of personnel administration consistent with personnel standards prescribed by the Office for positions engaged in carrying out such programs. The standards shall—

"(1) include the merit principles in section 2 of this Act;

"(2) be prescribed in such a manner as to minimize Federal intervention in State and local personnel administration."; and

(3) by striking out the last subsection and inserting in lieu thereof the following new subsection:

"(h) Effective one year after the date of the enactment of the Civil Service Reform Act of 1978, all statutory personnel requirements established as a condition of the receipt of Federal grants-in-aid by State and local governments are hereby abolished, except— *(Grants-in-aid, abolition of certain requirements.)*

"(1) requirements prescribed under laws and regulations referred to in subsection (a) of this section;

"(2) requirements that generally prohibit discrimination in employment or require equal employment opportunity;

"(3) the Davis-Bacon Act (40 U.S.C. 276 et seq.); and *(40 USC 276a-276a-5.)*

"(4) chapter 15 of title 5, United States Code, relating to political activities of certain State and local employees.".

(b) Section 401 of such Act (84 Stat. 1920) is amended by striking out "governments and institutions of higher education" and inserting in lieu thereof "governments, institutions of higher education, and other organizations". *(5 USC 3371 note.)*

(c) Section 403 of such Act (84 Stat. 1925) is amended by inserting "(a)" after "403.", and by adding at the end thereof the following new subsection:

"(b) Effective beginning on the effective date of the Civil Service Reform Act of 1978, the provisions of section 314(f) of the Public Health Service Act (42 U.S.C. 246(f)) applicable to commissioned officers of the Public Health Service Act are hereby repealed.".

(d) Section 502 of such Act (42 U.S.C. 4762) is amended in paragraph (3) by inserting "the Trust Territory of the Pacific Islands," before "and a territory or possession of the United States,".

(e) Section 506 of such Act (42 U.S.C. 4766) is amended—

(1) in subsection (b)(2), by striking out "District of Columbia" and inserting in lieu thereof "District of Columbia, the Commonwealth of Puerto Rico, Guam, American Samoa, and the Virgin Islands"; and

(2) in subsection (b)(5), by striking out "and the District of Columbia" and inserting in lieu thereof ", the District of Columbia, the Commonwealth of Puerto Rico, Guam, American Samoa, and the Virgin Islands".

AMENDMENTS TO THE MOBILITY PROGRAM

SEC. 603. (a) Section 3371 of title 5, United States Code, is amended—

(1) by inserting "the Trust Territory of the Pacific Islands," after "Puerto Rico," in paragraph (1)(A); and

(2) by striking out "and" at the end of paragraph (1), by striking out the period at the end of paragraph (2) and inserting a semicolon in lieu thereof, and by adding at the end thereof the following:

"(3) 'Federal agency' means an Executive agency, military department, a court of the United States, the Administrative Office of the United States Courts, the Library of Congress, the Botanic Garden, the Government Printing Office, the Congressional Budget Office, the United States Postal Service, the Postal Rate Commission, the Office of the Architect of the Capitol, the Office of Technology Assessment, and such other similar agencies of the legislative and judicial branches as determined appropriate by the Office of Personnel Management; and *("Federal agency.")*

"Organization."

"(4) 'other organization' means—

"(A) a national, regional, State-wide, area-wide, or metropolitan organization representing member State or local governments;

"(B) an association of State or local public officials; or

"(C) a nonprofit organization which has as one of its principal functions the offering of professional advisory, research, educational, or development services, or related services, to governments or universities concerned with public management.".

(b) Sections 3372 through 3375 of title 5, United States Code, are amended by striking out "executive agency" and "an executive agency" each place they appear and inserting in lieu thereof "Federal agency" and "a Federal agency", respectively.

(c) Section 3372 of title 5, United States Code, is further amended—

(1) in subsection (a)(1), by inserting after "agency" the following: ", other than a noncareer appointee, limited term appointee, or limited emergency appointee (as such terms are defined in section 3132(a) of this title) in the Senior Executive Service and an employee in a position which has been excepted from the competitive service by reason of its confidential, policy-determining, policy-making, or policy-advocating character,";

(2) in subsection (b)(1), by striking out "and";

(3) in subsection (b)(2), by striking out the period after "agency" and inserting in lieu thereof a semicolon;

(4) by adding at the end of subsection (b) the following:

"(3) an employee of a Federal agency to any other organization; and

"(4) an employee of an other organization to a Federal agency."; and

(5) by adding at the end thereof (as amended in paragraph (4) of this subsection) the following new subsection:

"(c)(1) An employee of a Federal agency may be assigned under this subchapter only if the employee agrees, as a condition of accepting an assignment under this subchapter, to serve in the civil service upon the completion of the assignment for a period equal to the length of the assignment.

"(2) Each agreement required under paragraph (1) of this subsection shall provide that in the event the employee fails to carry out the agreement (except for good and sufficient reason, as determined by the head of the Federal agency from which assigned) the employee shall be liable to the United States for payment of all expenses (excluding salary) of the assignment. The amount shall be treated as a debt due the United States.".

(d) Section 3374 of title 5, United States Code, is further amended—

(1) by adding at the end of subsection (b) the following new sentence:

5 USC 8301, 8701, 8901.

"The above exceptions shall not apply to non-Federal employees who are covered by chapters 83, 87, and 89 of this title by virtue of their non-Federal employment immediately before assignment and appointment under this section.";

(2) in subsection (c)(1), by striking out the semicolon at the end thereof and by inserting in lieu thereof the following: ", except to the extent that the pay received from the State or local government is less than the appropriate rate of pay which the

duties would warrant under the applicable pay provisions of this title or other applicable authority;"; and

(3) by striking out the period at the end of subsection (c) and inserting in lieu thereof the following: ", or for the contribution of the State or local government, or a part thereof, to employee benefit systems.".

(e) Section 3375(a) of title 5, United States Code, is further amended by striking out "and" at the end of paragraph (4), by redesignating paragraph (5) as paragraph (6), and by inserting after paragraph (4) the following;

"(5) section 5724a(b) of this title, to be used by the employee for miscellaneous expenses related to change of station where movement or storage of household goods is involved; and".

TITLE VII—FEDERAL SERVICE LABOR-MANAGEMENT RELATIONS

FEDERAL SERVICE LABOR-MANAGEMENT RELATIONS

SEC. 701. So much of subpart F of part III of title 5, United States Code, as precedes subchapter II of chapter 71 thereof is amended to read as follows:

"Subpart F—Labor-Management and Employee Relations

"CHAPTER 71—LABOR-MANAGEMENT RELATIONS

"SUBCHAPTER IV—ADMINISTRATIVE AND OTHER PROVISIONS

"SUBCHAPTER I—GENERAL PROVISIONS

5 USC 7101.

"§ 7101. Findings and purpose

"(a) The Congress finds that—

"(1) experience in both private and public employment indicates that the statutory protection of the right of employees to organize, bargain collectively, and participate through labor organizations of their own choosing in decisions which affect them—

"(A) safeguards the public interest,

"(B) contributes to the effective conduct of public business, and

"(C) facilitates and encourages the amicable settlements of disputes between employees and their employers involving conditions of employment; and

"(2) the public interest demands the highest standards of employee performance and the continued development and implementation of modern and progressive work practices to facilitate and improve employee performance and the efficient accomplishment of the operations of the Government.

Therefore, labor organizations and collective bargaining in the civil service are in the public interest.

"(b) It is the purpose of this chapter to prescribe certain rights and obligations of the employees of the Federal Government and to establish procedures which are designed to meet the special requirements and needs of the Government. The provisions of this chapter should be interpreted in a manner consistent with the requirement of an effective and efficient Government.

5 USC 7102.

"§ 7102. Employees' rights

"Each employee shall have the right to form, join, or assist any labor organization, or to refrain from any such activity, freely and without fear of penalty or reprisal, and each employee shall be protected in the exercise of such right. Except as otherwise provided under this chapter, such right includes the right—

"(1) to act for a labor organization in the capacity of a representative and the right, in that capacity, to present the views of the labor organization to heads of agencies and other officials of the executive branch of the Government, the Congress, or other appropriate authorities, and

"(2) to engage in collective bargaining with respect to conditions of employment through representatives chosen by employees under this chapter.

5 USC 7103.

"§ 7103. Definitions; application

"(a) For the purpose of this chapter—

"(1) 'person' means an individual, labor organization, or agency;

"(2) 'employee' means an individual—

"(A) employed in an agency; or

"(B) whose employment in an agency has ceased because of any unfair labor practice under section 7116 of this title and who has not obtained any other regular and substantially equivalent employment, as determined under regulations prescribed by the Federal Labor Relations Authority;

but does not include—

"(i) an alien or noncitizen of the United States who occupies a position outside the United States;

"(ii) a member of the uniformed services;

"(iii) a supervisor or a management official;

"(iv) an officer or employee in the Foreign Service of the United States employed in the Department of State, the Agency for International Development, or the International Communication Agency; or

"(v) any person who participates in a strike in violation of section 7311 of this title;

"(3) 'agency' means an Executive agency (including a nonappropriated fund instrumentality described in section 2105(c) of this title and the Veterans' Canteen Service, Veterans' Administration), the Library of Congress, and the Government Printing Office, but does not include—

"(A) the General Accounting Office;

"(B) the Federal Bureau of Investigation;

"(C) the Central Intelligence Agency;

"(D) the National Security Agency;

"(E) the Tennessee Valley Authority;

"(F) the Federal Labor Relations Authority; or

"(G) the Federal Service Impasses Panel;

"(4) 'labor organization' means an organization composed in whole or in part of employees, in which employees participate and pay dues, and which has as a purpose the dealing with an agency concerning grievances and conditions of employment, but does not include—

"(A) an organization which, by its constitution, bylaws, tacit agreement among its members, or otherwise, denies membership because of race, color, creed, national origin, sex, age, preferential or nonpreferential civil service status, political affiliation, marital status, or handicapping condition;

"(B) an organization which advocates the overthrow of the constitutional form of government of the United States;

"(C) an organization sponsored by an agency; or

"(D) an organization which participates in the conduct of a strike against the Government or any agency thereof or imposes a duty or obligation to conduct, assist, or participate in such a strike;

"(5) 'dues' means dues, fees, and assessments;

"(6) 'Authority' means the Federal Labor Relations Authority described in section 7104(a) of this title;

"(7) 'Panel' means the Federal Service Impasses Panel described in section 7119(c) of this title;

"(8) 'collective bargaining agreement' means an agreement entered into as a result of collective bargaining pursuant to the provisions of this chapter;

5 USC 7311.

5 USC 2105.

"(9) 'grievance' means any complaint—

"(A) by any employee concerning any matter relating to the employment of the employee;

"(B) by any labor organization concerning any matter relating to the employment of any employee; or

"(C) by any employee, labor organization, or agency concerning—

"(i) the effect or interpretation, or a claim of breach, of a collective bargaining agreement; or

"(ii) any claimed violation, misinterpretation, or misapplication of any law, rule, or regulation affecting conditions of employment;

"(10) 'supervisor' means an individual employed by an agency having authority in the interest of the agency to hire, direct, assign, promote, reward, transfer, furlough, layoff, recall, suspend, discipline, or remove employees, to adjust their grievances, or to effectively recommend such action, if the exercise of the authority is not merely routine or clerical in nature but requires the consistent exercise of independent judgment, except that, with respect to any unit which includes firefighters or nurses, the term 'supervisor' includes only those individuals who devote a preponderance of their employment time to exercising such authority;

"(11) 'management official' means an individual employed by an agency in a position the duties and responsibilities of which require or authorize the individual to formulate, determine, or influence the policies of the agency;

"(12) 'collective bargaining' means the performance of the mutual obligation of the representative of an agency and the exclusive representative of employees in an appropriate unit in the agency to meet at reasonable times and to consult and bargain in a good-faith effort to reach agreement with respect to the conditions of employment affecting such employees and to execute, if requested by either party, a written document incorporating any collective bargaining agreement reached, but the obligation referred to in this paragraph does not compel either party to agree to a proposal or to make a concession;

"(13) 'confidential employee' means an employee who acts in a confidential capacity with respect to an individual who formulates or effectuates management policies in the field of labor-management relations;

"(14) 'conditions of employment' means personnel policies, practices, and matters, whether established by rule, regulation, or otherwise, affecting working conditions, except that such term does not include policies, practices, and matters—

5 USC 7321.

"(A) relating to political activities prohibited under subchapter III of chapter 73 of this title;

"(B) relating to the classification of any position; or

"(C) to the extent such matters are specifically provided for by Federal statute;

"(15) 'professional employee' means—

"(A) an employee engaged in the performance of work—

"(i) requiring knowledge of an advanced type in a field of science or learning customarily acquired by a prolonged course of specialized intellectual instruction and study in an institution of higher learning or a hospital (as distinguished from knowledge acquired by a general academic education, or from an apprenticeship, or from training in the performance of routine mental, manual, mechanical, or physical activities);

"(ii) requiring the consistent exercise of discretion and judgment in its performance;

"(iii) which is predominantly intellectual and varied in character (as distinguished from routine mental, manual, mechanical, or physical work); and

"(iv) which is of such character that the output produced or the result accomplished by such work cannot be standardized in relation to a given period of time; or

"(B) an employee who has completed the courses of specialized intellectual instruction and study described in subparagraph (A)(i) of this paragraph and is performing related work under appropriate direction or guidance to qualify the employee as a professional employee described in subparagraph (A) of this paragraph;

"(16) 'exclusive representative' means any labor organization which—

"(A) is certified as the exclusive representative of employees in an appropriate unit pursuant to section 7111 of this title; or

"(B) was recognized by an agency immediately before the effective date of this chapter as the exclusive representative of employees in an appropriate unit—

"(i) on the basis of an election, or

"(ii) on any basis other than an election,

and continues to be so recognized in accordance with the provisions of this chapter;

"(17) 'firefighter' means any employee engaged in the performance of work directly connected with the control and extinguishment of fires or the maintenance and use of firefighting apparatus and equipment; and

"(18) 'United States' means the 50 States, the District of Columbia, the Commonwealth of Puerto Rico, Guam, the Virgin Islands, the Trust Territory of the Pacific Islands, and any territory or possession of the United States.

"(b)(1) The President may issue an order excluding any agency or subdivision thereof from coverage under this chapter if the President determines that— **Presidential order.**

"(A) the agency or subdivision has as a primary function intelligence, counterintelligence, investigative, or national security work, and

"(B) the provisions of this chapter cannot be applied to that agency or subdivision in a manner consistent with national security requirements and considerations.

"(2) The President may issue an order suspending any provision of this chapter with respect to any agency, installation, or activity located outside the 50 States and the District of Columbia, if the President determines that the suspension is necessary in the interest of national security. **Presidential order.**

5 USC 7104.

"§ 7104. Federal Labor Relations Authority

"(a) The Federal Labor Relations Authority is composed of three members, not more than 2 of whom may be adherents of the same political party. No member shall engage in any other business or employment or hold another office or position in the Government of the United States except as otherwise provided by law.

"(b) Members of the Authority shall be appointed by the President by and with the advice and consent of the Senate, and may be removed by the President only upon notice and hearing and only for inefficiency, neglect of duty, or malfeasance in office. The President shall designate one member to serve as Chairman of the Authority.

"(c)(1) One of the original members of the Authority shall be appointed for a term of 1 year, one for a term of 3 years, and the Chairman for a term of 5 years. Thereafter, each member shall be appointed for a term of 5 years.

"(2) Notwithstanding paragraph (1) of this subsection, the term of any member shall not expire before the earlier of—

"(A) the date on which the member's successor takes office, or

"(B) the last day of the Congress beginning after the date on which the member's term of office would (but for this subparagraph) expire.

An individual chosen to fill a vacancy shall be appointed for the unexpired term of the member replaced.

"(d) A vacancy in the Authority shall not impair the right of the remaining members to exercise all of the powers of the Authority.

Report to President.

"(e) The Authority shall make an annual report to the President for transmittal to the Congress which shall include information as to the cases it has heard and the decisions it has rendered.

"(f)(1) The General Counsel of the Authority shall be appointed by the President, by and with the advice and consent of the Senate, for a term of 5 years. The General Counsel may be removed at any time by the President. The General Counsel shall hold no other office or position in the Government of the United States except as provided by law.

"(2) The General Counsel may—

"(A) investigate alleged unfair labor practices under this chapter,

"(B) file and prosecute complaints under this chapter, and

"(C) exercise such other powers of the Authority as the Authority may prescribe.

"(3) The General Counsel shall have direct authority over, and responsibility for, all employees in the office of General Counsel, including employees of the General Counsel in the regional offices of the Authority.

5 USC 7105.

"§ 7105. Powers and duties of the Authority

"(a)(1) The Authority shall provide leadership in establishing policies and guidance relating to matters under this chapter, and, except as otherwise provided, shall be responsible for carrying out the purpose of this chapter.

"(2) The Authority shall, to the extent provided in this chapter and in accordance with regulations prescribed by the Authority—

"(A) determine the appropriateness of units for labor organization representation under section 7112 of this title;

"(B) supervise or conduct elections to determine whether a labor organization has been selected as an exclusive representative by a majority of the employees in an appropriate unit and otherwise administer the provisions of section 7111 of this title relating to the according of exclusive recognition to labor organizations;

"(C) prescribe criteria and resolve issues relating to the granting of national consultation rights under section 7113 of this title;

"(D) prescribe criteria and resolve issues relating to determining compelling need for agency rules or regulations under section 7117(b) of this title;

"(E) resolves issues relating to the duty to bargain in good faith under section 7117(c) of this title;

"(F) prescribe criteria relating to the granting of consultation rights with respect to conditions of employment under section 7117(d) of this title;

"(G) conduct hearings and resolve complaints of unfair labor   Hearings.
practices under section 7118 of this title;

"(H) resolve exceptions to arbitrator's awards under section 7122 of this title; and

"(I) take such other actions as are necessary and appropriate to effectively administer the provisions of this chapter.

"(b) The Authority shall adopt an official seal which shall be judicially noticed.

"(c) The principal office of the Authority shall be in or about the District of Columbia, but the Authority may meet and exercise any or all of its powers at any time or place. Except as otherwise expressly provided by law, the Authority may, by one or more of its members or by such agents as it may designate, make any appropriate inquiry necessary to carry out its duties wherever persons subject to this chapter are located. Any member who participates in the inquiry shall not be disqualified from later participating in a decision of the Authority in any case relating to the inquiry.

"(d) The Authority shall appoint an Executive Director and such regional directors, administrative law judges under section 3105 of this title, and other individuals as it may from time to time find neces-   5 USC 3105.
sary for the proper performance of its functions. The Authority may delegate to officers and employees appointed under this subsection authority to perform such duties and make such expenditures as may be necessary.

"(e)(1) The Authority may delegate to any regional director its authority under this chapter—

"(A) to determine whether a group of employees is an appropriate unit;

"(B) to conduct investigations and to provide for hearings;

"(C) to determine whether a question of representation exists and to direct an election; and

"(D) to supervise or conduct secret ballot elections and certify the results thereof.

"(2) The Authority may delegate to any administrative law judge appointed under subsection (d) of this section its authority under section 7118 of this title to determine whether any person has engaged in or is engaging in an unfair labor practice.

"(f) If the Authority delegates any authority to any regional director or administrative law judge to take any action pursuant to subsection (e) of this section, the Authority may, upon application by any interested person filed within 60 days after the date of the action, review such action, but the review shall not, unless specifically ordered by the Authority, operate as a stay of action. The Authority may affirm, modify, or reverse any action reviewed under this subsection. If the Authority does not undertake to grant review of the action under this subsection within 60 days after the later of—

"(1) the date of the action; or

"(2) the date of the filing of any application under this subsection for review of the action;

the action shall become the action of the Authority at the end of such 60-day period.

"(g) In order to carry out its functions under this chapter, the Authority may—

Hearings.   "(1) hold hearings;

Administer oaths.   "(2) administer oaths, take the testimony or deposition of any person under oath, and issue subpenas as provided in section 7132 of this title; and

"(3) may require an agency or a labor organization to cease and desist from violations of this chapter and require it to take any remedial action it considers appropriate to carry out the policies of this chapter.

"(h) Except as provided in section 518 of title 28, relating to litigation before the Supreme Court, attorneys designated by the Authority may appear for the Authority and represent the Authority in any civil action brought in connection with any function carried out by the Authority pursuant to this title or as otherwise authorized by law.

"(i) In the exercise of the functions of the Authority under this title, the Authority may request from the Director of the Office of Personnel Management an advisory opinion concerning the proper interpretation of rules, regulations, or policy directives issued by the Office of Personnel Management in connection with any matter before the Authority.

5 USC 7106.   **"§ 7106. Management rights**

"(a) Subject to subsection (b) of this section, nothing in this chapter shall affect the authority of any management official of any agency—

"(1) to determine the mission, budget, organization, number of employees, and internal security practices of the agency; and

"(2) in accordance with applicable laws—

"(A) to hire, assign, direct, layoff, and retain employees in the agency, or to suspend, remove, reduce in grade or pay, or take other disciplinary action against such employees;

"(B) to assign work, to make determinations with respect to contracting out, and to determine the personnel by which agency operations shall be conducted;

"(C) with respect to filling positions, to make selections for appointments from—

"(i) among properly ranked and certified candidates for promotion; or

"(ii) any other appropriate source; and

"(D) to take whatever actions may be necessary to carry out the agency mission during emergencies.

"(b) Nothing in this section shall preclude any agency and any labor organization from negotiating—

"(1) at the election of the agency, on the numbers, types, and grades of employees or positions assigned to any organizational subdivision, work project, or tour of duty, or on the technology, methods, and means of performing work;

"(2) procedures which management officials of the agency will observe in exercising any authority under this section; or

"(3) appropriate arrangements for employees adversely affected by the exercise of any authority under this section by such management officials.

"SUBCHAPTER II—RIGHTS AND DUTIES OF AGENCIES AND LABOR ORGANIZATIONS

"§ 7111. Exclusive recognition of labor organizations   5 USC 7111.

"(a) An agency shall accord exclusive recognition to a labor organization if the organization has been selected as the representative, in a secret ballot election, by a majority of the employees in an appropriate unit who cast valid ballots in the election.

"(b) If a petition is filed with the Authority—   Petition.

"(1) by any person alleging—

"(A) in the case of an appropriate unit for which there is no exclusive representative, that 30 percent of the employees in the appropriate unit wish to be represented for the purpose of collective bargaining by an exclusive representative, or

"(B) in the case of an appropriate unit for which there is an exclusive representative, that 30 percent of the employees in the unit allege that the exclusive representative is no longer the representative of the majority of the employees in the unit; or

"(2) by any person seeking clarification of, or an amendment to, a certification then in effect or a matter relating to representation;

the Authority shall investigate the petition, and if it has reasonable   Hearing.
cause to believe that a question of representation exists, it shall provide an opportunity for a hearing (for which a transcript shall be kept) after reasonable notice. If the Authority finds on the record of the   Election.
hearing that a question of representation exists, the Authority shall supervise or conduct an election on the question by secret ballot and shall certify the results thereof. An election under this subsection shall not be conducted in any appropriate unit or in any subdivision thereof within which, in the preceding 12 calendar months, a valid election under this subsection has been held.

"(c) A labor organization which—

"(1) has been designated by at least 10 percent of the employees in the unit specified in any petition filed pursuant to subsection (b) of this section;

"(2) has submitted a valid copy of a current or recently expired collective bargaining agreement for the unit; or

"(3) has submitted other evidence that it is the exclusive representative of the employees involved;

may intervene with respect to a petition filed pursuant to subsection (b) of this section and shall be placed on the ballot of any election under such subsection (b) with respect to the petition.

"(d) The Authority shall determine who is eligible to vote in any election under this section and shall establish rules governing any such election, which shall include rules allowing empoyees eligible to vote the opportunity to choose—

"(1) from labor organizations on the ballot, that labor organization which the employees wish to have represent them; or

"(2) not to be represented by a labor organization.

In any election in which no choice on the ballot receives a majority of the votes cast, a runoff election shall be conducted between the two choices receiving the highest number of votes. A labor organization which receives the majority of the votes cast in an election shall be certified by the Authority as the exclusive representative.

"(e) A labor organization seeking exclusive recognition shall submit to the Authority and the agency involved a roster of its officers and representatives, a copy of its constitution and bylaws, and a statement of its objectives.

"(f) Exclusive recognition shall not be accorded to a labor organization—

"(1) if the Authority determines that the labor organization is subject to corrupt influences or influences opposed to democratic principles;

"(2) in the case of a petition filed pursuant to subsection (b)(1)(A) of this section, if there is not credible evidence that at least 30 percent of the employees in the unit specified in the petition wish to be represented for the purpose of collective bargaining by the labor organization seeking exclusive recognition;

"(3) if there is then in effect a lawful written collective bargaining agreement between the agency involved and an exclusive representative (other than the labor organization seeking exclusive recognition) covering any employees included in the unit specified in the petition, unless—

"(A) the collective bargaining agreement has been in effect for more than 3 years, or

"(B) the petition for exclusive recognition is filed not more than 105 days and not less than 60 days before the expiration date of the collective bargaining agreement; or

"(4) if the Authority has, within the previous 12 calendar months, conducted a secret ballot election for the unit described in any petition under this section and in such election a majority of the employees voting chose a labor organization for certification as the unit's exclusive representative.

"(g) Nothing in this section shall be construed to prohibit the waiving of hearings by stipulation for the purpose of a consent election in conformity with regulations and rules or decisions of the Authority.

5 USC 7112.

"§ 7112. Determination of appropriate units for labor organization representation

"(a)(1) The Authority shall determine the appropriateness of any unit. The Authority shall determine in each case whether, in order to ensure employees the fullest freedom in exercising the rights guaranteed under this chapter, the appropriate unit should be established on an agency, plant, installation, functional, or other basis and shall determine any unit to be an appropriate unit only if the determination will ensure a clear and identifiable community of interest among the employees in the unit and will promote effective dealings with, and efficiency of the operations of, the agency involved.

"(b) A unit shall not be determined to be appropriate under this section solely on the basis of the extent to which employees in the proposed unit have organized, nor shall a unit be determined to be appropriate if it includes—

Post, 1215.

"(1) except as provided under section 7135(a)(2) of this title, any management official or supervisor;

"(2) a confidential employee;

"(3) an employee engaged in personnel work in other than a purely clerical capacity;

"(4) an employee engaged in administering the provisions of this chapter;

"(5) both professional employees and other employees, unless a majority of the professional employees vote for inclusion in the unit;

"(6) any employee engaged in intelligence, counterintelligence, investigative, or security work which directly affects national security; or

"(7) any employee primarily engaged in investigation or audit functions relating to the work of individuals employed by an agency whose duties directly affect the internal security of the agency, but only if the functions are undertaken to ensure that the duties are discharged honestly and with integrity.

"(c) Any employee who is engaged in administering any provision of law relating to labor-management relations may not be represented by a labor organization—

"(1) which represents other individuals to whom such provision applies; or

"(2) which is affiliated directly or indirectly with an organization which represents other individuals to whom such provision applies.

"(d) Two or more units which are in an agency and for which a labor organization is the exclusive representative may, upon petition by the agency or labor organization, be consolidated with or without an election into a single larger unit if the Authority considers the larger unit to be appropriate. The Authority shall certify the labor organization as the exclusive representative of the new larger unit.

"§ 7113. National consultation rights

5 USC 7113.

"(a)(1) If, in connection with any agency, no labor organization has been accorded exclusive recognition on an agency basis, a labor organization which is the exclusive representative of a substantial number of the employees of the agency, as determined in accordance with criteria prescribed by the Authority, shall be granted national consultation rights by the agency. National consultation rights shall terminate when the labor organization no longer meets the criteria prescribed by the Authority. Any issue relating to any labor organization's eligibility for, or continuation of, national consultation rights shall be subject to determination by the Authority.

"(b)(1) Any labor organization having national consultation rights in connection with any agency under subsection (a) of this section shall—

"(A) be informed of any substantive change in conditions of employment proposed by the agency, and

"(B) be permitted reasonable time to present its views and recommendations regarding the changes.

"(2) If any views or recommendations are presented under paragraph (1) of this subsection to an agency by any labor organization—

"(A) the agency shall consider the views or recommendations before taking final action on any matter with respect to which the views or recommendations are presented; and

"(B) the agency shall provide the labor organization a written statement of the reasons for taking the final action.

"(c) Nothing in this section shall be construed to limit the right of any agency or exclusive representative to engage in collective bargaining.

"§ 7114. Representation rights and duties

"(a)(1) A labor organization which has been accorded exclusive recognition is the exclusive representative of the employees in the unit it represents and is entitled to act for, and negotiate collective bargaining agreements covering, all employees in the unit. An exclusive representative is responsible for representing the interests of all employees in the unit it represents without discrimination and without regard to labor organization membership.

"(2) An exclusive representative of an appropriate unit in an agency shall be given the opportunity to be represented at—

"(A) any formal discussion between one or more representatives of the agency and one or more employees in the unit or their representatives concerning any grievance or any personnel policy or practices or other general condition of employment; or

"(B) any examination of an employee in the unit by a representative of the agency in connection with an investigation if—

"(i) the employee reasonably believes that the examination may result in disciplinary action against the employee; and

"(ii) the employee requests representation.

"(3) Each agency shall annually inform its employees of their rights under paragraph (2)(B) of this subsection.

"(4) Any agency and any exclusive representative in any appropriate unit in the agency, through appropriate representatives, shall meet and negotiate in good faith for the purposes of arriving at a collective bargaining agreement. In addition, the agency and the exclusive representative may determine appropriate techniques, consistent with the provisions of section 7119 of this title, to assist in any negotiation.

"(5) The rights of an exclusive representative under the provisions of this subsection shall not be construed to preclude an employee from—

"(A) being represented by an attorney or other representative, other than the exclusive representative, of the employee's own choosing in any grievance or appeal action; or

"(B) exercising grievance or appellate rights established by law, rule, or regulation;

except in the case of grievance or appeal procedures negotiated under this chapter.

"(b) The duty of an agency and an exclusive representative to negotiate in good faith under subsection (a) of this section shall include the obligation—

"(1) to approach the negotiations with a sincere resolve to reach a collective bargaining agreement;

"(2) to be represented at the negotiations by duly authorized representatives prepared to discuss and negotiate on any condition of employment;

"(3) to meet at reasonable times and convenient places as frequently as may be necessary, and to avoid unnecessary delays;

"(4) in the case of an agency, to furnish to the exclusive representative involved, or its authorized representative, upon request and, to the extent not prohibited by law, data—

"(A) which is normally maintained by the agency in the regular course of business;

"(B) which is reasonably available and necessary for full and proper discussion, understanding, and negotiation of subjects within the scope of collective bargaining; and

"(C) which does not constitute guidance, advice, counsel, or training provided for management officials or supervisors, relating to collective bargaining; and

"(5) if agreement is reached, to execute on the request of any party to the negotiation a written document embodying the agreed terms, and to take such steps as are necessary to implement such agreement.

"(c)(1) An agreement between any agency and an exclusive representative shall be subject to approval by the head of the agency.

"(2) The head of the agency shall approve the agreement within 30 days from the date the agreement is executed if the agreement is in accordance with the provisions of this chapter and any other applicable law, rule, or regulation (unless the agency has granted an exception to the provision).

"(3) If the head of the agency does not approve or disapprove the agreement within the 30-day period, the agreement shall take effect and shall be binding on the agency and the exclusive representative subject to the provisions of this chapter and any other applicable law, rule, or regulation.

"(4) A local agreement subject to a national or other controlling agreement at a higher level shall be approved under the procedures of the controlling agreement or, if none, under regulations prescribed by the agency.

"§ 7115. Allotments to representatives

5 USC 7115.

"(a) If an agency has received from an employee in an appropriate unit a written assignment which authorizes the agency to deduct from the pay of the employee amounts for the payment of regular and periodic dues of the exclusive representative of the unit, the agency shall honor the assignment and make an appropriate allotment pursuant to the assignment. Any such allotment shall be made at no cost to the exclusive representative or the employee. Except as provided under subsection (b) of this section, any such assignment may not be revoked for a period of 1 year.

"(b) An allotment under subsection (a) of this section for the deduction of dues with respect to any employee shall terminate when—

"(1) the agreement between the agency and the exclusive representative involved ceases to be applicable to the employee; or

"(2) the employee is suspended or expelled from membership in the exclusive representative.

"(c)(1) Subject to paragraph (2) of this subsection, if a petition has been filed with the Authority by a labor organization alleging that 10 percent of the employees in an appropriate unit in an agency have membership in the labor organization, the Authority shall investigate the petition to determine its validity. Upon certification by the Authority of the validity of the petition, the agency shall have a duty to negotiate with the labor organization solely concerning the deduction of dues of the labor organization from the pay of the members of the labor organization who are employees in the unit and who make a voluntary allotment for such purpose.

"(2)(A) The provisions of paragraph (1) of this subsection shall not apply in the case of any appropriate unit for which there is an exclusive representative.

"(B) Any agreement under paragraph (1) of this subsection between a labor organization and an agency with respect to an appropriate unit shall be null and void upon the certification of an exclusive representative of the unit.

5 USC 7116.   **"§ 7116. Unfair labor practices**

"(a) For the purpose of this chapter, it shall be an unfair labor practice for an agency—

"(1) to interfere with, restrain, or coerce any employee in the exercise by the employee of any right under this chapter;

"(2) to encourage or discourage membership in any labor organization by discrimination in connection with hiring, tenure, promotion, or other conditions of employment;

"(3) to sponsor, control, or otherwise assist any labor organization, other than to furnish, upon request. customary and routine services and facilities if the services and facilities are also furnished on an impartial basis to other labor organizations having equivalent status;

"(4) to discipline or otherwise discriminate against an employee because the employee has filed a complaint, affidavit, or petition, or has given any information or testimony under this chapter;

"(5) to refuse to consult or negotiate in good faith with a labor organization as required by this chapter;

"(6) to fail or refuse to cooperate in impasse procedures and impasse decisions as required by this chapter;

Ante, p. 1114.   "(7) to enforce any rule or regulation (other than a rule or regulation implementing section 2302 of this title) which is in conflict with any applicable collective bargaining agreement if the agreement was in effect before the date the rule or regulation was prescribed; or

"(8) to otherwise fail or refuse to comply with any provision of this chapter.

"(b) For the purpose of this chapter. it shall be an unfair labor practice for a labor organization—

"(1) to interfere with, restrain, or coerce any employee in the exercise by the employee of any right under this chapter;

"(2) to cause or attempt to cause an agency to discriminate against any employee in the exercise by the employee of any right under this chapter;

"(3) to coerce, discipline. fine. or attempt to coerce a member of the labor organization as punishment, reprisal, or for the purpose of hindering or impeding the member's work performance or productivity as an employee or the discharge of the member's duties as an employee;

"(4) to discriminate against an employee with regard to the terms or conditions of membership in the labor organization on the basis of race. color, creed. national origin. sex, age, preferential or nonpreferential civil service status. political affiliation, marital status, or handicapping condition;

"(5) to refuse to consult or negotiate in good faith with an agency as required by this chapter;

"(6) to fail or refuse to cooperate in impasse procedures and impasse decisions as required by this chapter;

"(7)(A) to call. or participate in, a strike, work stoppage. or slowdown, or picketing of an agency in a labor-management dispute if such picketing interferes with an agency's operations, or

"(B) to condone any activity described in subparagraph (A) of this paragraph by failing to take action to prevent or stop such activity; or

"(8) to otherwise fail or refuse to comply with any provision of this chapter.

Nothing in paragraph (7) of this subsection shall result in any informational picketing which does not interfere with an agency's operations being considered as an unfair labor practice.

"(c) For the purpose of this chapter it shall be an unfair labor practice for an exclusive representative to deny membership to any employee in the appropriate unit represented by such exclusive representative except for failure—

"(1) to meet reasonable occupational standards uniformly required for admission, or

"(2) to tender dues uniformly required as a condition of acquiring and retaining membership.

This subsection does not preclude any labor organization from enforcing discipline in accordance with procedures under its constitution or bylaws to the extent consistent with the provisions of this chapter.

"(d) Issues which can properly be raised under an appeals procedure may not be raised as unfair labor practices prohibited under this section. Except for matters wherein, under section 7121 (e) and (f) of this title, an employee has an option of using the negotiated grievance procedure or an appeals procedure, issues which can be raised under a grievance procedure may, in the discretion of the aggrieved party, be raised under the grievance procedure or as an unfair labor practice under this section, but not under both procedures.

"(e) The expression of any personal view, argument, opinion or the making of any statement which—

"(1) publicizes the fact of a representational election and encourages employees to exercise their right to vote in such election,

"(2) corrects the record with respect to any false or misleading statement made by any person, or

"(3) informs employees of the Government's policy relating to labor-management relations and representation,

shall not, if the expression contains no threat of reprisal or force or promise of benefit or was not made under coercive conditions, (A) constitute an unfair labor practice under any provision of this chapter, or (B) constitute grounds for the setting aside of any election conducted under any provisions of this chapter.

"**§ 7117. Duty to bargain in good faith; compelling need; duty to consult**   5 USC 7117.

"(a)(1) Subject to paragraph (2) of this subsection, the duty to bargain in good faith shall, to the extent not inconsistent with any Federal law or any Government-wide rule or regulation, extend to matters which are the subject of any rule or regulation only if the rule or regulation is not a Government-wide rule or regulation.

"(2) The duty to bargain in good faith shall, to the extent not inconsistent with Federal law or any Goverment-wide rule or regulation, extend to matters which are the subject of any agency rule or regulation referred to in paragraph (3) of this subsection only if the Authority has determined under subsection (b) of this section that no compelling need (as determined under regulations prescribed by the Authority) exists for the rule or regulation.

"(3) Paragraph (2) of the subsection applies to any rule or regulation issued by any agency or issued by any primary national subdivision of such agency, unless an exclusive representative represents an appropriate unit including not less than a majority of the employees in the issuing agency or primary national subdivision, as the case may be, to whom the rule or regulation is applicable.

"(b)(1) In any case of collective bargaining in which an exclusive representative alleges that no compelling need exists for any rule or regulation referred to in subsection (a)(3) of this section which is then in effect and which governs any matter at issue in such collective bargaining, the Authority shall determine under paragraph (2) of this subsection, in accordance with regulations prescribed by the Authority, whether such a compelling need exists.

"(2) For the purpose of this section, a compelling need shall be determined not to exist for any rule or regulation only if—

"(A) the agency, or primary national subdivision, as the case may be, which issued the rule or regulation informs the Authority in writing that a compelling need for the rule or regulation does not exist; or

"(B) the Authority determines that a compelling need for a rule or regulation does not exist.

Hearing.

"(3) A hearing may be held, in the discretion of the Authority, before a determination is made under this subsection. If a hearing is held, it shall be expedited to the extent practicable and shall not include the General Counsel as a party.

"(4) The agency, or primary national subdivision, as the case may be, which issued the rule or regulation shall be a necessary party at any hearing under this subsection.

"(c)(1) Except in any case to which subsection (b) of this section applies, if an agency involved in collective bargaining with an exclusive representative alleges that the duty to bargain in good faith does not extend to any matter, the exclusive representative may appeal the allegation to the Authority in accordance with the provisions of this subsection.

Appeal.

"(2) The exclusive representative may, on or before the 15th day after the date on which the agency first makes the allegation referred to in paragraph (1) of this subsection, institute an appeal under this subsection by—

"(A) filing a petition with the Authority; and

"(B) furnishing a copy of the petition to the head of the agency.

Petition.

"(3) On or before the 30th day after the date of the receipt by the head of the agency of the copy of the petition under paragraph (2)(B) of this subsection, the agency shall—

"(A) file with the Authority a statement—

"(i) withdrawing the allegation; or

"(ii) setting forth in full its reasons supporting the allegation; and

"(B) furnish a copy of such statement to the exclusive representative.

"(4) On or before the 15th day after the date of the receipt by the exclusive representative of a copy of a statement under paragraph (3)(B) of this subsection, the exclusive representative shall file with the Authority its response to the statement.

"(5) A hearing may be held, in the discretion of the Authority, before a determination is made under this subsection. If a hearing is held, it shall not include the General Counsel as a party.

"(6) The Authority shall expedite proceedings under this subsection to the extent practicable and shall issue to the exclusive representative and to the agency a written decision on the allegation and specific reasons therefor at the earliest practicable date.

"(d)(1) A labor organization which is the exclusive representative of a substantial number of employees, determined in accordance with criteria prescribed by the Authority, shall be granted consultation rights by any agency with respect to any Government-wide rule or regulation issued by the agency effecting any substantive change in any condition of employment. Such consultation rights shall terminate when the labor organization no longer meets the criteria prescribed by the Authority. Any issue relating to a labor organization's eligibility for, or continuation of, such consultation rights shall be subject to determination by the Authority.

"(2) A labor organization having consultation rights under paragraph (1) of this subsection shall—

"(A) be informed of any substantive change in conditions of employment proposed by the agency, and

"(B) shall be permitted reasonable time to present its views and recommendations regarding the changes.

"(3) If any views or recommendations are presented under paragraph (2) of this subsection to an agency by any labor organization—

"(A) the agency shall consider the views or recommendations before taking final action on any matter with respect to which the views or recommendations are presented; and

"(B) the agency shall provide the labor organization a written statement of the reasons for taking the final action.

"§ 7118. Prevention of unfair labor practices

5 USC 7118.

"(a)(1) If any agency or labor organization is charged by any person with having engaged in or engaging in an unfair labor practice, the General Counsel shall investigate the charge and may issue and cause to be served upon the agency or labor organization a complaint. In any case in which the General Counsel does not issue a complaint because the charge fails to state an unfair labor practice, the General Counsel shall provide the person making the charge a written statement of the reasons for not issuing a complaint.

"(2) Any complaint under paragraph (1) of this subsection shall contain a notice—   Complaint.

"(A) of the charge;

"(B) that a hearing will be held before the Authority (or any   Hearing.
member thereof or before an individual employed by the authority and designated for such purpose); and

"(C) of the time and place fixed for the hearing.

"(3) The labor organization or agency involved shall have the right to file an answer to the original and any amended complaint and to appear in person or otherwise and give testimony at the time and place fixed in the complaint for the hearing.

"(4)(A) Except as provided in subparagraph (B) of this paragraph, no complaint shall be issued based on any alleged unfair labor practice which occurred more than 6 months before the filing of the charge with the Authority.

"(B) If the General Counsel determines that the person filing any charge was prevented from filing the charge during the 6-month period referred to in subparagraph (A) of this paragraph by reason of—

"(i) any failure of the agency or labor organization against which the charge is made to perform a duty owed to the person, or

"(ii) any concealment which prevented discovery of the alleged unfair labor practice during the 6-month period,
the General Counsel may issue a complaint based on the charge if the charge was filed during the 6-month period beginning on the day of the discovery by the person of the alleged unfair labor practice.

"(5) The General Counsel may prescribe regulations providing for   Regulations.

informal methods by which the alleged unfair labor practice may be resolved prior to the issuance of a complaint.

Hearing.

"(6) The Authority (or any member thereof or any individual employed by the Authority and designated for such purpose) shall conduct a hearing on the complaint not earlier than 5 days after the date on which the complaint is served. In the discretion of the individual or individuals conducting the hearing, any person involved may be allowed to intervene in the hearing and to present testimony. Any such hearing shall, to the extent practicable, be conducted in accordance

5 USC 551.

with the provisions of subchapter II of chapter 5 of this title, except that the parties shall not be bound by rules of evidence, whether statu-

Transcript.

tory, common law, or adopted by a court. A transcript shall be kept of the hearing. After such a hearing the Authority, in its discretion, may upon notice receive further evidence or hear argument.

"(7) If the Authority (or any member thereof or any individual employed by the Authority and designated for such purpose) determines after any hearing on a complaint under paragraph (5) of this subsection that the preponderance of the evidence received demonstrates that the agency or labor organization named in the complaint has engaged in or is engaging in an unfair labor practice, then the individual or individuals conducting the hearing shall state in writing their findings of fact and shall issue and cause to be served on the agency or labor organization an order—

"(A) to cease and desist from any such unfair labor practice in which the agency or labor organization is engaged;

"(B) requiring the parties to renegotiate a collective bargaining agreement in accordance with the order of the Authority and requiring that the agreement, as amended, be given retroactive effect;

"(C) requiring reinstatement of an employee with backpay in accordance with section 5596 of this title; or

"(D) including any combination of the actions described in subparagraphs (A) through (C) of this paragraph or such other action as will carry out the purpose of this chapter.

If any such order requires reinstatement of an employee with backpay, backpay may be required of the agency (as provided in section 5596 of this title) or of the labor organization, as the case may be, which is found to have engaged in the unfair labor practice involved.

"(8) If the individual or individuals conducting the hearing determine that the preponderance of the evidence received fails to demonstrate that the agency or labor organization named in the complaint has engaged in or is engaging in an unfair labor practice, the individual or individuals shall state in writing their findings of fact and shall issue an order dismissing the complaint.

Rules and regulations, interpretation.

"(b) In connection with any matter before the Authority in any proceeding under this section, the Authority may request, in accordance with the provisions of section 7105(i) of this title, from the Director of the Office of Personnel Management an advisory opinion concerning the proper interpretation of rules, regulations, or other policy directives issued by the Office of Personnel Management.

5 USC 7119.

"§ 7119. Negotiation impasses; Federal Service Impasses Panel

"(a) The Federal Mediation and Conciliation Service shall provide services and assistance to agencies and exclusive representatives in the resolution of negotiation impasses. The Service shall determine under what circumstances and in what manner it shall provide services and assistance.

"(b) If voluntary arrangements, including the services of the Federal Mediation and Conciliation Service or any other third-party mediation, fail to resolve a negotiation impasse—

"(1) either party may request the Federal Service Impasses Panel to consider the matter, or

"(2) the parties may agree to adopt a procedure for binding arbitration of the negotiation impasse, but only if the procedure is approved by the Panel.

"(c)(1) The Federal Service Impasses Panel is an entity within the Authority, the function of which is to provide assistance in resolving negotiation impasses between agencies and exclusive representatives.

"(2) The Panel shall be composed of a Chairman and at least six other members, who shall be appointed by the President, solely on the basis of fitness to perform the duties and functions involved, from among individuals who are familiar with Government operations and knowledgeable in labor-management relations. *Membership.*

"(3) Of the original members of the Panel, 2 members shall be appointed for a term of 1 year, 2 members shall be appointed for a term of 3 years, and the Chairman and the remaining members shall be appointed for a term of 5 years. Thereafter each member shall be appointed for a term of 5 years, except that an individual chosen to fill a vacancy shall be appointed for the unexpired term of the member replaced. Any member of the Panel may be removed by the President.

"(4) The Panel may appoint an Executive Director and any other individuals it may from time to time find necessary for the proper performance of its duties. Each member of the Panel who is not an employee (as defined in section 2105 of this title) is entitled to pay at a rate equal to the daily equivalent of the maximum annual rate of basic pay then currently paid under the General Schedule for each day he is engaged in the performance of official business of the Panel, including travel time, and is entitled to travel expenses as provided under section 5703 of this title.

"(5)(A) The Panel or its designee shall promptly investigate any *Investigation.* impasse presented to it under subsection (b) of this section. The Panel shall consider the impasse and and shall either—

"(i) recommend to the parties procedures for the resolution of the impasse; or

"(ii) assist the parties in resolving the impasse through whatever methods and procedures, including factfinding and recommendations, it may consider appropriate to accomplish the purpose of this section.

"(B) If the parties do not arrive at a settlement after assistance by the Panel under subparagraph (A) of this paragraph, the Panel may—

"(i) hold hearings;

"(ii) administer oaths, take the testimony or deposition of any person under oath, and issue subpenas as provided in section 7132 of this title; and

"(iii) take whatever action is necessary and not inconsistent with this chapter to resolve the impasse.

"(C) Notice of any final action of the Panel under this section shall be promptly served upon the parties, and the action shall be binding on such parties during the term of the agreement, unless the parties agree otherwise.

5 USC 7120.

"§ 7120. Standards of conduct for labor organizations

"(a) An agency shall only accord recognition to a labor organization that is free from corrupt influences and influences opposed to basic democratic principles. Except as provided in subsection (b) of this section, an organization is not required to prove that it is free from such influences if it is subject to governing requirements adopted by the organization or by a national or international labor organization or federation of labor organizations with which it is affiliated, or in which it participates, containing explicit and detailed provisions to which it subscribes calling for—

"(1) the maintenance of democratic procedures and practices including provisions for periodic elections to be conducted subject to recognized safeguards and provisions defining and securing the right of individual members to participate in the affairs of the organization, to receive fair and equal treatment under the governing rules of the organization, and to receive fair process in disciplinary proceedings;

"(2) the exclusion from office in the organization of persons affiliated with communist or other totalitarian movements and persons identified with corrupt influences;

"(3) the prohibition of business or financial interests on the part of organization officers and agents which conflict with their duty to the organization and its members; and

"(4) the maintenance of fiscal integrity in the conduct of the affairs of the organization, including provisions for accounting and financial controls and regular financial reports or summaries to be made available to members.

"(b) Notwithstanding the fact that a labor organization has adopted or subscribed to standards of conduct as provided in subsection (a) of this section, the organization is required to furnish evidence of its freedom from corrupt influences or influences opposed to basic democratic principles if there is reasonable cause to believe that—

"(1) the organization has been suspended or expelled from, or is subject to other sanction, by a parent labor organization, or federation of organizations with which it had been affiliated, because it has demonstrated an unwillingness or inability to comply with governing requirements comparable in purpose to those required by subsection (a) of this section; or

"(2) the organization is in fact subject to influences that would preclude recognition under this chapter.

Filing of reports.

"(c) A labor organization which has or seeks recognition as a representative of employees under this chapter shall file financial and other reports with the Assistant Secretary of Labor for Labor Management Relations, provide for bonding of officials and employees of the organization, and comply with trusteeship and election standards.

Regulations.

"(d) The Assistant Secretary shall prescribe such regulations as are necessary to carry out the purposes of this section. Such regulations shall conform generally to the principles applied to labor organizations in the private sector. Complaints of violations of this section shall be filed with the Assistant Secretary. In any matter arising under this section, the Assistant Secretary may require a labor organization to cease and desist from violations of this section and require it to take such actions as he considers appropriate to carry out the policies of this section.

"(e) This chapter does not authorize participation in the management of a labor organization or acting as a representative of a labor organization by a management official, a supervisor, or a confidential employee, except as specifically provided in this chapter, or by an employee if the participation or activity would result in a conflict or apparent conflict of interest or would otherwise be incompatible with law or with the official duties of the employee.

"(f) In the case of any labor organization which by omission or commission has willfully and intentionally, with regard to any strike, work stoppage, or slowdown, violated section 7116(b)(7) of this title, the Authority shall, upon an appropriate finding by the Authority of such violation— **Strike.**

"(1) revoke the exclusive recognition status of the labor organization, which shall then immediately cease to be legally entitled and obligated to represent employees in the unit; or

"(2) take any other appropriate disciplinary action.

"SUBCHAPTER III—GRIEVANCES

"§ 7121. Grievance procedures

5 USC 7121.

"(a)(1) Except as provided in paragraph (2) of this subsection, any collective bargaining agreement shall provide procedures for the settlement of grievances, including questions of arbitrability. Except as provided in subsections (d) and (e) of this section, the procedures shall be the exclusive procedures for resolving grievances which fall within its coverage.

"(2) Any collective bargaining agreement may exclude any matter from the application of the grievance procedures which are provided for in the agreement.

"(b) Any negotiated grievance procedure referred to in subsection (a) of this section shall—

"(1) be fair and simple,

"(2) provide for expeditious processing, and

"(3) include procedures that—

"(A) assure an exclusive representative the right, in its own behalf or on behalf of any employee in the unit represented by the exclusive representative, to present and process grievances;

"(B) assure such an employee the right to present a grievance on the employee's own behalf, and assure the exclusive representative the right to be present during the grievance proceeding; and

"(C) provide that any grievance not satisfactorily settled under the negotiated grievance procedure shall be subject to binding arbitration which may be invoked by either the exclusive representative or the agency.

"(c) The preceding subsections of this section shall not apply with respect to any grievance concerning—

"(1) any claimed violation of subchapter III of chapter 73 of this title (relating to prohibited political activities); **5 USC 7321.**

"(2) retirement, life insurance, or health insurance;

"(3) a suspension or removal under section 7532 of this title;

"(4) any examination, certification, or appointment; or

"(5) the classification of any position which does not result in the reduction in grade or pay of an employee.

"(d) An aggrieved employee affected by a prohibited personnel practice under section 2302(b)(1) of this title which also falls under the coverage of the negotiated grievance procedure may raise the matter under a statutory procedure or the negotiated procedure, but not both. An employee shall be deemed to have exercised his option **Ante, p. 1114.**

Ante, p. 1140.

Ante, p. 1133, 1136.

Ante, p. 1138.

Ante, p. 1143.

5 USC 7122.

under this subsection to raise the matter under either a statutory procedure or the negotiated procedure at such time as the employee timely initiates an action under the applicable statutory procedure or timely files a grievance in writing, in accordance with the provisions of the parties' negotiated procedure, whichever event occurs first. Selection of the negotiated procedure in no manner prejudices the right of an aggrieved employee to request the Merit Systems Protection Board to review the final decision pursuant to section 7702 of this title in the case of any personnel action that could have been appealed to the Board, or, where applicable, to request the Equal Employment Opportunity Commission to review a final decision in any other matter involving a complaint of discrimination of the type prohibited by any law administered by the Equal Employment Opportunity Commission.

"(e)(1) Matters covered under sections 4303 and 7512 of this title which also fall within the coverage of the negotiated grievance procedure may, in the discretion of the aggrieved employee, be raised either under the appellate procedures of section 7701 of this title or under the negotiated grievance procedure, but not both. Similar matters which arise under other personnel systems applicable to employees covered by this chapter may, in the discretion of the aggrieved employee, be raised either under the appellate procedures, if any, applicable to those matters, or under the negotiated grievance procedure, but not both. An employee shall be deemed to have exercised his option under this subsection to raise a matter either under the applicable appellate procedures or under the negotiated grievance procedure at such time as the employee timely files a notice of appeal under the applicable appellate procedures or timely files a grievance in writing in accordance with the provisions of the parties' negotiated grievance procedure, whichever event occurs first.

"(2) In matters covered under sections 4303 and 7512 of this title which have been raised under the negotiated grievance procedure in accordance with this section, an arbitrator shall be governed by section 7701(c)(1) of this title, as applicable.

"(f) In matters covered under sections 4303 and 7512 of this title which have been raised under the negotiated grievance procedure in accordance with this section, section 7703 of this title pertaining to judicial review shall apply to the award of an arbitrator in the same manner and under the same conditions as if the matter had been decided by the Board. In matters similar to those covered under sections 4303 and 7512 of this title which arise under other personnel systems and which an aggrieved employee has raised under the negotiated grievance procedure, judicial review of an arbitrator's award may be obtained in the same manner and on the same basis as could be obtained of a final decision in such matters raised under applicable appellate procedures.

"§ 7122. Exceptions to arbitral awards

"(a) Either party to arbitration under this chapter may file with the Authority an exception to any arbitrator's award pursuant to the arbitration (other than an award relating to a matter described in section 7121(f) of this title). If upon review the Authority finds that the award is deficient—

"(1) because it is contrary to any law, rule, or regulation; or

"(2) on other grounds similar to those applied by Federal courts in private sector labor-management relations;

the Authority may take such action and make such recommendations concerning the award as it considers necessary, consistent with applicable laws, rules, or regulations.

"(b) If no exception to an arbitrator's award is filed under subsection (a) of this section during the 30-day period beginning on the date of such award, the award shall be final and binding. An agency shall take the actions required by an arbitrator's final award. The award may include the payment of backpay (as provided in section 5596 of this title).

"§ 7123. Judicial review; enforcement

5 USC 7123.

"(a) Any person aggrieved by any final order of the Authority other than an order under—

"(1) section 7122 of this title (involving an award by an arbitrator), unless the order involves an unfair labor practice under section 7118 of this title, or

"(2) section 7112 of this title (involving an appropriate unit determination),

may, during the 60-day period beginning on the date on which the order was issued, institute an action for judicial review of the Authority's order in the United States court of appeals in the circuit in which the person resides or transacts business or in the United States Court of Appeals for the District of Columbia.

"(b) The Authority may petition any appropriate United States court of appeals for the enforcement of any order of the Authority and for appropriate temporary relief or restraining order.

Petition.

"(c) Upon the filing of a petition under subsection (a) of this section for judicial review or under subsection (b) of this section for enforcement, the Authority shall file in the court the record in the proceedings, as provided in section 2112 of title 28. Upon the filing of the petition, the court shall cause notice thereof to be served to the parties involved, and thereupon shall have jurisdiction of the proceeding and of the question determined therein and may grant any temporary relief (including a temporary restraining order) it considers just and proper, and may make and enter a decree affirming and enforcing, modifying and enforcing as so modified, or setting aside in whole or in part the order of the Authority. The filing of a petition under subsection (a) or (b) of this section shall not operate as a stay of the Authority's order unless the court specifically orders the stay. Review of the Authority's order shall be on the record in accordance with section 706 of this title. No objection that has not been urged before the Authority, or its designee, shall be considered by the court, unless the failure or neglect to urge the objection is excused because of extraordinary circumstances. The findings of the Authority with respect to questions of fact, if supported by substantial evidence on the record considered as a whole, shall be conclusive. If any person applies to the court for leave to adduce additional evidence and shows to the satisfaction of the court that the additional evidence is material and that there were reasonable grounds for the failure to adduce the evidence in the hearing before the Authority, or its designee, the court may order the additional evidence to be taken before the Authority, or its designee, and to be made a part of the record. The Authority may modify its findings as to the facts, or make new findings by reason of additional evidence so taken and filed. The Authority shall file its modified or new findings, which, with respect to questions of fact, if supported by substantial evidence on the record considered as a whole,

5 USC 706.

shall be conclusive. The Authority shall file its recommendations, if any, for the modification or setting aside of its original order. Upon the filing of the record with the court, the jurisdiction of the court shall be exclusive and its judgment and decree shall be final, except that the judgment and decree shall be subject to review by the Supreme Court of the United States upon writ of certiorari or certification as provided in section 1254 of title 28.

"(d) The Authority may, upon issuance of a complaint as provided in section 7118 of this title charging that any person has engaged in or is engaging in an unfair labor practice, petition any United States district court within any district in which the unfair labor practice in question is alleged to have occurred or in which such person resides or transacts business for appropriate temporary relief (including a restraining order). Upon the filing of the petition, the court shall cause notice thereof to be served upon the person, and thereupon shall have jurisdiction to grant any temporary relief (including a temporary restraining order) it considers just and proper. A court shall not grant any temporary relief under this section if it would interfere with the ability of the agency to carry out its essential functions or if the Authority fails to establish probable cause that an unfair labor practice is being committed.

"SUBCHAPTER IV—ADMINISTRATIVE AND OTHER PROVISIONS

5 USC 7131.

"§ 7131. Official time

"(a) Any employee representing an exclusive representative in the negotiation of a collective bargaining agreement under this chapter shall be authorized official time for such purposes, including attendance at impasse proceeding, during the time the employee otherwise would be in a duty status. The number of employees for whom official time is authorized under this subsection shall not exceed the number of individuals designated as representing the agency for such purposes.

"(b) Any activities performed by any employee relating to the internal business of a labor organization (including the solicitation of membership, elections of labor organization officials, and collection of dues) shall be performed during the time the employee is in a non-duty status.

"(c) Except as provided in subsection (a) of this section, the Authority shall determine whether any employee participating for, or on behalf of, a labor organization in any phase of proceedings before the Authority shall be authorized official time for such purpose during the time the employee otherwise would be in a duty status.

"(d) Except as provided in the preceding subsections of this section—

"(1) any employee representing an exclusive representative, or
"(2) in connection with any other matter covered by this chapter, any employee in an appropriate unit represented by an exclusive representative,

shall be granted official time in any amount the agency and the exclusive representative involved agree to be reasonable, necessary, and in the public interest.

5 USC 7132.

"§ 7132. Subpenas

"(a) Any member of the Authority, the General Counsel, or the Panel, any administrative law judge appointed by the Authority under

5 USC 3105.

section 3105 of this title, and any employee of the Authority designated by the Authority may—

"(1) issue subpenas requiring the attendance and testimony of witnesses and the production of documentary or other evidence from any place in the United States; and

"(2) administer oaths, take or order the taking of depositions, order responses to written interrogatories, examine witnesses, and receive evidence.

No subpena shall be issued under this section which requires the disclosure of intramanagement guidance, advice, counsel, or training within an agency or between an agency and the Office of Personnel Management.

"(b) In the case of contumacy or failure to obey a subpena issued under subsection (a)(1) of this section, the United States district court for the judicial district in which the person to whom the subpena is addressed resides or is served may issue an order requiring such person to appear at any designated place to testify or to produce documentary or other evidence. Any failure to obey the order of the court may be punished by the court as a contempt thereof.

"(c) Witnesses (whether appearing voluntarily or under subpena) shall be paid the same fee and mileage allowances which are paid subpenaed witnesses in the courts of the United States

"§ 7133. Compilation and publication of data

5 USC 7133.

"(a) The Authority shall maintain a file of its proceedings and copies of all available agreements and arbitration decisions, and shall publish the texts of its decisions and the actions taken by the Panel under section 7119 of this title.

"(b) All files maintained under subsection (a) of this section shall be open to inspection and reproduction in accordance with the provisions of sections 552 and 552a of this title.

5 USC 552, 552a.

"§ 7134. Regulations

5 USC 7134.

"The Authority, the General Counsel, the Federal Mediation and Conciliation Service, the Assistant Secretary of Labor for Labor Management Relations, and the Panel shall each prescribe rules and regulations to carry out the provisions of this chapter applicable to each of them, respectively. Provisions of subchapter II of chapter 5 of this title shall be applicable to the issuance, revision, or repeal of any such rule or regulation.

"§ 7135. Continuation of existing laws, recognitions, agreements, and procedures

5 USC 7135.

"(a) Nothing contained in this chapter shall preclude—

"(1) the renewal or continuation of an exclusive recognition, certification of an exclusive representative, or a lawful agreement between an agency and an exclusive representative of its employees, which is entered into before the effective date of this chapter; or

"(2) the renewal, continuation, or initial according of recognition for units of management officials or supervisors represented by labor organizations which historically or traditionally represent management officials or supervisors in private industry and which hold exclusive recognition for units of such officials or supervisors in any agency on the effective date of this chapter.

"(b) Policies, regulations, and procedures established under and decisions issued under Executive Orders 11491, 11616, 11636, 11787, and 11838, or under any other Executive order, as in effect on the effective date of this chapter, shall remain in full force and effect until revised or revoked by the President, or unless superseded by specific provisions

5 USC 7301 note, 7701 note.

of this chapter or by regulations or decisions issued pursuant to this chapter.".

BACKPAY IN CASE OF UNFAIR LABOR PRACTICES AND GRIEVANCES

SEC. 702. Section 5596(b) of title 5, United States Code is amended to read as follows:

"(b)(1) An employee of an agency who, on the basis of a timely appeal or an administrative determination (including a decision relating to an unfair labor practice or a grievance) is found by appropriate authority under applicable law, rule, regulation, or collective bargaining agreement, to have been affected by an unjustified or unwarranted personnel action which has resulted in the withdrawal or reduction of all or part of the pay, allowances, or differentials of the employee—

"(A) is entitled, on correction of the personnel action, to receive for the period for which the personnel action was in effect—

"(i) an amount equal to all or any part of the pay, allowances, or differentials, as applicable which the employee normally would have earned or received during the period if the personnel action had not occurred, less any amounts earned by the employee through other employment during that period; and

"(ii) reasonable attorney fees related to the personnel action which, with respect to any decision relating to an unfair labor practice or a grievance processed under a procedure negotiated in accordance with chapter 71 of this title, shall be awarded in accordance with standards established under section 7701(g) of this title; and

Ante, p. 1191.

Ante, p. 1138.

"(B) for all purposes, is deemed to have performed service for the agency during that period, except that—

"(i) annual leave restored under this paragraph which is in excess of the maximum leave accumulation permitted by law shall be credited to a separate leave account for the employee and shall be available for use by the employee within the time limits prescribed by regulations of the Office of Personnel Management, and

"(ii) annual leave credited under clause (i) of this subparagraph but unused and still available to the employee under regulations prescribed by the Office shall be included in the lump-sum payment under section 5551 or 5552(1) of this title but may not be retained to the credit of the employee under section 5552(2) of this title.

5 USC 5551, 5552.

"(2) This subsection does not apply to any reclassification action nor authorize the setting aside of an otherwise proper promotion by a selecting official from a group of properly ranked and certified candidates.

"(3) For the purpose of this subsection, 'grievance' and 'collective bargaining agreement' have the meanings set forth in section 7103 of this title, 'unfair labor practice' means an unfair labor practice described in section 7116 of this title, and 'personnel action' includes the omission or failure to take an action or confer a benefit.".

Ante, p. 1192.

TECHNICAL AND CONFORMING AMENDMENTS

SEC. 703. (a) Subchapter II of chapter 71 of title 5, United States Code, is amended—

(1) by redesignating sections 7151 (as amended by section 310 of this Act), 7152, 7153, and 7154 as sections 7201, 7202, 7203, and 7204, respectively;

5 USC 7152-7154, 7201-7204.

(2) by striking out the subchapter heading and inserting in lieu thereof the following:

"CHAPTER 72—ANTIDISCRIMINATION; RIGHT TO PETITION CONGRESS

"SUBCHAPTER I—ANTIDISCRIMINATION IN EMPLOYMENT

"Sec.
"7201. Antidiscrimination policy; minority recruitment program.
"7202. Marital status.
"7203. Handicapping condition.
"7204. Other prohibitions.

"SUBCHAPTER II—EMPLOYEES' RIGHT TO PETITION CONGRESS

"7211. Employees' right to petition Congress.";

and

(3) by adding at the end thereof the following new subchapter:

"SUBCHAPTER II—EMPLOYEES' RIGHT TO PETITION CONGRESS

"§ 7211. Employees' right to petition Congress

5 USC 7211.

"The right of employees, individually or collectively, to petition Congress or a Member of Congress, or to furnish information to either House of Congress, or to a committee or Member thereof, may not be interfered with or denied.".

(b) The analysis for part III of title 5, United States Code, is amended by striking out—

"Subpart F—Employee Relations

"71. Policies_____ 7101";

and inserting in lieu thereof—

"Subpart F—Labor-Management and Employee Relations

"71. Labor-Management Relations_____ 7101
"72. Antidiscrimination; Right to Petition Congress_____ 7201".

(c) (1) Section 2105 (c) (1) of title 5, United States Code, is amended by striking out "7152, 7153" and inserting in lieu thereof "7202, 7203".

(2) Section 3302(2) of title 5, United States Code, is amended by striking out "and 7154" and inserting in lieu thereof "and 7204".

(3) Sections 4540(c), 7212(a), and 9540(c) of title 10, United States Code, are each amended by striking out "7154 of title 5" and inserting in lieu thereof "7204 of title 5".

(4) Section 410(b) (1) of title 39, United States Code, is amended by striking out "chapters 71 (employee policies)" and inserting in lieu thereof the following: "chapters 72 (antidiscrimination; right to petition Congress)".

(5) Section 1002(g) of title 39, United States Code, is amended by striking out "section 7102 of title 5" and inserting in lieu thereof "section 7211 of title 5".

(d) Section 5315 of title 5, United States Code, is amended by adding at the end thereof the following clause:

"(124) Chairman, Federal Labor Relations Authority.".

(e) Section 5316 of such title is amended by adding at the end thereof the following clause:

5 USC 5316.

"(145) Members, Federal Labor Relations Authority (2) and its General Counsel.".

MISCELLANEOUS PROVISIONS

5 USC 5343 note.

5 USC 5343 note.

Ante, p. 1191.

SEC. 704. (a) Those terms and conditions of employment and other employment benefits with respect to Government prevailing rate employees to whom section 9(b) of Public Law 92–392 applies which were the subject of negotiation in accordance with prevailing rates and practices prior to August 19, 1972, shall be negotiated on and after the date of the enactment of this Act in accordance with the provisions of section 9(b) of Public Law 92–392 without regard to any provision of chapter 71 of title 5, United States Code (as amended by this title), to the extent that any such provision is inconsistent with this paragraph.

(b) The pay and pay practices relating to employees referred to in paragraph (1) of this subsection shall be negotiated in accordance with prevailing rates and pay practices without regard to any provision of—

(A) chapter 71 of title 5, United States Code (as amended by this title), to the extent that any such provision is inconsistent with this paragraph;

5 USC 5301, 5501.

(B) subchapter IV of chapter 53 and subchapter V of chapter 55 of title 5, United States Code: or

(C) any rule, regulation, decision, or order relating to rates of pay or pay practices under subchapter IV of chapter 53 or subchapter V of chapter 55 of title 5, United States Code.

TITLE VIII—GRADE AND PAY RETENTION

GRADE AND PAY RETENTION

5 USC 5301.

SEC. 801. (a) (1) Chapter 53 of title 5, United States Code, relating to pay rates and systems, is amended by inserting after subchapter V thereof the following new subchapter:

"SUBCHAPTER VI—GRADE AND PAY RETENTION

5 USC 5361.

"§ 5361. Definitions

"For the purpose of this subchapter—

"(1) 'employee' means an employee to whom chapter 51 of this title applies, and a prevailing rate employee, as defined by section

5 USC 5342.

5342(a)(2) of this title, whose employment is other than on a temporary or term basis;

5 USC 5102.

"(2) 'agency' has the meaning given it by section 5102 of this title;

"(3) 'retained grade' means the grade used for determining benefits to which an employee to whom section 5362 of this title applies is entitled;

"(4) 'rate of basic pay' means, in the case of a prevailing rate employee, the scheduled rate of pay determined under section 5343

5 USC 5343.

of this title;

"(5) 'covered pay schedule' means the General Schedule, any prevailing rate schedule established under subchapter IV of this

Ante, p. 1180.

chapter, or the merit pay system under chapter 54 of this title;

"(6) 'position subject to this subchapter' means any position under a covered pay schedule; and

"(7) 'reduction-in-force procedures' means procedures applied in carrying out any reduction in force due to a reorganization, due to lack of funds or curtailment of work, or due to any other factor.

"§ 5362. Grade retention following a change of positions or reclassification

5 USC 5362.

"(a) Any employee—

"(1) who is placed as a result of reduction-in-force procedures from a position subject to this subchapter to another position which is subject to this subchapter and which is in a lower grade than the previous position, and

"(2) who has served for 52 consecutive weeks or more in one or more positions subject to this subchapter at a grade or grades higher than that of the new position,

is entitled, to the extent provided in subsection (c) of this section, to have the grade of the position held immediately before such placement be considered to be the retained grade of the employee in any position he holds for the 2-year period beginning on the date of such placement.

"(b)(1) Any employee who is in a position subject to this subchapter and whose position has been reduced in grade is entitled, to the extent provided in subsection (c) of this section, to have the grade of such position before reduction be treated as the retained grade of such employee for the 2-year period beginning on the date of the reduction in grade.

"(2) The provisions of paragraph (1) of this subsection shall not apply with respect to any reduction in the grade of a position which had not been classified at the higher grade for a continuous period of at least one year immediately before such reduction.

"(c) For the 2-year period referred to in subsections (a) and (b) of this section, the retained grade of an employee under such subsection (a) or (b) shall be treated as the grade of the employee's position for all purposes (including pay and pay administration under this chapter and chapters 54 and 55 of this title, retirement and life insurance under chapters 83 and 87 of this title, and eligibility for training and promotion under this title) except—

Ante, p. 1180.
5 USC 5501.
5 USC 8301,
8701.

"(1) for purposes of subsection (a) of this section,

"(2) for purposes of applying any reduction-in-force procedures,

"(3) for purposes of determining whether the employee is covered by the merit pay system established under section 5402 of this title, or

Ante, p. 1181.

"(4) for such other purposes as the Office of Personnel Management may provide by regulation.

"(d) The foregoing provisions of this section shall cease to apply to an employee who—

"(1) has a break in service of one workday or more;

"(2) is demoted (determined without regard to this section) for personal cause or at the employee's request;

"(3) is placed in, or declines a reasonable offer of, a position the grade of which is equal to or higher than the retained grade; or

"(4) elects in writing to have the benefits of this section terminate.

"§ 5363. Pay retention

5 USC 5363.

"(a) Any employee—

"(1) who ceases to be entitled to the benefits of section 5362 of this title by reason of the expiration of the 2-year period of coverage provided under such section;

"(2) who is in a position subject to this subchapter and who is subject to a reduction or termination of a special rate of pay established under section 5303 of this title; or

5 USC 5303.

"(3) who is in a position subject to this subchapter and who (but for this section) would be subject to a reduction in pay under circumstances prescribed by the Office of Personnel Management by regulation to warrant the application of this section;

is entitled to basic pay at a rate equal to (A) the employee's allowable former rate of basic pay, plus (B) 50 percent of the amount of each increase in the maximum rate of basic pay payable for the grade of the employee's position immediately after such reduction in pay if such allowable former rate exceeds such maximum rate for such grade.

"(b) For the purpose of subsection (a) of this section, 'allowable former rate of basic pay' means the lower of—

"(1) the rate of basic pay payable to the employee immediately before the reduction in pay; or

"(2) 150 percent of the maximum rate of basic pay payable for the grade of the employee's position immediately after such reduction in pay.

"(c) The preceding provisions of this section shall cease to apply to an employee who—

"(1) has a break in service of one workday or more;

5 USC 5101,
5301.
Ante, p. 1180.

"(2) is entitled by operation of this subchapter or chapter 51, 53, or 54 of this title to a rate of basic pay which is equal to or higher than, or declines a reasonable offer of a position the rate of basic pay for which is equal to or higher than, the rate to which the employee is entitled under this section; or

"(3) is demoted for personal cause or at the employee's request.

5 USC 5364.

"§ 5364. Remedial actions

"Under regulations prescribed by the Office of Personnel Management, the Office may require any agency—

"(1) to report to the Office information with respect to vacancies (including impending vacancies);

"(2) to take such steps as may be appropriate to assure employees receiving benefits under section 5362 or 5363 of this title have the opportunity to obtain necessary qualifications for the selection to positions which would minimize the need for the application of such sections;

"(3) to establish a program under which employees receiving benefits under section 5362 or 5363 of this title are given priority in the consideration for or placement in positions which are equal to their retained grade or pay; and

"(4) to place certain employees, notwithstanding the fact their previous position was in a different agency, but only in circumstances in which the Office determines the exercise of such authority is necessary to carry out the purpose of this section.

5 USC 5365.

"§ 5365. Regulations

"(a) The Office of Personnel Management shall prescribe regulations to carry out the purpose of this subchapter.

"(b) Under such regulations, the Office may provide for the application of all or portions of the provisions of this subchapter—

"(1) to any individual reduced to a grade of a covered pay schedule from a position not subject to this subchapter;

"(2) to individuals to whom such provisions do not otherwise apply; and

"(3) to situations the application to which is justified for purposes of carrying out the mission of the agency or agencies involved.

"§ 5366. Appeals

5 USC 5366.

"(a)(1) In the case of the termination of any benefits available to an employee under this subchapter on the grounds such employee declined a reasonable offer of a position the grade or pay of which was equal to or greater than his retained grade or pay, such termination may be appealed to the Office of Personnel Management under procedures prescribed by the Office.

"(2) Nothing in this subchapter shall be construed to affect the right of any employee to appeal—

"(A) under section 5112(b) or 5346(c) of this title, or otherwise, any reclassification of a position; or

"(B) under procedures prescribed by the Office of Personnel Management, any reduction-in-force action.

"(b) For purposes of any appeal procedures (other than those described in subsection (a) of this section) or any grievance procedure negotiated under the provisions of chapter 71 of this title—

Ante, p. 1192.

"(1) any action which is the basis of an individual's entitlement to benefits under this subchapter, and

"(2) any termination of any such benefits under this subchapter, shall not be treated as appealable under such appeals procedures or grievable under such grievance procedure.".

(2) Sections 5334(d), 5337, and 5345 of title 5, United States Code, are hereby repealed.

Repeal.

(3)(A) Chapter 53 of title 5, United States Code, is amended—

(i) by redesignating subchapter VI as subchapter VII, and

(ii) by redesignating sections 5361 through 5365 as sections 5371 through 5375, respectively.

(B)(i) The analysis of chapter 53 of title 5, United States Code, is amended by striking out the items relating to subchapter VI thereof and inserting in lieu thereof the following:

"SUBCHAPTER VI—GRADE AND PAY RETENTION

"Sec.
"5361. Definitions.
"5362. Grade retention following a change of positions or reclassification.
"5363. Pay retention.
"5364. Remedial actions.
"5365. Regulations.
"5366. Appeals.

"SUBCHAPTER VII—MISCELLANEOUS PROVISIONS

"Sec.
"5371. Scientific and professional positions.
"5372. Administrative law judges.
"5373. Limitation on pay fixed by administrative action.
"5374. Miscellaneous positions in the executive branch.
"5375. Police force of National Zoological Park.".

(ii) The analysis of such chapter is further amended by striking out the items relating to sections 5337 and 5345, respectively.

(iii) Sections 559 and 1305 of title 5, United States Code, are each amended by striking out "5362," each place it appears and inserting "5372," in lieu thereof.

(C) Section 3104(b) of title 5, United States Code, as redesignated by this Act, is amended by striking out "section 5361" and inserting "section 5371" in lieu thereof.

Ante, p. 1178.

(D) Section 5102(c)(5) of title 5, United States Code, is amended by striking out "section 5365" and inserting "section 5375" in lieu thereof.

(E) Sections 5107 and 8704(d)(1) of title 5, United States Code, are each amended by striking out "section 5337" and inserting in lieu thereof "subchapter VI of chapter 53".

5 USC 5361.

(F) Section 5334(b) of title 5, United States Code, is amended by striking out "section 5337 of this title" each place it appears and inserting in lieu thereof "subchapter VI of this chapter".

(G) Section 5334 of title 5, United States Code, is amended by redesignating subsections (e) and (f) as subsections (d) and (e), respectively.

(H) Section 5349(a) of title 5, United States Code, is amended—

(i) by striking out "section 5345, relating to retention of pay," and inserting in lieu thereof "subchapter VI of this chapter, relating to grade and pay retention.";

(ii) by striking out "section 5345 of this title" and inserting in lieu thereof "subchapter VI of this chapter"; and

(iii) by striking out "paragraph (2) of section 5345(a)" and

Ante, p. 1218.

inserting in lieu thereof "section 5361(1)".

(I) Sections 4540(c), 7212(a), and 9540(c) of title 10, United States Code, are each amended by inserting after "of title 5" the following: "and subchapter VI of chapter 53 of such title 5".

(J) Section 1416(a) of the Act of August 1, 1968 (Public Law 90-448; 15 U.S.C. 1715(a)), and section 808(c) of the Act of April 11, 1968 (Public Law 90-284; 42 U.S.C. 3608(b)), are each amended by striking out "5362," and inserting in lieu thereof "5372,".

5 USC 5361 note.

(4)(A) The amendments made by this subsection shall take effect on the first day of the first applicable pay period beginning on or after the 90th day after the date of the enactment of this Act.

(B) An employee who was receiving pay under the provisions of section 5334(d), 5337, or 5345 of title 5, United States Code, on the day before the effective date prescribed in subparagraph (A) of this paragraph shall not have such pay reduced or terminated by reason of the amendments made by this subsection and, unless section 5362 of

Ante, p. 1218.

such title 5 (as amended by subsection (a)(1) of this section) applies, such an employee is entitled to continue to receive pay as authorized by those provisions (as in effect on such date).

5 USC 5362 note.

(b)(1) Under regulations prescribed by the Office of Personnel Management, any employee—

(A) whose grade was reduced on or after January 1, 1977, and before the effective date of the amendments made by subsection (a) of this section under circumstances which would have entitled the employee to coverage under the provisions of section 5362 of title 5, United States Code (as amended by subsection (a) of this section) if such amendments had been in effect at the time of the reduction; and

(B) who has remained employed by the Federal Government from the date of the reduction in grade to the effective date of the amendments made by subsection (a) of this section without a break in service of one workday or more;

shall be entitled—

(i) to receive the additional pay and benefits which such employee would have been entitled to receive if the amendments made by subsection (a) of this section had been in effect during the period beginning on the effective date of such reduction in grade and ending on the day before the effective date of such amendments, and

(ii) to have the amendments made by subsection (a) of this section apply to such employee as if the reduction in grade had occurred on the effective date of such amendments.

(2) No employee covered by this subsection whose reduction in grade resulted in an increase in pay shall have such pay reduced by reason of the amendments made by subsection (a) of this section.

(3)(A) For purposes of this subsection, the requirements under paragraph (1)(B) of this subsection, relating to continuous employment following reduction in grade, shall be considered to be met in the case of any employee—

(i) who separated from service with a right to an immediate annuity under chapter 83 of title 5, United States Code, or under another retirement system for Federal employees; or

5 USC 8301 *et seq.*

(ii) who died.

(B) Amounts payable by reason of subparagraph (A) of this paragraph in the case of the death of an employee shall be paid in accordance with the provisions of subchapter VIII of chapter 55 of title 5, United States Code, relating to settlement of accounts in the case of deceased employees.

(4) The Office of Personnel Management shall have the same authority to prescribe regulations under this subsection as it has under section 5365 of title 5, United States Code, with respect to subchapter VI of chapter 53 of such title, as added by subsection (a) of this section.

Ante, p. 1104.

TITLE IX—MISCELLANEOUS

STUDY ON DECENTRALIZATION OF GOVERNMENTAL FUNCTIONS

SEC. 901. (a) As soon as practicable after the effective date of this Act, the Director of the Office of Management and Budget shall conduct a detailed study concerning the decentralization of Federal governmental functions.

Study.
31 USC 18 note.

(b) The study to be conducted under subsection (a) of this section shall include—

(1) a review of the existing geographical distribution of Federal governmental functions throughout the United States, including the extent to which such functions are concentrated in the District of Columbia; and

(2) a review of the possibilities of distributing some of the functions of the various Federal agencies currently concentrated in the District of Columbia to field offices located at points throughout the United States.

Interested parties, including heads of agencies, other Federal employees, and Federal employee organizations, shall be allowed to submit views, arguments, and data in connection with such study.

(c) Upon completion of the study under subsection (a) of this section, and in any event not later than one year after the effective date of this Act, the Director of the Office of Management and Budget shall submit to the President and to the Congress a report on the results of such study together with his recommendations. Any recommendation which involves the amending of existing statutes shall include draft legislation.

Report to OMB,
President and
Congress.

SAVINGS PROVISIONS

SEC. 902. (a) Except as otherwise provided in this Act, all executive orders, rules, and regulations affecting the Federal service shall continue in effect, according to their terms, until modified, terminated, superseded, or repealed by the President, the Office of Personnel Management, the Merit Systems Protection Board, the Equal Employment Opportunity Commission, or the Federal Labor Relations Authority with respect to matters within their respective jurisdictions.

5 USC 1101 note.

(b) No provision of this Act shall affect any administrative proceedings pending at the time such provision takes effect. Orders shall be issued in such proceedings and appeals shall be taken therefrom as if this Act had not been enacted.

(c) No suit, action, or other proceeding lawfully commenced by or against the Director of the Office of Personnel Management or the members of the Merit Systems Protection Board, or officers or employees thereof, in their official capacity or in relation to the discharge of their official duties, as in effect immediately before the effective date of this Act, shall abate by reason of the enactment of this Act. Determinations with respect to any such suit, action, or other proceeding shall be made as if this Act had not been enacted.

AUTHORIZATION OF APPROPRIATIONS

5 USC 5509 note.   SEC. 903. There are authorized to be appropriated, out of any moneys in the Treasury not otherwise appropriated, such sums as may be necessary to carry out the provisions of this Act.

POWERS OF PRESIDENT UNAFFECTED EXCEPT BY EXPRESS PROVISIONS

5 USC 1101 note.   SEC. 904. Except as otherwise expressly provided in this Act, no provision of this Act shall be construed to—

(1) limit, curtail, abolish, or terminate any function of, or authority available to, the President which the President had immediately before the effective date of this Act; or

(2) limit, curtail, or terminate the President's authority to delegate, redelegate, or terminate any delegation of functions.

REORGANIZATION PLANS

5 USC 1101 note.   SEC. 905. Any provision in either Reorganization Plan Numbered 1 or 2 of 1978 inconsistent with any provision in this Act is hereby superseded.

TECHNICAL AND CONFORMING AMENDMENTS

SEC. 906. (a) Title 5, United States Code, is amended—

(1) in section 5347, 8713, and 8911, by striking out "Chairman of the Civil Service Commission" and inserting in lieu thereof "Director of the Office of Personnel Management";

(2) in sections 1301, 1302, 1304, 1308, 2105, 2951, 3110, 3304a, 3308, 3312, 3314, 3318, 3324, 3325, 3344, 3351, 3363, 3373, 3502, 3504, 4102, 4106, 4113–4118, 5102, 5103, 5105, 5107, 5110–5115, 5303, 5304, 5333, 5334, 5335(b), 5336, 5338, 5343, 5346, 5347, 5351,

Ante, p. 1218.   5352, 5371 (as redesignated in section 801(a)(3)(A)(ii) of this Act), 5372 (as redesignated in such section 801(a)(3)(A)(ii)), 5374 (as redesignated in such section 801(a)(3)(A)(ii)), 5504, 5533, 5545, 5548, 5723, 6101, 6304–6306, 6308, 6311, 6322, 6326,

Ante, p. 1216.   7203 (as redesignated in section 703(a)(1) of this Act), 7204 (as redesignated in such section 703(a)(1)), 7312, 8151, 8331, 8332, 8334, 8337, 8339–8343, 8345, 8346, 8347(a), 8348, 8501, 8701–8712, 8714, 8714a, 8716, 8901–8903, 8905, 8907–8910, and 8913, by striking out "Civil Service Commission" and inserting in lieu thereof "Office of Personnel Management";

(3) in sections 1302, 1304, 1308, 2951, 3304a, 3308, 3312, 3317b, 3318, 3324, 3351, 3363, 3504, 4106, 4113–4115, 4117, 4118, 5105, 5107, 5110–5112, 5114, 5333, 5343, 5346, 5545, 5548, 5723, 6304, 6405, 7312, 8331, 8332, 8337, 8339–8343, 8345, 8346, 8347(a)–(c)

and (e)-(h), 8348, 8702, 8704-8707, 8709-8712, 8714a, 8716, 8901-8903, 8905, 8907, 8909, 8910, and 8913 (as such sections are amended in paragraph (2) of this subsection), by striking out "Commission" each place it appears and inserting in lieu thereof "Office";

(4) in sections 1303, 8713 (as amended in paragraph (1) of this subsection), and 8911 (as amended in such paragraph), by striking out "Commission" and inserting in lieu thereof "Office";

(5) in section 3304(d), by striking out "a Civil Service Commission board of examiners" and inserting in lieu thereof "the Office of Personnel Management";

(6) in sections 1505-1508 and 3383, by striking out "Civil Service Commission" and "Commission" each place they appear and inserting in lieu thereof "Merit Systems Protection Board" and "Board", respectively;

(7) in section 1504, by striking out "Civil Service Commission. On receipt of the report, or on receipt of other information which seems to the Commission to warrant an investigation, the Commission shall" and inserting in lieu thereof the following: "Special Counsel. On receipt of the report or on receipt of other information which seems to the Special Counsel to warrant an investigation, the Special Counsel shall investigate the report and such other information and present his findings and any charges based on such findings to the Merit Systems Protection Board, which shall".

(8) in section 5335(c)—

(A) by striking out "Commission" the first place it appears and inserting in lieu thereof "Office of Personnel Management";

(B) by striking out "Commission" the second place it appears and inserting in lieu thereof "Merit Systems Protection Board";

(C) by striking out "Commission" the third place it appears and inserting in lieu thereof "Office"; and

(D) by striking out "Commission" the fourth place it appears and inserting in lieu thereof "Board";

(9) in section 8347(d), by striking out "Commission" the first place it appears and inserting in lieu thereof "Merit Systems Protection Board" and by striking out "Commission" the second time it appears and inserting in lieu thereof "Board";

(10) in section 552(a)(4)(F)—

(A) by striking out "Civil Service Commission" and "Commission" each place they appear and inserting in lieu thereof "Special Counsel"; and

(B) by striking out "its" and inserting in lieu thereof "his";

(11) in section 1303—

(A) by striking out "Civil Service Commission" and inserting in lieu thereof "Office of Personnel Management, Merit Systems Protection Board, and Special Counsel"; and

(B) in paragraph (1), by striking out "Commission" and inserting in lieu thereof "Office of Personnel Management";

(12) in section 1305, by striking out "For the purpose of sections 3105, 3344, 4301(2)(E), 5362, and 7521 of this title and the provisions of section 5335(a)(B) of this title that relate to administrative law judges the Civil Service Commission may" and inserting in lieu thereof "For the purpose of section 3105, 3344, 4301(2)(D), and 5372 of this title and the provisions of   *Ante,* p. 1131, 1219, 1137.

Ante, p. 1137.

section 5335(a)(B) of this title that relate to administrative law judges, the Office of Personnel Management may, and for the purpose of section 7521 of this title, the Merit Systems Protection Board may";

(13) in section 1306, to read as follows: "The Director of the Office of Personnel Management and authorized representatives of the Director may administer oaths to witnesses in matters pending before the Office.";

(14) in section 8344(a), by striking out "Commission" and inserting in lieu thereof "Office of Personnel Management";

(15) in section 8906, by striking out "Commission" each place it appears and inserting in lieu thereof "Office of Personnel Management" the first time it appears and "Office" the other times it appears;

5 USC 2901 *et seq.*

(16) in the section heading for section 2951 and in the item relating to section 2951 in the analysis for chapter 29, by striking out "Civil Service Commission" and inserting in lieu thereof "Office of Personnel Management"; and

(17) in the section heading for section 5112 and in the item relating to section 5112 in the analysis for chapter 51, by striking out "Civil Service Commission" and inserting in lieu thereof "Office of Personnel Management".

Repealed.

(b)(1) Section 5109(b) of title 5, United States Code, is hereby repealed.

(2) Section 5109 of such title is further amended by redesignating subsection (c) as subsection (b).

Ante, p. 1161.

(c)(1) Subchapter VIII of chapter 33 of title 5, United States Code (as in effect immediately before the date of the enactment of this Act) is amended—

(A) by striking out the subchapter heading and inserting in lieu thereof the following:

"CHAPTER 34—PART-TIME CAREER EMPLOYMENT OPPORTUNITIES

"Sec.
"3401. Definitions.
"3402. Establishment of part-time career employment programs.
"3403. Limitations.
"3404. Personnel ceilings.
"3405. Nonapplicability.
"3406. Regulations.
"3407. Reports.
"3408. Employee organization representation.";

and

(B) by redesignating sections 3391 through 3398 as sections 3401 through 3408, respectively.

(2)(A) Section 3401 of such title 5 (as redesignated by this section) is amended by striking out "subchapter" and inserting in lieu thereof "chapter".

(B) Section 3402 of such title 5 (as redesignated by this section) is amended—

(i) in subsection (a)(1)(B), by striking out "section 3393" and inserting in lieu thereof "section 3403";

(ii) in subsection (b)(1)—

(I) by striking out "Civil Service Commission" and inserting in lieu thereof "Office of Personnel Management"; and

(II) by striking out "subchapter" and inserting in lieu thereof "chapter"; and

(iii) in subsection (b)(2), by striking out "Commission" and inserting in lieu thereof "Office".

(C) Sections 3405 and 3406 of such title 5 (as redesignated by this section) are amended by striking out "subchapter" each place it occurs and inserting in lieu thereof "chapter".

(D) Section 3407(a) of such title 5 (as redesignated by this section) is amended—

(i) by striking out "Civil Service Commission" and inserting in lieu thereof "Office of Personnel Management";

(ii) in paragraph (1), by striking out "section 3392" and inserting in lieu thereof "section 3402"; and

(iii) in paragraph (2), by striking out "subchapter" and inserting in lieu thereof "chapter".

(E) Section 3407(b) of such title 5 (as redesignated by this section) is amended—

(i) by striking out "Commission" and inserting in lieu thereof "Office"; and

(ii) by striking out "subchapter" each place it appears and inserting in lieu thereof "chapter".

(F) Sections 8347(g), 8716(b)(3), 8913(b)(3), and 8906(b)(3) of such title 5 are each amended by striking out "section 3391(2)" and inserting in lieu thereof "section 3401(2)".

(G) Section 8716(b)(3) of such title 5 is amended by striking out "section 3391(2)" and inserting in lieu thereof "section 3401(2)".

(H) Section 8913(b)(3) of such title 5 is amended by striking out "section 3391(2)" and inserting in lieu thereof "section 3401(2)".

(3) Section 5 of the Federal Employees Part-Time Career Employment Act of 1978 is amended by striking out "section 3397(a)" and inserting in lieu thereof "section 3407(a)".   5 USC 3407 note.

(4) The analysis for chapter 33 of title 5, United States Code, is amended by striking out the items (as in effect immediately before the date of the enactment of this Act) following the item relating to section 3385.

(5) The chapter analysis for part III of title 5, United States Code is amended by inserting after the item relating to chapter 33 the following new item:

"34. Part-time career employment opportunities_____ 3401".

EFFECTIVE DATE

SEC. 907. Except as otherwise expressly provided in this Act, the provisions of this Act shall take effect 90 days after the date of the enactment of this Act.   5 USC 1101 note.

Approved October 13, 1978.

LEGISLATIVE HISTORY:

HOUSE REPORTS: No. 95-1403 accompanying H.R. 11280 (Comm. on Post Office and Civil Service) and No. 95-1717 (Comm. of Conference).
SENATE REPORTS: No. 95-969 (Comm. on Governmental Affairs) and No. 95-1272 (Comm. of Conference).
CONGRESSIONAL RECORD, Vol. 124 (1978):
     Aug. 11, H.R. 11280 considered in House.
     Aug. 24, considered and passed Senate.
     Sept. 7, 11, 13, H.R. 11280 considered and passed House; proceedings vacated and S. 2640; amended, passed in lieu.
     Oct. 4, Senate agreed to conference report.
     Oct. 5, 6, House agreed to conference report; receded from amendment.
WEEKLY COMPILATION OF PRESIDENTIAL DOCUMENTS, Vol. 14, No. 41:
     Oct. 13, Presidential statement.

O

Contributors

ABOUT THE EDITORS

PATRICIA W. INGRAHAM is the Commissioner of the Department of Planning and Economic Development, Broome County, New York. She received her Ph.D. in Policy Science from the State University of New York at Binghamton. She has been employed by various agencies at the state and local levels of government and by the U.S. Department of Housing and Urban Development, Washington, D.C. She was the first director of the undergraduate Program in Public Policy and Administration at the State University of New York College at Cortland. Her primary interests include the role of public bureaucracies in the public policy process and change in public organizations.

CAROLYN BAN is an Assistant Professor in the Department of Public Administration and Director of the Evaluation Research Group at the State University of New York at Albany. She has taught at Ohio State University, worked for several consulting firms and was a member of the staff and Acting Chief of the Civil Service Reform Act Evaluation Management Division, U.S. Office of Personnel Management. She has published several articles on civil service reform.

ABOUT THE CONTRIBUTORS

MARK ABRAMSON is presently Staff Director of the Center for Excellence in Government in Washington, D.C. The papers in this volume are based on his research while employed by the U.S. Department of Health and Human Services.

CHARLES A. BANN is a software engineer in research and development with Wang Laboratories, Inc. in Lowell, Massachusetts.

SANDRA BAXTER is project director of the three-year evaluation study of the Civil Service Reform Act in the U.S. Department of Health and Human Services. She received her Ph.D. in Sociology from the University of Michigan and has taught research methodology and statistics at the Universities of Michigan and Detroit. She is currently a Senior Principal Analyst at Advanced Technology, Inc., in Reston, Virginia.

CURTIS BERRY is a Ph.D. candidate at the Maxwell School, Syracuse University. His primary interests are Labor Relations/Personnel Management and Bureaucratic Politics and Democratic Theory.

DAVID L. DILLMAN received his Ph.D. from the University of Massachusetts in 1982 and is Assistant Professor of Political Science at New England College, Henniker, New Hampshire.

GREGORY H. GAERTNER is a senior analyst at Westat, Inc. He received his Ph.D. from the University of Chicago. He has been involved in the evaluation of civil service reform for several years, as an Assistant Professor of Organizational Behavior at the Weatherhead School of Management, Case Western Reserve University and as a principal in Gaertner Research.

KAREN N. GAERTNER is an Assistant Professor in Business at Georgetown University. She received her Ph.D. from the University of Chicago. She has been involved in the evaluation of civil service reform for several years, as an Assistant Professor of Behavioral Sciences at Case Western Reserve University and as a principal in Gaertner Research.

JERALD A. JOHNSON is an Assistant Professor of Political Science at the University of Vermont. Professor Johnson was a Fulbright Fellow in Brazil (1974–5) and a NASPAA (National Association of School of Public Affairs and Administration) Fellow in 1979–80. His research interests and publications are in the personnel and general administration areas.

TONI MARZOTTO is an Associate Professor of Political Science at Towson State University, Baltimore, Maryland. She has also been associated for several years with civil service reform evaluation efforts at the U.S. Office of Personnel Management, Washington, D.C., where she had responsibility for developing the strategy to evaluate the Senior Executive Service.

B. RUTH MONTGOMERY is a doctoral candidate in the Organizational Behavior and Industrial Relations program at the Graduate School of Business Administration, the University of Michigan.

DONALD F. PARKER is an Assistant Professor of Organizational Behavior and Industrial Relations in the Graduate School of Business, the University of Michigan. He served formerly for twenty four years as a naval officer holding line and staff management positions, where he was responsible for both uniformed and civilian personnel of the Navy Department.

DAVID ROSENBLOOM is Professor of Public Administration at the Maxwell School, Syracuse University. His works include *Federal Service and the Constitution* and *Public Administration and Law.*

RICHARD E. SCHMIDT is Associate Director of the Office of Evaluation and Technical Analysis in the Office of the Assistant Secretary for Planning and Evaluation, U.S. Department of Health and Human Services. He has written extensively in the area of evaluation and improving government management. Previously, he was a Senior Researcher at the Urban Institute where he pioneered the concept of evaluability assessment.

SUSAN J. SCHURMAN is a doctoral candidate in the School of Education at the University of Michigan.

DAVID T. STANLEY, Chairman of the Panel on the Public Service of the National Academy of Public Administration, is a consultant on government matters. He was formerly a Federal management official, then a senior fellow at the Brookings Institution.

FREDERICK C. THAYER is on the faculty of the Graduate School of Public and International Affairs, University of Pittsburgh. He has been a visiting faculty member at the Maxwell School, Syracuse University, the University of Calgary and, in 1983–84, the Washington Public Affairs Center of the University of Southern California.

Index